ROAD SCRIBBLER

DAVID STANDISH

1FIRST BOOKS • CHICAGO, IL

1FIRST BOOKS
AN IMPRINT OF 1FIRST PUBLISHING, INC.

FRONT COVER PHOTO BY TERENCE MOORE
DESIGN & PRODUCTION BY NICK ACCARDI

3100 DUNDEE ROAD, SUITE 307,
NORTHBROOK, IL 60062

ISBN: 978-1-61855-335-5

PRINTED IN THE UNITED STATES OF AMERICA

VISIT US ONLINE AT WWW.1FIRSTCOMICS.COM

"Laugh, for Christ's sake—it's a humor magazine!"

Jerry Bovim
(1939-1968)

PRELUDE

Sometimes my magazine writing students at Medill will say, after I've told them some war story or other, "You should write your autobiography." My answer is that I already have—in the form of many magazine articles over the years. I have done stories on what interested me at the time, what seemed important or funny or just odd enough to write about. Together the articles collected here form a sort of photo album memoir spanning thirty years, since each is a snapshot of what I was doing, feeling, and thinking when I wrote them. They chart my curiosities, my concerns, what turned me on, made my heart leap up, scared the hell out of me, made me wonder, made me dream.

I tell my students too, that while there is seldom much money in journalism, it offers the opportunity to have one of the most interesting lives there is—that as a kid growing up on the west side of Cleveland I couldn't have even *imagined* all the things I would do and the people I would meet in my years as a journalist. Or of all the fun I would have doing it.

Being a journalist is an excuse to poke your nose into anything that interests you, to learn about anything you're curious about, meet anyone who intrigues you, do anything you ever wanted to try.

Largely through a stroke of luck, I got a job at *Playboy* magazine straight out of graduate school—thanks to an off-campus humor magazine some friends and I had started at Miami University—as the very first full-time Party Jokes Editor. Submissions had been piling up, and none of the regular editors, understandably, wanted to spend the time going through them. That quickly proved a thoroughly depressing task (surprisingly straight out of *Miss Lonelyhearts*), but after a few months I begged for a change, eventually moving to editing the letters to the editor page and various unsigned house copy—and, incidentally, replaced as Jokes Editor by Harold Ramis. For a couple of years we were terrorized by the same senior editors, before he went on to Second City, SCTV, and *Ghostbusters*, *Groundhog Day*, etc.

One of my main interests back then (and today) was good old rock & roll—having grown up in its birthplace listening to Alan Freed on the radio in Cleveland, before he sold out and went to New York—and so during my ten years at *Playboy* I wrote a lot about music. My earliest article for them was a story about a Virginia bluegrass festival in 1971 that was in its way as landmark as Dylan's 1965 Newport Folk Festival debacle—with icon Earl Scruggs practically being booed offstage for having the temerity to go electric. I also toured briefly with Led Zeppelin, and happened to be with them in New York when they were robbed of $180,000, receipts from their three-night stand at Madison Square Gardens. And my first truly exotic assignment—touring Japan for three weeks with Kiss. Clouds of groupies passing through Gene Simmons' hotel rooms, and poor guitarist Ace Fraley pretty much drunk the whole time (it was his first time out of the US, and he was scared shitless).

Then there was the strange bleak trip to Argentina with Queen during the "Dirty War" there, an uneasy mixture of stadium rock and sinister political events. A far happier experience was chasing Willie Nelson around off and on for about eight months trying to get him to sit still for the *Playboy* interview—he never did—but it resulted in the profile here, which recounts my week with him and the band on the band bus, including one night when bassist Bee Spears insisted I have a go at his new invention, a "pillowcase bong," which left me about as stoned as I'd ever been in my life, much to Willie's amusement. I found out later that "burning 'em down"—seriously oversmoking visiting journalists—is his amusing standard procedure for avoiding lengthy interviews.

I was also lucky enough to be the only journalist to cover the making of *Animal House*. This too was something of a fluke. One of the writers, Chris Miller, had been a pal of mine for several years, and invited me out to Eugene, Oregon, to hang out for a week while they were shooting it. I did so, and wrote the piece here about it, threading recollections of my own Animal House through it. I was then a Staff Writer at *Playboy*, and when Arthur Kretchmer, the Executive Editor, called me into his office about the piece in June, months before the movie opened, he said that he really liked it, that I was getting better at my "riffy style," as he character-ized it, but that he didn't want to publish the piece. His reason? In his opinion the movie wasn't *important* enough to merit the space. So it never ran. I remind him of this whenever I get the chance.

But that is one reason for this collection: a few of the pieces here, for one reason or another, never were published. And others, alas, were brutalized in the editing, victims of the prevailing "shorter is better" mentality. I have had many terrific editors over the years, and I thank them heartily, but a few have used a steamroller instead of a pencil, so in a number of cases here, I have *un*-edited them into restored versions that seem more pleasing. Also it has always been my feeling that each story has a natural size, and I generally write them as long (or short) as they seem to want, which is often beyond available space limits, which in turn often leads to cutting. So what's here is sort of my "Writer's Cut"—the pieces I feel hold up the best, and in my best versions.

But back to movies. Another on-set piece here is about the shooting of the first *Blues Brothers* movie. I had known John Belushi slightly while he was still in Chicago's Second City, and he figures in the *Animal House* piece as well. Lamentably, by the time of the *Blues Brothers* movie he was deep into his steep cocaine-fueled decline, and when we met during the shooting of the concert scene in LA, a sad mess. He was supposed to play one of the leads in a movie that Chris Miller and I wrote about this time. Our working title was *Club Sandwich*, about a pair of scruffy pot dealers on the lam trying to hide out in a square Caribbean resort.

Any similarity to Club Med was a complete accident. Honest. The movie came out in 1986 as *Club Paradise*, starring Robin Williams and Peter O'Toole, and directed by my old officemate, Harold Ramis. The difference in the titles said it all. But Harold invited me to Jamaica for a week to watch them shoot it and be an extra, and the piece here, *From Club Sandwich to Club Paradise*, recounts the long strange trip. It was sort of a look-at-what-they-done-to-my-song, but it also included one of the highlights of my life as a journalist, a two-hour-long interview with Peter O'Toole at his beach villa, during which he was completely gracious while telling one hilarious and often scandalous story after another.

So that's a brief taste of what's in here. One more personal confession: As a college student, when I first became serious about writing, my plan was to become William Faulkner #2. He is still my favorite writer. But after a few forays into fiction (any editors out there looking for a really nifty unpublished coming-of-age novel set in 1956?), I discovered that I didn't have the imagination required to do it very well, and sensibly drifted over to nonfiction. But my love for literature has never gone away, and I try to bring that to my articles. I have always been as interested in the *art* of writing good nonfiction as I have been in the information being conveyed. I think the best nonfiction can become literature (see *Walden*, now continuously in print for 163 years). It remains to be seen whether I even come close to that, but I've done my level best. I like to think, anyway, that at my best, I am a bad enough journalist that my stuff holds up. I hope you will agree.

I would like to thank a few people who helped this book happen.

First, Ken Levin. We have been pals for many years, since he was just finishing law school at Northwestern. We met when we found ourselves neighbors sharing a small courtyard in a townhouse building in Chicago, both checking each other out to make sure that the other wasn't a narc—we weren't. We quickly discovered that we had both attended Miami University (the one in Ohio, as we always explain apologetically), and, better, both had studied under the same brilliant iconoclastic English professor, John Weigel, who warped our young minds in ways we still remain thankful for. Ken is the best of friends, and has supported me in any number of harebrained enterprises over more than forty years now. In the 60s my college buddy Jerry Bovim and I co-wrote a deranged radio soap opera parody called *Secret Saga*, and a few years later Ken convinced several dentists to invest in it, and let us do it as a comedy album. So with a few friends from Second City and a couple of others, we made it in a little local studio. We never did sell it, but we couldn't have done it without Ken. In the 80s he became publisher of First Comics, which went on hiatus, as they say, in the 90s, but which he revived about ten years ago, and now publishes both comics and graphic novels—and this collection of my articles here. He went in this knowing the conventional wisdom that collections never sell worth a shit. But he wanted to publish it anyway. He believed it was worth doing it. I am hoping for his sake that we'll at least break even on the cost of printing it. And if it doesn't, well, it will be yet another example of Ken's continuing pro bono work.

I also had a lot of help from Maude and Wilson Standish, two of my remarkable children. They have always been in my corner, even when I wasn't there myself. Their belief in me has been a north star that has kept me true when I was wavering—*and* I have been flagrant about using them as characters in many of my articles, including several here. Both got degrees in journalism, which warmed my old heart, though both have semi-wised up, heading for strategic digital and social media spaces, although they continue writing. Maude is currently working on a young adult mystery, and Wil has been working a memoir about a six-month backpacking trip through Southeast Asia he and a friend did a few years ago. Today they have jobs I can only *sort of* understand, much of the time, but they are creative and innovative, and they both have had lots of terrific ideas about this book that helped me, both improving it and improving me. Also Maude has written the introduction to the book here—so thanks for that, too, darling!

I also want to thank my oldest daughter, Lisa Stewart, who has also seen me through many downs and ups, happily ups for a long time now. With her husband Rich, she has raised two sparkling daughters, Molly and Bailey, and in Bailey's face especially, I see shining through three generations back to my own mother's sunny aspect. And a hatlo tip of a hat too to Lisa's mother, Beth Meredith. We have now been divorced a shade under 50 years, and time will tell, because I couldn't love her more, and we couldn't be better friends. She has also thanked me for the divorce any number of times, because otherwise she would have never married George Meredith, her lifelong partner (and a longtime friend of mine as well—it's all just too *modern*, you know?). Beth was too good-hearted and sensible for me truly to appreciate her back then—but I sure do now. Beth has been reading my writing for many years now, and has always given me thoughtful feedback, as well as her eagle-eyed proofreading.

And last, I owe heaps and bunches and bushels of thanks to Patricia Kroll. Where to start? We met at an AA meeting more than ten years ago—what better place to find the best people!—and over time we realized we couldn't be better for each other. We have an amazing and unforced confluence of things we love, from bluegrass and dark mysteries and Thomas Hardy and Joseph Conrad and much else. She is a ferocious reader. She has been the best helpmeet I have had in my whole life, and I need a *lot* of that. I can be crabby, impatient, willful, blind to the obvious, dumb as a box of rocks, the list goes on, and Patricia rolls with it all with love and ease, and great humor. We have a lot of fun together. She often calls me her Brave Old Dog. Her compassion is far beyond that of mortal men (and women), caring more for people and creatures and the sorry world than anyone I've ever known.

Selfishly, I get a lot of this, especially when it comes to my writing. Cheerfully she reads everything I read, often more than once, and couldn't be a better thoughtful cheerleader for my work. She has her own medical difficulties, but when I had a stroke in February 2014, struck with aphasia, Patricia was right there for me. The doctor would point to everyday objects in the hospital room and ask me to identify them. I couldn't say "window," or "pen" or "button." I confess that days after the stroke, in the hospital, I curled into a pathetic ball in the bed, weeping and weeping, wanting to die. Three of the things I had cared the most about—reading and writing and talking—had been taken away from me. When I got home, I found I couldn't even read *Green Eggs and Ham* and understand it, when I had been reading Proust right before the stroke. My attempts at writing were a garbled hash. I was a mess. But, well, Patricia took me in hand. She worked with me, and worked, finding some online elementary reading program that we fought with day after day, having to start back in *second grade*. Over months we made it all the way to eighth grade (we had planned to have a graduating party at Chuck E. Cheese's, but didn't get to it). Today—summer 2017—I'm pretty much back to where I was before the stroke[1], and I owe most of this remarkable recovery to her. So I love her batches, and I am still trying to convince her to wear that grade school uniform for me!

[1] I had finished writing all the articles here before the stroke, but I wrote many of the introductions to the articles, post-stroke. And in full disclosure, I still haven't tried tackling Proust again. Once I regained my capacity for reading, I began going through all of John Cheever, and am now pleasurably devouring a few Jim Harrison novels I had missed.

INTRODUCTION

BY MAUDE STANDISH

Three years ago my dad had a stroke, which left him at a loss for words. I don't mean that he ran out of things to say, but that he was diagnosed with aphasia, a condition that took away his ability to match words, very simple words like "door," "window," and "daughter," with the things they represented. Words, which for so long had been the thing that came easiest to him, were suddenly strangers evading his every linguistic move.

When I arrived at the hospital, a nurse ushered me into his room, where he lay in his skinny metal bed, dressed in the terrible paper clothing they insist patients wear, tubes coming out of his hands, while a football game played out silently on a small TV hanging in the corner. His famous smile was still there, but above it, his eyes asked me the same thing that they asked everyone that came into the room: "Are my words coming home to me?"

A nurse took me outside to update me. "He is actually very lucky," she said. "It could have been his legs, not *just* his words." I nodded politely, but inwardly I wanted to shout at her, "If that's what you think, you know nothing about my dad!"

My earliest memory of my dad is the sound of clicking. He would sit up in his brown office, typing out whatever story he was currently obsessing over. While most people spend their lives trying to just get their own story straight, my dad spent his life using words to capture our story. I say "our story" because his articles are really a catalog of American culture during its lanky teenage years, told from the eyes of a boy fresh from the suburbs of Cleveland, in awe that the world could have so many delicious moments of crazy to offer him.

Though personal honesty is a theme that runs through his writing, my dad never shared these stories because he wanted you to know about him. His writing comes from a place of generosity. He knows how lucky he is to have spent decades backstage with musicians that changed the world, and with his stories, he generously invites us to share his luck.

As my dad got incrementally healthier, a speech therapist suggested that one way words can come back is by just plain practice. He was told to play a game of listing of "types" of things as a way to lure his words back home to his brain. First, we started with farm animals—I think he remembered what a cow and horse were before looking away in frustration and boredom. Not to give up on the game, someone suggested he name types of cars, which again was abandoned rather quickly. Never one to give up, Patricia said, "Well, maybe you should list something you love."

First came the authors: Faulkner, Kerouac, Vonnegut, Melville, Crane. Next came the musicians: The Rolling Stones, Bob Dylan, The Grateful Dead, Willie Nelson. Slowly the writers that taught him to love storytelling and musicians he spent his life chronicling brought his words back to him. And then of course for a little dose of black humor, he listed all his favorite forms of alcohol from his drinking days… Wild Turkey, Old Style, Heineken… Little by little, his words returned home and he welcomed them back with open arms.

The stories that fill these pages are a love letter to American culture from a man who respects words above all else—though Rock & Roll is a close second. They are stories of a boy from Cleveland who grew older during journalism's golden years, but never quite grew up and still thinks that around every corner you turn, there is a story worth telling waiting for us all.

CONTENTS

I was the only journalist who covered the making of Animal House, *largely I guess because nobody else thought it was worth the trouble—a low budget effort by a bunch of scruffy hippies, with an unknown first-time director. Not counting a cameo by Donald Sutherland, the only person in it anyone had even heard of was John Belushi, then in his second season at Saturday Night Live, and not yet JOHN BELUSHI. I had made my way to Eugene, Oregon that rainy October 1977 because my pal Chris Miller, one of the three writers (and the one whose life most of the movie was drawn from), had invited me out there for a few days to watch them shoot it. Chris of course was all excited. As a voice of sanity I kept reminding him that most movies came and went without making a dent, didn't make money, failed. Little did I know.*

And neither, it turns out, did my editor back at Playboy, *the usually astute Arthur Kretchmer, easily the smartest editor I had ever had. I came back from Eugene, and spent a month or more writing the article, even though no one had asked me to do so, one of the luxuries of being a Staff Writer for the magazine that I didn't fully appreciate at the time. I had written the article in time to have the magazine publish it in an issue before the movie's release, as a preview of the upcoming movie. Which is to say, nobody had seen the movie when I turned it in.*

A couple of days later Arthur called me into his office.

"I like it," he said. "You're actually getting your riffy style down."

"Great," I said, beaming.

He went on. "But I don't want to publish it."

"Huh?" I gulped. "Why?"

"Don't get me wrong," Arthur went on, "I do like the article. I just don't think the movie is important enough to be worth the space. Sorry."

So this likeable piece about this unimportant movie never ran.

I try to remind Arthur of his impeccable editorial judgment about this whenever I get the chance.

TOGA TOGA TOGA
HIGH TIMES ON THE SET OF *ANIMAL HOUSE*

It is an almost ordinary Saturday afternoon on the University of Oregon campus. Dark clouds spill down the low mountains surrounding Eugene. The sky is various dismal shades of gray, and it's raining lightly. It is full-flush autumn, which, here in the Northwest rainforest, means dapples of yellow and orange scattered through evergreen trees. Of the few students walking around campus, most wear flannel shirts, sleeveless down-filled vests, Levi's, hiking boots. The girls look like cute lumberjacks. Over at the stadium, the UCLA football team is once again kicking the shit out of the Oregon Ducks.

Like most large universities its age, Oregon began small a hundred or so years ago, and exhibits irregular growth rings, a time-lapse of architectural styles, dreary or terrific depending on how things were going at the moment (one, built during the burn-'em-down heyday of the Sixties, is thick black stone and has only a few squinty windows, clearly a fortress, victory for Our Side), all spreading around an old central campus straight out of an Andy Hardy movie: stately ivy-covered Georgian brick buildings arranged around wide lawns shaded by ancient trees, and crossed by intersecting slant walks, with a legendary alum or two done up in bronze on pedestals, stone benches placed beneath to encourage meditation upon their shining example. Fat speedy squirrels zipping about, birds chirping ... collegiate heaven, even in the rain.

It's too good. It looks like a ... movie set.

And on this day at least, that's what it is.

Parked along the tree-lined streets near one of these idyllic quadrangles are several semi-trailers with white corrugated sides. They're so out of place they're startling, like finding Allis-Chalmers tractors in a Monet barnyard. Near a slant walk, under huge trees, lighting men in see-thru slickers coil black cables on the grass. Two complicated cameras peer down the walk, toward a sitting statue of some renowned old lady, and the ivied brick buildings beyond. A yellow slicker has been thrown over one camera, since the weather keeps waxing and waning through a thin spectrum of damp, mist and drizzle.

Standing around watching, in an uneven down-filled arc behind the cameras, are thirty or forty student lumberjacks. But they are from the present, or aren't the cause of these lowlevel twilight-zone jolts I'm getting as I walk with Chris Miller to join in them gawking.

I'm getting these jolts because standing among the students and crew, and at various points around the quad, are all these disturbing visions from 1962. I've read the script for the movie, called *Animal House*, so I already knew, in theory at least, that it's about fraternity life on a college campus in 1962. These palpable blasts from the past are in fact young actors wearing period clothes and haircuts. I know this, but somehow it doesn't register. They look so … genuine, it's a little … jarring. *Too real*, as The Platters sing.

This is because in 1962, like my friend Chris, who co-wrote the screenplay with Harold Ramis and Doug Kenny, I was wandering around a campus even more gorgeous than this one; and I looked at the time exactly like all three of those actors out there on the quad leaning against the bronze old lady's stone chair – alarmingly clean-looking, in knife-creased chinos & crewnecks & white socks & penny loafers & short JFK haircuts, which we called "Princetons" in the culturally insecure Midwest.

The 19-year-old actresses wear perfect pageboys and French twists and ponytails; some in then-regulation beige camels-hair coats, others wearing so-called "car coats," new and *tres chic* in 1962, very popular in loden green and navy blue wool, with rope loops and wooden toggles as buttons, and, which, with their hoods up, made everyone look like Russian monks on ski vacations at Tahoe. One girl with hair below her shoulders and large thoughtful eyes has on an actual pleated red tartan plaid skirt featuring a single big silver safety pin, black knee socks, loafers. I knew all of you, especially you girls.

So I stand there as they set up for this short scene, under a heavy assault of hard *déjà vu*, blam blam blam, not entirely sure I'm ready or able to jump through the Wayback Machine for that one again, since for me and everyone I knew, 1962 was a banner year for frustration and boredom, hanging out waiting without knowing it for the Beatles, grass, acid, free love, Vietnam, assassinations, riots, Nixon and everything else that made the Sixties so much fun. In the winter of 1962, three pitchers of beer and two hours of dry-humping standing up in the black cold against a tree (O Kathy Allmon, where are you now?) were considered a wonderful night. Go back to bleak country like that?

"Back up twenty feet!"

"Here we go! Looking through the hole!"

"Go to your #1, guys!"

They're finally ready to shoot. Nearly an hour of setting up for maybe thirty seconds in the movie.

The scene is another small attempt to help Pinto part with his innocence. He's a pledge to Delta Tau Kai, a.k.a. Animal House. There used to be one at most schools. It was the house that seemed to exist solely to sully the good name of the fraternity system. It was always filled with charming young derelicts and drunks, R&B freaks, pleasant incompetents, fatsos, psychos and crooks.

At Miami (of Ohio, as we say, apologetically), where I went through this stuff, it was the Dekes. They provided an ongoing parody of the solemn rituals of fraternity life. At Homecoming, all the fraternities used to decorate the outsides of their houses, according to some annual "theme." One year it was "Animals," and while all the other houses were going gung-ho to out-bigger-than-thou each other, constructing great colorful kleenex-tufted-chickenwire sculptures of Thumper and Donald and Mickey, each more enormous than the last, the Dekes gave comment by digging a deep rectangular pit in their front yard and placing a live donkey in it. Get it? Har har. That summer the Army Corps of Engineers finished drowning a few hundred acres of gentle valley a few miles from town, and we had a murky new lake. The Dekes got in on the craze of going to the beach by building a two-foot-high cement wall around their front porch, filling it with water, once, and then lounging about in it for hours on end, drinking beer among the floating empties and emerald clots of algae. It was made better by the fact that Miami, then and now, takes these matters very darn seriously, mister. Not for nothing does Miami call itself "the cradle of fraternities." It is the birthplace of three heavy-duty Alpha Chapters. Right there in little nowhere Oxford, Ohio, began no less than Beta Theta Pi, Phi Delta Theta and Sigma Chi—sort of the fraternal equivalent of General Motors, Chrysler and Ford. Miami is very proud of this, but I spent a lot of time there, and I'm not so sure it should be.

DAVE'S VERY SHORT HISTORY OF FRATERNITIES

During the 1840s and 1850s, when the Big Three were started (and when many of our other national fraternities were begun), Miami was hardly more than a sparse stand of brick buildings shivering on a hilltop. There wasn't a lot of what you could call to *do*, especially in winter. Things were so thrilling back then that a snowball fight from the 1840s continues as a juicy legend. And so it is easy to see these smart young guys, eagerly putting the farm behind them as fast as they can, sitting around hallowed old Eliot Hall in someone's room one night, everybody bored shitless. Outside an icy wind howls through bare leafless branches. Since they're all trying very hard to be hip young intellectuals, despite the woods and cornfields on all sides, another wind of the currently fashionable ideas blows through each of their brains, blown out here to the frontier in copies of the bright British quarterlies and New York's sassy *Knickerbocker*, named in homage to W. Irving and the platonic model for *The New Yorker*. Their intellectual breeze is scented by an increasingly popular and thoroughly florid Persian-tinged romanticism that often tended to take the form of secret societies.

If they'd had any other way to amuse themselves, we might have been spared Beta Theta Pi. But at dull Miami, it was almost inevitable that one of these guys would finally jump up and exclaim, "Say fellows! I've a thought! Let's find a barn and get together and start a secret society!"

"We'll call it Beta Theta Pi!"

"Good title!"

"My Dad's got a barn!"

"We got any more beer?"

They shoot the scene with Pinto a dozen times and ways.

Pinto is sort of a freshman Candide, with a teenage Stan Laurel face, and in this scene he's walking across campus with a fraternity brother named Boone, and Boone's girlfriend Katy. As they walk, Boone is doing his best to con Katy into finding a date for Pinto, who follows along blushing a step or two behind.

Suddenly Katy stops, pissed, turns to Boone and says, "You just want someone he can screw on the first date!" Boone shrugs and smiles. "Nicely put. You see, Pinto's never been laid."

For the ninth or seventeenth time director John Landis shouts "Cut!" and like a baseball manager heading for the mound, goes out to do some coaching.

"Tom, I like that when you hesitate and pick your nose," he tells Tom Hulce, who plays Pinto. Hulce is the young actor who got raves on Broadway for his part in *Equus* a couple of years ago.

When they're done talking it over, Landis heads back behind the cameras, saying, in parting, "If you don't get it right this time, no lunch for two weeks!" This in reference to the fancy continental cook they've hired to man the lunch wagon, who's been wowing everybody every day with hot gourmet chow, much appreciated in wet, clammy Oregon.

Landis is a good-looking bearded 27-year-old, up and coming on the strength of *Kentucky Fried Movie*, today another lumberjack in a blue sweater, sleeveless down vest, saggy Levi's. The black neo-Buddy Holly glasses give him the aspect of a grad student in Paper & Pulp Tech. His boots appear to be L.L. Bean rubberized Li'l Abner shitkickers.

As he walks back toward the cameras, and the ritual sequence of preliminary shouts again tumbles toward action, Chris, beaming, something he does a lot, turns to me and says, "See? It's just like summer camp."

Behind us, a very California member of the crew, who appeared, over the course of the afternoon, to have that tall lean blonde surgically attached to him, says to his buddy, "There's a good fight on tonight." Buddy asks straight-faced, "Oh yeah? You and Donna?"

Chris and I spent the lunch break pursuing our roots in the nearest pinball parlor, a log-cabin-style bungalow on a sidestreet near campus, entered across a wooden front porch, pinball machines in the ex-living room and kitchen, pool table in the ex-dining room, makeshift plywood change stand as you come in from the door. A house whose time has come. It's right down the street from the barber shop where everybody in the cast had their hair cut back in time fifteen years, bringing out of hiding those old styles lurking there all along. As we walked by on our way back, three people working inside recognized Chris and smiled and waved. On the tranquil lake of student life, the movie company is an unexpected powerboat roaring through: proof of life beyond.

By mid-afternoon the clouds have shouldered together overhead in an ominous huddle, and it is for all practical photographic purposes dark outside – even darker over at the stadium, where the UCLA Bruins are laying it on without mercy right to the end (the final score will be UCLA 38, Oregon 7). But the remaining shot today is an interior, the reception area of a girls' dorm. They're using a turn-of-the-century building that had really been a dorm for years, but is at the moment gutted and abandoned, Miss Havisham awaiting renovation. Inside, in the midst of emptiness and rubble left behind, a few clean, well-lighted square feet of 1962 have been recreated in the reception area, detailed to handmade posters on a bulletin board announcing ADVANCED POTTERY SEMINAR and EXISTENTIAL DANCE FORMS WORK-SHOP.

This is supposedly a dorm at a girls' school called Emily Dickinson College, somewhere in the cultured wilds of New England. Any similarity to Bennington is just one of those crazy, one-in-a-million accidents. Otter (Tim

Matheson) and crew are here on a Road Trip, such a sacred institution at eastern men's colleges that it was referred to, even verbally, in capital letters. They are in search of the elusive quiff, and in this scene, Otter has just read in a campus newspaper that one of the girls has been killed in some gruesome fashion—so he hotfoots it over to the dorm and asks for her at the reception desk, claiming to be her fiancee who's come for a surprise visit. Unable to stand the tragic irony, the desk girl runs upstairs weeping, and then down comes Shelly, the dead girl's pretty roommate.

Shelly (played by Lisa Bauer) is another dead-center 50-point bullseye. She's wearing a skintight gray sweater, and what must be an authentic vintage bra: it forces her breasts into those Dixie Cup points I had so mercifully forgotten. (As one of the actresses remarked to Chris after he commented on the difference in bra construction then and now, "Yeah, torpedoes aren't in these days.") Shelly also wears a tight black wool skirt, black tights, shoes that were then called "flats" and may still be. Her eyes are large and brown and innocent as Bambi's, her hair suggests Leslie Caron in *The L-Shaped Room*, and yes, dear Lord, I knew her, too. She was a French major from Piqua, Ohio, who wrote poetry in the style of e.e cummings and Ferlinghetti; and sometimes, much to her own astonishment, found herself desperately horny beneath those Isadora Duncan leotards, and after sending up a few small flags in the name of Art and Decency, welcomed a chance to do something about it.

At Miami this wasn't easy, even worse in the winter, because the University had a web of rules that effectively prohibited the mixing of sexes indoors in groups less than forty. The dorms were obsessively segregated by sex (a friend of mine was thrown out of school for spending the night with his girlfriend in her room), no apartments or cars, all women locked up at ten p.m. on weeknights. We cheerfully broke all these rules, of course, but this is still another world we're talking about. Things were so difficult that many of us who went there remember with great fondness a forlorn little cemetery on the south side of town, right across from Miami Manor, a dolorous complex of Fifties-modern brick apartments for married students, carefully designed with divorce in mind. The cemetery was the place closest to several women's dorms where you could lay carnal hands on each other without an audience (in a strange suspension of grim Ohio morality, there was a steamy halo zone around each dorm entrance where, as the hour approached ten, the bushes and dark sides of trees were alive with couples in an assortment of heated tableaux, each writhing pair acting as if they were quite alone, and one were leaving in moments, never to return, *Casablanca* ending again and again all around you). I liked the cemetery. It was there, behind the caretaker's shed, in the lee of a brisk twenty-mile-an-hour March wind, that my Shelly and I at last consummated our respect. She sang a folk song afterward.

I am, as you can see, time-tripping like crazy by now.

Back in the present, that is, the 1977 recreation of 1962, Otter tells this Shelly he's Frank Lymon from Amherst, her roommate's fiancee. (His alias is an obscure tribute: Why *do* fools fall in love?)

She says, "I don't know any other way to tell you this, so I'll just tell you. Faun is dead."

Otter laughs. "Dead? Did she put you up to this? That minx. What a lively sense of humor."

Shelly, trembling, hands him a copy of the newspaper, and we see the headline: SOPHOMORE DIES IN KILN EXPLOSION. Touching his knee, she says, "I'm terribly, terribly sorry, Frank."

Stunned, heartbroken, Otter says, "I just spoke to her a week ago … she was going to make a pot for me …" He buries his face in his hands. Misty-eyed, Shelly puts an arm around him. "If there's anything I can do …"

"You're very nice. I really shouldn't impose on you."

"No," insists Shelly, "please, anything."

"I don't think I should be alone tonight … would you … go out with me?" asks Otter, still shaken.

She smiles. "I'll get my coat."

Shelly is partway up the stairs when Otter yells after her, hopefully, "And could you get three dates for my friends?"

They shoot this two-minute scene again and again, for a couple of hours. Even at the final take, after hearing it all afternoon, the assembled crew & gawkers give up a ripple of laughter at Otter's last line.

With one not-ready-for-prime-time exception, the whole cast and crew are staying at The Rodeway Inn, conveniently located a mile north of downtown Eugene, right off the cloverleaf, at the intersection of Belt Line Road and Interstate 5. The setting, out here in God's country, is nearly as picturesque as it sounds. The Rodeway is part of a *2001* sprawl village that exists exclusively to serve this spigot in the four-lane pipeline: the buildings are all gas stations, motel complexes, coffee shops, fast pizza and Mex, a fake 7-11, a few new quickie apartments offering instant elegant townhouse living with a good view of the Interstate. Not half a mile away, the clear cold water of the McKenzie River boils into icy foam over its one-lane roadway of water-smoothed boulders, and on the banks the aspens are gold pointillist clouds against the dark cedars. But over at The Rodeway & Environs you'd never guess. This blister on the Interstate could be outside of Newark or Dayton or St. Louis or Birmingham or three dozen other cities in America. Another Utopia. Nowhere. A free glimpse of the future while you fill 'er up and check the oil.

The Rodeway itself is perfect: less like camp than a small college from the late 21st Century. Microwave University. The buildings are all pre-fab cost-accountant Mount Vernon. All outside walls sheeted with authentic colonial-style brick siding, towering white Georgian pillars of painted plywood, lush healthy plastic evergreens growing out of gravel gardens on each side of the main entrance. Where Thomas Jefferson had a spacious green lawn before him to gaze out upon, The Rodeway has an equally spacious parking lot. Some day, son, all the asphalt as far as the eye can see will be yours. So big is The Rodeway that beyond the black sea of the parking lot is another long two-story row of rooms, also pre-fab Mount Vernon, and that's where practically everyone in the movie is staying for the duration. Two weeks or so into shooting, when I got there, it was already turning into a college dorm.

When you're living on the moon, as we learned at Miami, one salvation from suicidal boredom is a semi-communal hanging out together. It's true in futureshock cinderblock dorms painted neurotic shades of institutional green; true for gypsy rock 'n roll entourages, endlessly touring; for the good southern Ohio folks on the annual Rev. Kash D. Amburgy Christmas Pilgrimage to the Holy Land, probably; and for sure for a movie company on location. Especially one making a nostalgic movie about college, even if the good old days are being remembered in all their glorious technicolor horror.

When I got in Friday night, I went looking for Chris Miller's room in yet another satellite of the Big House. Out of a room by the stairwell I was aiming for burst several people obviously from the movie company, happy, laughing, leaving a party inside. One of them, a man in his fifties, had a face that sent my Celebrity Trivia switch going boing boing boing. He's been the villain, at least once, on every television cop show I've ever seen. Clint Eastwood movies, others. The icewater executive who'd stop at nothing to tote that coke, lift that incriminating mail. The clever international flesh merchant who forces Pepper to go undercover as a white slave. Evil in a tailored suit. His name, Chris told me later, is John Vernon. He plays, naturally, dread Dean Wormer in *Animal House*. The room he and the others were leaving was still full of people, and inside someone was playing an acoustic guitar. All but the oversmoked were singing along to something from the classic folkie hit parade, *Hard Travelin'* or *Wildwood Flower…*

Dear Lord with a green bookbag: it's a "hoot," or a direct descendent. I haven't seen a real one since 1961, when with their shades and beards and Student Peace Union buttons and 12-strings and mimeographed books of chord changes to all known Carter Family songs, except the popular ones, the folkies would gather on Friday nights in the YMCA lounge of the Student

Union, to spend the evening drinking coffee, exchanging snappy anecdotes about 18th-Century ballads, and planning their trips with SNCC to darkest Mississippi. Since I was and am of the loud bars and Chuck Berry persuasion, I didn't manage to catch many of these. The only time I distinctly remember joining the Friday night hoot I was slightly on the lam from the university security cops (known fondly as the "Seekies"), who didn't think several of us should have been processing pictures for our off-campus humor magazine in a darkroom belonging to the student newspaper. My Friday nights usually went more like those in *Animal House*: pursuing sweet weekend oblivion through prolonged application of beer. Usually in a bar, preferably with a SeeBurg jukebox so loud the bass tickled your dick when you stood there picking out tunes, pinball machines dinging and ringing and counting in cascading clicks, the place jammed, smoky, all conversations carried on at a shout, no matter how vile or intimate, chasing whatever we could imagine.

On Saturday night the party, one anyway, is again in the same room. The room and the acoustic guitar, a beautiful Martin, belong to Bruce McGill, who plays the all-purpose Animal House scrounger, criminal activity a special-ty, a son of Milo Minderbinder named D-Day. For the part McGill sports a handlebar mustache and what we used to call a "New Yorker," although it was known as a "Detroit Boxcar" or a "San Diego Freeway," depending on where you were from. It's a crewcut on top, and a greasy D.A. on the sides and back. The only more courageous style from the period, not counting the walking wounded wearing Mohawks, substituted a single long clotted curl for the crewcut; the good ones spilled down over the forehead like carefully combed sludge.

The theoretical point of tonight's gathering is to watch the Saturday night fights, because there's an insistent dark attraction to seeing Ali go through the paces in decline, the same way it must have been to see fat old Babe Ruth waddling around the field in the early Forties. Also there's nothing else to do.

The glamorous movie life: ten of us strewn around a standard-issue motel room watching Ali doze and sweat through another one on the tube. Bruce under the circumstances is the perfect host. He's set up the basic bar on a vanity next to the john: vodka, Scotch, ice, a few sacks of beer. Sitting on the floor, wearing the same Levis she wore for the day's shooting, is Karen Jane Allen, Boone's delectable girlfriend Katy, who in the movie likes hanging around with the guys in Animal House. Tonight she's strumming Bruce's guitar, lightly singing a phrase here and there (while every man in the room explains to her nearly in chorus how the fight is going and why), hanging around with some of the guys who play in *Animal House*. True to her school. And Chinese boxes everywhere. I'd tell you more, but there suddenly appeared a joint of what must have been Indonesian Ultraviolet, and it was good night ladies for the group of us. We sat there jabbering for another two hours, but I don't remember a word of it. I called Chris recently to see if he was any clearer on that night. He didn't even remember the fight, so he called Bruce McGill, our host. He couldn't either. Another night lost to laughter.

At nine Sunday morning, while the cast sleeps, I've been invited to join Landis, crew and staff in watching the week's rushes. The cast is specifically *not* invited because Landis believes it would change and perhaps ruin their performances if they were to see themselves—make them self-conscious to the point of screwing themselves up, like golfers who think too much about their swing. And it's highly unusual to let a writer in, I'm told, but chiefly on Chris' recommendation I get an early peek.

The screening is at a movie house somewhere in the labyrinth of a nearby mall, one of those new "tasteful" complexes with plenty of natural wood and modernist granite slabs, a streamlined Stonehenge with boutiques. After making several bad choices in the maze, our down-vest rat-pack locates and swarms upon the theater, which is, according to the marquee, currently showing *Fantasia*. Landis, our lead blue lumberrat, bursts exuberantly inside and inquires of anyone: "Is the popcorn ready?" Almost.

Watching Landis watch the rushes, what he said and didn't say, when, I got a glimmer why practically everyone, cast and crew, is almost gushy about how good making the movie feels. On the way over in the car, a woman hair stylist and makeup man were, unbidden, going on and on about how wonderful it is; and both have been in the business forever. This is roughly equivalent to having your hard grizzled secretary rush beaming into your office to tell you what a terrific memo you've just written. At the center of many reasons for this is Landis himself. He is flatout charming, in the best sense of that word. Somehow he manages to be in charge with no trace of punk or cop, a boss who's also in the running for Most Genial award, something most bosses cannot or don't care to pull off. He seems to do it naturally, like the general of an equal-rights army.

During a break Landis says, "You know the rock star Andy Gold?" This just generally offered, apropos of nothing, to any of the thirty or so of us who are to listening. "When we were fourteen, in Grauman's Chinese ..." and proceeds to describe how once when the theater was full he and Gold began down at the front row and systematically criss-crossed every row, all the way back, saying "Excuse me, excuse me, excuse me" as they went.

An inset shot of a clear glass bowl on the stairway inside Animal House, filled with little white pills, yes, good old white crosses, the real six-days-on-the-road thing.

The bowl bears this sign: STUDY AIDS 5¢

At increasing speed, hand after hand drops coins in an adjoining bowl and takes out the study aids by the handful.

Next we are in the apartment of a young cynical English professor named Jennings, a cameo character played with deadly subtle accuracy by Donald Sutherland. Sitting on the floor of his spare post-bohemian living room are Boone, Katy and Pinto. Jennings is about to turn them on to marijuana for the first time. Sutherland is perfect: that thirtyish Assistant Professor with two bad unpublished novels buried in the closet, who finds refuge from his boredom in soft-spoken irony and the prettiest of his students. He says to the three of them, through a friendly black smirk, quietly, "Wanna smoke some pot?" Portentous pause. Even more quietly: "It's very good stuff." Pause. Quieter still: "I got it from a guy who's close friends with a black jazz musician."

Sutherland is so good that Landis is at last moved to exclaim, "Next time I'll pay him more than scale!"

Shots of Jennings removing his stash from behind a set of books stolen from the library, numbers still on their spines, *The Complete Oscar Wilde*. While they're on, Landis inquires if anyone present knows Oscar Wilde's dying words. No one does. Landis tells us that Wilde was on his deathbed, in the home of an old friend. He'd been in the same room for a week when one afternoon his friend stopped in to ask how he was doing. Wilde looked slowly around the room, and said "Either this wallpaper goes, or *I* do!"—and died.

The Toga Party scene: and finally a glimpse of John Belushi.

Like me, you may have been wondering where he's been, since he's billed as the star of the movie. On Saturday afternoon, he was at the football game. And he took less than a week in a so-called suite at The Rodeway before bailing outward and upward to a redwood modern house in the hills above Eugene. So he hasn't been hanging out with everyone else at Microwave U. Also, despite the star billing and the fact that his character was breathed to life with him in mind, Belushi doesn't have the biggest part. It may seem that he does in the final cut, but there isn't really a main star. The script by Harold Ramis (currently of *Second City TV*), Doug Kenny (co-founder of *National Lampoon*) and Chris Miller (whose cheerfully depraved collegiate life at Dartmouth inspired all this) is in its way populist: there isn't really a single central character—more like fifteen of them.

When Belushi is on the screen, though, he sometimes seems like all fifteen. When he was in Second City, other people in the company used to mutter sometimes that he wasn't above wrecking a scene to grab a big laugh for himself. That may be, but it's a crime of lower magnitude if you happen to be in the audience cracking up. And I think it may be more a matter of *inten-*

sity, anyway. Belushi burns out at you. Samurai comedy: zen explosives inside, ticking. Here he's Bluto, a yet-grosser incarnation of his namesake from *Popeye*, the animal of Animal House. He can crush beer cans against his bare forehead, open bottles with his teeth, is able to steal midterm exams from professors' offices in a single bound. But Belushi doesn't play him entirely as an ape in a grubby sweatshirt. Close, but not entirely. There are glints and gleams of something else as well, that seem to come from the same place inside where he gets his Brando, circa *On The Waterfront*. Bluto could be a pure unregenerate slob, but through Belushi he's less raw lout than lusting full-bore for life. Bluto comes at it *all* ready to roar. Even in this toga party scene, where he's just supposed to be monkey drunk but still dancing. Bluto to the end, he's wearing a foul lethal tee-shirt visibly beneath his toga. And *really* gets into the music: thrashing spastic rhythm on the floor, sweating, burning that famous *intensity*, invisible but there, a quasar blasting out x-rays, that suggestion that madness may call at any moment, no fucking around this time, folks, and that this foolishness has the utmost seriousness, meaning.

The fraternity's unanimous reaction to learning that vile Dean Wormer has put the house on "double secret probation" has been to light the boogie lamp, Roman r & b style, in their basement party room: inhaling beer and dancing in togas to a live band called Otis Day & The Knights, who hoot and wail and trill in falsetto through *Shout*, the grand old Isley Brothers anthem. Another perfect touch. Back then no self-respecting low-rent bar band dared take the stage without playing *Shout* some time during the night—and sometimes for most of the night. At Miami we had our choice among Tony & The Bandits, Maurice & The Rockets (sometimes The Mystics, Sultans or Galaxys, since Maurice was an Aries), or C.J. & The Disciples, depending on which bar one called home. All three groups usually murdered it, with enthusiasm, each in their fashion, but C.J. & The Disciples definitely held the endurance record. If we wanted it pure and undiluted straight from the fountain, fifteen miles away in Hamilton, Ohio, there was Spatz's Show Bar, a seedy roadhouse by the tracks, a true fightin-n-dancin' club where the Isleys themselves, local heroes from nearby Cincinnati, could be seen tearing it up on a regular basis. If you didn't mind flirting with a few parking lot switchblades and fistfights hoping to happen. And if nobody looked too closely at your fake I.D. that said you were 41 years old and weighed 268 pounds.

Chris Miller used to frequent a similar joint. But there was nothing so … common as a roadhouse anywhere near Dartmouth. His was on 45th Street in New York. It was called The Peppermint Lounge, and the house band was Joey Dee & The Starliters. This was 1961, well before the Beautiful People showed up there to twist a few trendy nights away. Chris and friends got the bright idea to bring The Starliters up to Dartmouth, to be the band for Spring Weekend at their fraternity house. In doing so they met an agent, and soon were regularly breaking an unspoken color line among the fraternities, which hired only white local bands (the squarer houses still bringing in Dixieland groups) or white bozos from Boston who imitated the black doo-wop sound. Chris' fraternity began bringing The Flamingoes, The Five Satins—even had Chuck Berry signed up to play their basement one Saturday, but Chuck had a gig the night before at Mount Holyoke, and apparently spent the weekend singing *Good Mornin' Little School Girl* to a very small but responsive audience in South Hadley, so they held over Joey Dee & The Starliters.

Which is why the band and music are what they are. Landis, showing considerable faith and charity, has given Chris and Doug Kenny minor parts in the movie as members of the fraternity. Chris has called himself Hardbar, and in these rushes of everyone dancing in increasing alcoholic frenzy to *Shout*, who should I spot but Chris, twisting in a toga, right next to the bandstand, unredeemed, close to the band as he can get, the old rock junkie shooting up once again.

Once more the steel jaws of the Wayback Machine are gobbling at my brain: through the dancing chaos four drunk young Romans wearing togas carry the bombed wife of Dean Wormer, her legs, as they used to say, akimbo. One I had blanked out comes rushing back: a Road Trip I took in dead of winter, 1962, from southern Ohio to semi-upstate New York, object Winter Weekend at Colgate. My friend Scott had been in school there for a while before landing at Miami, and wanted to go back to see the guys in his ex-fraternity. It seemed logical to me. Our final exams were an entire week away, it was only something like 1200 miles round trip, and we'd promoted a fine car—a terminal '54 Ford short with no heater or first gear. Starting from a stop, especially at railroad tracks, in second gear, and since the clutch wasn't too tricky either, it would lunge, heave and die. A couple of times before coughing and choking onward, all ninety-two tubercular horses. My girlfriend Beth, showing more good nature than sense, was convinced to go with us. We convulsed and froze 300 miles to Cleveland, where we picked up Scott's date. She was a pretty, quiet and refined girl named Valerie from Clifton Park, a fancy old suburb along the lake. Valerie wasn't really prepared for this. Upon stepping out the door of her Greek revival mansion and first laying eyes on the car, painted three noisy shades of primer and no hubcaps either, she involuntarily recoiled just a fraction, in spite of her good breeding, and turned a whiter shade of pale even as she smiled and said hello to us. I didn't blame her a bit. The rest of the drive to Colgate was uneventful. Scott courageously drove most of the way, through falling snow, while Beth and I made like squirrels in the back seat, constructing as best we could a nest from old newspapers, towels and a few ripe blankets I'd borrowed from my fraternity house. Valerie sat in front, shivering in her fur car coat, staring out at the snow.

It was gray late Saturday afternoon when we got in. First we located the rooming house where eventually Beth and Valerie would be spending the night, since we were already putting a severe strain on decency even to drive this far together without a priest in the trunk, or one parent strapped to the roof. The rooming house was an ancient frame farmhouse on the edge of town, presided over by a crabbed woman in her seventies whose mad rheumy eyes pulsed and flashed TILT! every few seconds. While the girls put their stuff in the room, Mrs. Tilt told Scott and me how, very soon, she was going to get away from all this, that her …*secret patents*…would any day now make her filthy rich as she deserved and allow her to retire to the Ozarks where she belonged.

Scott gave us a quick tour of campus and town, being certain to point out the diner with the best chili and pinball machine, then drove over to his old fraternity house. From the street we could hear the band in the basement. And love at fifteen degrees: in the dying light lay a couple glued in an embrace behind a bush in the front yard, accented rather than hidden by its leafless branches, heaving and groaning in passionate spasms on the frozen grass, fully clothed; and from an upper window, someone was throwing up, or, from our point of view, down. Definitely the place.

The rest of the weekend returns mostly as images scattered and scrambled, vivid but lacking coherence, just like *Last Year At Marienbad*, the 1962 season's hit among the arty grad student set, who always found higher merit in anything artistic that achieved quintessential incomprehensibility, especially if it was foreign, preferably French. One thing I remember clearly from *Last Weekend at Colgate* is that both Scott and I struck out cold in the all-important Scoring Division. Or was he the one in there with the naked redhead when the Dean threw open the closet door, as the lights went out? Could be. By then I was well beyond that desired peak of drunk where you feel like you've swallowed a big neon sign, still on, and your whole body is alight, buzzing CHEESEBURGER CHEESEBURGER CHEESEBURGER, brain off somewhere in a basket of fries. I know that *I* struck out. First we had all danced to the band in the basement. Beth, who never drank very much, and then only 3.2 beers because that's all Oxford had to offer, kept quenching her twisting thirst with smooth tumbler after tumbler of Scotch-and-water, on an empty stomach. Soon she found herself on her knees staring at fate in a low oval bowl of white porcelain. We drove her back to Mrs. Tilt's to sleep it off. In a burst of altruism, Valerie volunteered to stay there and take care of her.

Before or after that, maybe considerably before or after, to be precise,

Scott directed us to the room of a friend of his, known for no reason as Rickshaw, a guy from New York whose collection of Fifties 45s was legend. I remember drooling inwardly and then on my madras sportcoat as he showed us three black steamer trunks filled with carefully alphabetized grease. A selection from I to L, on a tape I still have: *Tick-Tock* by The Innocents. *I'm So Sorry* by Jimmy Inman & The Impollos (no, not Brenda Lee, or the Impalas). *VooDoo Doll* by The Interiors. *Bad Boy* by The Jive Bombers. *Stormy Weather* by The Leaders (*the* classic r&b version). *Come Into My Palace* by Lee & The Leopards … give, oldies buffs? I did right away. He'd begun collecting as soon as it started happening, helped along by a jacket whose pockets, strangely enough, were two shades larger than a 45 record. Mister Rock 'n Roll, if anyone deserved the title.

It was in Rickshaw's room—as he deftly played requests and mixed drinks while basically continuing to make out with his date on the couch—that I found myself suddenly turned to furniture. One moment, sitting in an overstuffed chair. Gooned and reeling, certainly, but still conscious and digging the music. The next, I *was* the chair. Insensate. Gone. The difference between me and the other furniture essentially one of internal body temperature. Except that I could still see. I seem to have passed out with my eyes open. Nobody appeared to mind, or notice. I fit right in with the glassy-eyed moose head wearing stereo headphones and a cigarette draped from its lips, Bogart style, above me on the wall. Even in my furniture state, it registered that I'd never seen a fraternity party like this one before. A wild night at my straight house occurred when someone spiked his date's Pepsi and managed some fleeting bare tit in the dark parlor full of couches known accurately and tenderly as The Grinding Room. Here another couple had replaced Rickshaw & date on the couch and oh, Cisco! Had I been able to move a muscle I would have left the room. Really. And somewhere in there, in the blur of my peripheral vision, a guy who looked vaguely familiar led a serious amount of hips and red hair into the room, opened the closet door, and with a grand sweeping gesture escorted her inside, closing the door after them. And at some point there was definitely a motorcycle roaring down the hallway outside the room. It must have been just after that that the Dean showed up. An angry older fellow in a suit, as I recall, who exploded into the room and my freeze frame snarling something corny like "What's the meaning of this?" He'd been working at a men's school too long. The meaning was perfectly clear. And provoked the female member of the couple on the couch to empty her mouth with a *pop*!, while her date still stared off toward heaven, and ask: "I suppose you want me to get pregnant?" and then returned to the business at hand. The Dean looked her over carefully before saying, in measured tones, "No, I suppose not." He turned to a rodent assistant who'd appeared behind him and said: "Take all their names." I still couldn't move, but I remember thinking gleefully: *Fuck you! I don't go to school here! My name is U Thant!* The Dean was leaving to view other bloody moral battlefields when from the closet a high throaty voice began beating its wings upward and ever faster toward joyous pagan *getting off*, a flight he shot down in mid-ascent when he flung open the closet door, which sent all this freckled pink skin and red hair reeling out onto the rug, just as the lights went out. Some wise saint had killed the electricity by taking an axe to the fusebox, and in the darkness everybody scrambled to have been somewhere else while all this was happening.

Leaving the theater into the bright Sunday sunlight is like returning to the surface after being down in some grotto fifteen years deep. Even in rough repetitive pieces, the movie has done a job on me, and I'm glad to be on my way to a brunch at John Belushi's house in the hills, for selected cast, crew and staff, in the present, which I prefer, hard and dull as it sometimes gets.

One thing better about the present is the food. Judy Jacklin, Belushi's wife and, today, hostess, greets me at the door and aims me straight for it: eggs & avocados, caviar, lox & bagels, sweetrolls, abundant bloody marys and coffee… The house is G.I. modern, natural and open, lots of bare wood and windows. In a bright room off the kitchen, ten or so of the assembled are watching a color TV set, where John Belushi's and my Chicago Bears are getting creamed by the Green Bay Packers.

Belushi and I don't really know each other, but we've met several times—going back to the days when he was the new kid at Second City. Since Chicago is in its way a small midwestern village, we have quite a few mutual friends, so when he comes over to say hello, wearing a blue Japanese *hapi* coat over Levi's and a shirt, we start out talking about who's doing what where. Slim as our connection is, I can see that he's happy to run into someone from "home"—which good for him, appears still to be Chicago in his head. Further proof: the tape playing on his hotshit portable stereo with the works is gritty Chicago blues, and the short stack of albums he's brought along the road are all blues or r&b classics, many the Fifties originals, their covers worn gray in places from being handled. Someone is rolling joints on a vintage Ray Charles album.

Belushi begins telling several of us about a new bit he's working on with Dan Aykroyd for *Saturday Night Live*. It's a takeoff on *Fear and Loathing in Las Vegas* by Hunter Thompson. Aykroyd to play everyone's favorite Doctor, and Belushi his Brown Buffalo lawyer. Belushi flashes on the scene in the cocktail lounge, both tripping their brains out. Hard to top the original, where, in medias res: *Terrible things were happening all around us. Right next to me a huge reptile was gnawing on a young woman's neck, the carpet was a blood-soaked sponge—impossible to walk on it, no footing at all. "Order some golf shoes," I whispered. "Otherwise, we'll never get out of this place alive. You notice these lizards don't have any trouble moving around in this muck—that's because they have claws on their feet."* … Belushi's got Hunter's famous machine-gun mutter down perfectly, and I don't doubt they'll think of something. We all admire and trade stories about Doctor Thompson. My contribution is that once while doing a phone interview with him, he responded, when I asked the subject of his novel-in-progress, by pounding the phone repeatedly on a table, bang bang bang, shrieking hideously, then saying in a tense whisper: "Texas."

A little later I'm again standing near the food, part of a circle which for me features Lisa Bauer, yesterday's Shelly, roommate of poor dead Faun. Today's she's wearing a wine-colored sweater and poured-denim Levi's. I try not to fall into her large chocolate eyes while she tells us she's sad that she doesn't have a bigger part, because in two hours she's to be put on a plane for Hollywood, where she lives, not to return for two weeks.

Standing next to her is Doug Kenny, hair on the sides and back of his head cropped nearly to nonexistence, and stylish neo-mad bomber rimless glasses. He looks nothing like the long-haired hippie in a high school jacket who used to stare forlornly out of the pages of *National Lampoon*, begging to be sent to camp. The character he's created for himself in the movie is a clod engineering student named Stork, who distinguishes himself even at the toga party by wearing mechanical pencils clipped to his toga, a complicated ugly chronometer on his wrist, and those two-tone hornrims, black and clear-plastic, that supposedly made you look less like you were wearing glasses, but which in fact looked like regular hornrims cut off by shears at the eyeball. The rest of the circle are Chris Miller, who's fussing with his bloody mary, since he's among the select few who believe they know the True Secret Formula; Art Director John Lloyd; and Tim Matheson, the movie's handsome slippery Otter. Each of us a brilliant dazzling wit in his own right, of course. But we don't know each other very well, and so when Lisa leaves to catch her plane we soon fall for no reason to reminiscing fondly about firecrackers, enjoying the names, hammerhead, M-80, chinese ladies fingers… We agree in concert that cherry bombs were the *primo* kind, not only for name and look, but because they were waterproof—just right for those temperamental school toilets. Then it is cruising for burgers, joys of. Then the weather. How half the cast has colds or worse. I think we did manage, to our credit, not to compare the relative merits of New York and Los Angeles.

On Monday morning before leaving I walked around campus toward the building being used as Animal House. As I passed a women's dorm, above me through an open window I could hear someone playing a *lute* and, truly, singing *Born Free*. The river is always different but never changes: Shelly of 1977.

The house they've taken over is on fraternity row, but when it's not in a movie it's a halfway house for ex-convicts. Seems right. Landis & crew have turned it into a magnificent disaster area: rusting hulks of several dead cars and an ambulance decaying in the front yard; charred remains of a fire around one boarded-up window; a shopping cart on the roof, etc. The attention to detail is remarkable, right down to the smallest. Today on the front lawn, for instance, the still photographer is shooting pictures of extras recruited from several fraternities and put into early Sixties drag, for the Animal House composite picture of all the brothers. Supervising are Chris and Doug Kenny, who's decked out as Stork, in an outfit that includes scuffed desert boots, cheap chinos that stop three inches above his ankles, and a sliderule that he wears mounted gunfighter style from his belt, and which he uses to occupy dull moments by practicing his fast draw.

A kid shows up to be shot by the still photographer. Clothes are fine, but he's got his hair parted down the middle, in a fruity Beardsley style. Doug the classical purist notices the anachronism and walks over to him. Without thinking Doug says to him: "Don't you know *nobody* wore his hair that way in 1962?"

And also without thinking the extra answers: "Are you kidding? In 1962 I was *four years old*!"

- 1978

Before writing this article, I knew almost nothing about bluegrass beyond the Flatt & Scruggs theme song to The Beverly Hillbillies. *I talked* Playboy *into letting me go to Virginia to cover this bluegrass festival by a green river partly because I knew it would be a scene, but also an excuse to hang out with my longtime pal Scott Guthery, another sucker for scenes (we once drove all the way from Cleveland to Greenwich Village right after* On The Road *came out, because we had to see it firsthand), and probably my best friend ever, though now that is ancient history and he is long gone out of my life. So in many ways the piece for me today is a snapshot of that bright moment in our friendship, its sun at zenith, but unknown to either of us at the time, beginning to set. This one's for you, fuckhead.*

It was also my very first bylined piece for the magazine, and the very first long article I had ever written. I didn't have a clue how to go about doing it. So as usual I just faked it. I remember reading In Our Time, *Hemingway's early short story collection, as inspiration before starting, which was weird, since then and now he was never one of my favorite writers. But I think I wanted to absorb some of his famous economy, to counter my unfortunate tropism toward Faulkner, and it was also a great way to avoid having to actually begin writing it.*

And the long weekend at the Berryville Festival revealed to me a lifelong true love—for bluegrass music. Much of why I feel that way is in the article, but I would add I think too that the appeal is genetic. Both my mother and father traced their families back over many generations to origins on the Isle of Man, lying right between Scotland and Ireland. And this Scotch/Irish folk music was transplanted to new soil into the mountains of Virginia and Kentucky, nicely cooking along there for generations, until it become a high octane home brew called bluegrass.

So crank up a little Stanley Brothers, pop open a jug, and take a sip…

SHENANDOAH BREAKDOWN

AT A BLUEGRASS FESTIVAL IN OLD VIRGINIA, COUNTRY-FOLK AND FREAKS GATHER BY THE RIVER FOR THREE DAYS OF DOWNHOME MUSIC

You turn at the fruit stand on Route 7. The country road curls slowly downward through wooded east Virginia hills to the Shenandoah River. Ridges of rock poke their backs through thin topsoil in the scattered fields, and to be knee high by the Fourth of July, the corn crop will have to double its size in two days.

The road abruptly becomes a gooey mix of tar and dust and gravel, twists with the land through a few final bends and spills out onto a 40-acre patch of bottom land bordering the green river. Beyond the fence that runs along the road are two big fields divided by a tree line, and one is already filling up with pickup trucks, campers, trailers, converted school buses and cars. Alongside many of them, orange and green and brown tents have already sprouted.

The folks are settling in for three days of at the Fifth Annual Berryville, Virginia, Blue Grass Music Festival.

The sign above the gate says:

WATERMELON PARK
NO ALCOHOLIC BEVERAGES PERMITTED

A dozen campers and cars are strung out along the road in front of the gate, waiting to pay the admission price— $12 a head for all three days—and then politely scramble for a good spot to camp. Inside on the field, a couple of jolly Georgia boys with epic beer bellies and genuine red necks spot a driver in the line with hair like you'd expect to see on a city boy.

All smiles. "Hey, there, buddy, hey you there," one yells, rubbing his barbershop bald head, "how about loanin' me some of that hair of yours?" Grins.

"Sure thing," shouts the city boy, also all smiles. He grabs a handful and waves it. "How much you want?"

Everybody smiles as hard as he can, and finally the line moves up a long notch.

*** *** ***

The blue-and-white concrete bandstand, about the size of a boxcar, sits to the right of the gate on the shaved top of a little knoll, facing the river through a grove of old sycamores. The Shenandoah here is clean and fast, waist-deep in the middle. Where it bends, the park ends in a spear-shaped tip with a tiny sandless beach. Two dozen kids have already discovered the pool of quiet water there, held by a wide rock ridge that rises and runs barely underwater across the river. Below the ridge lies 30 yards of soft rapids, just wild enough to tempt any kid with an air mattress into shooting them, but about as dangerous as sunning on the bank with the bluegrass widows who sit there watching their kids swim, talking about everything but bluegrass.

Onstage, The Lewis Family is winding up the three hours of hymn singing that opened the festival. It's hymn singing bluegrass style, naturally, get-up-and-go Gospel, banjo picking for the Lord. In front of the stage, in the shade between the big trees, a ragged rainbow of aluminum chairs is growing in arched rows. You're supposed to bring your own seats, but in case you didn't, there's a flatbed truck full of empty apple crates over to the side, and they'll do better than the ground. There aren't more than 300 people watching the show now, but by nine o'clock Saturday night, when The Earl Scruggs Revue comes on, the number will nudge 8000. The space up close to the bandstand has been staked out and claimed for hours, and there might as well be a sign: SERIOUS BLUEGRASS LOVERS ONLY—damn little talking in that section, filled mostly with middle-aged country people in drip-dry Dacron shirts and cotton shifts. Many of the men study the picking and fiddling with eyes squinted and jaws set, like hanging judges hearing evidence at a murder trial, cassette tape recorders whirring on their knees. You don't get to hear live bluegrass much, and they're going to hear it all.

Over to the right of the stage, a tired-looking long-hair stands by a board covered with the buttons and bumper stickers he has for sale. He's a student at Ann Arbor and in the summer covers the bluegrass circuit, having just gotten in from Bill Monroe's weeklong Festival in Bean Blossom, Indiana. He digs bluegrass, he says, doesn't know why, he just digs it. The buttons say I LUV BLUEGRASS, and his bumper stickers invite everyone to GET HIGH ON BLUEGRASS.

*** *** ***

"We've got a big family Bible that's usually marked for fifty-nine-nine-ty-five," Little Roy of The Lewis Family reminds everybody from the stage, "but we're sellin' it here for twenty-five dollahs."

*** *** ***

The concession stand is to the right of the stage, and to its right is a small white fruit stand that's temporarily become the festival office. Inside, Carlton Haney, the downhome promoter who invented bluegrass festivals six years ago, is talking over a minor problem with one of The Country Gentlemen, while a mandolin player named Frank Wakefield, unattached, looks on. Haney is short and solid, a friendly man in his mid-50s. After bluegrass, he most dearly loves talking to people and does it in a backthroat North Carolina accent undisturbed by the patch of top front teeth he's missing.

The Country Gentleman is mid-30, handsome and serious. If Merle Haggard had had a really hard life, he'd look like Charlie Waller. He's pointing to a row of tents and tables piled and hung with bluegrass goods for sale, a back-woods shopping mall running 100 yards toward the river. It seems The Country Gentlemen have a table where they're selling Country Gentlemen records, but some independent capitalist is selling everybody's records, including records by The Country Gentlemen, and he's underselling them by a quarter.

"You just tell 'em, Charlie, that they can't do that," Haney says. "You can't tell 'em what to charge for other people's albums, of course, but you can tell 'em that they can't do that to you. I told them people last year I didn't want 'em to come back."

*** *** ***

Ralph Stanley is introducing a song to the Friday-afternoon crowd. He's been on the road playing banjo for 25 years, and you can hear every mile in his voice. He was half of The Stanley Brothers until brother Carter died five years ago, and you can hear that in his voice, too.

"We want to do a sacred song now, we always include some hymns on our program, and this one that's in our latest album we get a lot of requests for it, and it's the title of the album. Jack Cook, you got a lot of albums on the table over there, why don't you tell 'em about a couple of the albums."

"Thank you, Ralph, we do have a new hymn album out, the one Ralph just said. It's got a lot of good songs on it, it's been out about three weeks, and we also have an album over here, the last show that Carter and Ralph did together, recorded live onstage from Bean Blossom, Indiana. And it's on Ralph's private label, you can't get in the store, and it'd be a good keepsake. Carter does the m.c. on it and the applause is on it, so if you'd like to have one of the albums, why, we'll have 'em on sale right here. If you'd like to, come by, and like Little Roy says, if you come by and shake hands with us, have some money in your hand..."

*** *** ***

The pantheon of bluegrass is a long list of unfamiliar names: Bill Monroe and The Blue Grass Boys, The Stanley Brothers, Reno & Smiley, The Lilly Brothers with Tex Logan and Don Stover, Jimmy Martin, The Osborne Brothers, The Country Gentlemen. As a national American obsession, their music ranks right up there with hog calling. The few people who care about it live mostly in the Southeast, with a few others scattered about the Ohio Valley and east Texas. For the rest of the country, bluegrass consists entirely of the theme song from *The Beverly Hillbillies* and the soundtrack from *Bonnie and Clyde* — both performed by Flatt & Scruggs, the only bluegrass group that people who live in high-rises have ever heard of.

Which makes sense. Bluegrass goes back to the country, a country that barely exists anymore. The sound is out of the mountains, high lonesome harmonies sung in a rough moonshine blend above a galloping banjo and a hard-running guitar, sweetened with a mandolin and a fiddle that chugs in and out of the thick of things, all in time to the string bass. Many of the songs are traditional, some dating back to English ballads, and many celebrate values just as old. The sacred songs are strictly fundamentalist: You stay right with the Lord and He'll stay right with you, and it's part of His plan when He takes a loved one away. God isn't even sick, let alone dead, in bluegrass music. Of the non-sacred songs, the most memorable are about equally divided between absolute sentimentality, *Mother's not dead, she's only a-sleepin'*, and tough fuck-everybody-but-me anarchy, *Morphine run me crazy, cocaine'll kill my baby, nobody's business what I do*. Love your mother and fight all night.

It's not the sort of thing that's going to fill Shea Stadium, even though it may be the closest thing we've got to a living folk tradition — and a beautiful one if you listen right. But it's a music with such a limited appeal right now that even so-called country radio stations seldom play it. A hit single by Bill Monroe, the much-loved father figure who started it all, will sell about 50,000 copies.

When Ralph Stanley stands up in front of 8000 people at a festival, he's looking at nearly a sixth of his entire market.

*** *** ***

The Friday-afternoon sun slants through the trees. The crowd is bigger now, 500 or 600. In a back row, flanked by his wife and two restless kids, a crewcut fiddle lover in a white T-shirt raises his hands to whoop over a tasty fiddle break by Tex Logan. His kids look at him like it's just another crazy thing the old man does. His wife looks like she wouldn't mind if he didn't enjoy himself quite so much. They don't see it, but about 30 feet to their left, a girl in an Army shirt, looking too gray and somber not to come from New York, focuses her Nikon F with a 135mm lens on them. Click. Instant folklore.

A few minutes later, m.c. Fred Bartenstein, a good-looking kid in his 20s with a slight Southeast drawl, introduced the group. "Ladies and gentleman, this is a historic moment. This is the first time in over a year that The Lilly Brothers, Tex Logan and Don Stover will appear on the stage together, and the first time ever at a bluegrass festival." The group comes out, and Logan is the stylish stand-out with an L.B.J. Stetson, a prosperous bounty-hunter's mustache, string tie, dark neatly cut Western suit and cowboy boots. Fred Bartenstein is a junior at Harvard majoring in urban planning, and Tex Logan has a master's in electrical engineering from MIT. His current hitching post is a Bell Labs think tank in New Jersey.

*** *** ***

By Friday night, with the stage lit bright and the moon rising high above the hills, it wasn't hard to tell that this was something more than a gathering of Baptist dirt farmers. Most of the 4000 people in front of the bandstand had logged their share of miles in pickup trucks, and many had faces weathered by too much hot sun and raw wind. But scattered among them—isolated clumps of chaos in a field of well-mowed heads and white shirts—were 200 or 300 freaks, dread long-hair dope-smoking freaks with peace symbols and headbands and power-to-the-people handshakes. Weirdo radical revolutionaries sitting next to right-wing racist bigots. Always read the label first.

The small fields of energy where they came together seemed surreal in a hopeful way, even if the mood wasn't precisely lions and lambs. There was no hostility, but a lot of very interesting glances got exchanged, and a number of the freaks decided that staying on the edge of the crowd wasn't such a bad idea. For the most part, it was a musical truce: I come here to listen, and you come here to listen, so let's us listen.

*** *** ***

Depending on who you were, the hit of the evening was either Bluegrass 45 or the New Deal String Band. Bluegrass 45 consists of five good ole boys from Kobe, Japan, who play traditional bluegrass—or "brewglass," as they called it. They came out like a vision from a 1961 fraternity party—all madras sports coats, ties, black stovepipe slacks, white socks and penny loafers—and sounded just like a bluegrass band, shitkicking fiddle and all. The crowd immediately shifted gears from critical consideration to Southern hospitality, cheering and clapping for music they would have yawned at if it had come from Ralph Stanley. Like Samuel Johnson said of dogs walking on their hind legs, it's not that they do it well, it's that they do it at all.

*** *** ***

The New Deal String Band didn't come on until almost midnight, and people used to getting up at dawn just don't stay up that late, so the crowd had thinned considerably, leaving large patches of empty lawn chairs as territorial markers. The timing was no accident. Bluegrass 45 was one thing, but the New Dealers, with hair to their shoulders and East Village duds, look like a hard rock band with the wrong instruments. Hip bluegrass. They speeded up the bedtime of several good people with a bluegrass version of Bob Dylan's *One More Night*—greeted with the only genuine boos of the evening, from five or six offended purists—and told the longhairs who they were by introducing a song saying, "We're gonna do this one now, it's a old bluegrass tune we learned from the Coasters...

I took my troubles down to Madam Ruth
You know, that gypsy with the gold-capped tooth
She's got a pad down at Thirty-fourth and Vine
Sellin' little bottles of love potion number nine.

One long-haired couple gave up after 12 solid hours of bluegrass and walked slowly back along the dark rocky river path to their campsite, two sleeping bags spread out on the sandy ground between the saplings and the small trees along the riverbank. Two old friends they hadn't seen for a year were with them, and they sat around a little fire until late, drinking good cold prohibited beer and finding out about each other again, while the distant jam onstage echoed through the hills.

*** *** ***

It turned out Saturday afternoon that this was a convention, not a festival. The two fields next to the bandstand were packed with tight haphazard rows of pickup campers and tents, and late-comers were threading through them to a third field half a mile from the stage. And, like Julie Andrews says, the fields were alive with the sound of picking.

*** *** ***

A wide canvas flap has been strung between two campers, and in its shade two banjo players, two fiddlers, a mandolin player and a guy on guitar are making plenty of music. One of the fiddlers is a young skinny boy about 16, and at the moment he's seriously proving he has his licks down, paying to join up. The older fiddler encourages him by laying back on rhythm for two or three long tunes before showing him how a man does it. One banjo player is shirtless and shoeless, wearing only khaki cutoffs, wire glasses and a beard. He's trading runs with a guy who could be a small-town insurance salesman, well combed, in a plaid cotton shirt and ample trousers with cuffs. Between tunes, the insurance salesman comes over and asks to see a particularly pretty run that caught his eye, watching hard until he's got it down. The mandolin player has the slack jaw and tight eyes of a real red-neck, but it's doubtful that Lester Maddox would approve the shoulder strap on his mandolin, a gentle pale blue, embossed with alternating white doves and peace signs.

*** *** ***

At the end of the park downstream from the little beach, the woods along the bank start getting thick. In the last clearing, the sweetest music of the festival got played. It started late Saturday afternoon, at the campsite of a lean bearded guy who played a beat-up guitar that sounded valuable. He was sitting on an apple crate opposite a dobro player with a preposterous gut and a canary-yellow cowboy hat. A dobro is a beautiful instrument, a guitar inset with a shining circular metal plate that's got a complex pattern of openings cut into it, like an elegant Turkish hubcap. That was apparently why a media-looking friend of the guitarist was hovering around with a camera, and looking very handy at it, getting in there tight on the dobro. Another media-looking friend stood by close, puffing on a fat joint with chocolate papers—almost the only visible dope at the festival—and getting way into the music. Occasionally the dobro player caught a stray whiff of the grass and shot a puzzled glance at the joint, not like he smelled evil killer weed, more like, what kind of cheap tobacco you smokin', son?

They picked together for an hour. And just as the dobro player started shifting his ass like he'd have to be leaving shortly, Doyle Lawson of J.D. Crowe and The Kentucky Mountain Boys wandered in with his guitar. With the scar on his upper lip, Lawson looks a little like Stacy Keach. He said he'd been looking three hours for someone to do some real picking with. Two sets on stage apparently just got him going.

Word of good jams must travel fast. In ten minutes, other musicians started drifting in with black instrument cases, tuning up and jumping in. One of the first was a short, sun-tanned, 40ish fiddler with an electric-blue shirt and a toothpick in the corner of his mouth. He frowned and fiddled like a son of a bitch for two hours in the woods—and then turned up later onstage, backing none other than Earl Scruggs.

By sunset, a great golden shine on the river, so many musicians were circled around the two apple crates that they had formed layers, like uneven rings on a tree. A plump kid with horn-rimmed glasses and a pink eager face strolled over, casual-like, not too interested, not his fault he happened to be lugging his bass fiddle with him. The New Deal String Band, camped a little way upriver, one by one decided not to miss this, even though they had picked half the night before onstage.

Half a dozen guitars, as many banjos, two dobros, three mandolins and a fiddle—all lickety-picking along, fast and smooth and happy. It was clean, ain't-things-just-goin'-fine country music, not bluegrass, and the little crowd that sat and stood among the tents, slightly outnumbering the musicians, loved it. One of them, a young balding Pennsylvania lawyer named Pat, obliged a new acquaintance with a running who's who of the personnel: Tut Taylor, antique-instrument collector, in the canary-yellow hat; Vassar Clements on fiddle, doing sessions with John Hartford; Leroy Savage on guitar. The skinny guitarist who started the game was David Bromberg, a New York studio musician who turned up on the last two Dylan albums, now producing John Hartford's latest. "They're picking some hard stuff here," Pat said. "Not like that shit they're feeding the Okies on the bandstand."

*** *** ***

When Bob Dylan showed up at the 1965 Newport Folk Festival with electric guitars and a new sound laced with rock, the hard-core folkies tried to boo him off the stage. Maybe that was in the back of Carlton Haney's head Saturday night as he introduced Earl Scruggs, the Special Guest Star of the festival.

"He's one of the world's greatest musicians. Now, we're gonna ask you to listen to the show, or if you don't want to, you can go over to the side. If you're stayin' here, you're gonna listen and show respect for the show… Twenty-five or thirty years ago, there was a man took a banjo and played it different from other men, and they told him then it wouldn't work, they told him then he didn't know what he was doin'. The banjo never could be played like that. It was not to go with singin', it was to go with square dancin'. But he didn't believe 'em, they never convinced him. He went to work with Bill Monroe, and he's the man that taken the only native American instrument and adapted it so it could be used in country music, and music around the world. And when the history of music is written, this man's name will be among the Top Ten that's ever lived."

A ripple of noise down front jarred Haney out of his history. "You'll be quiet, or we'll ask you to leave now. If you want to hear what I've got to say, you can be quiet; if you don't, you don't have to stay. I've spent a lifetime bringin' you these, and you're gonna listen or be quiet! I want you to hear this man, we have longed to have him at a festival."

The cheers and whistles from the crowd meant that Haney had temporarily won. But there was something in the air. And anybody wondering why had only to look onstage, where the equipment men were setting up an electric piano, guitar amplifiers and a set of drums. Earl Scruggs wouldn't be playing pure bluegrass tonight.

Scruggs may have been remembering the 1965 Newport Festival, too. He came out—with his three sons on guitars, Vassar Clements on fiddle, and a pretty young lady on piano—and launched into *Nashville Skyline Rag*, a Dylan tune. The long-hairs, mostly far away on the edges of the crowd, let out a joyous surprised whoop the moment they recognized their old buddy Dylan, but closer up front the full-time bluegrass fans recognized that they didn't recognize the song and countered the whoop with a low moan of boos—while small groups of offended purists here and there showed how betrayed they felt by packing up their lawn chairs and marching through the audience toward their tents. They didn't come all this way to listen to rock 'n' roll.

You could feel it. It wasn't anything to fight about, but the tension crackled through the air for a few minutes before fading, and in some spots didn't fade at all. When Scruggs followed *Nashville Skyline* with Dylan's *You Ain't Going*

Nowhere—insult to injury—a couple of hefty farm boys feeling their beer began eyeing the crowd, looking for someone to slug, the music being as good an excuse as any. Toward the back of the crowd, a clot of would-be hippies were trying to re-create the wonders of Woodstock right behind a row of quiet country people who were trying to hear Scruggs. One of the little Woodstock Nation, a baby-fat teenage girl in hip new hitch-'em up overalls, was singing along loudly to the music and lurching around in a dance that was probably beautiful if you were on acid or mescaline like she was. If you weren't tripping, it wasn't so beautiful: a blast of artificial energy where it wasn't needed at all. Her girlfriend had a more subdued glaze in her eyes and sat on the ground tossing pebbles and rocks at two empty Coke bottles. She finally broke one, and everybody around her turned to look when it shattered, and the bright shards seemed out of place, too. But she kept working on the second bottle, and one rock, tossed too hard, took a fat bounce and hit the back of a lawn chair. The frail middle-aged man in it shot her a fast angry glance, which she didn't notice, and then turned to his wife. "Fuckin' hippies," he said. "Fuckin' hippies."

*** *** ***

In the cool silver moonlight, a 30-year-old newcomer to bluegrass wanders toward a fire surrounded by the New Deal String Band and friends. He has a Ph.D. in math from Michigan State and he's in the same Bell Labs think tank that Tex Logan swims in, but it's a big tank and they've never heard of each other. He leans against a Volkswagen bus, listening to the picking and singing, watching the instruments flash in the flying yellow light, grinning to himself. After a few minutes, his old grad school buddy appears at this shoulder, shoving a beer toward him. They sip their beer in the dark, and it's 200 years ago, mountain men coming together in the woods to break the months of silence, among people again, happy and letting loose, America like we wish it was.

*** *** ***

Early false dawn, with thick gray mist rising like cold steam off the river. A thin girl in her 20s sits by a dying fire talking quietly to an ex-academic in a Levi jacket and pants. Their conversation has that special late-night seriousness and intimacy, and they pass a bottle of Ripple back and forth, slowly. But the mood is abruptly brought into the daylight by a guy with hair to his shoulders and a good paunch shoving out his orange undershirt. He comes wandering toward them, smiling, and they recognize him as the mandolin player with the New Deal String Band. When he gets close, he smiles wider and says in a somehow surprising mountain accent, "Yew got any marywana? Ah been tryin' ta get stoned fer three days."

They laugh, and the night's all over.

*** *** ***

"Oh! Lordy!"

It's Sunday-morning shower time in the river for two beer-bellied good ole boys. They come rebel-hooting toward the water, wearing boxer bathing suits and trading hot-damn locker-room shoves. It is a joy to be a hillbilly and alive.

"Know what ah'm gonna do to yew?" hollers one with a grin as they get close to the water. "Ah'm gonna *baptize* your ass!"

They run unnoticing through the campsite of the same city boy they wanted to borrow some hair from two days ago. Shoving each other in, they splash shouting into the current.

"Ohhh, Lordy," hoots one, ducking his head. "Ah am saved!"

*** *** ***

If you have to leave early, you drive out the gate and up the road to Route 7 with the music from the bandstand still rolling out across the river. And you hear it for a long time after you can't hear it anymore: in random barely heard sounds lurk faint ghostly bluegrass runs. Even leaning back tired in your seat over the wing two hours later, with Washington's serious geometry quickly diminishing beneath you, you can hear hiding in the drone of the jet engines a distant banjo, racing with sweet steps toward home.

- 1971

I've been teaching at Medill for a number of years now, and I tell students the story here as a cautionary tale: This is how NOT to conduct a celebrity interview. As you'll see, I did just about everything wrong that I possibly could have.

But I had hardly interviewed anyone in my life up until then, and certainly not my very favorite rock band, Cream, which at the time I considered the best on the entire planet.

Before then, the only celebs I had interviewed, after a fashion, were Robert Wagner and Natalie Wood. I was in high school, this was 1959, and they were doing gang interviews with high school reporters in various cities. So it was me and about 40 other juvenile journalists packed into a small auditorium somewhere in downtown Cleveland. I didn't ask a single question of my own—but I did get to see fetching young Natalie, just 3 years older than I was, in the flesh, up close if not personal. Also while working for the high school paper—my only "official" training in journalism, incidentally—I was sent to a similar gang interview with Red Grange, of whom I had never heard (legendary Chicago Bear circa 1925-1934, I learned), who was on a twilight-round of a motivational speaking tour, and I definitely asked no questions in that one either.

So that was my background in celeb interviews going into this.

It would have to be qualified as an unqualified disaster, but I did get to *shake* the hand!

CREAMED BY CREAM
NEVER TRY TO INTERVIEW GOD

It was October 1968.

Cream's *Wheels of Fire* double album had been released in August—the silver one with the live version of *Crossroads* on it, the track which even after all this time I would take to the moon with me if I were exiled there and allowed only one rock and roll record. *Crossroads* is perfect, flawless and exciting even after the 9 millionth time you've heard it. Eric Clapton spilling notes over measures like a spring waterfall, that lambent sound of his; Jack Bruce on bass slugging it out with him for the lead, playing lead bass in spots; and crazy Ginger Baker back there showing the drumkit what amphetamines were invented for. For me *Crossroads* is the platonic model for rock and roll, the essence.

I mean, a few years ago I even made a pilgrimage to Rosedale, Mississippi, the sleepy little river town the singer is "goin' down to" in this seriously *electric* update of the old Robert Johnson acoustic blues from the 1930s. You might say that in 1968 when the album came out, I was a fan. No, worshiper might come closer. I guess for me there has never been a better rock and roll band.

At the time, I was fresh out of graduate school in American Studies and working as the most junior of editors at *Playboy* magazine, having somehow talked my way into the job of, yes, Party Jokes Editor. We would have weekly Articles meetings in the conference room, all the editors sitting at the big round mahogany table, though generally it was more like the Gunfight at the O.K. Corral than anything as dull and civilized as a business meeting. Each of the editors would arrive armed with a revolver loaded with story ideas and possible writers, and, when his turn came, would basically *fire* them at the other editors, while those on the receiving end shot back objections blam blam blam blam. The idea was to prevail, have your idea selected to live in the magazine, instead of lying there dead on the conference room floor. The best shots won the day.

As the lowliest of editors, I habitually kept my mouth shut and just enjoyed watching the bloodshed. But on this splendid October morning, having gotten my day started by blasting *Crossroads* while in the shower, I had the temerity to open my mouth.

"There's this new group, Cream, and they're fucking amazing…" I babbled on for a couple of minutes about how great and revolutionary they were. "And I really think we should do something on them, at least a short On The Scene."

I should add that I was just bringing this up as a general idea, something good for the magazine to cover, not stumping to do it myself—I wasn't *that* delusional.

But that afternoon, there I was, in my windowless office, digging through postcards largely consisting of unimaginably dumb and/or downright hateful Party Jokes submissions, when a Senior Editor appeared in the doorway telling me I was to cover the Cream concert on Saturday night and then interview them in their hotel suite the next morning.

My stomach did a little backflip, a spasm compounded of fear, dread, and excitement.

I should probably say here that I had never interviewed anyone in my life, much less anyone cool and famous. I'd gotten my job at *Playboy* on the strength of a college humor magazine that I'd started with a few friends at Miami University, and had ended up being the Editor/Publisher because I was the only one of us who was even marginally orderly. It was called *Plague*, and we put out about 20 issues in my time at Miami, never making more than beer and pizza money, but at least managing to get it published with a certain regularity. We ran jokes as filler for layouts and to keep the few ads apart—so when I showed up at *Playboy* in my cheap suit lugging a battered briefcase full of copies of *Plague*, saying here I am, hire me, they said, do we have a job for you, kid. At the time *Playboy* was paying $100 per published joke, which seemed like a lot of money for little effort to a *lot* of people, so the joke submissions were pouring in. The editors, understandably, wanted no part of reading this endless tidal wave of *dreck*, so the cards and letters had been piling up and piling up—until I came along. My job, 9 to 5, was to sit in a tiny windowless office stacked pretty much to the ceiling with transfer boxes filled with unread Party Jokes submissions, going through them all one by one, adolescent toilet joke by poisonous prejudiced thigh-slapper.

The point is that I had NO training or background in actual journalism. Zilch. They really should never have hired me. In truth I had up until then had a certain disdain for journalism—something a decent English major simply wouldn't stoop to, you know? My goal in life at the time, beyond avoiding the Vietnam war and getting stoned as much as possible, was to become William Faulkner #2.

So I didn't have a clue how to go about doing this.

The Saturday night concert was maybe the best I've ever seen, period.

It was at the crumbling old Coliseum on South Wabash, built in 1899. From 1904 it housed 5 consecutive Republican Conventions, and was where William Howard Taft was nominated for the presidency in 1908, and then Warren G. Harding in 1920. From the outside it looked like a 19th-century stone prison, and inside, like the grubby sports arena that it had been for many years, though in 1968 it had been recently rechristened "The Syndrome," in someone's tragic attempt to make the dank old joint sound hip, with it, cool, in keeping with its final brief incarnation as a rock venue, before it closed forever in 1971 on a fire violation, sitting ghostfilled but otherwise empty until 1982, when it was flattened and forgotten.

The opening act was Frank Zappa & The Mothers of Invention.

They were also up at the top of my rock pantheon. "Call any vegetable" and "Brown shoes don't make it" and many other Zappa phrases were a regular part of my everyday vocabulary. This was in Zappa's *Lumpy Gravy* period. So he did these moon unit rock symphonies interspersed with some of his "hits"—*The Duke of Prunes*, *America Drinks and Goes Home*, *Who Are The Brain Police?*, *Motherly Love*, *Plastic People*, and other early classics.

And then came Cream. All of them in big-collared big-floral hippie-dippie shirts and jeans and boots. And all of them sort of slight. Ginger Baker skinny and red-haired and looking possessed as he pounded the drums. Jack Bruce the short guy who doesn't put up with any guff, and Clapton thin and ethereal-looking but with fingers of fire.

They started out with *Spoonful*, their 20-minute-plus thunderous jam on the old Howlin' Wolf classic. It was more like musical war than a band. All three of them battling for space and supremecy, almost all the time, and each a black belt on their different instruments. It was both bloody and wonderful. Next came *White Room*, *Politician*, *I'm So Glad*, *Sitting On Top Of The World*, and *Sunshine Of Your Love*—building of course to *Crossroads* as a finale. On *Crossroads* it seemed like a boxing referee might be helpful, and that points should be awarded after the round. It was more like a fistfight than not, and a rush such as I cannot describe. They broke up not long after this concert, and for good reason—the mix was just too intense.

And I had to interview this shooting star the next morning.

You know how people don't remember automobile wrecks they've been in?

It was a sunny crisp Sunday morning, and I was let into the very first fancy hotel suite I'd ever seen. Jack Bruce was sitting on a white couch with a cup of tea in front of him. The road manager introduced us, and I sat down across from Bruce in the center of a small couch that would barely fit three people if need be. Someone brought me tea. I fumbled with my tape recorder, terrified that it wouldn't work.

It started out all right.

Bruce was the perfect English gentleman. Quickly realizing that I hadn't the vaguest idea how to conduct such an interview, that he had a green fish on his hands, but being the polite Brit, he began telling me how the band got together, and about how they loved American blues—chatting along on his own and basically interviewing himself, because I was finding myself awestruck to be sitting there across from him and couldn't think of a single question to save my life.

And then appearing from a hallway, looking tousled and sleepy and quickly dressed, in jeans and a t-shirt, came Eric Clapton himself. He said hullo and put out a hand, and I looked down and, well, gulped. And my brains whirled, as if in a blender set to Scramble.

It's like this: At the time, a common *graffiti* in London, and spreading to New York and elsewhere, was *Clapton is God*. And you see, I was one of the people who believed that. Also, one of his nicknames at the time, tribute to the speed and unbelievable dexterity of his playing, was *Slowhand*. And he was sticking out that very hand, appendage of myth and legend, to shake my own unworthy mitt. I mean, it was *the hand*, you know? The very one that made all that incredible music. But bravely I stuck out my own and shook hands with him—one of the big moments of my life.

I sat back down again, trying to be cool, my mind reeling.

I think my first incisive, penetrating, thoughtful question to him was: "What's your favorite album?" Clearly well on my way to a Pulitzer here!

He looked at me like he couldn't quite believe how lame I was, but politely so, and answered that it was *B.B. King Live at the Regal*, an auditorium on Chicago's South Side, and started talking about what an influence B.B. King had been on his own guitar playing.

I began to relax a bit. I might live through this after all.

No chance.

There was a loud pounding on the door, and cheery shouts outside.

The road manager opened the door, and standing there, arms around one another, an electric gleam in their eyes, were Frank Zappa and Ginger Baker. They hadn't been to sleep yet, had rather been goofing around Old Town much of the night and then had found a party. It was Sunday morning for the rest of us, but very late Saturday night for them. They were swacked and roaring, buoyant and lit with artificial energy—or at least Baker was. His habits at the time rather famously tended toward the all-speed diet, and his eyeballs were down to swirling pinpricks agleam. But Zappa as famously was anti-drug of all kinds, and, being strange enough on his own, didn't need any chemical help.

Immediately they scoped out what was going on, and like sharks smelling blood they surged into the room, sensing easy prey. Zappa and Baker sat down flanking me on the little couch, one on each side, and then began interviewing *me*.

"Have you always worn shoes?" asks Zappa.

"How long has there been madness in your family?" asks Baker.

"Is there life after Tuesday?" Zappa inquires.

"How do you like your eggs?" wonders Baker.

"Why is the moon?" adds Zappa. "And who is France?"

Remember the party game in *Who's Afraid of Virginia Woolf?* The one called "Get The Guest?" Well, this was "Jape the Journalist." In nothing flat they had me totally flustered, and the only thing I could think of to do was flee.

I packed up my tape recorder and tried not to run for the door, to chuckles behind.

I had lasted maybe 15 minutes in my first celebrity interview.

By the time I had written my piece and it was ready to be published, they had broken up, and it never ran.

- 1983

As I mentioned in a previous introduction, I got my start as a writer on my high school newspaper. I'm pretty sure the editor, Mary Pat, had a little crush on me—in any case she gave me my own weekly humor column, based on pretty slim evidence that it might be any good. Well, back in 9th grade I had been voted funniest kid at Harding Junior High School. The column was called—are you ready?—Grandstandishing. Awful, right? But no worse than my byline back then. Taking a note from Fitzgerald, I floridly signed this alleged humor column, and my other pieces in the paper, D. Roman Standish. My remaining friends from back then still call me "D.Roman." Who knows? Maybe I'll go back to it.

This actually led, in a tangled way, to my first real job in publishing. After Lakewood High School I had gone to Miami University (of Ohio, as we always add apologetically), chasing after lost Charlene—she had dumped me for a returning college guy at the end of our senior year. But hope springs eternal, and I was too dumb and smitten to give up, and when I found out that she was going to Miami, without revealing my reasons to anyone, especially not to her, I followed her there, chiefly to conduct long siege on her affections. It didn't work, of course. I took some of the same classes she did in order to be near her, and contrived other ways to be around her, but she never budged, She married the same college dork after graduation, and a year after that, went with him in Paris, where he was studying French (what a dipstick!). It was there that she caught some mysterious illness, and was dead at age 23. I still miss her, 50 years down the line. But if I hadn't chased her to Miami, none of the rest would have followed.

In my sophomore year, three or four friends and I decided it would be fun to start an off-campus humor magazine. And thanks to my splendid track record of two dozen not-particularly-funny humor columns in high school, and also, I soon *realized, because I was the only one who was even marginally orderly, they named me Editor—which also meant being Publisher, Ad Salesman, Circulation Director (taking the copies to the five stores that carried it in this tiny cow town), and Head Writer. We called it* Plague, *after the Camus novel—existential despair was very big in our healthy apple-cheeked young crowd back then. We didn't have any bylines because we didn't want anyone to know how few of us were producing it—by the third issue or so, it was pretty much written by two of us, me, and Jerry Bovim, who was lightyears smarter and funnier than I was, but who had little patience for revising and editing and such dull tasks, so a lot of what I did was simply put spit and polish on the products of his wonderful twisted mind. He too died far too young, in the spring of 1968, not yet 29, and I still miss him too. When our first issue came out in December 1960, to our relief and astonishment, the 1000 copies we had optimistically printed (there were only 8000 students total—what were we thinking?) sold out in about 5 hours, proof less of how terrific our magazine was than of how desperate everybody was for a laugh there in the depths of the Cold War at the end of the Eisenhower Years, and in southern Ohio to boot! We made enough to pay the printer, and celebrate with pizza and beer at Mac 'n Joe's, our student saloon of choice.*

Flash forward to spring 1967. On the strength of, yes, Plague *magazine, I had talked my way into a job—of sorts—at* Playboy *magazine in Chicago. In* Plague *we used to run jokes—cheerfully stolen from other college humor magazines—as filler, to complete layouts and keep the ads apart. Well,* Playboy, *then and now, has what they call the Party Jokes page. These jokes are drawn from reader submissions, and back then they were paying $100 per pubished joke. That's the equivalent of $680 today. That's right. For one stupid joke. So as you might imagine, the submissions were pouring in. And as you also might imagine, the editors understandably wanted no part of—and had little time for—reading this ceaseless torrent of dreck. So the submissions were piling and piling up. The editor who interviewed me took one look at* Plague *and said, boy, do we have a summer job for you, kid! So I found myself in a windowless office with boxes of unread jokes rising to the ceiling, a cardboard humor mausoleum. I could not have conceived what a dreary soul-draining task this would be, day after day of it.*

At the end of the summer they told me I could stay full time if I wanted to. My choice was to go back to Indiana University to finish my Ph.D in American Studies, or work for Playboy. *Seemed like a no-brainer. So I hung in there—for a while. Gradually they gave me other more regular assistant editor jobs—editing the letters column, writing captions for pictorials, that sort of thing—and after a year I was off the jokes entirely.*

By 1969 I had gotten married for a second time, to Margaret, a girl I had known back at Miami—well, all right, we had had just a little *affair, even though I was married at the time. I had stayed on at Miami for a master's degree, continuing to put out* Plague. *My first wife, Beth, was the Art Editor for the magazine and was and is simply the most decent person I have ever known. We had an adorable little daughter, Lisa. I should have been happy, and responsible, but like the soap opera, I was young and restless. This is not the place to detail the lapses in sense and propriety that have pretty much characterized my whole life, and it would fill a book of its own anyway. Beth and Lisa and I moved to Bloomington in 1965, and I began Ph.D.*

work there, but Margaret was now in grad school at the University of Chicago, and I couldn't seem to get her out of my mind. So in 1967 Beth and I got divorced. Chasing another girl, I followed Margaret to Chicago.

For reasons I'm a little unclear on after all these years, in 1969 I took a year-long leave from Playboy, and Margaret and I went back to IU so I could by god finish that Ph.D—partly because it seemed wrong to waste all those years in school after getting so close, but mainly I think it was just more of that lifelong restlessness. I could go off on another adventure—even if it meant sitting through some dull classes—and still have a job waiting for me afterward. Truth is, I wasn't all that interested in finishing the Ph.D; by then I was certain I wanted to be a writer, and it looked like I might be able to make a living at it. Heading back to IU was just something different to do. Because we had a plan. No dull dreadful Bloomington for us.

We were right in tune with the back-to-the-land spirit that was going around back then. Wasn't Dylan living in the country outside Woodstock? We rented a plain modest farmhouse on an old back road 12 miles outside of Bloomington, with a vast soybean field as a back yard and acre upon acre of state forest beyond that, with little quiet wooded lakes nearby where I went fishing some afternoons and usually brought a few bass and bluegill home for dinner. I bought a nice Honda 350 from my pal Tom Corcoran, let my hair and sideburns grow, and Easy Rided serene curving country roads back and forth to school. Margaret put in a huge wonderful garden, and our two cats, Meat and Potatoes, thought they had gone to heaven.

It couldn't have been more idyllic, and we couldn't have been more broke. We made the move with zero savings and were trying to scrape along on the pittance of my T.A. pay.

So I had the idea for this piece. I'd write it for Playboy, they'd pay me a generous fee, and we could stop wondering if we'd have the money for Lowell Bohaul to bring his truck out and fill our cistern with water when rainfall off the roof failed.

The newspapers were full of the youth culture wars back then. The epic and now-legendary mess remembered as the Woodstock Festival had happened the month we moved to the farm. I had thought of going—another scene, I knew—but seeing the footage, all that mud and bad acid, and indifferent performances in the rain, even though by groups and performers I loved, I felt lucky I hadn't tried. Even so, it was a major event that everybody had an opinion about. In the press, mostly negative. Stoned hairy hippies having sex in the mud while such agents of the Devil as Jimi Hendrix and the Grateful Dead and Mountain incited them toward ecstasy and anarchy, a violation of true American values, blah blah blah…

So while I was glad I wasn't actually there with them, I rather admired the peace love dope ethos of it all—and had never been a fan of Nixon and Agnew and that crowd. So I had this flash: What if there had been a similar huge festival thrown by and for the upright wholesome youth of Nixon's cherished Silent Majority? What would that have been like?

And that's what you have. It's an anomaly among all the other pieces here, in that it's a piece of premise humor, completely made up satire, a reversion to Plague magazine.

The editors who read it at Playboy were encouraging, really liked it, and it seemed to be a sale. Margaret and I began planning some non-poverty-level purchases.

We made the mistake of starting to spend the money before the check was in hand.

It never came.

The piece was scheduled to be published, and was sent to our publisher, A. C. Spectorsky, typically just a formality. But no. Reading it he decided that Playboy *had rather been picking too much on conservatives and right-wingers lately, and further decided to act on that thought by nixing my piece. And, of course, my paycheck.*

Thanks again, Spec.

So this one never ran either. Some of the cultural jokes and jabs in it could probably use some footnoting all these years later—I wrote it early in 1970—but hey, that's what Google's for!

THE GUNSTOCK MUSIC FESTIVAL

A RIGHT-THINKING GENERATION GATHERS TO CELEBRATE

Gunstock.

Until recently, it was only an obscure village halfway between Scylla and Charybdis, Kansas, known chiefly as the site of General George Custer's famous 1867 attack of dysentery. Local folks called it "Custer's Runs," and the only people who visited were the occasional souvenir hunter and biographers of Custer's alimentary canal. But now, the gas station, four roadhouses and local VFW post that are the hamlet of Gunstock can boast of a new legend: The Gunstock Music Festival of 1969.

By the thousands, the hundreds and the dozens they came, half a million strong, to Gunstock, Kansas. This was no gathering of freaks, weirdos, hippies, liberals, and other degenerates come together, as they would casually put it, to "drop Mary T" or "shoot acid." Nor was this a gathering of those who would "fuzz out" on their responsibilities to society: This was the first tribal gathering of the youth that make America great.

From bowling alleys they came, from silos and fraternity houses, church basements and locker rooms, libraries and slumber parties, student council meetings and movies rated "G." They came in their winedark GTOs, in station wagons lent to them by self-sacrificing mothers, in chartered county school buses and on Honda 50s. There were license plates on many of their pickup trucks from as far away as West Virginia and Georgia. And one enthusiast actually drove his John Deere harvester cross country all the way from Rapture, North Dakota, setting a new interstate baling record in the process.

They began arriving on Thursday, converging on the hastily-chosen area. The promoters, two right-thinking entrepreneurs named George Washington Shuck and Esau Carp, had originally planned to hold the festival in upstate New York, near the home of legendary culture hero Kate Smith; but local zoning ordinances and threats on their lives forced them to shift its location somewhat, to an abandoned strip mine just outside of Gunstock. The ex-mine was now owned by a World War I veteran who had plans to turn it into the Sunny Valley Home For The Nearly Worn Out. Seeing in Shuck and Carp men with vision to match his own, he readily rented them his property.

Having settled on the site just a week earlier, Shuck and Carp barely had time to set up the facilities necessary to make their idealistic dream of a youth festival come true—essential services like ticket booths, storm fences, concession stands, camping equipment rental tables, pay toilets and 24 hour parking meters. But everything was miraculously ready by Thursday, and easily accommodated the first wave of the coming flood.

But out on the highways that night, an epic traffic jam was brewing. By sundown, cars and tractors alike were creeping along the sclerotic asphalt arteries; at midnight, a ten-mile bumper-to-bumper standstill had bloomed, but in the true spirit of the occasion, no one seemed to care—they simply dipped into their coolers of cold beer and enjoyed their common predicament. Everyone, that is, except the president of the Joe McCarthy Memorial Fan Club from Bob Jones University, who celebrated finishing his second case of beer at four a.m. by screaming "Buy American! Buy American!" as he patriotically demolished a Volkswagen with a tire iron. Witnesses said that he finally passed out, murmuring "Protective tariff, protective tariff ..."

At dawn, traffic began creeping forward again, a beautiful pilgrimage in the early morning sun, made even more vivid by the colorful beer cans gleaming by the roadside like some shimmering silver trail to the center of America—or slightly to the right of it, at any rate. By mid-morning, progress was only fitful, but still, as one girl explained in the argot of her generation, "Everyone was having a *swell* time; it was *sharp* to be stuck like that!" Group sings were spontaneously generated, and the unpolluted air rang with *their* songs:

> *Fighting soldiers from the sky*
> *Fearless men who jump and die*
> *Men who mean just what they say*
> *The brave men of the Green Beret...*

One busload of Eagle Scouts trapped in the traffic jam, though, didn't join in the infectious fun—instead they worked on their Merit Badges in

Advanced Knots by tying a contingent of teenage 4-H'ers into an imaginative if somewhat suggestive tableau. Quickly setting up a tent around it, the ever-alert Scouts charged curious peers a quarter each to check it out. Before traffic got moving again they had earned $57 and had given the 4-H'ers the time of their lives. As 4-H'er Mary Baker Finger from Doom, Nebraska, later remarked: "I better not tell Daddy—he'd be jealous!"

But when Mary Baker and her friends got to Gunstock that afternoon, after more than a day of inching along highways that sliced through lush Kansas wheat fields, she had something better to tell the gang back home: There, looking at the awe-inspiring expanse of crushed rocks and rubble from the edge of the soon-to-be legendary strip mine, she could see thousands of youths like herself pouring into this symbolic site, turning the burnt ochre of its surface into a kaleidoscope of color, a swirling patchwork of beiges, charcoal grays, blackwatch plaids and bleeding madras prints. "It's like halftime at the greatest football game in the world," sighed one Big Ten coed in happy wonder. "No, it's even neater than that…it's … it's like halftime at *two* of them!"

Then, as the sun set behind the gravel mounds, the Gunstock Festival officially began. In a moving tribute to their sense of community, nearly half a million young people stood up together and chanted:

I pledge allegiance to the Flag of the United States of America…

And from the moment they began, to the closing benediction by Billy Graham, it was clear that this was a revolutionary gathering.

The press was aware of its importance. Reporters from major media outlets were everywhere: the music critic from *National Review*, with his wire recorder; the Precious Bodily Fluids Editor from *Reader's Digest*; Paul Harvey's *Page Two* crew; the Fashion Editor from *Consumer Reports*, and an etching team from *American Heritage*. Rumor even had it that Norman Mailer had infiltrated, masquerading as a Topeka teenybopper; but since he never took over the stage to talk about himself, no one really believed it. Those who were there, though, had living history to report.

When the lights came up for the first time, the emcee—Cousin Whitey from radio station WASP in Quisling, Ohio—shouted: "And here he is, to open up the Gunstock Festival, none other than *the man*, Mister Charisma himself: *Wayne Newton!*"

The crowd went wild. Girls sobbed and hugged one another, quivering and moaning, "It's him! Oh, it's him! I can't stand it, I'm going to wet my—" As a girlfriend interrupted: "You don't *love* him! I already *did*!" Most of the boys scuffed the raw earth uncomfortably with their penny loafers, trying to hide the obvious lumps in their throats. When the pandemonium subsided, Wayne, so touched that only two of his dimples showed, tore right into the tune that made him famous, the tender *The Ballad of Shirley Temple Black*. Caught up in the music, the audience unconsciously began swaying, keeping time. Some of them couldn't help dancing, and for the rest of the night the wide expanse of the mine was scattered with festival-goers, lost in the music, instinctively doing their favorite dances, like the twist, the mashed potatoes and the gravy.

Six much begged-for choruses later, Wayne followed up *Shirley* with *It's A Heck Of A Country* as an electrifying encore. While the next group was setting up, the first of the many generous acts that characterized the festival occurred: Elated by the tremors of joy that the big Newton's voice sent through her, a self-less young girl opened one of her samsonite suitcases and began passing out that precious commodity—cigarettes—free to everyone around her. Others joined in, following her lead, and soon nearly everyone was "lit up," as they call it.

Said April Weaselton, who began the nicotine & tar offering: "It was wonderful to see everybody, all openly smoking cigarettes together, filters and regulars and menthols and extra-longs all mixing, with no hassles, no problems. It had to be the high point of my life, at least until everybody started coughing and almost drowned out the music, and the smoke got so thick I started crying. But even that didn't really matter, because we were all doing it together."

What they missed during the smoke-in was a smooth, professional Mantovanti set that was highlighted by his lyrical interpretation of the *Theme Song From The Kiplinger Report*. The smoke was still thicker than the haze over Gary when Pat Boone next took the stage, and so it may have accounted for some of the tears shed during his poignant *Love Letters In Your Dossier*, but by the time he got to a medley of his greatest hits—including the immortal *White Bucks*, *Capped Teeth* and *Two-Button Suit*—the air had cleared, and the already familiar hiss of opening beer cans provided sibilant counterpoint to the music.

And to the tune of the choicest hops, rice and best barley malt, the dazzling lineup of names and talent went on into the chill Kansas night. But just as the crowd began to accept the succession of such superstars as Don Ho, Andy Williams, Rosemary Clooney, and all eleven generations of The King Family— and when requests for *Melancholy Baby* were on the rise—a previously unheard-of group appeared, and left the bandstand as stars.

Making its debut as a group on its own that night, The Canned Band was the product of a decade's association. Starting out as a backup group to the Ray Coniff Singers during the Fifties, they were eventually discovered by Muzak. After gaining anonymous renown in dentists' waiting rooms across the country, they decided to try their luck as a name group. What happened is now history. Hardly a record collection in America is missing their smash single, *You're My White Bread, Baby*.

Shuck and Carp, however, knew how to stack climax upon climax, and to close the live part of the night's entertainment, they brought out the guru of the Nixon Years, Rod McKuen. With the rugged, raspy he-poet's voice that makes him unique, superbard McKuen read his famous poem, *I Like Your Brown Hair And The Moon*, taken from his best-selling collection (soon to be a major motion picture), *Parking Meter Mind*. Begged for an encore by the hundreds of plump girls crowding around the bandstand sweating, McKuen, accompanied only by his voice, sang his own composition for a lengthy ten minutes—a sensitive musical chronicle of all his published and recorded works, complete with Library of Congress numbers. Cheers could be heard over the snores before he was through.

Then the flood lights dimmed. Except for a stray goat someone had playfully set fire to, and a small candleabra on the piano (where Liberace couldn't resist leading quiet improvised cocktail tunes), the strip mine was bathed in quiet darkness. Everyone settled down under the communal blanket of night, and all that could be heard were the occasional, disembodied voices of contented festival-goers:

"I think I'm gonna puke …"

"You don't love him—I did already …"

"Who you calling a drunk, you wise ass?"

"… and, get this now, then she actually let him see her underwear, right there in her own dresser drawer …"

"I figure I'll get the old man's used car lot anyway, so why study?"

"Come on, Emily. I *promise* I'll respect you. Didn't I tell you that you reminded me of Tricia Nixon? Now, please don't cross your legs."

"Where's the church key?"

"Are you number sixteen, or seventeen?"

As the respected Joplin, Missouri, newspaper, *The Janus*, editorialized about the day's events:

> *Those cynics who think our younger generation is nothing but a bunch of long-haired, drug-taking, effete pointy headed commies should look to the Gunstock Music Festival. There, congregated in an old strip mine, they have proved the cynics wrong—and shown that strip mines aren't the useless eyesores that godless liberals claim. For nearly two days now, close to half a million people have come together in Gunstock, Kansas, and there has not been a single instance of wrong trips, speed crashes, acapulco smack, brown dimes, franking out, or any other of the unintelligible but dangerous things associated with drugs. And those few causes of delerium tremens, bleeding ulcers and suicide that did come up were far*

below the average for a city of half a million …

At sunrise the next morning the music began again, right after flag raising. Many of the celebrants, still huddled together in ones and fives, continued to sleep. They would have missed an unbelievable workout by the latest supergroup—Fabian, Avalon & Rydell (who have since added Jimmy Clanton to their musical law firm)—if it hadn't been for a small eight-year-old boy with a receding hairline and jowls, who was wearing a shifty grin and a shiny blue suit. Somehow knowing what they wanted better than the people themselves, he somberly worked his way through the crowd, pouring stale beer onto sleeping faces to wake them up. It was easy to see that the tyke was a budding leader.

As it turned out, he needn't have bothered. Before Fabian, Avalon & Rydell could get into its current chartbuster, *Gooey Chewy Louie Baby*, the clouds rolled in.

The first sign of the coming clouds was a distant hum, like the sound of the current coursing through an electric chair; but then it became a drone, a buzz, and suddenly the sky was dark with them—a swarm of locusts.

It rained grasshoppers; they fell in torrents, forming puddles in depressions on the ground, flowing in small streams to the lowest part of the abandoned mine. At first, people sought what shelter they could find, erecting tents of fraternity blankets and zipping themselves inside sleeping bags. But soon, most everyone resigned themselves to their plight and simply plopped down in the pools of grasshoppers to wait for the music to begin again. One girl even celebrated the event by stripping off her shoes and running through the puddles. "I guess it sounds funny," she said, "but they're so squishy, I mean, it's *exciting*!"

The rain subsided after about an hour, and after another most of the puddles and streams had hopped away.

"I swan," swanned the local historian, Private Wayne Johns, Ret., "that's the darndest thing's happened in these parts since the Great Groundhog Stampede right after the Big War. In 1923, it was—they et one of my favorite saloons, right down to the poker chips. Tragedy."

But the Gunstockers weren't about to be daunted by this, or many others that quickly followed. When the concession stands ran out of food in the afternoon, privates stores were passed around—corn chips, beer nuts, pretzels, and space food sticks. And when the pay toilets could no longer be paid, the festival-goers didn't, until an emergency team from the Gunstock Custer Memorial Septic Tank Company remedied the situation. And even when the sound system went out during the the much-awaited George Gobel-Arthur Godfrey-Tennessee Ernie Ford guitar jam, they waited patiently, for an hour, until the epochal musical experience could resume.

In fact, not until much later did the violence break out.

At first, it seemed only that a few purists were protesting the act on stage. The experimental section of the festival had just begun. Shuck and Carp had generously wanted to give the audience a taste of the way out, of the avant-garde in popular music, but it seemed they went too far when Sonny and Cher walked out on stage. Gasps of shock, mixed with groans and belches, greeted them. They led off with a far-out number called *We're Not Hip, But We Can't Sing*," from Cher's latest album, *Hype*!

Before they reached the bridge, fistfights erupted.

Only when Sonny and Cher were hurriedly replaced by Barbra Streisand in an attempt to calm things down, did it become apparent that the music wasn't the most important factor. Barbra belted out her show-stopping theme song, *Funny Face*, better than she ever has before, but the fighting only increased.

Within seconds, it seems, half a million young people mystically shared the same thought: The beer's almost gone. With a common idea and a common goal in mind, sharing a need and a dream, it was every man for himself.

At first the fighting was fiercest near the stage, where a group of college students belonging to FFNCC (Fraternities For Nice Clothes Committee) had stockpiled several kegs. Moving swiftly, however, Shuck and Carp dropped a platoon of Andy Frain ushers from waiting helicopters, and the Frainers soon had established a firm Demilitarized Zone between the stage and the crowd. With the good of the people and the film rights in mind, Shuck and Carp continued the show.

While Julius Wechter and the Baja Marimba Band provided a latin beat with *The Gringo Mariacha*, the beer battle raged; as Julius shifted into bossa nova tempo for *El Dinero, Mi Amor* the first automobiles burst into flames, sending grisly tongues of fire into the black heartland sky. Unfortunately for the band, an exploding gasoline tank obscured their driving finish.

The papers said later that almost everyone was involved in the fighting, but that is simply an exaggeration. At the very peak of the violence, not more than two-thirds were participating directly—many didn't have the proper weapons, and many had beer safely hidden away. Furthermore, as anyone who was there can swear, fighting practically reached a standstill when the closing act, Glen Campbell, took the stage behind the line of grim ushers and barbed wire to sing the song that touches a soft spot in the heart of all Americans, *I'll Be A Hobo On The Train To Tuscaloosa Of Your Memory By The Time You Find Your Underwear Beneath The Bed This Morning*.

A stranger, walking through the area, would have found it a depressing spectacle: an abandoned strip mine, once more abandoned; on the rough grounds, only silent reminders of what transpired here—an ocean of beer cans and crumpled cigarette packs, dotted with bloody shreds of button-down shirts and chinos, discarded aerosol deodorants, soap wrappers, mouthwashes, foot powders, hair tonics, toothpaste tubes, teeth; and here and there, a well-thumbed copy of *Valley of the Dolls* or *The Police Gazette*, turned to a story headlined HITLER ALIVE IN ARGENTINA, all punctuated by random bodies sprawled in the mud. Yes, a stranger would have called it a fiasco.

The Kansas director of public safety, Col. Biff "Biff" Biff—a former Marine, Green Beret, Storm Trooper and Boy Scout—could only shake his head in amazement. "Been around the world three times, been to two dogfights and a whorehouse in Steubenville, and I ain't seen nothing like this. Those were the meanest damn kids I'd ever seen. Good Americans, every one, but boy did they give us a time. I hope they hold the next one of these damn things at Parris Island, where they have the facilities for it," he said.

But to the festival-goers, slowly limping toward their remaining cars, it was a smashing success, a milestone in their lives. As one young man put it, wincing as he walked: "The Gunstock Festival a failure? Man, you got to be kidding. I wouldn't miss the next one if you paid me. Man, this was the best fight I've had in two years."

- 1970

Poor Led Zeppelin. When their first album came out early in 1969, the critics pretty much dumped all over them. I remember my own disappointment. Many of us were still mourning the (inevitable) self-destruction of Cream a few months earlier—whose live version of Crossroads from their Wheels of Fire *album, after somewhere in the neighborhood of 470,000 listenings on my part (a conservative number), still raises the hair on the back of my neck and gives me a rush. It is the one track I would want to have with me on a desert island. With Cream gone, Led Zeppelin had promised to be the Next Big Heavy Thing. Certainly in Jimmy Page it had a guitar wizard right in there with Clapton—and both had done time with the legendary Yardbirds, arguably the ur-progenitors of metal rock. But that first album! What were they thinking? Patches of any track lit up like fireworks when Page attacked his guitar, exciting, amazing, but then there was all this…meandering…wandering dungeons and dragons baloney, with Robert Plant's vocals veering too often toward sounding like a choked chicken squawking in pain. (Check out the end of* You Shook Me *in particular. As one critic wrote: "Please, for the love of God, someone cut out Robert Plant's vocal chords.") An even more maddening track was* Dazed And Confused*—an absolutely stunning gritty moment, then drifting into the fog, before eventually reappearing. Didn't they know great rock songs are supposed to build, not burn and fizzle, burn and fizzle?*

So I didn't know what to make of Led Zeppelin. They combined hair-raising kickass monster guitar rock with some of the dippiest treacle imagineable, and it did not help that Page became increasingly enamored with the occult, Aleister Crowley-influenced mystical esoterica and magic—and that Plant was fascinated by Norse mythology, Welsh mythology, Celtic folklore, and, god help us, J.R.R. Tolkien—or that a mishmash of this stuff found its way too often into Led Zeppelin's music.

But they became the Next Big Heavy Thing anyway, since nobody pays any attention to critics, and over the first few albums produced several classics—topped for me by Whole Lotta Love *and* Rock and Roll—*that refuse to die on vintage rock radio. Despite the fruity bits, the pointless voyages into uncharted seas, there was enough metal and thunder to make me a convert.*

They also established a reputation for being Debauchery and Excess Incarnate while on tour—and it's hard to fault that, you know? They turned that last up a few notches for their 1973 American tour, with the centerpiece being the Starship—a Boeing 720 reimagined as a combination hotel suite and bar/lounge—which they were using to fly to gigs, an aerial jetset tour bus.

They were mega-rock royalty by then, and their mega-manager, Peter Grant, a huge hulking presence, former bouncer and wrestler, decided to rub the noses of the snooty press in it by inviting a bunch of us rock writers to come along for the ride with them, aboard the Starship from New York to a Pittsburgh concert at Three Rivers Stadium and back, followed by three consecutive nights blowing out the fuses at Madison Square Garden—what better proof that Led Zeppelin's critics had their heads up their asses? It would be the epitome of cool glitz.

Well, maybe. You'll see what I mean.

MISSING PLANKS ON THE STAIRWAY TO HEAVEN

ABOARD A BUMPY FLIGHT
WITH LED ZEPPELIN

The bent old lady caromed around the lobby, ranting vigorously at anyone who seemed to need it. She was wearing a faded flowered dress and carried a bludgeon-size purse. It was getting to be quite a group.

We were in the Drake Hotel, New York. Normally it's sedate enough, seemingly content to linger under the Top Ten and behave otherwise. The lobby looks like a dim memory of a Bavarian court in slight decline, the sort of place where threadbare Counts and despondent aging Pretenders ought to hang out.

But it was at the moment filling up with another sort of royalty; or, more accurately, royalty's fallout. Somewhere in suites above us, languishing or sniffing through Ben Franklin or romping in a puddle of nymphets or putting on one last touch of mascara or God knows what, were Led Zeppelin. In three hours they were due on stage in Three Rivers Stadium, Pittsburgh. Collecting down here were the thirty or so people they apparently couldn't go to Pittsburgh without: roadies, groupies, photographers, Atlantic records people, friends, security and a film crew, plus those of us present for purely morbid reasons, as reporters.

It gave Flower Lady plenty to choose from.

Cowards, Eugenie and I leaned against a gold-gilt pillar we hoped was out of her range, and watched. I was drab bordering on invisibility anyway, standard cheeseburger urban cowboy, but Eugenie wasn't exactly easy to miss. She'd decided the occasion merited Medium-Low Groupie Drag; and since she's acted for years at Second City (lately quit to play bass in a band), and since she is, conservatively, stunning, she knew how to do it: a black tee-shirt top glittering with sequins, Levi hotpants, platforms and black nylon tights, through which shone on her right thigh a sunburst tattoo newly healed there.

Flower Lady moved in on one of the roadies, wagging a bony finger in his blank hairy face. "Disgusting. I had nine sons, every last one a hero. Not one of them would do anything like this"—flicking at his prince valiant gone long— "to his mother. And your pants"—a real hotdog pair of bells, with hand-stained leather appliques, silver spangles, fringe, Christmas tree lights—"You poor, poor boy. Didn't your mother love you?"

Blank stood uncomprehending. He was a roadie for Led Zeppelin, for Christ sake. What was this shit?

When he didn't answer she sighed like she was seeing his soul sink into Hell, right there on the spot, and turned abruptly away from him.

Straight for Eugenie.

"You look like a nice girl at heart—why do you dress like this? Aren't you ashamed?" she demanded, almost sadly.

Eugenie answered in that calm sanitarium voice she uses in conversations of this sort. "I enjoy dressing this way; there's nothing wrong with it."

"But my child, does it really seem *decent* to you?" She seemed to be veering toward coherence.

"*Legs* indecent? It's style, it doesn't have anything to do with morality."

Naturally, we'd been waiting here since 4:30 for "the boys," as people in the entourage tend to call them. Outside six Cadillac limos had sat for an hour in a solemn black row, ready to rush everybody to the Newark airport and the famous jet, Starship I. It was now much past five, and still no boys. People were glazing over with boredom or, depending on their function, beginning to twitch. And Eugenie was engaging in meaningful dialog with the Flower Lady. Easier to raise the consciousness of scrambled eggs. For the next five minutes or so, Eugenie told her charmingly that people these days are *allowed* to have different values and that a pair of hotpants do not necessarily a killer lesbo hooker make, while she told Eugenie about her nine sons and a trip she once took to Phoenix. As communication it seemed average.

Maybe higher. Suddenly, staring Eugenie hard in the eye, she took a large handful of dress in her right hand, and, raising it regally well above her knees, left us to ponder her ancient road-mapped thighs as she spun smiling away into the first of several creaky pirouettes—a Zen lesson stopped when she collided with the practically bare and much lusted-after chest of Robert Plant, first of the boys to show up. He looked amused.

I'd never seen him in the flesh before, so I was halfway expecting another frail androgynous wisp in the image of Jagger and Clapton and Daltry.

Rolling Stone had not yet done 30,000 words on the subject, and who can tell from the cover of *Hit Parader?* So it was surprising to see that he is *big*, upwards of six feet and 180—much less the soulful lost waif than a Phi Delt gone wrong. With short hair and a cheap suit he would look like somebody who sold a lot of insurance in Columbus, Ohio and daydreamed wistfully about wife-swapping.

Healthy.

His arrival was about the same as dropping a fox into a chicken coop. Road Manager Richard Coles, who in beard and manner has the presence of a prissy Rasputin, was among the earliest of the twitchers, since it was *his* job to get everybody and everything to Pittsburgh before the crowd started setting fire to the Astroturf. Coles immediately began snapping orders and gesturing at his roadies; the film crew burst into Lights Camera Action, zooming and panning and poking mikes on long poles into random conversations; most of the ladies clicked from Dim to Full Glow, an aurora borealis of sexual energy suddenly lighting up around each one; and we, having so far laid distant eyes on one Zep, were directed outside toward the right limo by Danny Goldberg, the publicist. He's a friendly lank longhair who formerly edited *Circus* and wrote for the *Voice*, which may explain his sympathy for people who compulsively write about rock & roll. On the way out he assured us that there'd be plenty of time to talk to the boys on the plane; that there'd be less confusion at 20,000 feet, don't worry.

Danny led us to the last limo in the six-pack. It was for the press. The boys would be riding together in the first. There was apparently a prescribed seating arrangement for each of the others—as we guessed by watching Coles lurch up and down the black line directing bodies like a Drill Instructor filling in for Pearl Mesta—but if so it was according to some murky court logic undecipherable to us. All that was clear, by accident or design, was what constituted the head and tail of this fancy snake.

Leaning inside, Danny introduced us to the two people already there, a British journalist and an American photographer he'd hired from a New York agency. The photographer, smiling back at us from the front seat, looked right, sporting a work shirt and round glasses with clear plastic frames. But The Journalist decidedly didn't. Admittedly, you don't see many English rock writers when you live in Chicago, but I had an idea they didn't look like him—confirmed by Eugenie, who turned toward me choking down a giggle. It wasn't just that his carefully razor-cut and processed hair might have been sculptured out of Fortrel and dry-varnished; or even the coordinated blazer-tie-and-slacks, which were fine for anyone with a longing to look like Johnny Carson—it was the shoes. He honest-to-God had on a pair of those two-toned patent numbers, caramel on the sides and shiny white on top, just like the conventioneers cruising Rush Street currently favored back home. He looked twice at Eugenie, himself amazed; then at his wristwatch; then out the window, in fascination at the plain gray side of a delivery van stopped there.

The snake was finally ready to go. In the movie version, a gleaming string of limos goes sailing through the city, melting traffic away by its sheer odd majesty. In our version, we sped elegantly away from the curb and onto Fifth Avenue—right into a solid clot of rush hour traffic, which was not impressed. Like regular rude beasts, we slouched toward Jersey.

The Journalist kept looking at his wristwatch and frowning. Finally he asked Eugenie, "Have you heard this Led Zeppelin?"

Hmmm... She said she had.

"What do they sound like?"

Nurse Ross back in action, communicating with the cabbages.

"It's a real heavy metal sound, you know, thousands of amplifiers, energy."

"Sounds smashing." He checked his wristwatch again. Then looked out the window. "Tell me something, would you please? Are there still groupies?"

The Journalist, it turned out, was not here to cover the band; he had come to interview the airplane.

The stretch between New York and the Newark airport is one of my favorite scenic routes, eighty lanes of concrete snarled and roaring through swamps and smoldering junk heaps and refineries looming like mutant aluminum mushroom patches—landscape straight out of *After the Big Nuke*; so I enjoyed the ride, even the part at the end when the driver couldn't find the plane and took us tearing in search through parking lots and past AUTHORIZED PERSONNEL ONLY signs.

But The Journalist was not pleased. The sun, rudely, was beginning to set, which in turn was causing him to experience, with admirable British restraint, a severe fit. What good would an interview with the airplane be without pictures of the bloody thing? His photographer seemed entirely unconcerned; he'd just finished three weeks in Washington, recording at the Watergate hearings the nervous sweat of various trusted government servants, and now sat up front beatifically digging the sights, as photographers will.

We found the Starship parked alone on a huge cement field. Clustered randomly around it were the other limos, with the entourage scattered among them in several bright bouquets. The moment we stopped, The Journalist bounded and made straight for one containing Richard Coles; he would have his pictures.

Eugenie and I decided to cruise the inside of the plane before it filled up. It was, after all, part of the hype, intended as proof that this was *the* hotshit flash tour of all time; that Led Zeppelin walked empyrean regions shared by only a few; that they like the Stones & the Beatles & Dylan were not mere rock & rollers; that they, too, were Mythic. Ordinary mortals on tour schlepped equipment and changed tires in the mud and ate fast grease for days on end; not Led Zeppelin. They had a magic plane of their very own.

Or at least were renting one, at five dollars per mile. The rock papers had been gushing about it since the beginning of the tour, so there was no way to not know the story: What had started life as a drab spinsterish Boeing 720, it went, had been transformed with great taste and lavish expense into a supersonic lady of pleasure, with a fur bedroom, a long copper bar, couches, color TVs, an artificial fireplace, flowing champagne—a seductive Liza Doolittle who's been taught how to talk and fuck and fly.

So Ms. Starship was intended to be the embodiment of the high rock & roll life, a fantastic mechanical groupie. But as Eugenie and I snooped through her interior organs, the hit we got was not Bianca Jagger; it was closer to high-class Vegas hooker, the product of a K-Mart imagination given too much money to play with but too little taste. Everything advertised was there, including an electric organ built into the bar...but maybe the organ did it, conjuring images of boozy Syndicate types gathered round late at night, crooning *My Melancholy Baby* and fighting back the tears...but even so it considerably beat being stuck in coach in the middle seat praying to God that your drinks will arrive.

The boys, meantime, were accommodating The Journalist, and at the moment stood smiling together outside, on top of the wing. Down below, the film crew was going into heat, while The Journalist's photographer and several others machine-gunned away with their Nikons. The man from the hometown paper, even as he was, carried some clout with the boys. Enough, at least, to get them up a mobile 30-foot stairway and onto a curving slice of wing. They even seemed to be getting off on it. Plant truly was, raising his arms like a happy Jesus and lifting his head to the wind, grinning; and Page, in a shirt green as an electric lizard, mainly was too, but he carries around an expensive set of hands, and at least once I saw his eyes flash to the ground and come up full of broken bones.

*** *** ***

For the next twenty minutes people drifted into the plane, most heading straight for the bar, where magnums of champagne and beer from Thailand were in abundant supply. Eugenie and I stationed ourselves on a couch in the main cabin and watched everybody slowly settle, land where they figured they belonged in the natural order of things. Ahmet Ertegun sat talking genially across from us, flanked on each side by a fascinated lady. With his sleek suit and handsomely suntanned balding head and precision-trimmed beard he looked like what he was—most of Atlantic Records—and not much like what he used to be, the hip kid with a label so small that he was himself nine of the original Coasters. Then down the aisle from the cockpit came the huge and genuinely intimidating Peter Grant, Led Zeppelin's manager, hulking in a Hawaiian shirt, like an enormous Jurassic reptile shaped like a football and harboring a mean streak. He has a reputation as being a cross between Albert Grossman and *Godzilla*, and tells a story about the time he was a bouncer and singlehandedly lunched half a dozen cops one night during a misunderstanding. He's said to love as fiercely as he fights. He kept right on going to the back, where the bedrooms were—turf tacitly off limits to everybody but the true intimates, that small solar system within the system, since in constant attendance even thirty of your dearest friends can get to be a drag after a while.

By now Eugenie and I, in the guise of having a quiet and slightly boring conversation, were whispering various flashes, chiefly slanderous, to each other.

"Did you pick up on that chick in the pink silk playsuit?"

"The one hanging around those seats by the bar?"

"Loser."

At which point we were drenched in light. A cameraman has spotted Eugenie's tattoo, and he's moving in on it; we discover that a mike on a pole is suspended above our ears. We are *on*.

"As I was saying," Eugenie said brightly, adroitly shifting gears, "Plato's dialog between Socrates and Dostoyevsky has always interested me."

"Absolutely," I agreed, "Especially the part about the poet as tortured artist and bass player..."

I was strapped down for takeoff across from what looked, to all outward appearances, like the original Monster Hippie. I'd seen him first back in the lobby and inadvertently flinched, since muscled brutes six and a half feet high wearing headbands and black sprung-fishnet tee-shirts generally have that effect on me. He was obviously one of the security guys, and it wasn't hard to picture him on a stage cheerfully pitching screaming teenagers back toward the crowd like horseshoes, in long frenzied arcs.

Wrong again. We introduced ourselves over the rush of the take-off blast. His name was Joe, and because he looks like some paranoid's vision of a Hell's Angel come to stomp, he naturally turned out to have a master's degree in history and was probably the gentlest person I ran into all day. He usually teaches junior high school in New York, and when it gets too dreary trying to make horny eighth-graders really care about the Franco-Prussian War, he tends bar. He was even getting tired of that, so he took the Led Zeppelin gig. "I'm *big*, you know?" he told me matter-of-factly, by way of explaining how he'd stumbled into the bodyguard business—and went on to say that he was mainly getting off on the tour. "The only thing I don't like about it," he said, "are some of the kids. It's a drag to see them so fucked up they're paralyzed. Or not showing any respect for each other in the crowds, jamming people against the stage, throwing firecrackers at each other...There's no mutual respect, and that's not a good sign."

*** *** ***

On the ground the deep green hills of the Appalachians were turning slowly black in the increasing twilight; and at twenty thousand feet things weren't all that much brighter. The party kept trying to get going, but there were too many strangers and too much chaos for anything much to happen, too many people wandering and being interrupted and zapped by the film crew—all of us come to record the behavior of this special little tribe were instead close to trampling it senseless.

Jimmy Page, in the midst of it all, was holding distracted court at a group of seats by the bar; with him were a selected batch of ladies and B.P Fallon, a lean gnarled chap in a patchwork sport coat, friend of the group and for vague reasons famous back in England. Fallon was telling what, judging from the ladies, was a terrifically funny story, but Page was clearly uncomfortable, and had his mind on other things. Like Clapton, Page is one of those guitarists who always looks a little sad and pained, even when he's ecstatic—which is what, Eugenie tells me, makes rock & roll women fall apart over them, lost little boys who are absolute motherfuckers on a guitar—but even so this obviously wasn't his idea of a good time.

He kept glancing around the plane, the fastest gun in town, but jumpy anyway, and a lot of his glances were aimed our way. As far as we knew, he didn't have the slightest idea who we were, since we hadn't yet had a chance to talk to him, so I figured he was just properly marveling at Eugenie. But that was just half of it. When Eugenie interviewed him the next afternoon he told her that he'd already known who we were, such is court intelligence, and he was watching the writers from the *Playboy* organization watch him. He's not overly in love with the press, probably for good reason.

*** *** ***

PAGE: Over the years the press hasn't known or understood what we're into. Each of our LPs are completely different, purely because of evolution. And each LP is just a statement of where we are at that time. A lot of reviewers don't know what to make of us. If they've seen us at the time of our second record, when we were doing really hard rock, and then when they're faced with something like our fourth album...well, some of them completely wrote it off. They couldn't see the wood for the trees. I've come down hard on the press for judging us. I once said that a lot of reviewers were frustrated musicians; and through their own paranoia, they came down on me personally, slamming me—and I was glad, because I knew I hit their weak point because of the truth of my statement.

EUGENIE: Anyone in particular?

PAGE: This one person gave us a really bad hammering, John Mendelsohn. I didn't know why, and then I discovered he had a record out. So I sent a message indirectly to *Rolling Stone*: I'll make my one and only contribution to *Rolling Stone*—I'll review his record. But they obviously wouldn't have it. They haven't the guts. And I wouldn't just tear it apart, I'd be fair. No one can make better judgments on what you're doing than you yourself; you're your own worst critic. What happens if one night I try something new in a solo and it doesn't come out all that well? A critic hears it and says, well, he's lost it. But that was just one night.

EUGENIE: Is anyone preserving some standard of excellence outside the artist?

PAGE: I wouldn't have thought so. There are no critics harsher than the artist himself. When you're doing an album you live it. You sweat it out for months, no one knows it inside out like you do. And somebody who plays it and tries to relate or compare it to other statements on earlier albums misses the point. It all comes down to the same thing: the press just aren't important to us. The *Rolling Stone* magazines of this world don't mean anything. It's the *people* out there that one cares for, and they obviously care for you. That's why people turn up and see the concerts. We always do the best we can possibly do. And then it gets down to the people again, who turn up at the concerts, who buy the record and expend the time listening to it.

*** *** ***

It was a little after eight, nearly dark, as we came down toward the early city lights for a landing. Eugenie, looking out the window, wasn't exactly thrilled. "It looks like an open sewer."

"Some day I'll take you to Cleveland."

*** *** ***

Led Zeppelin is very proud of the fact that they do a three-hour show, without an opening act, and that they get there on time—unlike the Just One More Pound Of Coke First school of rock performers. But they were supposed to go on in half an hour, and the Pittsburgh airport is a pretty good haul down the expressway from Three Rivers Stadium, which sits near the center of town in a concrete valley where the Allegheny and the Monongahela rivers become the Ohio—a confluence which in Pittsburgh is apparently not seen as two rivers turning into one, but rather as *three* separate rivers. Frontier metaphysics.

Anyway, we were late. But outside another string of limos awaited us, complete with a police escort. *This* was going to be the movie version, zooming to the stadium behind a wailing wall of sirens, while the good citizens of Pittsburg looked on and marveled. Practically everybody on the plane had moved up a few notches on the Energy-Frenzy scale. Richard Coles and his lieutenants were zipping around telling everyone to haul ass the second the door opened; before we'd even come to stop a knot of fifteen people were crowded in front of it, just *waiting* for those stairs to roll up. The limo drivers were already going into gentlemen, start your engines. The race, for reasons that remained a little obscure to us, was on.

We erupted from the plane like cereal shot from guns. Eugenie and I dutifully ran for the last limo, figuring that everybody would head for the spot they had on the way out. Wrong again. In the Mission Impossible urgency to get going—as if Led Zep were professional assassins late for work—the police had revved up their sirens and were taking off, followed by the first few limos, leaving too many people to scramble for too little space in the ones that remained. As each one filled up it lurched away, peeling rubber to catch up with the pack. Since we were last, we took up the slack. Putting the film guy's equipment in the trunk took a little time, and so did figuring out precisely how to fit that many people in one car, but we, too, finally tore out of there—all twelve of us. In the front seat: the driver; a publicist from Atlantic; on his lap, B.P. Fallon; riding shotgun, the film crew's bearded sound man. In the jump seat: myself; on my lap, Eugenie; and a pair of roadies. In the back seat: three of the group's lady friends and another guy from the film crew. This was the life.

Our driver floored it out of the airport, encouraged by Fallon—who had apparently decided he was on top of this particular pecking order—telling him politely that he'd fucking well better catch up with everybody if he knew what was good for him. We turned on to I-22 and went barreling east toward the city, twenty miles over the posted speed limit, slippin' and slidin' through traffic—nice stuff, but the pack was nowhere in sight, and we were coming up on a genuine jam, without any sirens to tell it how important we were.

Indeed. Both lanes down to a flat stop. A rush hour *into* the city on a warm Tuesday night—things certainly are different in Pittsburgh. Stuck in traffic we are no longer black streaking magic; we're more of a side show. Cars in slowly shifting ribbons move past and gawk at the pile of people in that slick funereal automobile. Who could blame them? We looked like some debauched steel magnate's delivery truck, loaded with a new shipment of white slaves from the East Village, with faithful servant Igor at the wheel.

Our driver intended to remain cool. He pushed for every inch he could get, threading his way from lane to lane, looking for openings. He didn't flinch when Fallon began joking with the Atlantic publicist about not expecting to get a blowjob this early in the evening; or when the first joint was lit and passed; or when the ladies called for music, and somebody up front found the loudest Top 40 station in Pittsburgh, turning it up until you could hear the speakers shredding, while the ladies went into their Ledettes act, harmonizing backup vocals with plenty of enthusiasm; or even when Fallon implied that a Four-Star Shit-Fit was forthcoming if he didn't figure out some way to get us to the concert on time. Actually, that may have unhinged him a little bit. He fought his way over into the right-hand lane and, with the inspiration granted the desperate, created a new lane for himself out of the narrow gravel shoulder and a few leftover feet of road—and we were off again, bottoming out in chuckholes and whizzing past semis with inches to spare, leaving behind us a stream of people eating exhaust because they weren't Stars.

Igor knew a shortcut. He curled onto a cloverleaf doing fifty, up a hill into an old backstreet neighborhood of frame houses aging grimly on a bluff above all those rivers. He had clearly cruised these streets as a punk kid in a hot car, making clever time on a complicated path to the burger stand, and was now in his shorthaired forties reverting to teenage delinquent wisdom in the middle of a professional disaster. He drove like he had hungry dogs snapping at his ass, blowing through stop signs and charging against the grain up the gray channels of one-way streets.

*** *** ***

We came honking up to the truck-sized metal door at the back of the stadium like a black maria gone nuts, but Led Zeppelin had started without us. From blocks away we'd been able to hear *Rock & Roll* rising and spreading like summer thunderclouds into the night. The best laid mice...

When we pulled onto the outfield, Danny came running over to us looking considerably relieved. "Jesus Christ, I thought you were lost. Come on."

The green plastic sward where the Pittsburgh Pirates usually worked had been sealed off just about at second base. A six-foot high wire fence ran across it there, reinforced by a double row of oil drums filled with water. Behind it in the center of the field sat the twenty-foot platform of the stage, flanked by black skyscrapers of speakers on each side. It looked more like a Fellini space launch than not, yellow equipment trucks parked randomly around the outfield, the entire infield and stands beyond nothing but layer upon layer of young faces, forty thousand of them, and all that energy directed toward a single alien jumble of junk...which at the moment was producing some remarkable rock & roll.

Danny led us to a spot onstage behind some trunks and giant amplifiers where we could watch the act. They were doing *Black Dog*, and Page moved transformed. Changed into a white linen suit with a black silk shirt, his red Gibson slung down around his crotch, the gunfighter at work, his face in a tough pout, strutting and slinking into dirty boogie dips, the fastest and meanest guitar in the west...while Plant, still in skintight levis and a vest that was mainly bare chest, shook and himself strutted, stamping his snake boots and grinning up to the heavens, absolutely getting off on it, as the stadium filled with the high soaring waves of his voice, jumping and climbing to keep up with Page's guitar.

It is a carefully orchestrated evening. They play for three hours nonstop, with complex lighting changes and an array of special effects—all handled by the crew with the precision of crack S.S. troops. And they are *not* heavy metal punks turned up to ten and blasting out a thick blue buzz. If anything, they put too many changes into their music. John Paul Jones, along with the bass, plays three different keyboards during the night, one of which can simulate an inter-orchestra scrimmage between the London and Berlin Philharmonics. Page, playing magnificently in every style known to man, uses three different guitars, and assaults and teases one of them with a violin bow until the white resined strands shred and snap—and additionally tackles a theremin, a sonic black box which reacts to a hand interrupting its signal at various distances by producing a changing feedback wall that sounds like Martian police calls; and Plant's voice is sometimes shoved through some enigmatic machine to become warped and echo back upon itself, as if he were belting it out in an underwater cave. The show, Plant told me the next day, is supposed to be magic, should send you somewhere fine and pleasant and strange; and even if they do occasionally try to get you there by wandering off into deep space and playing the Pick Hits from the Asteroid Belt, it sometimes does just that.

*** *** ***

I would probably have enjoyed it more if I hadn't been in terminal need of a piss. All that good cold Thai beer. Danny was standing next to me, and I shouted in his ear over the music that I would very much like a john. He pointed to the trailer on the field below us. "There's one in there." I ran not walked down the stairs and over to it, but Peter Grant was entertaining a bunch of friends inside, and I wasn't about to talk my way past him just to take a piss, particularly when there was all that empty black Astroturf behind the trailer and the trucks.

So there I was, as the fella says, standing in deep right field at Three Rivers Stadium, pissing on renowned plastic grass, probably the same spot where the immortal Lefty Lemon leaped nineteen feet to make the catch that won the '37 Series, while behind me Led Zeppelin filled the air with *Misty Mountain Hop* and forty thousand high lean teenagers boogied their brains out. There was no doubt a lesson there.

And there certainly was when I tried to get back onstage. I was nailed by the security guy, Joe's boss, at the top of the stairs.

"Where's your stage pass?"

He looked like one of those guys who would kill to be a real cop, with a badge and everything, but had been forced to reluctantly settle for this.

"I don't have one."

"Then get the fuck out of here!"

We were right next to the tower of amplifiers, so communication could have been better. I tried to shout the tale of getting stuck in traffic and them running out of passes before we got here, and he promised immediate bodily harm if I didn't get my ass off the stage. Ten feet away Jimmy Page curled toward the crowd in a sensual grind, lost in his guitar.

*** *** ***

With some help from Nurse Ross, who'd joined our discussion just about the time I'd told Fosdick to go screw himself and he'd grabbed me by the Levi jacket and started to shove, we ended that installment of *Kafka Komics* with a truce of sorts. While Fosdick and I were calmly and rationally moving up on attempted murder, she managed to find Danny, who finally cooled everything out and sent us off to neutral corners. So I was standing on the side of the stage that didn't belong to Fosdick, next to The Journalist.

He was looking a little wilted. In the thick Midwest summer heat his meticulously sculptured hair had gone soft and then in places sprung; his tie was loose and he was sweating inside his blazer. He looked like he'd just been mugged.

"How do you like it?"

Plant presently was prancing and shaking his ass and doing his very best to get on down. The sort of moves that send high school cheerleaders to bed at night for weeks with ambiguous heated dreams.

"He's a bit stiff, don't you think? Not much rhythm." Then he looked at his watch. "Do you think they'll play much longer?"

*** *** ***

They did, for another hour, through amazing changes of mood and energy, echoed perfectly by the subtle and precise choreography of the lights in saffron and blue and emerald green response, all building toward the final old monster, *Whole Lotta Love*, and the release of two hundred white doves into the night sky, the Old Testament and Freud all wrapped into one. Behold! The Blessed Ascent of the Lord's Feathery Seed!

While Led Zep moved toward this final bit of magic, Fosdick or someone ordered another stage-cleaning. They missed me this time, but a lambent-eyed girl, so delicate and innocent she made me sad, who'd been standing in the hollow of the red tubular steel superstructure that held the lights, sharing a joint with her boyfriend and nearly glowing, was busted right out of there by Richard Coles, who was closer to foaming at the mouth than not. Peace love dope.

*** *** ***

The moment: Page and Jones are into the slamming final throbs of *Whole Lotta Love*, giant barbwire heartbeats pounding slow with Bonham's drums, and the doves are freed to soar. The first few rise in eager swirls and gyres, and then more follow, sending a surprised cheer through the crowd as by wingbeats they curve up, up and away until they fade into the darkness high above.

A truly fine spectacle, and no one's fault, certainly, that white doves are as dumb as they are symbolic, and that fully a third of them couldn't get it together to fly off into the sunset, and instead plopped like feathered grenades into the crowd and onto the stage. One blammed down right at Plant's feet, and he used it beautifully, gently lifting it in his right hand and holding it out above him, where it sat content until he tossed it into the air toward freedom, a perfect last gesture for a rock & roll Jesus. But another had landed on a speaker five feet away, and was clearly not having a nice day: the feathers on its head ruffled and awry, it stood dazed and confused, like a drunk who just woke up in the wrong city, trying to focus on Plant, shaking its head to stop the buzz, swaying on its feet, stunned, goofy, forlorn.

- 1973

This was my first exotic assignment: Me and 10 other alleged rock writers on tour in Japan for three weeks with Kiss, all paid for by their record company. Back in the 70s we didn't really worry much about the ethics involved in taking such free rides. Their reason for laying out all this money was similar to that of Led Zeppelin's, though far more extreme. By 1977 Kiss were the fave-raves of disaffected teens the world over—I...want to rock and roll all night, and party every day!—but the rock press treated them like a loud joke, comic book escapees in reptilian sci-fi drag, blasting out mindless garage rock beneath consideration. So this was their attempt to buy a little respect.

I confess—no surprise—that I was a lot more interested in spending three weeks in Japan than I was in Kiss, though they proved to be pretty good guys I came to like, and realized by the third concert or so, as I say in the piece, that once you stripped away the sci-fi costumes and pyrotechnics, they were basically a pretty good bar band, no better or worse than dozens playing in college bars everywhere. Theirs was a triumph of packaging and marketing.

But Japan...at the risk of sounding soppy, it was lifechanging. I had never experienced anything like it, especially the mindbending contrasts—the 23rd century slamming again and again against glimpses of simple traditional beauty. Many of these moments are in the article, which kept threatening to turn into a travel piece more than one about Kiss, but despite its length I was unable to squeeze in the most moving, and unsettling moment, an afternoon excursion a bunch of us took, by bullet train to Hiroshima. We had all read John Hersey, and knew that the A-bomb was dropped there in 1945, ending WWII, but I at least was not prepared for the lovely setting, streams meandering through downtown, a low circle of mountains in the distance. We went to the Hiroshima Memorial Peace Museum, and for me it was *like getting kicked in the stomach. To see these relics of this awful destructive force, unparalleled in human history, was visceral, shocking and saddening. One image stays with me: a 3-step stone stairstep, bleached white by the A-bomb, except for the dark shadow, clearly a cringing human form, left there by a body burned to a crisp by the blast.*

But I mentioned contrasts. We also spent three days in Kyoto during cherry-blossom season, whose shrines and Buddhist monastaries with their parks and ponds and zen gardens evoked a peace I had also never experienced before. And I will always be grateful to Kiss for being the unlikely vehicle that allowed me to sit quietly on the long dark cedar planks facing the Ryoangi Garden, a zen stone garden dating to the 15th century, and to lose all thought for a time, serene. It is something I still carry with me.

HOW I SPENT MY SPRING VACATION: ON TOUR WITH KISS IN JAPAN

BULLET TRAINS, CASES OF KIRIN,
AND GROUPIES BY THE DOZEN

On one edge of Ueno Park sits a lake-sized pond. It's bisected by a wide, slightly meandering footpath lined with cherry trees. Half the pond is overgrown thinly by reeds, brown and dead-looking this time of year, home for dozens of small ducks paddling around among them. The other half is clear water, rippled this Sunday afternoon by batches of amateur boaters in rental rowboats painted bright primary colors, yellow and red and blue; they splash about happy to be alive. A great pond you can stroll across the way you'd cruise the Met. On your left, *Wild Ducks Among the Reeds*, Momoyama Period (1573-1615), Kano School; and on your right, *Apremidi Bateaux* by Pierre-Auguste Renoir. Very Japanese.

This is also the season and the spot where the old gents sitting on benches, sipping their saké from paper sacks, have been known from time to time to burst into heated geriatric fistfights while disagreeing over which of the blossoming cherry trees is most beautiful. Also very Japanese.

Among us, however, it's Stan Mack's *Real Life Funnies*.

While we're resting on a bench by the pond, Barbara-still-suffering-from-jet-lag decides that she would, after years of avoiding it in New York, like to try some sushi for lunch. Terrific idea, agrees Jack of *Circus* magazine. Carl of *The Detroit Free Press*, amiable enough to try anything that doesn't go too hard against his Mormon upbringing, also agrees. I can already taste the cold Kirin beer that goes with it.

So we wander, we hope, in the direction of the Kokusai Theater. There are, we remember from yesterday's Dynamic Tokyo bus tour, bunches of sushi bars near it. But as we learn after walking for fifteen minutes, it is unfortunately nowhere near us.

But this is Tokyo, after all. How far can we be from a sushi bar?

By actual count, 45 minutes, a two-mile walk, and a long subway ride to Ginza—where we still have trouble finding one that's open, since most are shut down for the spring holiday or Sunday or something.

At last, though, we find one on the corner of a narrow sidestreet and an alley, with a bamboo façade and mouthwatering plastic replicas of the goods in the windows—from tasty acrylic varieties of nigiri sushi and sashimi to oversize bottles of Kirin that hold nearly a liter.

Genuine greenhorns, without so much as a single pidgin Japanese phrasebook among us, off Pan Am #1 from New York less than 48 hours, we duck anyway through the curtains in the doorway. We are greeted, as our confusion of heads appear on the other side, by a fierce shout of *Haiii!* And then a fast volley. *Hai! Hai! Hai!*

Good Christ. Is this samurai for gonna cut yo ass, mothafuckah? The proprietor saying hello in karate? What?

Both. A grinning sushi chef in white apron is standing proudly before the glass cases holding his array of raw fish, esthetically arranged on beds of crushed ice. Wiping with a white rag and great vigor, he is ceremonially cleaning his instrument—a foot-long sushi knife shaped like the shadow of a spruce—and shouting *hai!* at each of us as we come in.

I soon learned that *hai* (pronounced h-eye-eee, the last rhyming with tree, though in practice the syllables are fused nearly to one) means nothing more sinister than *yes*. But *hai* is also linguistic glue that holds all sorts of conversations and transactions together.

It indicates any sort of agreement, no matter how vague; and it's used as ambiguous punctuation as well, to fill up the spaces, the way leftover hippies say you know, man, and some of us wave our hands in the air. Whole telephone conversations can consist of one party softly repeating *hai* in a continuous stream. Taxi drivers smile and say *hai, hai* when they don't have the slightest idea where you're asking to be taken but want to be polite anyway.

Who knew at the time, but our sushi chef was saying, roughly, "Yes! Yes! Good fish! Yes! Come in! Yes!"

We sit down in front of him at the counter, on stools not built for us *gaijin* (roughly, "foreign devils") that leave my knees wondering where to go.

With a great show of Midwestern confidence and optimism, I ask, smiling, "Does anyone here speak English?"

"*Hai!*" sez our sushi man right back, nodding and smiling.

"English?"

"*Hai!*" smiling and bowing a little this time.

"English?"

"*Hai*!"

No need to go on.

He produces a menu. It's entirely in Japanese characters. "Hai??" hopefully this time. No, sorry, no help. Time to draw on my extensive background in linguistics.

"Kirin beer?" I ask, holding up four fingers, and add, giving no quarter, "and tekka maki?"

Pachinko! He finally heard sounds that connected.

A single finger in the air, he asks, "Tekka maki? One odah?"

My four fingers up again I say, "No, four," since the group by now had decided for openers to settle for whatever we can get first, and tekka maki is a good start.

"*Foah* odah?"

I should have listened to the faint gust of surprise and hesitation that blew by in his voice. It was the same I heard once from a Chinese laundryman when I asked for heavy starch in my shirts, and he agreed, reluctantly, returning my clean shirts so stiff with starch my fingers bled trying to button them.

Instead, I just nodded and smiled and said, "Yes, foah odah," pointing one-one-one down the line.

"Foah odah," he repeated, and then commenced growling and cutting and rolling tekka maki with incredibly deft, graceful movements—and like tekka maki was going out of style. Heaps of it before each of us, and more on the way.

I'll leave out the grim details. If you've ever seen Mickey Mouse as the Sorcerer's Apprentice in *Fantasia*, you don't need to hear it. To make him stop, after shaking heads & waving hands and saying no over and over failed, we finally resorted to covering the bar with our arms and shoulders, to keep him from giving us any more. At last, as a treat, he insisted that we take the pound or so of leftover tekka maki with us in a sushi bag—he wasn't going to cheat us. I put mine, unopened, in my hotel room refrigerator as a present for the maids.

That night I went with Stan Meises (of the *New Yorker* and *New York Daily News*) and Francis Schoenberg (of the German magazine *Bravo* and the soft Bavarian accent) out to the Shinjuku district, billed to us as Tokyo's version of Greenwich Village. Stan has connected with a local artist named Kenji, who's going to show us the sights.

Our taxi lets us out on a wide street roaring with neon and little shops still going full blast at 8 p.m., selling everything you can think of and some things you can't. Somehow it's just not my idea of Bleecker & McDougal—more like a smaller, transistorized Times Square, but scrubbed clean, without the porn or the pervos, if that can be imagined.

It turns out that Shinjuku shares only two things with the Village.

There's a small park, where the few brave Japanese hippies gather to get high on glue fumes. And much of Tokyo's gay scene is clustered here, in clubs and bars, sometimes so small the whole place is two tables crammed together and a bartender crouched in one corner. Shinjuku is otherwise mainly a network of bright narrow sidestreets full of discount shops.

Kenji manages to find us in a few minutes—easier for him than us, since we're the only *gaijin* on the block. He's got a scraggly beard and wears universal bohemian costume, sweater and Levi's-style black pants. He introduces us to his beautiful wife Meiko, who has the first frizzed hair I've seen on a woman here, and her equally beautiful companion, a shy heartbreaker of 17 or so. He suggests that we might hurry, since he'd like to get back home later to see something on television.

He leads us to a nearby tempura joint, which, like everywhere else, since tomorrow is a national holiday (to celebrate, naturally, the arrival of spring), is crammed. But Kenji advises patience, so we get in line.

Slowly we advance, first inside, then across an arched wooden bridge next to the cash register, and finally upstairs, where we kick off our shoes and sit at a low table in a room full of them.

My ligaments never were very elastic even when I was on our high school swimming team, so I am left, again, wondering what to do with my knees, since no matter how I sit they seem to rise like mountains just beyond the horizon of the table. I like Frances even better when I notice her knees in white slacks form a snowcapped range next to mine.

After dinner, some of which does *not* drop into my lap, we head next for one of the two supposedly hot discos in town, called Mugen's. There are too many of us for Kenji's little compact, so it's decided that us fearless men will go there by taxi and the women will take the car—which is the last time we'll see them for hours.

Mugen's is in the Akasaka district, back near the huge Hotel Okura where we're staying. It's the fancy tourist area. Like Shinjuku, it's a maze of identical sidestreets and alleys—only these are crammed with cabarets, pachinko parlors and occasional vast geisha houses announced by much neon and sprawling over the better part of a block.

When Kenji and the driver in concert can't find Mugen's, we abandon the taxi and search on foot, without much success. Addresses are so confused all over the city that people have given up really caring about it. Mail is routed, at the end, by word of mouth. And your deal with any taxi driver is that he'll get you to the general area, but after that you're on your own.

This is fine with me, since discos are right in there with stockyards on my places to stay away from. But finally we find Mugen's. So long have we been stumbling around, we assume the ladies have long since arrived and gone inside, so we pay up and go right in to look for them.

They're nowhere to be found. We wait it out for 20 minutes, then hitting the street again—where Kenji finds a note tacked on the front door, missed in our first rush to get in. They'd waited in the street, getting colder, until Frances went back to the hotel, unable to convince them, she said later, to go inside without the men. Kenji's wife and young friend were at home, not missing the TV show.

We three Marx-san Brothers hail a cab for Tokyo's north country. Stan and I, obvious *gaijin*, hide in the shadows while Kenji does the flagging. Some customs are the same everywhere. The ride is a long blur of lights diminishing, down to quiet streets packed with gray concrete boxes, apartments and houses. Miles from the center of town, it's the first residential neighborhood I've seen in two days of running around Tokyo. It really is *big*. Kenji directs the driver through a geometric maze of identical narrow streets, leader of the "A" Rat Team in the black Toyota.

At his apartment we leave our shoes in a strawmatted entranceway and walk up the stairs into a narrow utility kitchen, then through a sliding doorway of burlap and wood into the family room. Half the size of a handball court, it has a low couch, lower coffee table, books and magazines piled everywhere, beyond eclectic at a glance, sound system and records covering one wall, a red portable TV sitting cockeyed on a table, fighting a lamp for space.

When we come in, Meiko and her shy friend are watching the TV with the sound off. Stan and I find comfortable places on the floor. Kenji plops on the couch and begins shortly to roll a sparse but serious joint of buddah stick, known as Thai stick back home. Meiko disappears into the kitchen and comes back with a plateful of late-night munchies, the most striking proving to be midget smelt dried and candied whole, zonked eyes and all. I tried a couple, they were good, and now I'm ready for insects.

Meiko also brings hot saké, cold wine and Kirin in those giant bottles. After all the feminist wars back home, all this cheerfully submissive service is a little unsettling. I want to get up and wash the dishes or repair the roof to keep things even. But as always it's more complicated than that.

While we wait for the show to start, Meiko tells us about the business she owns and manages—a geisha house. Her shy companion is an undergrad or fledgling or whatever they are called. So Meiko's attentiveness is in fact a profession, her instrument, played tonight for us and as incidental instruction for her young friend—who is presently exploding, silently, with embarrassed giggles as

Stan throws every comic flirt-move he's ever learned her way.

I'm flipping through Japanese comic books and photo magazines with color layouts of Kenji's pictures in them, when our much-waited TV show comes on. So there I was, as the fella says, moving up on Buddha in the boonies of Tokyo, stoned out of my gourd, when who should appear on the TV before me but Bob Dylan?

It's the *Hard Rain* special, complete with Japanese subtitles. Zimmerman's burnoosed Arabs reach farther than they know. It occurs to me during their twosome close-ups, that Dylan should visit his dentist, and that cold Joan Baez has waxed sexy in her middle age, the smartly coifed guerilla housewife. Yes, Joan, any time.

We drift in and out of the Dylan show, which is followed, of course, by *Soul Train*.

Here we are in the mysterious Orient.

So far I've seen so little of Kiss, our hosts, that I barely have all their names straight. Except for watching them clown for us during the long flight over, and a solid rumor that they all ordered spaghetti from room service when we got to the Okura—one of the world's very best hotels, with several fabulous restaurants ranging from a sushi bar to A+ French restaurant to a Kobe beef steakhouse, which many regard as the best in the world, and these guys stay in their rooms and order spaghetti—the only thing new I've learned about them is that drummer Peter Criss is a gun fancier, and has a large pistol collection that leans toward James Bond models.

This tidbit came from a short unplanned interview I conducted with him at the Okura late Saturday night, in the hallway in front of bass player Gene Simmons' room, both of us lying on the floor.

Carl and I had been sitting in Simmons' room while he showed us, one at a time, a suitcase full of Japanese Kiss memorabilia—their painted alien faces on the covers of magazines, guest appearances as comic book characters, hand-inked portraits done by lovelorn artistic teenagers.

As background through the open door we could hear occasional manic outbursts in the hallway. For reasons of security—the hotel's—we'd been given the whole floor to ourselves. The seed of college dorm life in the setup was blossoming into full freshman bloom.

So we're looking through his stuff, marveling in the right places, when in the hall we hear laughter, the muffled clumpclumpclump of feet running in short bursts, periodic airy pop pop pops, more laughter.

The BB wars have flared up again. While we of the press were sitting in traffic Saturday afternoon, on our Hato Bus Tour of Dynamic Tokyo, most of the band and friends were cruising the famous five-story toy store here, buying everything in sight. Japanese toys are terrific because many of them, used right, are still fairly dangerous. Especially nice are the futuristic Buck Rogers pistols that shoot small plastic BBs shaped like miniature champagne corks. The band bought several.

When we got back from seeing Dynamic Tokyo in the afternoon, in moods ranging from grumpy to dangerous, the hallway on our floor was already reel three of *Gunfight at the Hard Rock Hotel.*

We apparently came in just as they were getting bored with tracking and shooting each other. We were fresh game. And, as an additional bonus, the press.

So I'd earned my battle scars earlier in the day, one each on arm and thigh before making my getaway. A close-range hit leaves you with a light bee-sting that fades quickly and a matching welt that doesn't. Harmless anywhere but the eyes, but not so much fun that I was eager to do it again right away.

But just then a phantom in white terrycloth sped by Simmons' open door and got off two low quick ones faster than Lee Harvey Oswald. Pop pop at our feet. He flies by again, laughing, pop, hitting Carl's shin.

Maybe ignoring him will work?

Nope. At floor level in the doorway a black plastic gun barrel is slowly poking its nose around the corner. I know this is only good-natured fooling around, but it really has been a long day, and I'm really tired of it—or so this occurs to me during my diving leap for the gun—tired, as well, of our side having no firepower. Our phantom is surprised but streetwise and doesn't lose his grip on the piece as I lunge. I'm trying to wrestle it away from him when flash I get a look at his face and see that here I am on the floor with one of our stars, trying to steal his toy gun from him.

On Monday morning comes our first real chance to see Kiss vs. The Orient, at a press conference in the Tokyo Hilton. This was to be no somnolent PR gathering of the same seventeen rock writers to hype the new product, as it would be back home. Kiss in Japan is news.

We'd had our first inkling back in the Tokyo airport three days earlier, getting off the plane, groggy from a flight so long some of us got drunk twice. We were greeted by a flashing phalanx of motoclicking Nikons, the Japanese paparazzi in full force, or so we thought at the time. Behind them, beyond the glass-enclosed customs area, were a thousand teenagers, most there in hopes of just a glimpse.

Kiss was ready to oblige, and had spent the last hour of the flight putting on full makeup and drag, ready to give the kids what they wanted.

But the sensible fellow in charge of customs wasn't having any. These crazy Americans could walk around dressed up like monsters if they wanted to, but famous or not they didn't look a bit like the people in their passport pictures to him. And he wanted to see their real faces before letting them into the country.

Triumphal entry turned anticlimax. The boys go wash up.

So eager were the teenagers by then, like wind gusting on a rice field, the sight in customs of any western face beneath long hair sent excited screams washing through them.

The band, their faces inspected and then repainted, ducked out a side way. Most of the kids never laid eyes on them. The true believers were left at last with following our bus full of press and roadies in taxis, on a long expensive ride into the city, in hopes of trailing us to the band's lair.

Every once in a while, as gray ugly Tokyo unfolded before us—provoking shouts of "Newark!" "Detroit!" "Cleveland!" inside the bus—I'd see a taxi alongside, blossoming with young girls waving & giggling & peeing their pants. Big Al, our friendly publicist, kept comparing it to the Beatles. And like it or not, in some ways he was right.

The press conference, for example, provided a few echoes of those golden old hard day's nights, or was supposed to.

Outside the Hilton as we pulled up, there were maybe 60 or 70 girls, standing around in small bunches on both sides of the street, patiently waiting for that magic glimpse…

We were directed to a featureless meeting room, past security right up there at Manhattan Project levels. Inside sitting around tables were a hundred or so select photographers, journalists and a few well-connected groupies. Cameras and tape recorders of every expensive description lay in black heaps on white tablecloths, alongside trays of little bald crustless sandwiches and glasses filled with cola and orange pop.

Lead guitarist Ace Frahley's wife was turned out in a gorgeous silk kimono, bought the day before, and looked like Madeline Kahn in a remake of *Sayonara*. Bill Aucoin, the band's manager, trimly 30ish, persistently rumored to be the brains behind Kiss, although it is as persistently denied, was taking picture after picture of her—trying out his spiffy new Nikon, a gift from Mr. Udo, the Japanese promoter, of whom more later.

The show opened with dimmed lights and … mixed media! A short color film of the band live on stage, dressed like Delirium Tremens 2000, prancing & leaping & leering through four songs. This time through, probably because I've been primed to think Beatles, *Beth*, the hit Kiss single that invaded my car radio too often last winter, even sounded like it might actually be descended from early lamenting McCarthy. Certainly what happened at the press conference was right in there with Beatlemania.

Lights up after the film, and in strolled the band wearing full battle dress. They sauntered theatrically toward the long low dais in front, and the photographers went nuts. There are almost 100 rock magazines published in Tokyo alone, some of them fat as phone books, and new close-ups of Kiss must pay handsomely. In ten years of wasting my life this way I'd never seen such a prolonged electric-storm of flashes. It lasted nearly fifteen minutes, a remarkable photo frenzy, with the photographers swarming around the band like giant stroboscopic lightning bugs.

Eventually they were coaxed reluctantly back to their seats, and the Q & A began, moderated by an attractive bilingual young woman, who did her best to translate everything back and forth. The tone the band seemed to be aiming for was classic charming Beatles put-on, and in scattered moments they pulled it off. But mostly they didn't. Here's how it began:

MODERATOR: We would like to ask each one of you to give us a few words to start off. Would you like to start off, Peter, please?

PETER: A few words? … A few words.

(Laughter) (Translation) (More laughter)

MODERATOR: Would you like to take over, Ace, then?

ACE: I'd just like to say that I'm very happy to be in Japan. So far the country is very beautiful and we're having a very good time, and we're looking forward to the concerts. Thank you.

MODERATOR: Would you please, Gene?

GENE: I'll try not to be repetitious, but everybody in Japan has been tremendously nice to us, and from us to you, *domo arigato.*

PAUL: It's amazing, we've just gotten here, the tour hasn't even begun yet, and already we're looking forward to the next tour.

(While he talks, the photo frenzy flares up again)

GENE: We've never seen so many cameras. It's amazing.

ACE: This is like when the amplifiers blow up on stage.

They give up on talk for the moment. Girls in kimonos present extravagant bouquets of roses to each band member, courtesy of Victor Records, Japanese Division. Paul reads a thank-you note in Japanese, bravely murdering the language. Questions are tried again. Who does your makeup? Were you influenced by traditional Japanese kabuki theatricals? We do our own, and no, not really. Then there's a brief lag in the questions. Big Al on the way over had asked if we would fill any such gaps with questions of our own, should the Japanese press prove too timid or awestruck or something.

PAUL: Tell them not to ask all the questions at once.

(A local to the rescue)

Q: Do you have any particular reason why you don't show your real faces, you're always with makeup?

GENE: We're too beautiful. (Laughter)

PAUL: More seriously, we have a chance to live our fantasies, and everybody in our audiences wishes that they could live the way we do. We live our audience's fantasies for them.

(Another dread lag, then one of us to the rescue)

STAN: If your makeup is part of your fantasies, we're all very curious whether you have sex with your makeup on.

GENE: We don't understand English, I'm sorry.

(Laughter) (Pause) (No question)

GENE: Your television is magnificent. In America we don't have television shows like this. You have superheroes that are magnificent. We've never seen anything like them.

ACE: I like the toy stores. Kiddieland.

PAUL: And we wanted to take this opportunity to thank Mr. Udo…

It went on like that.

From the Hilton, after a lavish lunch bash thrown by Victor, featuring bite sized chunks of broiled this and that, served perched like cooked little Billy goats on small hot boulders suggesting lunch-sized Alps or Rockies, we were taken to the airport and put on a packed flight for Osaka, 250 miles southeast.

During lunch the distinguished-looking president of Victor stood and addressed us briefly in Japanese. Translating for him was a skinny PR man whose business card read "HUSTLE" HONDA.

As "Hustle" relayed it, the president was saying that in this propitious cherry blossom season, it was his hope that this tour would cause the sales of Kiss albums to spread across Japan like cherry blossoms blown before spring wind.

Half the buildings in Osaka were bombed to smithereens during the war, but the city has been built back in industrial-strength concrete and draped in futureshock neon to make sure you notice. Much of it looks like the issue of a ménage a trois among downtown Chicago, Century City in LA, and Las Vegas. The view from my room at the Osaka Grandé consists of an elevated expressway soaring above a six-lane bridge crossing a river long since become a cement-sided canal, a SUNTORY sign dominant among the neon, low Euclidian mountains of high-rise office buildings rising behind.

Osaka isn't one of Japan's biggest hits.

It's second after Tokyo in size, but it's so devoted to business that the pleasures are chiefly for businessman—miles of cabarets and many fabulous bath houses, where those knots in the stomach vanish like vapors in the steam, with the help of course of a cold beer and a warm geisha.

Otherwise there just isn't much to *do* in Osaka.

The guidebooks usually advise that if you find yourself stuck in Osaka, you should daytrip elsewhere. Which is what most of us did.

We had two days to hang out while the band rehearsed and got used to the new set. Then after two Osaka concerts, it would be life on the road, forty of us moving together on trains and planes and buses, a series of one and two-nighters that would go like this:

From Osaka to Kyoto, then to Nagoya for two concerts, back to Osaka for one more, then down south to Fukuoka, and then back to Tokyo for four concerts at Budokan, the last of which will tie or break a record for attendance established by the Beatles.

I spent Tuesday temple-hopping in Kyoto with Carl Arrington and Michael Gross, covering the tour for *Swank*.

To get there we took the famed Shinkansen, which translates variously as Bullet Train or Rocket Train. It can do upwards of 150 mph without swirling your tea, and the lead car suggests a voyage to the moon circa 1952. The Shinkansens connect most cities in Japan like railroad superhighways. And they are always on time. It's a terrific way to get around.

The Osaka-Kyoto run is so short, though, about fifteen minutes, that our Shinkansen never quite got cranked up and wailing—but we got that the next day on the way to Hiroshima.

In Kyoto we made our rounds of the necessary stations.

Kyoto was never bombed during the war, in part because it was the ancient imperial capital. Scattered around town are nearly a thousand shrines and temples, some tucked into spots on thriving business streets, others spread thoughtfully over acres, ponds and gardens tended with Buddhist care since the thirteenth or fourteenth century, our time.

At the Ryonaji Temple on the southwest outskirts of the city there's a celebrated stone garden created five hundred years ago by a Zen monk with strange things on his mind. It is mainly a long rectangular expanse of white gravel raked lengthwise meticulously into many parallel rows. Cornfields under snow, a limestone sea in light chop. Whatever you see. This combed expanse is broken only in five places, deliberately random, by craggy small groups of black boulders.

That's the garden, rocks and gravel. I loved it.

As the temple brochure explained:

"We can view the garden as a group of mountainous islands in a great ocean, or as mountain tops rising from a sea of clouds ... Absorbed in this scene, we, who think of ourselves as relative, are filled with serene wonder as we intuit Absolute Self, and our strained minds are purified. In Zen, everything, even a leaf of grass, expresses ultimate Reality. Thus we can say that this simple garden of itself suggests to us absolute value."

Running the full length of the garden on one side are three rows of bleachers made from fine Japanese cedar. On them sit people in their socks, holding clear plastic bags provided by the temple and containing their shoes, contemplating the garden in silence. The crowd at a Zen football game. I added my own invisible silent cheer for a while.

On the grounds of the same temple there's a decorative pond, surrounded by trees and flowering bushes, that's a thousand years old, which is also something to think about. Back about then my ancestors were living without villages or roads in the forests and swamps of northern Germany-to-be, chased around like wild goats by Charlemagne, while in Japan in A.D. 900 there was a bureaucracy already so advanced that one government bureau was designated the Department of Poetry.

Tuesday night, Bob Weiner, a pleasantly grumpy sort who works as gossip columnist for the *Soho Weekly News*, was determined by god to see The Bottom Line—*the* hot disco in Osaka, according to no less an authority than "Hustle" Honda. Stan Meises and I decided to go along for the ride. The only problem was that none of us knew where to find the place.

Down to the hotel lobby to ask.

The scene at the Osaka Grandé is considerably looser than things had been at the Okura, so there are groupies hanging out—some of whom we're beginning to recognize as regulars, our camp followers. Some of them will follow us hundreds of miles in the next week or so, paying their own way, on trains and airplanes with us, and with rooms in the same hotels.

We manage to ask two of them where we might find The Bottom Line. They giggle and don't know, they live in Tokyo. The desk clerk tries several phone books but no luck. We ask the young cashier at the coffee shop, but this is a breach in the pecking order and her boss turns up immediately to answer any questions we might have. He doesn't know either. Weiner persists. Down to the Pine Bar in the basement, which is quickly becoming Osaka's biggest attraction to most of our entourage. On his red uniform tonight the bartender is sporting a redder pair of enamel KISS lips, one of the pins we've all been giving away as small gifts, courtesy of Big Al's bagful of them. The bartender's not sure but he'll check. Soon there's a consortium of waiters & waitresses at the bar. After much discussion they agree that it's in the basement of what sounds to me like the Haiku Department Store. A map of the city is produced. The bartender traces imaginary paths on it with a raised pen. The best one is then drawn. He confirms this with Weiner. We *domo arigato* him practically senseless, but he's not finished. He leaves his station and leads us up to the taxi stand, where he sticks his head in the first one and gives the driver a shotgun slew of instructions. We are off.

It would have been perfect if the driver had understood. He's courteous but completely mystified. Our increasingly frantic questions and directions in the pidgin phrasebook don't help. After fifteen minutes of driving uncertainly around downtown Osaka, we pay and abandon him in what Weiner is sure is the right area.

As we walk I notice a neighborhood police gazebo the size of a 42nd St. hot dog stand. Inside is a bench and two desks and three cops. They're wearing 30s-military uniforms and white chauffeur's gloves and no guns. They look so quaint I walk right in to ask the whereabouts of The Bottom Line, something I'd never do back home. Might Japanese cops actually serve and protect? They indicate politely that we should sit on the bench. Weiner shows them our piece of paper with The Bottom Line written out in Japanese characters. They consult, amused. Another map is drawn and explained to us with much pointing and gesturing.

Turns out we're just a ricochet away.

Our official handmade police map takes us down an alley into a *lit* network of arcades. On the main drag where we turn, it's a quarter-mile blast of sushi joints and shoe shops and fun fun fun strung along a street hardly wider than Mama Cass at her best.

On each side at blazing intervals are pachinko parlors wrapped in neon bright as doomsday. The bouncing, falling steel balls in row after row of machines sound like distant waterfalls of dimes as we hurry past.

The cops have steered us right.

On the left in big English letters is the sign.

The entrance is a space-age escalator done in shining stainless steel and avant plastic. We're happy that we've managed to do this silly thing, in the best tradition of Hemingway, and climb on. But at the top we're met by several slim young fellows in black suits who aren't so sure they want to let us in. We flash all our press cards and Kiss IDs, which don't help much. But Weiner hands over the ace—the business card of our friend "Hustle" Honda.

They walk back and forth conferring, passing the card for inspection. There isn't a fleck of hostility in all this. Finally they decide we're all right, but we're told we have to pay regular rates—1500 yen each, about $6—and thank the owner, who's standing by the cashier's cage.

Fine.

Inside a soul group called Prime Cut is slinking through passable replicas of current hits. They're on stage at the far end of the room, beyond the dance floor. Except for the rhythm section, they're all black. Running the length of the walls on each side are red-lit glass cases, filled with neat dark rows of whiskey bottles. Two enormous white parachutes are draped from the ceiling. All the tables downstairs by the dance floor are taken, so we're led up to a booth on the mezzanine, with a good view of one parachute. A waiter appears with glasses, ice, and a full bottle of whiskey. "The bottle is free," he explained over the music, "a gift from the owner," smiling broadly now, "because you are foreigners."

Prime Cut's set includes *Rubberband Man* and *Car Wash*.

On the packed dance floor most of the girls wear pleated skirts cut below the knee, V-neck sweaters and blouses with the collars out. Hip fashion in Osaka has made it up to 1958.

Weiner jumps bravely in and transforms all his nervous energy into thrashing limbs, with an effect that suggests a chicken during shock therapy.

As I watch the dancers I realize that something else is wrong. The anarchy's missing. Instead of slugging it out for space as it's done back home, the dancers have all aligned themselves in rows, and almost everyone is politely facing the band—as if they're in the front rows at a rock concert, boogieing in their seats. Only a few turn their backs to face the mirrors and dance with the perfect partner.

A banner hung from the mezzanine shouts to all in big English capitals:

WELCOME TO
THE BOTTOM LINE
DANCING EVERY NIGHT
BURN YOUR SOUL
*** *** ***

The world's thinnest teenager had a jagged scarlet lightening bolt streaking diagonally across his face. The bolt was edged in silver glitter. From the ground up he was platform shoes, silver tights, black leather hot pants and cling shirt. His poor mother. Three pretty girls stood near him, talking, their black hair spilling without flaw onto the shoulders of their white coveralls, each with the KISS logo sewn in spangles across the back. Also in spangles they had duplicated exactly the signature of each band member. The autograph of Paul Stanley curved gleaming around one athletic rump.

A few kids had on UCLA sweatshirts. One with a Playboy rabbit. A T-shirt that said on the back, in graceful English script, Lonely Boy. Another in the same style that read Young Blood. Scattered here and there were the mad devout, their faces painstakingly painted in the image of their heroes.

We were all hanging out in the lobby of the concert hall, waiting for Kiss to start the first of ten concerts in Japan. Most of the crowd was already inside. The opening act, a Japanese metal group called Bow Wow, had just finished its set and been rewarded for its efforts with a bored pitter-pat of applause. In a few minutes we went in to find our seats. The usual intra-act muzak was being piped loud and clear through the monstro amps on either side of the stage, stereo headphones of the gods.

Could it be? Yes. To warm up this audience of 2500 Japanese teenyboppers out here in the Osaka sticks, Kiss before going on was feeding them tapes of flower-top primo Led Zeppelin. *Whole Lotta Love, Black Dog, Rock & Roll ...*

They did it every night of the tour. I never figured out whether it was bravado or ingenuousness or just plain dumb—whether it mattered to Kiss at all that they were, musically speaking, blowing themselves out of the water every night by playing these Zeppelin tapes.

Silvery machinegun bursts from a bad angel, Jimmy Page's guitar was nicely carving up the place when two live roadies appeared on stage. Urged on by increasingly excited screams, they began lethargically removing the black sheets draped over the Kiss set—a new, cut-down version of the one they use in the States. The old one wouldn't fit on the lone 747 they'd chartered to carry cargo, and they wanted a new one anyway.

It only cost $150,000. Twenty-five feet high, it's wide as the stage and consists chiefly of black stacked Marshall amps. Peter Criss's considerable drum kit is inset in the center of this loud honeycomb. It's flanked on each side by a Busby Berkeley stairway to heaven, ascending steps big as dream sequence dominoes that light up when they're stepped on. Much fancy prancing will occur here. At the top over the Marshalls there's a runway on each side. The drum kit itself is on a platform that moves up and down like a lube rack. During the drum solo it's sent zipping pneumatically to stage front. And there are also the smoke bombs and flash pods and eerie dry ice fog and confetti canisters artillery-launched over the crowd, exploding in fireworks bursts that fall like showers of spring snow.

As the lights go down, the screaming goes up.

Weiner has brought along a box of gum wad earplugs, and passes them out among us. As Gene Simmons said quietly a few days earlier, "The kids like it loud." I guess. When I'd seen Kiss at Chicago Stadium back in January, they were putting out a measured 140+ decibels to the first twenty rows or so. It's an effect you can reproduce almost exactly by sticking your head inside a jet engine. If you're under 15, it's very stimulating.

The considerably more sensible Japanese have set an upper limit of 110 or so, and were metering the concert halls every night to keep Kiss honest, but that's still high enough to leave you with a head full of ghostly telephones ringing away for hours.

Everybody is standing and screaming as Kiss take their carefully choreographed battle stations in the semi-gloom. Then lights, camera, flash bombs, music...

Simple slamming Gibson chords. Paul pouts and leaps and shouts out lead vocal. Gene is the prowling evil lizard, horny and looking for something to ravage. Ace, playing lead in a Flash Gordon outfit, is of the Bill Wyman performing school. The self-proclaimed "master of space and time" seems to have left his body playing guitar while his spirit is far off on the planet Zorg, in another dimension, duking it out with Ming the Merciless. Or he's drunk. Somewhere behind the jungle of drums is Peter Criss, a regular guy from an Italian section of Brooklyn, with his face painted up to look like a cat's—although a friend of mine said she thought he looked like Minnie Mouse.

By the end of the tour I'd seen eight concerts.

Night after night the show varied only in minor details, including Paul's spontaneous intro raps. The crowds and their response were also nearly identical every night. Some more up than others, but that's all.

In the midst of all this sameness, I was changing my opinions about the band more often than my socks. Are they a threat to mankind and harbinger of apocalypse? Minstrels for the new barbarians? Carny for the 70s? Four nice guys with a very commercial idea? Boring? Terrific? All of the above?

Some of my concert notes:

OSAKA #1:

They're doing *Meet You in the Ladies Room*. The kids know the lyrics, singing along behind us. The Japanese show enthusiasm by throwing long streams of crepe paper, instead of firecrackers, toilet paper, cherry bombs, or each other, as at home.

Ace's solo is, well, underwhelming. But then his guitar does give off actual smoke, billowing out of some contraption wired inside. The rock-critic cliché brought vividly to life, sort of. And then the guitar is left alone on stage, spotlit in a rack, wailing feedback just about as well on its own as it had been under the direction of Ace.

But *good* apparently doesn't matter to the fans. It has more to do with sentiments than songs, such as "You got nothin' to lose!" and Paul screaming into the mike, "I wanna rock and roll all night, and party every day!"

That's what you want to hear if you're in ninth grade in No Falls, Indiana or Ennui, Ohio—your major centers of boredom and repression, that is—and apparently in Osaka, too. The snow machine cranks up, Paul does the obligatory guitar-smash and throws it—and gently—into the audience. The kids commence shouting in unison, "Encora, encora, encora …"

OSAKA #2:

The show's a return engagement for a number of the fans. The world's thinnest teenager is back, sans red lightning bolt, but back. Also the girls in white overalls, and Tough Blondie in the front row again.

Gene doing his nightly troglodyte blood-spitting act, with the dry ice smoke rolling out. Throughout the drooling and snarling under exorcist-green lights, Bavarian Frances holds her head in her hands, so as not to see it. Paul's pinwheeling arm during *Rock & Roll All Night* is a straight cop from The Who— as is the guitar-smashing bit, of course. Kiss is like a collection of other people's moves and chops. The lowest common denominator. Which is fine if you're 14, I guess. But by the end of the show I find myself thinking, who needs it?

KYOTO #3:

Saturday. A HIBINO SOUND truck sitting outside the Kyoto hall, which is the nicest we've seen so far. A gaggle of kids made up in KISS face, one with a crewcut done up as Gene. I spot four of the same girls who were hanging around the Osaka Grandé. True love knoweth no limits, I guess. Inside, the hall is a modernist horseshoe with what look like schools of cubist sea biscuits flying ten feet below the angled plane of the roof, acoustic deflectors of some sort.

There are slightly sinister overtones to all the "security" on the tour— especially as applied to crowd control, which is about six times more efficient than in the States, and depends in large part on the abundance of black belts & such in these parts. So instead of getting knocked in the jaw by some ex-road-house ape when you get too excited and rush the stage, here that impulse can lead to a quick chop that can leave you looking for scattered parts.

So crowd control is thus: One security guy each on each side of the first 20 rows, Mr. Udo's boys in pink armbands, ready to keep you seated. Two or three guys in suits at the sides give warning blasts at potential transgressors with high-powered flashlights. And the beam usually manages to put them right back down in their seats.

Cops in squads of six cruise the lobby. Several come down the stairs, sticking their little white-gloved index fingers into their ears, shaking their heads at each other and smiling.

Walking up to the top balcony as the band does *Rock & Roll All Night*, as I look down to the stage I realize something is wrong. It takes a few moments to figure it out. It's is the air. After two hours of music, it is still clear as a cold autumn night. No pot haze, no cigarette smoke. And still no lethal missiles hurled through this clear air.

Then standing right by the stage, watching Gene's antics and playing.

They seem even more comic up close—and much more overtly & deliberately sexual. Wagging the silver scaled codpiece that shines between his legs against black tights, that looks like a biker's fantasy of a chrome-studded cock. Symbolically licking every girl in the first five rows with his fat long serpent's tongue.

The truth is, it *is* a great costume. Thigh-length silver-scaled boots, each scale twice the size of a silver dollar, scales evolving at the ankle into a boot shaped to be the face of a sour monster with red rhinestone eyes, and 10-inch platform heels.

It's a little too much for the plump schoolgirls in the first row, who react as most Japanese girls seem to when tremendously embarrassed, by putting their hands to their mouths and lowering their eyes while they giggle like mad.

SUNDAY TO NAGOYA BY TRAIN:

On the Shinkansen to Nagoya, ridin' that train, high on Suntory…

And there's Honey, the 15-year-old groupie who's been following us everywhere. All day during the photo shootings at various temples around Kyoto today, she and her friends followed us in cabs. And tonight as we attacked the Shinkansen platform there she was again, in her white denim jacket with a cloth Kiss decal sewn on the back, pouting, on the platform with a bunch of her friends.

Later Sunday night she will appear in that same outfit in the fancy rooftop restaurant of the Nagoya Grandé, wanting Michael Gross, who it appears she has fallen in love with, to tell him that she's out of money and light years from home and would he, gulp, help?

Michael two nights earlier on arrival at the Kyoto Grandé had connected with her. They'd been eyeing each other since Osaka, which is where I noticed her first. He was on his way up with her to better things when he found out that she was 15 and never been kissed. So he'd said polite goodbyes and grabbed his hat. Now, rejected, she was deeply in love. And broke.

Back on the train, we have now taken over one entire 1st class Green Car, blitzed the bar car and come away with Suntory pints. Too bad for the few other folks sharing the car with us, at least if they were expecting a quiet ride to Nagoya.

But what's this?

There sitting a few seats away with an average-looking mom are two little girls of eight or nine or so. Mom has dressed them both in high red plastic go-go boots, silver tights, black satin hot pants and red tops—with a decorative gold cocaine razor blade hanging from a gold chain around each of their little necks. Our Lolita twins suck shyly on lollipops. They certainly get the tour's Roman Polanski Award.

NAGOYA #4:

The biggest hall yet — a sports arena. On the way to our seats we pass stacks of Kiss albums sitting unattended on tables in an aisleway. At home they would have been ripped off and sold twice by now.

And I'm actually beginning to enjoy the show—through earplugs.

Kiss is all right if you think about them in the right way. Musically, I mean. It's the clockwork orange costumes and huge halls and bombs going off and pervo Walt Disney staging that fools you. If you close your eyes and get past all that, you can hear the secret of Kiss.

They are a bar band from outer space.

Simmons had told me in January, "Any bar band in the country could learn all our tunes in one day."

I didn't get it then, but I do tonight. They're a paradigm of the form. And that's one reason they're so adored. Their fans know, sense that *they* could be up there prancing around instead, that what Kiss does musically is Jacksonian democracy, proof that you can still make it in America with energy, that genius isn't required.

If Kiss were in jeans and sweatshirts and I had a flat draft beer in front of me, I could be back in college in southern Ohio at Al & Larry's Bar, listening to Tony & The Bandits do cheery off-key versions of current Stones and Beatles hits. Or visiting friends in East Lansing, at some joint that featured Terry Knight & The Pack, soon to be known as Grand Funk Railroad, doing pretty much the same. And that is after all where the members of Kiss come from—the bar band circuit in Queens & Brooklyn & Jersey.

OSAKA #5:

Back at the Osaka Grandé, after two nights in Nagoya. Our camp-following groupies become more and more familiar. Sad-eyed Honey is still with us, as are the two who have come to be known by the band as Nabisco and Bosco.

So boring was Nagoya that most of us spent late nights at an ersatz casino and game parlor across the street from the Nagoya Grandé.

Gene Simmons decided to conquer the Badger Game. It consists of an array of holes big as coffee cans in a flat knee-high surface. When you put in your 100 yen, mechanical badgers begin popping up randomly. The object is to bash as many in the head as you can with the mallet provided. It takes speed and a fairly high level of aggression.

After several tries, Simmons made 22 and drifted off to other things, leaving the machine to Mitsu, one of the black-belt security guys who's also the author of a published book of poetry, and who spent a year studying art in the United States—in Cleveland, where I grew up, something we discovered to our mutual amusement. At the concerts Mitsu often stands, taciturn, in the pit, ready to shred anyone who gets too eager, but probably dreaming as he stands of snow on Mt. Fuji or cranes in flight over silver ponds.

Mitsu has decided to tackle Gene's record of 22.

His crewcut lieutenant, also a black belt in bear-trap shape, feeds the machine coins as Mitsu takes it on. He actually hits a third more than Simmons has, in precise startling flashes, but you have to really slam the daylights out of these fast little fuckers for it to register. For game after game, New York street moves were beating out a thousand years of martial arts. Mitsu managed 22 twice, but gave up sweating at last.

Then it was the lieutenant's turn for a while, also no luck. Arrington, our amiable Mormon, also tried his luck, revealing hints of a mean streak I liked a lot.

Peter Criss was toward the back, by the bar, playing blackjack against a live dealer with his wife and Barbara-finally-over-her-jetlag, for chips worth five dollars. At the table next to them, Ace was working on getting drunk and winning at 7-card stud. I happened to be standing next to him as he won a big pot. He laughed and sighed, and looked at me and said quietly, "I wish I was home."

On this return engagement at the Osaka Grandé, we find we aren't the only group in the hotel. We are sharing it with the Moscow Opera. There's a blackboard hanging in the lobby, a timetable scribbled in Russian characters. Dour Russians stand around the lobby smoking, along with a scattering of teenybop groupies in various scandalous outfits hanging out waiting to be noticed. One opera member especially is doing a great imitation of Peter Bull playing the Russian ambassador in *Dr. Strangelove*.

In the elevator I find myself with several people dominated by a fellow a head taller than all of us, with a chest like a bass fiddle. Stan Meises smiles and sings deeply, "Bass …" The big Russian laughs and booms out a couple of low notes in response.

In the lobby as I went back up to my room, having forgotten something, just before the concert, were some of the wives and girlfriends of our entourage, sitting on couches facing the bank of elevators. Dressed to the rock & roll teeth, they're bored. gossiping fitfully, hanging out, waiting for the gig to start.

A few minutes later when I came back down, the elevator doors parted at the lobby, and there, sitting on those same couches, the wives of the other group. Stolid Russian women in drab solid clothing, bored, gossiping fitfully, hanging out while their husbands in the Moscow Opera got ready for their gig …

The next morning both groups were leaving and mingled in the coffeeshop and lobby. Like Kiss, the Moscow Opera had brought along enam-elled buttons to give away. Usually through mutual broken German or French, or simply through sign language, we all traded buttons back and forth—our smackeroo red KISS lips for frowning Lenin buttons.

FUKUOKA #7:

Wednesday. After the concert we're all invited to a party at the Honey Pot #2, a private club across from the Fukuoka Grandé. The owner is one Gan, a short, shoulder-heavy wedge of muscle who taught four of our black-belt security guards everything they know. Gan is something of a martial arts grand master, and owns a few cabarets around Japan on the side. He is also something of a groupie, and has invited the whole Kiss entourage to Honey Pot #2 for an after-hours party.

But Paul Stanley is in a mood to talk, and so are Arrington, Frances, Meises and me. So we're sitting in his hotel room, tapes rolling bob, while Stanley sits in a towel taking off the last of his makeup and telling us stories about his days as a New York City cab driver. There's still an afterimage of his famous star over his right eye as he tells us these tales in New York street accents. We're collectively working on a fifth of Japanese green tea liqueur, a delicacy we've all grown fond of.

After a while Weiner appears to report that the party across the street is a dud. "I advise you not to go. It is an empty club filled with Michael Gross, Al Ross and Bob Gruen and that was all. And a few Japanese, and a loud 50s-style band and some cold chicken. Nothing."

We believe Weiner's unsolicited testimonial, but after talking through another side of the tape, we decide to go check it out anyway. The black wet street shines in a cold mist of rain as we cross toward what proves to be the bolted steel security door of Honey Pot #2.

Much banging and shouting. The door is mounted garage-style. Unlocked, it's shoved upward but sticks halfway, and looks like a cartoon guillotine poised for a man-sized mouse. One by one we bend and scurry inside.

The club holds maybe a hundred, in two low tiers of tables and booths facing a stage and dance floor in one corner. The stage is full of rock & roll weaponry, but nobody's using any of it. We've missed the show—an oldies band, according to Weiner, fronted by a Japanese imitator of Elvis, authentic right down to the sahdberns & hillbilly sneer.

Weiner had barely understated the crowd, which was bored and going terminal when we came in. But Paul Stanley, leader of our pack, is up and energized by the gangbang interview, and ready to rock & roll all night. Gan, accommodating, starstruck, sends someone to fetch the 50s band. Not to play another set, but to borrow their instruments. Stanley is in a mood to jam, and quickly is everyone else. Hope yet for something to do in bleak rainy Fukuoka. It's hardly after midnight, and everywhere else is long closed. We don't seem to be in tune with local rhythms.

Mr. Udo, impeccable in an expensive suit, stands near the back and smiles as the instruments arrive and are claimed. Since Ace and Peter Criss aren't here, we are treated to a jump-shift in the pecking order right before our eyes. Paul straightaway claims lead guitar slot, moving up from rhythm, and is already plugged in playing bits of this and that while a roadie tinkers with Gene Simmons' amp. Simmons has moved up from bass to rhythm guitar. A roadie named Barry jumps right on the bass; and another roadie who first claimed the drums is replaced amid cheers by one B. Posthlewhaite, function unknown.

Mr. Udo smiles and smiles.

Paul Stanley tries to kick this jury-rigged group into *Honky Tonk Women*, and runs nicely through the lead part like a bat out of Keith Richards, not bad at all. But the confusion reigns around him, and it collapses with a thud.

Back to the basics. They to start up again with a slow *Wild Thing*. Dual vocals are provided by Hollywood Richard, the costume caretaker, clearly a star in his own shower, and the Japanese Elvis, who's back, wearing a striped sports coat and white slacks.

They try to fight it, but *Wild Thing* slides inevitably downhill, like mud, into *Louie, Louie*, anthem of every bar band that ever dodged a flung bottle.

On *Louie, Louie* they begin to cook.

Mr. Udo smiles and smiles, even as an associate leans toward his ear and tells him something in urgent tones. I drift their way to find out what's up—and overhear Gan telling Mr. Udo that the police have thoughtfully called to say they will be raiding the joint shortly.

Mr. Udo smiles and smiles while thinking about this.

The jam is actually on the verge of cranking up, and we crazy Americans are beginning to smell a party till dawn in the air, with a portion of the highest-paid bar band in the world providing the music.

But Gan has a license to lose and is not so cool as Mr. Udo.

After a few more loud minutes, when decency and subtle suggestion fail utterly, Gan commandeers the mike and announces a little frantically that we will all for sure spend the night in jail if the music doesn't stop immediately. But we don't have to go home, he says, because he has a demonstration that will please us.

It's another of those very Japanese moves, like the story in the paper a couple of days earlier. Two of the southern islands had voted, as an ecological move, to ban the use of chemical detergents. Wonderful. But how will they bring this about? From the paper: "The Kamajima Fishery Association has passed a resolution to 'seize every detergent found on the island from April.' They will confiscate any chemical detergents found at homes, and give out natural soap in exchange."

Yes, the detergent goons will burst uninvited into your home and tear things apart snooping for contraband. But if they find any, instead of fining you or carting you off to jail, they will give you the right thing, and put you on the proper path.

Gan and the police tonight are seizing our loud jam and giving us in exchange ... a ritual demonstration of classic samurai moves.

Bare to the waist, Gan kneels on the dance floor, gripping a samurai sword with both hands. Also bare to the waist, assisting him in this solemn ritual, is the Japanese Elvis, who is, truth be told, a little too drunk to pull this off it seems. But he will try mightily. Symmetrical roses are tattooed on his pecs. He kneels a few feet from Gan and begins the demonstration.

It is a fierce chop-&-kick ritual, or is supposed to be, punctuated by warrior shouts of "UUOUS!" that sound to my Ohio ear like what you might get by sneaking up on an unsuspecting cow and kicking it in the stomach.

Japanese Elvis is drunk but gaining concentration. He flashes through a series of steel-trap-moves, shouting "UUOUS!" with each change.

It's beautiful in its way, but it just isn't *Louie, Louie*, and is mainly hilarious to this drunk and stoned company. Mr. Udo is not smiling until we ugly Americans manage to stop hooting and cracking up. Then Gan goes into his ritual butcher act with the samurai sword, another brave repertoire of moves, executed above and around the head of the Japanese Elvis, who is feeling a bit loose by now, and bellowing "UUOUS!" whenever it feels right.

For several minutes Gan carves metaphysical air with his ancient sword, sweating, veins in his forehead ready to pop, slashing away his fizzled party and the cops and the bombed Japanese Elvis and whatever else is on his mind.

Mr. Udo is not smiling.

- 1977

Nobody remembers the Bay City Rollers—probably not even the kids who were in the group. But they were a teenybopper rock phenom in the 1970s, lads from Scotland decked out in tartan, which all their fans—99% of them girls, and most what would be called "tweens" today—all adopted, all of them swept up in "Rollermania."

Lisa, my 13-year-old daughter, was visiting Chicago (she now lived with her mother and stepfather in New Jersey), and on a whim I asked if she might be interested in going to their concert. To her credit, then and now Lisa was skeptical of many things, and wasn't so sure she was interested. But I convinced her. By then, among my duties as an editor at Playboy *magazine, was editing the front-of-the-book Music section, and I thought it might prove fun to write a short piece about attending the concert with her.*

I really wasn't ready for what we were getting into.

AN EVENING WITH THE BAY CITY ROLLERS

EEEEUUUUUU!

Bay City Rollers concerts ought to be outlawed for males over 18—because they attract more jailbait per square foot than most old hearts can stand. Worse, it is mainly jailbait of the Humbert Humbert persuasion, 12-year-old nymphets, 13-year-old heartbreakers; and, even worse, well, there is this phenomenon called Rollermania. . . .

At the Uptown Theater on a steaming summer night in Chicago, we can hear the pleading pubescent chorus all the way from the street, "We want the Rollers! . . . We want the *Rollers*!" . . .

Too old to do this safely alone, I have with me my own expert—a 13-year-old heartbreaker named Lisa, who's also my daughter. In the car on the way to the concert, she's being very cool about the whole thing. At her school, anyway, nobody has a dose of anything like Rollermania. She's never heard of the tartan business (the plaid is the band's trademark, and true believers supposedly *live* in shirts, scarves and cuffed Huck Finn jeans trimmed in the stuff), says she thought at first that *Saturday Night* (their biggest U.S. single) was all right, but then she got bored with it real fast, and, in truth, really wishes we were on our way to see Wings.

We are barely inside the lobby when the chorus, which has been rolling out in increasingly peaking singsong waves, suddenly leaps in pitch and resolves into mass shrieking—and our cool is melted as we see that it's for . . . a *stagehand*, wearing a grubby sweat shirt and a sour look, carrying a mike on stage. Keyed up, I think they call it.

By the time we find our seats, and I am wondering—not complaining, mind you, just wondering—what I'm doing in the middle of 4000 screaming teenagers on the hottest night of the year, when the lights have gone black. Then, abruptly, a slide is projected onto a screen high above the stage. It is a color photograph of a tartan plaid. Its appearance, I swear to you, jolts the screaming yet upward, toward canine regions, making my fillings vibrate. It feels wonderful. It is followed at heartbeat intervals by slides of each boy in the band, each with the same effect. And then, still in the dark, a neon gadget begins an actual countdown, ten . . . nine . . . eight . . . , timed to produce shrieks you could ride like a roller coaster. So far, we have seen a stagehand, a slide show and a neon sign, and there is more flat-out frenzy around me than anyone has seen since early Beatles or Stones concerts. And when the gadget hits the magic zero, and lights blast the stage with white, and the Rollers are there, hitting those uncertain first notes . . . I feel like I have been yanked back to the scene in *A Hard Day's Night* when the TV studio audience goes berserk and the Beatles play amused over the pandemonium.

From where we are, the Rollers look nearly as young as their teeny-bopper fans—which is, of course, the idea. The Stones, the Beatles or even apple-cheeked Herman's Hermits never looked as young and innocent as the Rollers do. One of them, Ian Mitchell, is the angelic image of a baby-teeny Jimmy Page who has not yet had an evil thought; and the rest are nearly as cherubic.

Their musical skills contribute to that image of freshness. They sound like they've been playing together for about six weeks, tops. But the band in various forms has been together for eight years. So there is apparently no danger of their sophisticating the energetically harmless primer-school Stones sound they've developed. In the studio, it comes out with a bit more accomplishment and complexity. Their latest album, *Dedication*, reveals a lyrical Manilow-romantic streak in them that must pierce the very hearts of seventh-grade girls. But the rockers on it sound better to my ear, and, old fogy I, of all the cuts, I like best their remake of Brian Wilson's *Don't Worry Baby*.

But, in concert, they seem mainly to be watering down the best—the Stones, The Who, et al. And the music doesn't seem to matter all that much, anyway. If you were born the same year *Time Is on My Side* first hit the States, Mick Jagger probably just doesn't do it for you. The Rollers aren't there to be *listened* to, they are there to be *adored*.

Which is what is happening.

The screaming doesn't stop during the entire 45-minute set. Lisa spends most of it standing delighted and wiggling (if not quite screaming, you understand) on the arms of her theater seat. Tartan objects of every description are waved and waved and waved in the air, certainly to be taken home later and venerated as sacred relics that have been in The Presence. Instamatic Magicubes pop and pop and sometimes catch, strobelike, a tear-filled girl-scout face, hair pasted to it by sweat, transported beyond. . . .

The lobby, during all this, is a scene all its own. So young are the fans that it's full of moms and dads just waiting for the concert to be over so they can take the kids home in their station wagons. One mom I like especially is in her best Sears patiowear, and paces, smoking, back and forth, staring into space, hardly noticing when other forlorn moms lead their hysterical daughters (all in tartan shirts, etc.) toward the exits.

But the best is last: As everybody files out when it's over, two boys of nine or so, in full tartan drag, soaked in sweat, clearly drained and worn out, come walking up the aisle. One—again, I swear—turns to the other wearily and says, with grim resignation, "You know, I guess we're just gonna have to get used to this."

Amen.

- 1976

I loved The Band long before they became The Band, *but I just didn't know it yet. Probably the only good thing about growing up in Cleveland in the Fifties, on the southern rim of Lake Erie, our first official Dead Lake, was the rock & roll on the radio. Alan Freed didn't exactly invent rock & roll there—the music itself I mean—but when his late night "Moondog House" show went on the air on WJW in July 1951, and he began playing r & b records by black performers, he found to everyone's surprise that the show was attracting an increasingly big audience of white teenagers—and so he gave this music the name "rock & roll". And on March 21, 1952, renting out the Cleveland Arena, usually home to basketball and hockey, he threw the "Moondog Coronation Ball"—the world's first rock concert. Fitting that the cops shut it down after only one act had performed. Hard to believe, but for a while at least, when it came to teen music, Cleveland was the hippest location in the nation. It quickly came to be considered a "breakout" market by the music industry, with several top DJs spinning platters on four or five stations—including Bill Randle, and, a little later, the all-time best, Mad Daddy. And for those of us hungry for more back then, there was the phenomenon of AM radio waves travelling farther at night, so we would sit huddled over our radios, turning the tuning dial with a precise careful surgeon's touch, trying to see how far away we could hear: CKLW in Windsor, Ontario, WJR in Detroit, sometimes WBZ in Boston, and, best, WLAC in Nashville, Tennessee—where John R. played true gritty r&b all night long sponsored by White Rose Petroleum Jelly. And that distant listening paid off.*

It was on CKLW, late one night long after I was supposed to be asleep, that I first heard Ronnie Hawkins. He was originally from Arkansas, but had landed in cold Toronto and was kicking it up there with a band he called The Hawks. He never made it on the level of Elvis or even Gene Vincent, but he loomed pretty large in my own list of rockers. His biggest hit was Forty Days—*adding ten days and a more driving beat to the Chuck Berry original—and* Mary Lou, *another amped-upped cover, both from 1959. He also did a version of* Mystery Train *that to my ears blew away Elvis's, thanks largely to its propulsive guitar and drumming. Back then we weren't yet paying much attention to the backup players, but I knew I sure dug The Hawks.*

Well, turns out so did Bob Dylan. And he famously stole The Hawks—by then consisting of Levon Helm (drums), Robbie Roberston (guitar), Garth Hudson (organ), Richard Manuel (piano) and Rick Danko (bass)—to make them his backup group for the 1965-1966 tour which outraged his folkie fans the world over: the tour where Dylan plugged in, went electric to a fare-thee-well, and turned it up to 10. For every pure folkie it offended, it drew a hundred of us lowlife rockers who hadn't been so sure about Dylan up until then. For years if you hadn't been lucky enough to see it live during the tour, you could only hear a sample on a notorious bootleg lp usually called Zimmerman Looking Back, *but generally known as* The Royal Albert Hall Concert *(though actually recorded in the Manchester Guild Hall during the same 1966 tour). This was blueburning rock & roll, transcendent, an amphetamine rush like none before it.*

But then Dylan had his motorcycle accident on a hill outside Woodstock in July 1966, and they all disappeared. Until—what was this? An album out in July 1968 called Music From Big Pink *by a group called The Band. What band? Oh, that Band! Dylan had written three of the songs, but it was their own sound and sensibility that came through—even in their mournful rendering of Lefty Frizell's* Long Black Veil. *They traded vocal lines like friends passing around a joint, and for all its roots-rock country sound, the musicianship was accomplished and had an understated virtuoso quality. Dylan too was striking out for the country about then, but they were clearly headed somewhere entirely different, and brand new, even though the overall effect was of some timeless traditional folklore being brought back to life. And the second album, simply called* The Band, *released a year later, was even better. By then Margaret and I were living on the farm outside Bloomington, Indiana, and we would just put one side on the record player, set it on auto repeat, and let it play again and again, and then turn it over and do the same, letting the music spill out our back door into the countryside, where it seemed to belong.*

We also went to see them live as often as we could—which was pretty often, once driving all the way from Bloomington to Chicago just to see them at the elegant old Auditorium Theater, which seemed like a perfect setting for their own ragged elegance.

I even had a chance to meet them once. They were headlining a big outdoor music festival just outside Austin, Texas, and I talked Playboy *into letting me cover it for the music section. Walking into the marbled lobby of the famed old Peabody Hotel in downtown Austin, heading for the check-in counter, I practically ran right into them—the whole Band, standing there not saying much, evidently waiting to check in too. So I was within breathing distance of all of them. And as a reporter, there covering the festival for* Playboy, *I had every excuse to go up and introduce myself, say hi, ask if I could maybe get a few minutes for an interview…etc.*

But I didn't. I just kept walking. Why, you might ask? Why not actually meet these heroes? Here's why: I loved their music too much. By this time—it must have been 1974 or 1975—I had interviewed my share of rock stars, truly more than I could ever have dreamed of. But in doing that I had found—no real surprise, but still no fun—that a certain proportion of these musicians whose music I found so splendid were, up close and personal, jerks. Not very many, certainly, but enough that I had become fearful of meeting someone whose music I found transcendent, who turned out to be a turkey. The few times it had happened, pretty much ruined listening to their music for me. So I had learned. I loved The Band's music too much to risk meeting them and find out they were mere regular mortals. So I kept walking.

Getting a chance to go to The Last Waltz *in San Francisco on Thanksgiving Day 1976, The Band's star-studded farewell to touring after nearly 20 years together, was another of those rare opportunities that make the downsides of being a journalist—don't get me started—worthwhile, or at least bearable. I had been following The Band since before they were The Band, and this proved, as you'll see in the piece, a gathering of rock royalty as well as a bittersweet farewell to many things we had all carried with us for many years.*

And I remained true to my school, just watching and hanging out, and not really interviewing anybody, and passing on the after party as well.

My favorite moment was at rehearsal the night before the show. Despite the above, I really couldn't resist going up to Ronnie Hawkins—we were both aiming for the cooler filled with beer on ice sitting on the main floor—and introducing myself, saying, "Mr. Hawkins, I just have to tell you that I've been a fan of yours since the 50s. I loved Forty Days *and* Mary Lou.*" He grinned, now a giant bear of a man, and clapped one large meaty arm around my shoulders, giving me a friendly hug. "Lord love ya, son," he said warmly. "Wish there was five million more like ya!"*

THE LAST WALTZ
NOTES FROM MY DANCE CARD

It's hard to make any enormous claims for the music at The Last Waltz—The Band's farewell fling at performing together, on Thanksgiving Day at Winterland, where they did it the first time under that name in 1968—but it was easily the rock social event of the season. And proof that we are now old & many enough to *have* our own society, like it or not, with *Random Notes* and *People* magazine as our Social Register.

Which is why I spent Thanksgiving having dinner with The Band and 5000 of their closest friends—including Eric Clapton, Joni Mitchell, Van Morrison, Paul Butterfield, Bob Dylan and many others…

*** *** ***

The night before at Winterland, a ruined old hulk in the Fillmore district of San Francisco, about a hundred people were hanging around watching rehearsal and being *very* cool about it. No obvious glad-handing, gawking, or particular overt interest in what's happening onstage.

Van Morrison has just finished when I get there, and Joni Mitchell, backed by The Band, is just beginning. Standing there ten feet from the stage, I could see at last why so many rock writers go into heat when they write about her. She's that upperclass skinny boarding school babe we all dreamed about and never got near. In a soft gray sweater and slacks of floppy clinging wool that show off her ass nicely—and which at this distance and trajectory appears to be one of the fine ones. And love them lank bony arms wrapped around her guitar, executing as she sings a complex dipping *fleur-de-lis* with her crotch…

Levon Helm, the while, pops up and down behind his drumkit like the light tick-ticking valve of a pressure cooker. He's in a Farm-All baseball cap, a shirt with blue & red stripes going sideways, and Sears-style jeans. Later standing near me during a break, he looked just like he'd just stepped down from a John Deere 4520 tractor. Robbie Robertson stands next to Joni, in French, not Sears, jeans and a Nik-Nik shirt with a large 1930s-imitation plaid pattern, mainly rust & black. He also sports a modified Borsalino fedora on his head. Rick Danko on bass moves like a loose set of bones, so barely connected he flops in the manner of the Scarecrow in Oz. Higher behind everyone is the serious balding dome of Garth Hudson, bent over the keyboards that fence him in on three sides. He reminds me of a character out of Jules Verne, piloting the whole thing through time, or Captain Nemo beneath the sea, or creating some new Nietzschean potion for Supermen. And Richard Manuel in full solemn beard & brown suede planter's hat sits calmly observing it all behind his piano on the far left.

The set they are playing before is a theatrical imitation of 18th century European splendor—gilt-edged *empire* flats rising thirty feet toward three huge faux crystal chandeliers hung above the stage, with several more hung high over the auditorium floor. It is the set for *La Traviata*, borrowed from the San Franciso Opera Company.

Joni's songs—*Coyote* and *Shadow and Light*—have that same sexy elliptical beat that *Jungle Line* did on her last album (and the first song of hers I ever heard that made me understand what all the shouting was about).

Robertson has clearly taken on the job of leading all this, so when there's trouble, he's the one who directs traffic and gives signals to the band, consulting with Levon on the tougher stuff. Later, as they work out the harmony on one, everybody involved goes into a huddle, smiling, trying to get it right. After he gets his part, Danko, now wearing his own flattop frontier hat straight out of the 1870s, sits flopped in a chair nearby, a blank country grin on his face, bass cuddled in his lap—it's not his problem any more. And he is the very first to don his long denim overcoat & split as soon as he's done playing, while Robertson & Levon hang in there to work some things out with the little horn section.

During all this the lighting crew has been working on *its* act as well, so the lights go up, down, melt from red to gold to third-degree white; the mirrored ball near the ceiling twirls for no reason, and falling teardrops of light shower the nearly empty hall.

And so by accident, when Joni Mitchell finishes her set and stands chatting onstage with Robertson, both still holding their guitars, all the houselights go suddenly black and the backlighting for the scrim that's behind everything goes suddenly scarlet—and they are caught in sharp black silhouette, the low red light sometimes glinting off Joni's guitar as she moves while talking. I am finding it beautiful and poetic, being a sucker for such things. But some rock & roll baby next to me says to her boyfriend, "*Yucchh*! The Red Death!"

That went with the hip business type with a clipboard who went up to the stage, beckoned Robertson forward, and said something at length to him. Robertson laughed several times and said with a sparkle in his eye at the end, "Free agent!" And Joni Mitchell, after her set, standing in a long gunblue trenchcoat a' la Bogart, with her back to the stage, where The Band is rehearsing alone, hooking a thumb back over her shoulder toward the stage, saying with humor in her voice, "*Those guys?*"

So The Band runs through their classics with ease, while down among us it's mainly Stan Mack's *Real Life Funnies*. A lighting man standing casually on top of a 20-foot stepladder, chatting with a guy in the lighting tower; Margo St. James, founder of COYOTE, hugging & grinning at everyone who's worth it, it seems, like an "outgoing" college girl circa 1961...and at my feet a cardboard box full of black walkie-talkies, and a list handwritten large on a piece of paper...

278—KEN
312—JOE
243—YOU

*** *** ***

The impression of course is that it is to be some final silver nail in the coffin of the Sixties. There are obvious—and almost obligatory—contrasts with Woodstock, where three days of eating acid in the mud symbolized New Dawn. That it was *called* Woodstock after the power Dylan & The Band had given the place, the spiritual power, that is...And so here today we say thanks and farewell—and do it nearly like grownups. Sit-down dinner and a concert afterwards—at $25 a ticket. But it is also a testament to the power of the music—that we gather, even at $25 a head, to give thanks to rock & roll...

*** *** ***

The backstage pass is a handstamp: MATILDA. I get there about 5:30 in the afternoon, and there's still a line stretching around the corner. Inside, the chandeliers are lit and the Berkeley Prominade Ballroom Orchestra is playing, cleverly enough, waltzes. And as many as the floor will handle are waltzing, while dinner is served from five separate lines.

Rock & roll babies out in force, many in floor-length black velvet dresses carrying flowers, some in high Sunset Strip hooker drag; one 45-year-old gent in a wildly flowered shirt and a large black halo of electric hair; a young longhaired Evening Magician in tophat & cane, his beautiful assistant in black floorlength and a white velvet cape…

The backstage area has been redecorated for the occasion by Bill Graham. Three long tables hold various fancy cheeses, pastries, nuts and wine. Empty gilt-edged picture frames on poles sticking out from one wall. In case anyone thought psychedelia was *entirely* dead.

As I go back to check it out the first time, I practically collide with David Bromberg, who's wandering around wearing a sheepskin coat and a red *Alaska Helicopters, Inc.* baseball hat. Then I spot Julia Cameron, whom I'd run into a few times but knew so casually I wasn't aware she'd married Martin Scorsese of *Mean Streets* and *Taxi Driver* fame—who's here filming it all. She and I say hi, and Julia tells me and some other writers who have gathered like magnetic particles to trade one-liners about The Event, and about her new game of Appropriate Punishments. I asked if this was the same one invented by Dante 600 years ago, and she said yes—only the punishment had to suit the fantasy life of the punishee. Her example: for Jann Wenner, to be snubbed on national television by Jackie Onassis.

We all worked on this premise for a while, but it never got going—there was too much going on around us to be clever. So Julia instead gave us a tour of the Cocteau Room, the name painted on the door. It had been a window-less 20x15 equipment storage room, probably. But Graham had had it painted entirely white inside, furnished only with a beige rug and a glass coffee table— and pink rubber noses stuck on the walls in various places. A little built-in loudspeaker hooked to a tape loop provided sound effects of actual prerecorded deep sniffs and snorts, just to get you going, apparently. So far, Julia told us, no one had done anything interesting in it.

*** *** ***

Wandering the balcony as the Waltz Orchestra plays on, I am struck again that everybody here, most in their early 20s or less, has paid $25 to be here. But more interesting, everyone is here having Thanksgiving without their *parents*, their families—making this for all of us here a Thanksgiving of a more primitive sort than is usually celebrated these days. Gathering not as family blood gathers for the holiday, but for the spirit, for the music.

So tonight the thankful waltz on, until the Waltz Orchestra finally calls it quits around 8:30, to a well-felt and warm ovation, which obviously delights the Orchestra and its young maestro.

*** *** ***

Backstage, a heartbreaker for Yrs. Truly, in floorlength lavender & a black velvet band about her neck, as if caught in amber after all these years, the face of my first Lonesome Suzie, the older high school sister of my best pal in junior high school, when we were 14-year-old hoods listening to *Rock Around The Clock* and reading *Blackboard Jungle* for the 7th time....and sister Suzie made me melt every time I saw her. Where are you now?

David Bromberg continues to wander about looking for someone to talk to, and now the Shower of Stars begins: Ringo Starr himself appears in a black velvet Edwardian coat and two slender gold bands in one ear. The hair is an overgrown crewcut on top, the beard is going gray, and he's plump. And over there in a fur-trimmed vest & beige bells is Ron Wood, late of The Faces, now a Rolling Stone, gassing with publicist Paul Wasserman about something. And who is leaning smoking against a wall, looking as scummy in life as he did in *Bonnie and Clyde*, but Michael J. Pollard? And over there, Kinky Friedman in black Mexican-style sportcoat with a rainbow topping the back, above three red crucifixes diminishing in size, all outlined in spangles, and on the right side, over his liver instead of his heart, a portrait of Our Lord done in leather and spangles. The hat is a sickly green stetson with red spangled trim. He is greeted by someone: "Hi, Kinky—you're looking subtle, as usual."

*** *** ***

Two songs into The Band's opening set, Robertson is getting cheers for stretching out a little on lead—"...and the rain don't fall any more..."—and I am sitting high in the last row of the balcony, The Band mostly obscured by chandeliers and bunting. They go into *I Shall Be Released*, with the horn section still a little shaky on the beginning.

Danko is decked out in charcoal preacher's coat & beige bells; Robertson similar in dark grays; Manuel in orange plaid sportcoat—and only Levon remains true to last night's school in a blue shirt with dark red stripes barely visible, and the same shitkicker jeans.

They move on to *W.S. Wolcott's Medicine Show*, and then to *Ophelia*, which stirs up some cheering & hooting as the horn section starts kicking ass and Robertson lets loose again to play Last Fling lead, it would seem. Next comes *King Harvest* and then *The Night They Drove Old Dixie Down*, as the cheers begin well before the end, in recognition of The Classics. Then *Stage Fright*, on which Danko rattles those loose bones; and Hudson wails, the arc of graying hair around his dome flying, Beethoven back there, solemn imperial chops.

The guest set is next, and to begin this musical biography, *This Is Your Life* with electric guitars, who else but Ronnie Hawkins, who brought them together as his backup band, The Hawks, and worked their asses off? Ronnie tonight is a big bear in a creamy bent straw cowboy hat, black western suit and a red bandanna around his neck, *his* black beard going gray as well. He gets them into a mean old version of *Who Do You Love*, moving half-seriously out to front them again, standing with his back to the audience, directing them with a grin, just to remind them of their beginnings, in case they had forgotten.

(And I realize that this is the jolly hilljack who laughed when I handed him a beer from the cooler last night at rehearsal. Later backstage I can't resist going up to him and telling him that I'd admired him ever since *Forty Days* and *Mary Lou*, back in the late 50s. He clapped a solid arm around my shoulders and said, "Lord love ya, son—I wish there was a million more like ya!"— and proceeded to introduce me to the little old lady standing with him, small and slight, something vaguely familiar about her—"This is Robbie Robertson's *mother*"—and by god, except for the mom hairdo and the plastic teardrop eyeglasses, she looks just like him, or rather he just like her, of course. She smiles and smiles, looking very happy but a little bewildered by it all—and I have met my favorite Star of the evening.)

Dr. John is next, doing *Such A Night* in his fey New Orleans accent, wearing a pink bowtie & black beret & a spangled red & black polkadot sportcoat—dressed a great deal like Jerry Lewis imitating some existential French philosopher of the Fifties. So Dr. John turns out to be the session man last night who looked like a weekend biker in leathers & shades.

After *Way Down Yonder In New Orleans* it's Paul Butterfield's turn, with some blooze. Butterfield looking the southside wino who's made it, in a 6-day beard and a brown leather shirt that looks like naugahyde except up close. Butterfield leads *Mystery Train*, and The Band is now rocking harder than anything I've heard since the *Zimmerman Looking Back* bootleg of them backing Dylan at the Albert Hall during the 1966 tour, when they were all cranked up on something and cutting loose.

Now Muddy Waters—*Caldonia, What Makes Your Big Head So Hard?* Dr. John doing serious business on the guitar, Butterfield blowing his brains out, and Bobby Charles on piano. Then into *I'm A Man*, and the blues chills fill the room. Manuel doubles on drums with Levon, and Dr. John is stripped down to…a brown body shirt and banlon slacks?? Without his duds he could be the manager of a Division Street singles bar instead of the sinister voodoo man…

Next Robertson announces: "Let's play a little electric guitar—Eric Clapton!"

Clapton in beard & black cut-velvet sportcoat sings *I Don't Want To Be The One* from his latest album. EC or not, it's still too slow & clunky, practically deadly until Danko takes over on vocal for him and shows him how it should be done, with more passion and texture. They follow it with *Further On Down The Road*, which opens with some nice lead trades between Robertson & Clapton. Old Slowhand is back, and Robertson is right with him. And trading off again at the end it gets so good they send the first real rush of the night through the crowd.

*** *** ***

It occurs, before returning to the blow-by-blow, that The Band going their separate ways is what has happened to most of us. In 1968 I tried to talk my friends into beginning a communal college with me, somewhere in the wilds of Vermont, where real education would take place, etc, etc, etc, blah blah blah. This year my wife, Margaret, and I bought a dead old house on the north side of Chicago and are bringing it back to life. I have a Sears credit card now, and wrote an actual check recently to Plywood Minnesota, that legendary city I've laughed about for so long. There's nothing wrong with that, but it sure is different. In a real sense without saying it much out loud we are trying to create what is supposed to be a soothing retreat. A hidcout. It remains to be seen if it will be. But that's just what The Band's doing—saying they now belong to themselves, not to us.

As an event this *does* seem related to Woodstock, if not a final parenthesis then a final elipsis toward something new… At Woodstock everybody went on down to Yasgur's farm and later called it heavenly apocalypse—and while there were at The Last Waltz a few Woodstock veterans, most were younger, their spiritual descendents, still aspiring toward the trinity of Peace, Love & Dope—but doing it, following The Band's lead, waltzing in evening clothes & floor-length dresses beneath crystal chandeliers.

*** *** ***

Since I was alone, like David Bromberg I wandered all night, and didn't see one mean-red drunk or oversoaped basket case—even the security people, wearing crimson Last Waltz sashes like Miss America candidates, were smiling, and, to use the dread word, mellow.

*** *** ***

And it occurs that The Band makes music you can listen to endlessly—which is as good a criterion for great music as I can think of. How many albums can you simply put on and play and play? In 1970, when their second album, *The Band*, came out—and Margaret and I were living on a farm (Organic!)—we would set the turntable to automatic return and weed Margaret's enormous garden while one side played again and again, listening for two or three hours before turning it over and doing the other side for four more. It is music that has the deeply felt, authentic ring of *Absalom! Absalom!* or *Huckleberry Finn*—which by me is as high as praise gets. Unmistakably *American*, this music by four Canadians and one displaced Arkie. And not quite like anything we'd ever heard before, as you could tell by the long sputtering lists of comparisons generated by rock writers who tried to describe it. To say that it's American is only to say that it seeps into those places in us that feel most like home. The Band are virtually the only rock & rollers who have stopped long enough to look hard at our culture, to use another dread word, past & present, to see the places most of us pass in a blur—and maybe they didn't need to do it, but it seems no accident that they created most of those first two remarkable albums by sitting for a year in an ugly pink house in the Catskills.

*** *** ***

After Eric it's Neil Young, in a limp sheepdog haircut and an army shirt, looking slightly wan and forlorn even as he smiles and says, "It's one of the great pleasures of my life to be here on this stage tonight."

I confess I had to ask an enthusiast next to me who this Superstar is. Young begins one of his hits which I don't recognize but learn later is *Helpless*. You can probably tell I'm not exactly a fan. I believe everyone who makes such huge claims for his songwriting etc, but I simply can't take the voice. Whiny adenoidal teenager is all I ever hear. As I take this opportunity to head for the backstage area for some wine and brie, some kid taps me and asks, "Who is that up there?" "Neil Young," I answer knowledgeably.

Backstage Kinky Friedman sits on a folding chair apparently making deals with an agent out of the Professor Irwin Corey school; Julia Cameron sits bored, ignoring the closed circuit broadcast of the show on the TV monitor above her; and there is an actual Hells Angel among us, arm in a sling & a tambourine slung around his neck like a fat necklace; silver-haired Albert Grossman hobbles by on crutches; and another silver-haired gent wearing the same KENT warmup jacket he had on at rehearsal...

*** *** ***

Standing now near the first-floor exits in the very shadow of Albert Grossman-on-crutches as Joni Mitchell goes into #2...She is wearing tonight a wine-colored sweater top & a light satinlike skirt, patterned and slightly full, falling soft to the floor. She is joined by Neil Young, which is almost a stand-off—and California has crept into The Band. And J. Mitchell, to amend, is not attractive so much because she suggests the cold beautiful unattainable beauty as because she simultaneously seems fragile & a little bit crazy, always a winning combination in my book, like she could use someone to take care of her but wouldn't *think* of asking. Maybe not fragile—finely tuned. There is also the surprise of seeing this highcheeked Bonwit's model in the midst of the grubby rock life, where most of the women are in the good ole girl mode of Janis Joplin, Linda Ronstadt, and Tracy Nelson.

Next comes Neil Diamond, and it's nearing midnight. It seems you can overdo this Canadian solidarity business. Real life criticism, overheard: "I don't know how much Neil Diamond's agent paid to get him up there, but he sure doesn't belong."

But he is followed by Van Morrison in pointy nose and wine-colored suit, doing *Tura Lura Lural*, the great old Irish barroom standard, in duet with Richard Manuel, harmonizing like happy drunks, *It's just an Irish lullabyyyyy...*

Now Joni Mitchell and Neil Young reappear to help on *Acadian Driftwood*, truly a boreal version of *The Night They Drove Old Dixie Down*. Hudson leaves his keyboard redoubt to be fitted for his melodian, a small old relative of the accordian that sounds like the boys sitting around a campfire in a John Ford western, held by a roadie who slings it on Hudson like a tailor fitting a bulletproof vest...

*** *** ***

And the whole thing seems so hopeful, a launching of something new more than a farewell to the old, proof that we veterans *can* drift on through our thirties and still be wonderful & attractive & hip—even more wonderful & attractive & hip because we have been through so much and are calmer now, more peaceful...we are *not*, of course, not all the time, but it's a good place to aim, and that's what The Last Waltz suggests...so it becomes, a little late, maybe, Rites of Passage, suggesting that we can grow up and not be like our parents, but still grow up—and the waltzing & the chandeliers are there to point the way a bit...

*** *** ***

End of the first two sets.

During the musical intermission, Bay Area poet and Digger Emmett Grogan introduces other Bay Area poets, beginning with...the Hells Angel I saw earlier backstage. His name is Sweet William, and he read his Angel poetry... "Every time you kill one of us, ten more spring up in its place...Hells Angels is the living truth...the fighters who never gave up and never gave in..." After his reading, Angel Sweet William limps off with a cane to whistles and cheers. Then some woman poet whose name I miss when it's announced. "The lion tamer shed his skin...I want to roll in sugar until the comets shine..."

Then poet Michael McClure appeared & recited without preamble, explanation or apology what seemed to be the first 600 lines of *The Canterbury Tales*—in the original Middle English, which seemed rather snobbish & pointless, although it did permit all of us dope-smoking ex-English majors in the crowd to pat ourselves on the back when we were the first to "get" it. On his part, a clear *tour de force* delivered without passion.

Diane di Prima next. I had read an early collection of hers called *Dinners and Nightmares* in the very early Sixties, so I liked it when she began with my favorite—and single remembered line of hers: "Get your cut throat off my knife!"

Meanwhile backstage, Slowhand holds court with a circle of ladies on folding chairs & one approving guy. And for what it's worth, Eric's crushed-velvet sportcoat gets *my* vote in the evening's Velvet Sweepstakes...

*** *** ***

The final set opens with Garth Hudson's ritual lengthy solo intro to *Chest Fever*, his soundtrack for the film *Sherlock Holmes Meets Godzilla & E.*

Power Biggs, at 12:30 a.m. Then into *The Last Waltz*, written for the occasion by Robbie Robertson—not one of their classics by any stretch, but just the right bittersweet tone and tempo for leaving. This is followed by a fast upbeat *The Weight*, and then Roberston announces: "We'd like to bring out a very good friend of ours—Bob Dylan."

Dylan comes out wearing a very snazzy Panama hat, emblem of his continuing interest in obscure tropical lands such as Mozambique and Black Diamond Bay—and they get into a rendering of *Baby, Let Me Follow You Down* that sounds like it's right off the famous Albert Hall bootleg, Robertson's characteristically shy lead guitar coming out of the closet, in that fleet barbedwire style that never sounds like anyone else.

Next Dylan sings *Forever Young*, a rabbinical blessing to all the kids he's singing to; and the song is still better as a message than music, a moral to the night's story if anyone needed one.

And at 1:15, here come everybody, and then some—the big production number finale, with Bill Graham filling in tonight for Ed Sullivan.

Ringo & Ron Wood both join the game. Neil Diamond & Dr. John *both* sit down at the piano, but are rapidly bounced by Richard Manuel. Joni Mitchell stays close to Neil Young while everybody comes on & gets arranged.

And then, right *heeere* on this stage, from left to right, interspersed among The Band: Dr. John, Neil Diamond, Joni Mitchell, Neil Young, Van Morrison, Dylan (center stage, natch), Ronnie Hawkins (patting an ample thigh & sipping a beer), Eric Clapton, Paul Butterfield, and Ron Wood. Together, mostly, they start into a version of *I Shall Be Released* that is exuberant if nothing else. Above all these others, Dylan, as our generation's acknowledged Sinatra, takes lead vocal.

*** *** ***

Then Robertson says, "We're gonna have a party now, and you're invited to the party."

So first we get Levon & Ringo doubling on drums as Carl Radle takes over Danko's bass. Ron Wood, Butterfield & Robertson return after the grand mass exit. Clapton is *carried* onstage by strong admirers...

Led by Dylan, everybody continued to jump into *I Shall Be Released*. Too bad these all-star jams usually turn out to be as exciting as the Pro Bowl—and this one rapidly does just that. Stephen Stills makes his first appearance and tries hard to save it, looking a little puffy in his gray blazer, like a wasted Phi Delt from OSU who's now bored selling insurance and drinking too much because of it. Stills does help, but it's Butterfield's harp, surprisingly, that continues to hold it together. If ever there was one, this is a jam in losing search for a groove.

Somewhere in here Jerry Brown appears on stage to flash his teeth at the crowd & remind everyone how groovy he is. Someone next to me in the crowd yells, "Get Jerry Brown on guitar!" We already know he's groovy.

And out, worn out, about 2:30 in the morning. Some animals take a while do die.

Backstage by now is crammed, parties & deals to be arranged, serious high-powered hobbing & nobbing, but unlike some I was without any help from our chemical friends, hadn't been invited *once* to use the Nose Room, so I missed all of it—and didn't mind a bit, having learned over the years that you can know too many things about these people whose music you love, or whose books move you. No point in spoiling it all now with The Band. They have been trying to teach us something, probably without really knowing it, and it's best learned in the clarity of distance.

*** *** ***

So as music it only had its moments. As an idea and a possible direction it seemed just right. Everyone in the rock & roll life has been haunted at times by the Who's punk-brave statement of metaphysics: *Hope I die before I get old.* What *does* a poor middle-aged boy do? Play in a rock & roll band? How do you remain a part of something that has until now been dedicated to Youth with a very big Y?

The loosely defined generation that Dylan & The Band belong to, are, many of them, still smoking dope & rocking right on—even though they are now lawyers & professors & housepainters & suburban housewives. They do it in different ways now, but they still do it.

The hard part is the style—*how* do you rock on at 36—or even 30?

Is it the Dylan lesson? That to live outside the law you must be honest? Or, turned halfway round, that you have to live inside the law to be an outlaw? How does that fit with the other Dylan lesson—don't follow leaders, and watch the parking meters…??

Well, you make your own lessons, just as tonight The Band has shown us all quite vividly how the river has changed in 15 years, and yet has stayed the same. So there are directions, not lessons, maybe.

Could be The Last Waltz was a direction for the people I saw the opening night of the '74 Dylan/Band tour at the Chicago Stadium. The good mezzanine seats were filled with prosperous & slightly balding young lawyers in three-piece suits & wives who substitute teach for the excitement of it—some of them exactly the same ones who six years earlier were in the streets in front of the Hilton eating teargas & billyclubs during the '68 Democratic Convention. At the concert that night, everybody sat down between songs. And I've never heard anything stranger than all 20,000 of us, singing along in unison...*Oh my God, am I here all alone?...*

I think The Last Waltz was for us.

- 1976

If you really don't have anything better to do, you can still see blurred watery clips of this on YouTube, but I don't recommend it. Some TV producer had a bright idea: Let's have a TV Special "Rock Olympics" featuring various rock stars competing in athletic events, with a sprinkling of other celebrities as emcees and commentators. Didn't he know that "rock stars" and "athletics" were elements never meant to be combined?

This was 1978, and the lineup of stars gathered for the show speaks volumes about fickle fleeting fame: The Runaways, The Jacksons, Alessi Bros., Earth, Wind & Fire, Electric Light Orchestra, Michelle Phillips, Boston, The Commodores, Seals & Crofts, Rod Stewart, Freddy Fender, Marilyn McCoo and Billy Davis Jr., Sha Na Na, Anne Murray, Gladys Knight and several Pips, Kenny Loggins, Barbi Benton, Joe Smith, Leif Garrett, Tanya Tucker, Susan Anton, Ed McMahon, Phyllis Diller, Alex Karras, Kristy McNichol, Fred Travelena and several of The Dallas Cowboy Cheerleaders.

Ten dollars to anyone under 40 who can tell me who the Alessi Brothers, Fred Travelina or Leif Garrett are. And five to anyone who can name a single track by Kenny Loggins, Boston or ELO.

It was dead of winter back in Chicago, and I was going through a second divorce, so I was happy to head for the Irvine Campus of the University of California to be diverted by this silliness for a few days. And who could fault getting to lay actual eyes on Michelle Phillips, the archetypal golden California Girl of all time?

The account of the events here is a fairly cinematic rendering of my experience at the Rock Olympics—a mixture of confusion, disbelief, more confusion, and a selection of groupie moments. It was one of the strangest events I have ever covered, and one Philip K. Dick would have enjoyed had he been there. He is one of my favor-

ite novelists, and was always wondering about the nature of reality. I think the Rock Olympics would have tested even his capacity for wonder. It was very weird, and pretty funny—just, come to think of it, like a PKD novel.

After all these years, though, knowing what has happened to so many of these people in all that time, certain of the snapshots here have a portent of melancholy they lacked then. And especially one: A 20-year-old Michael Jackson, still with the face his mother gave him, running hard in the 100-yard-dash, beat out at the end by his brother, Jackie Jackson. The watery U Tube video of the show has a closeup of Michael's face moments after the race: sweating, happy and healthy-looking, under a nimbus of afro, the picture of a regular young kid.

Time is not kind.

TV'S FIRST ROCK SPORTS CLASSIC

AND WITH ANY LUCK, THE LAST

Those of you who watched the *Rock and Roll Sports Classic* on television early in May know better than I do how it went. I was just actually there in mid-March for all three days of videotaping at the University of California's futuristic Irvine campus, deep in the heart of Orange County.

By the time I found the outdoor swimming pool on Friday morning, I'd already missed two events—the 50-yard men's freestyle, won by Kenny Loggins (formerly of Loggins & Messina) in an unsnappy 37 seconds; and the 50-yard women's freestyle, won by Sandy West of The Runaways ("Queens of Noise") in 33 seconds—but I came in on what proved to be the paradigm of all to come: On bleachers running the length of the pool, a crowd of a hundred or so students are cheering their brains out, whistling, jumping up and down, shaking rhythmic fists, urging on...no one. Nothing. Except for the shining water and giant pop cm-beads lane markers, the pool's empty. Very existential. No, very television.

Next for the cameras the East team, in blue warmup suits, similarly cheers a ghostly teammate on to victory. Then members of the West team, in gold, do the same. Sitting on the one-meter board in his navy-blue Commentator's blazer and tie is Alex Karras, easily the funniest killer defensive tackle ever to breathe air. He's billed as the "Host" of the Rock Classic. Two hours into a three-day gig, he lights another cigarette and says to someone sitting next to him, "I'm bored stiff." He's not feeling funny today. Three times he blows the chatty introduction to the upcoming relay race, stumbling over his improvised repartee with "Reporter" Michelle Phillips, in O-so-sexy satin running shorts and late of the Mamas & Papas.

Nearby on the pool deck another cameraman has his axe turned and whirring on East team "Captain" Phyllis Diller, who looks, well, even more like Phyllis Diller than on TV. In a blue plastic shortie dress, orange makeup, flamingo legs and white go-go boots, she looks like the most fetching stewardess on Air Bulgaria. The cameraman's after a series of closeup "fills." Asks Phyllis: "Flirts, is that what you want?" He nods. "Tell me when," she says, "so I don't waste it." And on signal puts her face through a two-minute close-order drill of expressions, cheese cheese cheese cheese cheese, a lifesize bionic fright doll set on Fast Forward.

That's how it went for three days.

But before plunging onward, let's set the teams. For the East: all ten members of Sha Na Na; some of Electric Light Orchestra; all of the Jacksons; three from Boston, group and town; Anne Murray; Marilyn McCoo, probably others. For the West: Earth, Wind & Fire; The Commodores; The Runaways; Gladys Knight and a few Pips; Kenny Loggins; Dash Crofts; Leif Garrett; Tanya Tucker; Rod Stewart; and Freddy Fender, who is truly something to behold in a bathing suit. "Captain" of the West team is Sandy Duncan, and Barbi Benton is "Assistant Captain." H-e-e-e-e-e-r-e-'s Johnny himself, Ed McMahon, is "Co-Host," and Kristy McNichol of *Family* is billed as another "Reporter." And let's not forget the Dallas Cowboys cheerleaders in their tight white hotter-than-thou hotpants and blue halter tops featuring decolletage that won't quit. Real Texas. I got a great picture of all of them inside the huge yellow-and-white-striped "hospitality" tent, sitting in uniform around a folding table, eating cold lunch.

Friday afternoon, at the outdoor basketball courts:

The game's supposed to start at two, but this is happening for television, not the mere humans gathered here watching, so we are all treated to an hour's wait while the cameras and fake Renaissance Tournament backdrops are set up.

Fred Travelina, the young comedian who will be doing the pre-game patter with Alex Karras during this segment, sits beforehand on a folding chair in his blazer & tie, with paper napkins forming a rough monk's yoke around his shoulders. No, it's not some wild prank—he's getting a light trim from a stylist before going on. Clip clip clip.

I am struck as the weekend progresses that these performers—as opposed to the musicians—are without shame. On Saturday, Sandy Duncan (who is, incidentally, considerably cuter in the flesh than while climbing *The $20,000 Pyramid*) will dash up to Ed McMahon in front of two thousand spectators at the stadium, sunlight gleaming off the rump of her golden satin running shorts, and announce breathlessly, "Well, I'm off to see how the swimming events are going!" before bounding away out of camera range. It leaves me thinking, hmmm, she's running off into *yesterday*, which isn't a bad trick. All the swimming events were taped on Friday morning. Reality and unreality intertwine to become a Big Event.

Finally the basketball game begins. Pussy rules: They're playing half-court, and laying hands on the ball constitutes team possession—they don't even have to take it back to the half-court line. During warmups tall bearded Kenny Loggins looked pretty good, but right at the start of this heroic ten-minute battle, Michael Jackson is the only one who looks at all competent. Everybody is travelling and fouling like mad, with little interference from the Ref. Any pickup playlot team in Chicago would have beaten all then of them silly. A kid in front of me comments, laughing, to no one in particular, "They're *terrible*."

Quickly it turns from basketball to showbiz: Several Sha Na Nas on the sidelines doing cheers: "Hold that line! Hold that line!" And a couple of mock fights, all team members from both sides streaming onto the court to fall laughing in a heap. Etc. At last Johnny Contardo of Sha Na Na wins it for the East with some dirty comic street moves and a final "key" layup. As sport, it was as exciting as watching my cat sleep; as television, it was right in there with *Gilligan's Island*. No, come to think it, *Gilligan* is better.

Late Friday afternoon, on the central campus, so-called:
This one is The Marathon.

It's a grueling one-mile walking race around a course of curving sidewalks that cross a rolling grassy declivity ringed at intervals by academic buildings. They're all done in tastefully understated Buck Rogers styles designed to bring you the future now. And look ma, no two alike. One so well imitates ten stories of stressed concrete straining toward Launch that it's nicknamed "The Space Ship." A student I start talking to tells me, striving to impress, that scenes from *The Planet of the Apes* were filmed on this very spot.

The course is marked by colorful plastic streamers on sticks. A gloomy wet chill has settled in under gloomier leaden clouds, rain threatening. During this one the stalling around and apparent confusion are so considerable that they nearly lose the light to rain and evening. Alex Karras spends much of the long delay sitting alone on a stone bench beneath a small tree. Much of that time he spends staring at the ground.

The All-Star Walkers are jammed together for so long at the starting line, all these million-dollar egos penned up and put on hold, that at last in chorus they begin going "Moo! Moooo! Bahhhh! Bahh! Moooooo!" and then burst into collective protest song, the old Animals classic....*We gotta get out of* *this place, if it's the last thing we ever do…we gotta get out of this plac*e… And this impromptu a cappella choir has to be the weekend's most historic event, a true special Ed Sullivan moment. Right here, on this sidewalk…

Finally the momentous Marathon begins. A glob of the superstars are off and furiously walking before the gun goes off. Near the starting line a student inquires of his buddy, "They're gonna have to do that over, aren't they? They screwed up." Sez his buddy, showing great insight into televison, "Who *cares?*"

Indeed. I can't tell you who won. The cameras had all the good seats. Which was fine, but nobody bothered to make any announcements afterward to those of us merely here in the flesh. It didn't matter. It was in the can.

Friday night, in my room at the Sheraton-Irvine, since there are no cheap motels within ten miles:

And on my television set is something called *The All-Star Anything Goes.* Are these things going around? Ye gods—Stacy Keach, one of my favorite actors, is wearing huge stage cherries on his head and has a rolling pin tied between his ankles. He's sitting in a round plastic pool full of balloons, and yes, now he's scooting around on his ass like a dog with worms, breaking balloons with the rolling pin. Interviewed later he says of the contest, "It's the most important thing I'm doing tonight." The Rock Classic seems dignified and significant by comparison. The big final event on *All-Star Anything Goes* is the Star Sack Race. Three stars per sack, hippety hopping. Barbi Benton is interviewed about how competitive she is. Then Stacy Keach and others are in their sack, hopping away. The narration: "That's Barbi Benton crawling into the sack with the other Singers…No question about it, the Singers are better in the sack than the Stars!" It really must be going around, and Barbi appears to be going around with it.

Saturday, at the track & field stadium:

I walk in on a voice booming over the PA system: "Throw it to Ed McMahon, Kristy!" Wait. Hold it. Throw *what?* I'll never know. Now the crowd is applauding an empty track. A morsel of action: The contestants are lining up for the men's 100-yard dash. In lane 6 is Leif Garrett, and at the end of the stands nearest the starting line, a clutch of his groupies—perhaps the highest concentration of 14-year-old girls with bad complexions I'd ever seen in California, where blemishes are outlawed according to Beach Boys Statute #14937B. They hover and giggle, fluttering butterflies of near-hysteria, barely able to contain themselves when he turns their way to wave and show them his upper gums.

Then bang! the race is on. No, it's not. A false start. William King of the Commodores has fallen down. They're going to retake it. As Leif comes back down the track, some of the pizzazz is gone. New boy wonder teenage heart-throb or not, he walks back sweating and winded. But youth will out, almost.

In the retake he's third. William King is second, and Jackie Jackson takes it.

Next is the women's 100-yard dash, featuring as favorites Marilyn McCoo, Ann Murray, Tanya Tucker, Sandy West and Joan Jett. Ms. Jett, in short straight crypt-black hair and deathmask eye makeup, appears to be cultivating the image of a tough guy with tits; to her credit she doesn't pull it off. She and fellow Runaway Sandy West—who seems to be shooting for the mean peroxide carhop look—come in a close first and second in the race. For girls who try so hard to radiate a sleazy, unhealthy aura, they're in very good shape—and placed in or won several of the women's events. Could it be they're not actually *bad girls*? Another dream shattered.

Saturday afternoon:

I confess. By now I do not give much of a shit who is winning or losing these races. Part of it is that no one yet has done anything physically—in public, anyway—that's more than mediocre. Life on the road doesn't breed Olympic material. Although I guess that's part of the idea: the Samuel Johnson's Dog effect. As he said of dogs walking on their hind feet, it's not that they do it well, it's that they do it at all. There's a curious appeal to watching one's heroes in a certain area prove themselves abysmally average in another. But I'm not getting the jolt today. Part of it is the absolute lack of momentum, that slow rising toward climax you get from most real sporting events, even junior high school volleyball. This is more of a sportsoid. It's posing as a sporting event—and the races certainly aren't rigged—but they're really making a movie. So being here is like watching an *autopsy* of an actual sporting event. The living whole has been systematically slashed into its component parts, and everywhere the dead pieces are being filmed. Except here there never was a living whole. The film editor will do the Lord and Lazarus one better by bringing back from the dead something that was never quite alive to begin with. It may make wonderful television, but it's impossible to care about here on the spot.

Oh, good: Ed McMahon is once more taking us with him into *The Twilight Zone*. To all of us here in the stadium, he's announcing the beginning of yesterday's Marathon. Next he begins to read from a prepared script. It's his voice-over commentary for invisible instant-replay slow-mo shots of the Marathon's finish. *Do do doo do do do doo do....*

Sunday:

A sunny warm morning after night rain. The grounds are a mud swamp in places. Just inside the fenced-off "backstage" area where three great tents have been set up (men's, women's, and "hospitality") sit several chauffeurs, variously uniformed, at a table, all in a row. The crowd is hooting & celebrating the arrival of a nonexistent Rod Stewart. He won't be here for a couple of hours yet. He's to compete in a low-hurdle relay and a soccer goal-defense, events which must have been conceived as a custom-made showcase for him, famously a former soccer player. Nearly until kick-time his opponent remains uncertain. Rumored superstar possibilities include Mick Fleetwood, John McVie, Elton John and others. It will prove to be someone named Tandy from the group Boston. And Stewart will beat him easily, making defenses that look almost… dare I say it?…professional. Strangely believe it: out of everyone here, Stewart is the only one who will turn in an athletic performance a few cuts above Sunday picnic. And Ed McMahon, during a lull before introducing him, standing live mike in hand in front of all those potential customers, won't be able to resist saying spontaneously, "Have a cold Budweiser…" just to fill the empty air.

Today many of us have discovered an interesting truth: that it's less muddy, and that much of this makes more sense when viewed inside the hospitality tent, on the color television monitor there that's showing what the cameras are seeing on the field. From their point of view it takes on a certain coherence, and even looks like fun. So while Milan Williams of The Commodores zips around the track outside on his ten-speed, on his way to winning the men's bicycle race, I'm inside watching it on television, along with a hundred or so stars/press/wives/girlfriends/kids/groupies/photographers/parents.

One is a 10-year-old Judy Garland, who's evidently the daughter of Somebody around here. She's wearing a red sweater and a red heart sewn over each denimed babycake, and cavorts and teases several adults right in front of the TV set—so everyone watching the set can't help watching her too. Kid learns fast. Twenty feet away, staring raptly at her performance, is a regular little girl with large dark eyes and long brown hair, in a blue ski jacket and white jeans. She sits unnoticed, silently watching and watching this creature her own breastless age behave like a boozy divorcee…

Outside, too, the people wandering and standing become the event.

I leave you with some real-life dialogue.

(1) Fellow in his fat late thirties to a friend: "Show ya what a guilt complex will do for ya. I woke up resisting coming down here, and here I am!"

(2) "How high you wanna go?"

"I'm high enough now," says the sleepy cameraman twenty feet above the ground on the yellow forklift-in-the-sky.

(3) "My kids hated my father from the second they met him."

(4) Over the PA system: "Could we have all the talent…Sandy Duncan… Phyllis Diller…"

(5) Three teenagers, two girls and a boy, stand talking next to the running track. Next to them is a 30ish father with a young kid. One of the girls is saying, "…and they were fucking like crazy right there on the couch."

"No!" says the other girl. "I thought he was a homo."

Father can't take it any more. He turns to them and says, "Nice language!"

"I'm sorry," says the first girl by way of explanation but with a snotty edge in her voice, "but I grew up in Hollywood."

- 1978

I didn't exactly have a front seat, but stray circumstance allowed me to watch the rise and fall of the skyrocket called John Belushi from several vantage points over his brief time, from the beginning until the end, really.

As I once said in a guidebook to Chicago I wrote part of in the late 80s, Chicago is the biggest small town in America. After a while, it seems you get to know, or at least bump into, just about everyone. Or know somebody who does.

For instance: My oldest Chicago friend today is Warren Leming. I met him in 1968 when I went looking for Paul Tyner, a guy I'd known from visiting the University of Illinois, a brilliant funny writer and mathematician who won an O. Henry Award for a short story he'd published in The New Yorker *at age 24, and who had written for the* Daily Illini *when Roger Ebert was Editor. Tyner was living in a townhouse near Orchard and Lincoln that they called "Fat Chance House," and Warren was one of his roommates. Warren at the time was a rock guitarist and also dabbled in improv with the Second City Touring Company, something he and Nate Herman (later a director at Second City and a writer for Saturday Night Live for a couple of seasons) combined into a rock group/satirical revue they called Wilderness Road in the early 70s.*

So what do they have to do with John Belushi?

Well, when I was interviewing him while working on the piece about the Blues Brothers *movie here, Belushi told me that Warren and Paul Tyner pretty much changed his life. He'd come in from Wheaton to a party in Hyde Park, and Warren and Tyner were also there. Belushi said he found himself sitting in some little room away from the main noise with Paul and Warren, listening to them riff and rap, do their shining improv chitchat, the bebop of fast, funny talk; listening to them, joining in himself, was what prompted him to leave Wheaton behind. They encouraged him to move to Chicago, and to have a go at Second City, which he did in 1971. So in a small way, Paul and Warren invented Belushi at that party, according to his own testimony.*

One member of that 1971 Second City company was Eugenie Ross-Leming, who was married to Warren at the time. She and Warren were by then—and remain—close friends of mine, and did I ever feel lucky. Parties at Margaret's and my apartment were often like after-hours Second City performances, everybody shining and then out-shining each other, and all I had to do was provide the beer and the joints and sit back and enjoy. Belushi only showed up once or twice, but it was memorable—or would have been, if we all hadn't been so stoned.

It should be said that members of the Second City company back then were hardly Stars. I mean, they were, but they were also struggling underpaid actors who also did "industrials"—corporate motivational performances—to bring in some extra cash. They were mainly leading regular lives like the rest of us. And the Second City shows during the week at least were often half-empty, so with a certain regularity Eugenie would slip me free tickets, and I'd often drop in a couple of times a week to see the true improv section of the nightly show—the part where they'd take suggestions from the audience and work out new sketches. And, no surprise, Belushi night after night would light up the room with bit after bit of inspired incandescent lunacy. Eugenie said the other cast members—her included—used to get pissed at him for being such a scene stealer. I remember one. The main action was going on stage left with three of the cast, and Belushi was standing stage right, not part of the action. But then just standing there watching, he began waggling his famous eyebrows, throwing in a few stray expressions, and quickly all audience attention swiveled to him—he almost couldn't help it. After those 1971 shows Eugenie and Belushi and I would occasionally go out for coffee, and I remember him as being a sweet mild-mannered kid—at least while only drinking coffee.

Then he went off to New York and soon joined the off-Broadway ensemble of National Lampoon's Lemmings, a blistering black humor sendup of Woodstock which opened in January 1973 at the Village Gate and ran for 350 performances. Just about as UN-PC as it was possible to get. It featured, among many other hilarious outrages, a Joan Baez protest-song parody called Pull Your Triggers, Niggers, We're With You All The Way, Just Across The Bay, and Belushi's first run-out of his devastating Joe Cocker annihilation, It's Lonely At The Bottom (Of The Barrel).

I managed to see one performance. It was a grubby space, which seemed perfect, since the production and the performers had a certain appealing grubby quality as well. You can find it still on YouTube, and it's worth a look—if only as a time capsule of what cutting-edge humor was like back then. I just watched it again while writing this, and was struck by a vein of mean-spiritedness running through the whole thing that I hadn't really noticed at the time. But by 1973 the peace-love-dope-flower-power-all-is-groovy vibe of the late Sixties had soured badly. We had had Altamont, and the Manson killings, and Chicago's Days of Rage, and Vietnam was dragging on, and fucking Nixon in the White House—all of it signs that the brief sweet dream of the Sixties, if it had ever existed at all, had pretty much curdled into fear and loathing. So Lemmings gave us, not hope, but the Woodshuck Festival of Death. Seemed right at the time, I guess.

From there Belushi moved over to the National Lampoon Radio Hour for a year or so, and then, along with other refugees from that show—including Chevy Chase, and, a little later, Bill Murray—in 1975 became one of the original cast members on Saturday Night Live. *Like everyone else I knew, that show drastically altered my Saturday night habits, and like everyone else, I watched and marveled week after week as Belushi carved out a larger-than-life brand of comedy that was totally new to television, if not totally new, period. Cheeseborger cheeseborger cheeseborger...*

We next crossed paths in Eugene, Oregon in fall 1977 on the set of Animal House. *You'll find that story in* Toga Toga Toga, *the first piece in this collection. One note on that: By then Belushi was getting Star Treatment, above and beyond that of the other cast members. Everybody else had standard-issue motel rooms at a big Rodeway Inn out by Interstate 5, but Belushi only put up with that for a day or so before insisting on getting a roomy rustic cabin up in the woodsy hills at the edge of town.*

It's tempting now to see in this time the beginning of the end. Belushi had oversize talents and oversize appetites, always the last man standing at every party. Chris Miller, one of the Animal House *writers and a friend of Belushi's in New York (for years Chris had a champagne persian cat sired by Belushi's cat that he named Otis), testified to the justice of Belushi's nickname among his friends: The Thing That Wouldn't Leave. It even got turned into a sketch on* SNL. *This isn't the place to go into the sad drug-fueled plunge that ended at the Chateau Marmont in 1982, and it has been said often before, but the perils of getting Star Treatment are real, and often deadly. And for Belushi that had begun by the time he was shooting* Animal House. *There are all those sycophants, many of them with dope they're more than willing to share; there is all that money, often an obstacle to staying loaded when there aren't piles of it; and then, maybe most insidious, there is living up to the public persona, being the Wild Man Belushi everyone expects, all the time. Friends close to Hunter Thompson say that he suffered from that as well, trapped by the creature he had created. In any case my few encounters with Belushi during the* Animal House *shoot seem to me in retrospect Belushi at his pinnacle, at his best, the top, the moment before the roller coaster goes roaring downhill. I mean, during a Sunday brunch at his woodsy cabin that he threw for the cast and I was invited to attend, the heaviest drugs were only bloody marys and a few primo joints (which Belushi rolled using a vintage Ray Charles album cover as a rolling board)—hardly worth mentioning, you know?*

But by the time he was shooting The Blues Brothers *Movie in 1980 that was no longer the case. Talking to him on the set of the concert scene in LA, I could see that some of the gleam was gone. Never in anything approaching athletic shape, he looked lumpier, puffy, gray. He could still ignite the spark when he wanted to, but sometimes it took a millisecond longer, needed a little jolt of energy to produce it, not the natural battery pack he always had been.*

So I felt a certain sadness while reporting this piece, especially during the doppelgänger moment described in the article, when the Blues Brothers make their entrance to the gathered crowd, and Jake says hello by doing a front flip that lands in a splits. Performing this, of course, is a stunt double. He looks remarkably like Belushi, except for the flat trim stomach and healthy muscle tone, that is. There is something uncanny in watching Actual Belushi watch Stunt Belushi doing take after take of the flip (even he had trouble landing it), and it may have been projection on my part, but I don't think so, when I caught Actual Belushi staring rapt at Stunt Belushi, as if he was seeing some phantom self that was flying faster and faster away from him.

SWEET HOME CHICAGO GETS L.A.ED

ON LOCATION WITH THE BLUES BROTHERS

I park my old wounded Mustang at a meter on 47th Street between Indiana and Prairie. In front of Queen of the Sea Fish—Gumbo—Filé—Chicken. Beyond the alley is the Welcome Day Care Center for Retarded Children. A few, their eyes sadly somewhere far away, are being directed aboard a double-parked school bus by a social worker. Across the street in a row are Sweetback's Cocktail Lounge, a dead iron-gated empty storefront, Honey Wigs, and Loans Palace, with an Aztec pyramid of fine unclaimed watches agleam in one window. Over an outdoor speaker from the record shop next to Queen of the Sea, disco gushes into the street.

I get out of my Mustang and lock it. No sane car thief would touch it with a stick, since it looks like it's been stolen and abandoned twice already, but I'm fond of it. And this is a tough neighborhood. I feel like *Kolchak: The Night Stalker*, a fellow Chicago reporter and pursuer of the bizarre and supernatural. I am in these unfamiliar precincts on this clear alpine October day because *unreality* has gripped 47th & Prairie. It's known by many names, but most call it...*The Blues Brothers Movie*.

It's been impossible to be in Chicago this autumn and not hear stray, horrible reports of the monster's movements. It's at Cooley High, breaking all the windows. It just dropped a Ford Pinto 200 feet into the Chicago River. At dawn one Sunday morning, it had all the cop cars in the world chasing a beatup ex-black-and-white around Lake Shore Drive. It's even gone marauding to the far burbs, reportedly destroying an entire shopping mall out near Rockford.

And now it's striking again at 47th & Prairie.

Using their best S.W.A.T. team tactics, the Chicago police have cordoned off the four square blocks surrounding the "event" and closed them to traffic. Squad cars sit in the middle of intersections, blue bubblegum lights silently bleep bleeping. Closer in, a police line of sawhorses keeps the gathered crowd a safe 30 yards distant from the corner storefront where the monster has momentarily stopped.

*** *** ***

On the outside, beyond the police sawhorses, there are all these black people, local folk doing what comes naturally, which is to say gawking like crazy.

Asks one guy of his buddies, rhetorically amazed, "They shootin' a *movie* here on 47th? What's the worl' comin' to? What's it *comin'* to?"

"Shit, I *grew up* on 47th! Why ain't I in no fuckin' *movie?*"

"'Cause yo' face break the fuckin' *lens*, that's why!"

Short Fat Fannie in an acre of polka dots: "I've *got* to see Robert Redford!"

*** *** ***

What's curious about this is that all these regular Chicago *black* people have gathered to gawk at all these *white* people from California, who, inside their charmed sawhorse circle, are running around, hollering at each other, talking urgently into two-way radios, messing with all this outer space equipment, making themselves a movie about...*black Chicago music.*

You tell me.

In the changing light, cameramen's assistants in Sassoon jeans keep putting thick monocles to their eyes and squinting into the sun.

Says one to another, passing the time, "D'ya know what a pygmy whore is?"

Other guy shakes his head no.

"A little fucker about *this* tall!" His hand measures off knee-height and he waits for his laugh.

Instead the other guy looks around nervously and pops right back, "Y'know, this isn't exactly the neighborhood for that."

"Whaddya mean? It's like a block party!"

"Oh, yeah? Well, watch your wallet!"

*** *** ***

And over on the corner where the real people are standing, there's a fading, monochromatic street mural painted on the brick wall, stylized WPA people standing around a large curled 2001 fetus floating in the middle of things. Not bad, but mere reality.

Across the street where the cameras are pointing, *wowie zowie*!

The corner storefront has become a Chicago pawnshop, Hollywood style. Ray's Music Exchange, Ray Charles, proprietor. The mural on its wall fairly leaps out and feels up your eyes. Portraits of r&b greats colorfully ablaze on a trippy background. The very best street art money can buy.

*** *** ***

Two director's chairs sit facing it in the middle of the street. JOHN LANDIS and ROBERT K. WEISS are written on their respective backs.

Weiss is the producer. He's the bearlike fellow wandering about in the fatigue cap, Chicago cop's leather jacket, CHICAGO POLICE patch still on it, and elaborately tooled cowboy boots.

This is the new Hollywood, you understand.

Landis is the one who's leaping about and shouting a lot. Still under thirty, with the enormous success of *Animal House* already to his credit, he's something of a wunderkind. But you'd never know it to look at him. He looks less like a hotshot young director than a grad student in Paper & Pulp Technology. With dark hornrims, a full beard, blue down vest, saggy-ass levis and long-haul hiking boots, he suggests Buddy Holly newly returned from a backpacking trip—not the head honcho on what, at $30 million-plus, is the highest-budgeted comedy in history.

*** *** ***

Between takes, when Saul the Publicist tells him I'm here, he comes bounding over to say hello. Landis is probably the most pleasantly manic individual I've ever met. My guess is there's a little Labrador retriever in him. My simple corny question, "How do you like Chicago?" launches him into an unsolicited testimonial on the visual wonders of the city. He tends to talk in machinegun bursts of !!!!!!

"It's a *great city*!" he tells me. "Beautiful! But nobody knows it! Do you know why? It's because Mayor Daley never let anybody make movies here! Back in the Fifties, they shot an *Untouchables* segment here, and it showed a cop taking a bribe. He saw it, and after that he wouldn't let anybody in! But Chicago's *great*! And this movie's gonna let people know that!"

145

*** *** ***

The scene I've been invited to watch them shoot isn't the usual felony-level mayhem. And it doesn't involve Belushi and Aykroyd, the actual Blue Brothers. It isn't even funny, at least not ha-ha.

But it *is* fairly strange, at least if you've lived in Chicago as long as I have.

This neighborhood is presently part of the South Side black ghettoes, Chicago boasting the distinction of having three of them. It's knifepoint poor and tough and gritty, the very stuff of horrible secret suburban nightmares about the lurking terrors of the city. It's turf that North Side white trash such as myself generally avoid, except for occasional expeditions to the blues clubs, excursions regarded by non-believer friends *not* as necessary religious pilgrimages to the source, the fountain, but rather as wantonly unhinged exercises in courting death. In Chicago mythology, these are some of the original mean streets.

So it is both wonderful and weird to hear playback speakers crank up a Ray Charles original that could have been yanked out of his *Hit The Road Jack* period in the early Sixties, to hear that fill the street, and then to see, pouring exuberantly from Ray's Music Exchange, *dancers*, dozens of them, spilling into the street, filling this rough intersection with joy unconfined and well choreographed.

Dear Lord, it's just as Martha & The Vandellas prophesied!

People actually *dancing in the streets!* Life as it ought to be!

Pardon me for showing my hippie-dippie roots. I know these people are getting paid to do this. And between takes, these spontaneous, happy-go-lucky creatures all stand around checking their watches, sipping coffee and shivering their asses off, since the temperature's been dropping all day, and white poofs of clouds increasingly interrupt the bright cold sunshine. I mean, on film this may look like just another Busby Berkeley *Singing in the Rain* production number extravaganza. We're all used to things like this suddenly happening in movies.

But live on the spot, it's terrific. People actually dancing in the streets! I can't get over it. Regular grim reality put on hold, suspended, while an alternate reality takes over, if only for moments on a single afternoon, just the way it happens in Philip K. Dick novels like *Time Out of Joint* and *Ubik*.

*** *** ***

Many weeks later I conduct a much-postponed interview with Dan Aykroyd, and ask him his version of how this fantasy world came about. He tells me, with little or no prompting:

"John and I used to do this act for the warm-up. We used to warm the audience up at *Saturday Night Live* with it. He used to sing rock stuff, and he introduced me to The Allman Brothers and Led Zeppelin. I introduced him to James Cotton and some of the white blues bands that were working up north, like the Lamont Cranston Band. He picked up on the blues thing, and I picked up on the rock thing, and we decided to put an act together.

"We just decided we'll go out and sing a couple of old blues numbers, and why don't we wear the suits that you wore when you were doing Roy Orbison? That was the discussion. John did Roy Orbison once. He wore the thin tie and white shirt and black suit. And then the shades, you know? And we just added the hat to it and digital watches and the locked briefcase…

"And from there, it was just kind of obvious. A sort of myth began to evolve about these characters. We talked about where they'd come from in Chicago, and everything. And I went away and thought about it, John went away and put together the band, I started to write it, and then we both came back to the city.

"He had a rough idea of who we wanted in the band, although the band wasn't set yet. At the time we sold the story to the movie, we didn't know who was gonna be in the band at all. It was just all sort of conceptual, you know? So we sold it on the phone. They said, fine, we'll do it. Then Landis came in and talked to me at *Saturday Night* one night, and said, well, I want this, this and this in the movie. I took some notes, and said, fine, you'll have it. And I sort of cut the script to what he wanted—including, of course, the thought and the myth that we knew.

"So from the beginning, it was like Landis and I putting it together. Landis saying, I want the biggest car chase ever at the end of the movie and I went, *o-kay*! And I said, well, I want to jump a swing bridge. And he said, fine, okay. And I wrote it down. And you know, I mean, I turned in a 300 and some-plus page script."

"They must have shit."

"Yeah. I said, I'm gonna give you guys a movie here that's gonna be four hours. So they were ready for a monster. And what Landis did was distill it, basically."

"What kind of qualities did he bring to it?"

"All kinds of things. He sort of turned it …you know, I sort of wrote a heavy, kind of, real sort of urban experience that was a little…a little *gritty*. What he did was, he put a little Disney flash into it—you know what I mean? And it worked really well. He loved the stuff that I did, and I loved the stuff that he did. He took it and…originally in the script, every band member had a story, and we went and searched them out. What he did was distill them down so that four were lumped together—and we could deal with that. Now only three of them have their own…quest that we go on."

"What would you say the movie is about? If, even by accident, it makes a point or has theme, what would you say it is?"

"It's about two guys who really want to go straight, and really want to straighten out, and really want to get redeemed and get saved and get right—but don't quite have it together. And so end up being criminal, recidivists. It's about good and evil, it's about black and white, devils and angels…it's kind of a Christian Crusader's tale in a sense, because they try to pull the orphanage where they grew up out of financial trouble. They go to great, extensive, even vandalistic lengths to get the money together to pull a nun, who is their surrogate mother, out of trouble. It's basically about all those things.

"It's got a Christian theme in it. It really does have a Christian moral and theme running through it. I know that sounds—to the press, you print that and…It's not really laid in, it's just an obvious…it's a real simple story. There's nothing complex about it. Your nose is taken right from the top of the film to the bottom. No problem.

"We don't have any hidden messages or meanings. There's a certain style and symbolism to it, you know? People are good and bad—they're both. And these guys are good some of the time—striving for salvation, or trying to straighten out.

"But they kind of stray from the path a little bit, and cause a lot of damage. And they receive their just rewards in the end—which is incarceration and correction."

*** *** ***

I next encounter the monster early in December. Like nearly everyone else I know, it has moved to Los Angeles.

I get on the plane under dismal slate skies and fly for four hours over a continent frozen solid and frosted with snow. Until the final western mountains, covered with a green fuzz of evergreens like a 3-day beard on pioneer cheeks, and then into…sunshine. That peculiar alien LA white, like spoiled mayonnaise, or essence of old refrigerator.

Flowering begonias and rampant ivy beds border the freeway, and there are blonde people with good cheekbones everywhere, strolling along at sweat-point in cutoffs and t-shirts—proof of a friend's theory that LA is populated by the descendants of generations of dumb, beautiful hillbillies who came to Hollywood to be stars and wound up instead as reborn dog groomers and gas station attendants and car battery salesmen.

I know it's corny to pick on L.A., but it really is a lot of fun. On the Budget rent-a-car radio—which, here on the rim of the future, is AM-FM stereo inside a stick shift Toyota hatchback wagon—the two pick hit FM stations seem to be one at the left that's into Terminal Mellow—when they really want to tear things up, they put on a J.J. Cale cut—and another at the far right among the other minorities, whose format seems to be All New New Wave Nonstop Marathon, the squarest they get being to put on Blondie. Welcome to southern California.

*** *** ***

They're shooting the climactic concert sequence at the venerable Palladium on Sunset. Among landmarks it forms a triangle with the nearby round Capitol Records tower and the low brown theater that's home to *The Merv Griffin Show*, in front of which I park my Rent-A-Toyota.

I walk into the Palladium lobby but am immediately stopped by a security guy, since I am not a real person to him without a pass or a work slip or a famous face. So I am detained near a card table serving as security headquarters, while someone goes off to find Saul the Publicist so he can declare me to be a real person, for today at least.

Much of the crowd seems to be splitting, drifting outside. Many end up in an accidental line, which sparks the interest of a blond surfer type. He asks, generally, "They getting' *paid*?"

This being Hollywood, the crowd, you see, isn't actually people—it's paid extras. Someone tells me shortly, with great pride, that while half the audience are winners of a listener's contest on KMET, the other half were recruited from a local unemployment office. Whispers my source, looking around first, "We wanted, you know, *black* people."

Once Saul designates me a real person, I go inside to very little happening. It's a long break in shooting to relight the stage.

Landis, rising, manic, comes bopping over, in the same saggy jeans but now sporting a complementary saggy blue blazer. He's all over the place explaining, with a dropping arm gesture, how Cab Calloway was terrific yesterday: "Fifty years, right on the floor!"

I take this to be high if somewhat obscure showbiz praise, and don't find out until seeing rushes the next day that he's referring to a low twirl during *Minnie the Moocher* which C.C. patented an easy 50 years ago, and which he still athletically executes.

"Even the crowd loved him," he tells me. "I thought they'd be disappointed."

He then relates that he's fooling them at the moment. The Blues Brothers are due to come out shortly. Indicating the audience he says, "They don't know it, but I've got every camera trained on them! John and Danny are going to do *Soul Man*—the *least* favorite of their songs—and I'm going to shoot reaction shots!"

Still lots of !!!! in Landis's vicinity.

*** *** ***

But first, the Door Prizes.

Since the rare reward of this experience for the members of the crowd is about $25 for the day and a lot of dull hanging out, the potential restless beast must be appeased. So they will feed it some door prizes during this one of many glacial lulls—and then there will be a song from the BBs…

*** *** ***

Saul, meanwhile, is introducing me to everyone in sight.

I am confronted with a white-haired gent with huge bony hands.

"This is Shotgun Britain. He did *Citizen Kane*, Grable, you name it."

Shotgun rips off a couple of opening blasts about how great Cab Calloway is, how he used to see C.C. right here in The Palladium years ago. Then he tells me, "Shit, I been doin' this fuckin' thing for 50 years. I'm comin' out with a fuckin' book. It's called *Quarterback With A Powerpuff*."

Shotgun is a veteran makeup man and what you'd call an easy interview.

"I was a football player. Hardin-Simmons in Abeline, Texas. Joan Crawford got me in this business. I knew her father. He used to live across the street from me Abeline, Texas. Tom LeSeur. Fuckin' Tom. He never left Texas in his life. I called up his wife when he died. And she said, 'Shotgun, he never left. He never saw his daughter.' And these motherfuckers are writin' about that. I'm one of the son of a bitches who signed the goddamn adoption papers for Christine—and that cunt writin' that book. I didn't even read it. I don't need anybody to tell me what Joan Crawford did. She did more for the poor goddamned working stiffs like me—cameramen, and electricians, and gardeners and grips and sound…than any son of a bitch in this motion picture business."

This I take as criticism of *Mommie Dearest*, which, like Shotgun, I haven't read. I try to get his considered assessment of how things are going on this one. "These two guys are a rare breed," he says of Aykroyd and Belushi. "The bright people. They're bright, you know. They can perform if they're bright." He speaks highly too of John Landis. I ask him if there have been any problems, fuckups, feuds, whatever, but Shotgun knows better than to piss in the tent. He does, however, say cryptically of Landis, "John's gonna step on his cock if he ain't careful. It's a jungle out there." He adds: "They're rookies, you understand? There's not a .200 hitter on the ball club. I'm very flattered that they call me the Stargell—in this league, if you know what I mean."

As a closer Shotgun says, "I was under contract to Jane Russell for ten years. And so I say, I've had ten years with Jane, ten years with Bob Hope, and ten years with Frank Sinatra. That's 30 years of my life, and I've got about 40 more. Somebody says, when you gonna retire? I say, when I get *your* age—if you want to try me, well, let's go to Fist City."

Colorful.

*** *** ***

Through the tall curtains at the back separating the lobby from the hall come uniformed troopers with bayoneted rifles at the ready, a mix of Illinois State Patrolmen and the National Guard. The crowd, like a good crowd, boos, whistles as they file in. Onstage, Landis through a bullhorn explains, "These are real people like yourselves—not the police! You don't really see 'em—they're just here to be scary!"

*** *** ***

The Blues Brothers hit the stage. As happens sometimes at rock concerts, a tangible *rush!* fills the air as they make their appearance in full sinister regalia, cheap black K-Mart parolee suits, shades & hats…

All seriousness, Elwood offers up the locked briefcase chained to his arm, while the band vamps and Jake produces the key, and Elwood's harp is ceremoniously produced from inside.

Jake reverts briefly to Belushi, who checks out the crowd and says through the mike, 'What an attractive crowd! They pass out those hash joints I rolled?"

Cheers, shouts of no, where are they?

For obscure reasons, it's more hurry up and wait.

Aykroyd, finding a live mike and a captive audience before him, launches into spontaneous *SNL* schtick, and begins auctioning off a Styrofoam coffee cup.

"We got $500, who'll gimme 6?…"

Guy in audience: "How much do *you* go for?"

Aykroyd, deadpan: "Seven dollars and 98 cents worth of chemicals. Just cut me open and see."

And Belushi can't help observing, through his live mike, "Cheesh! Lotsa good-looking girls here!" Hands in pockets. "How many here from Chicago?" Scattered cheers. Belushi: "Hyde Park? Elmwood? South Side?"

Beyond his comic talent, which is something of a precious natural resource, I like best about Belushi that he really loves Chicago, that somewhere in his brain it remains home to him.

Belushi, for the second time: "There's some *very* attractive women here. I can't believe it!"

Belushi & Aykroyd fill the dead time by introducing various luminaries, beginning with Landis. Then Shotgun is brought on stage and Aykroyd announces, all seriousness, *"Citizen Kane...Notorious...*Jane Russell's personal makeup man for years..." Like he's reciting a pedigree, which he is.

Then Belushi does the honors for John Candy, the very large former *SCTV* gourmet and Playboy, Johnny LaRue, playing Mercer the Warden in this one.

Much milling about.

For the third time, Belushi observes into the mike, "There's some very attractive women here. I can't believe it..."

*** *** ***

I can't, either.

Standing by the stage when—finally—they begin shooting the crowd reaction shots, I have a chance to check out the audience.

And something's wrong.

Exactly what doesn't register at first. And then I get it. There are no misshapen abnormal-psych case studies in Black Sabbath tee-shirts falling out on ludes or puking on the people in front of them. No sneering punks with faces blasted by new red craters and acne volcanoes, like we always have at real concerts in sweet home Chicago. Nobody really ugly and dangerous-looking, and the color of cave fish.

This is supposed to be an Illinois R&B show crowd. But they're all too cute, too clean. The vast majority even appear to be *healthy.* This is a *movie* crowd. Pick your fantasy heartthrob 19-year-old, and somewhere among these 2500 people, there she/he/it is—gorgeous people of all genders and persuasions.

The first few rows are salted with 150 professional extras, so the people in them are *especially* beautiful. There's a busty young Grace Kelly in the second row, and near her a tall thin darkly heartbreaking girl with a Modigliani neck and lean model's arms and denim honeybuns that won't quit, the very image of my Ruth from so long ago now, once again 19 as she was then…

Pick your fantasy, like I said.

I like especially the girls in what look like spray-on iridescent slacks. They look like sexy dragonflies and glow-in-the-dark green beetles in forties wraparound heels. One with, well, *tits*, is identified to me as a recent *Oui* magazine model, who, in the absolutely factual story accompanying her pictures, was definitely described as a bona fide Israeli, but today at least appears to be a would-be actress in Hollywood with a not so would-be chest.

*** *** ***

More waiting & milling.

Then it's Door Prize time, with Belushi and Aykroyd pulling slips of paper from a clear plastic globe; announcing the numbers, and waiting for the lucky winners to come up and claim their prizes, just like at Bank Nite.

Announces Aykroyd, "Mitch Bell will take home the stereo. He says he's going to burn it in celebration of the 1980s. And now, we have a…*live goat…*"

Instead they give away headphones.

"That's all for now," says Aykroyd, "but a little bit later we'll be giving out a few ounces of *radium…*"

*** *** ***

We all sit around some more and sweat some more while one light is adjusted in the back booth. David Sosna, the Assistant Director—his function being, among other things, to be some combination of drill sergeant/cop/managing editor/conveyor of bad news—takes this opportunity to inform the crowd of something:

"There's been a fire in the paper towel basket in the bathroom. So to be sure that the building doesn't burn down—*listen to what I say*—there will be a policeman outside the bathroom. So in case a lot of fire and smoke pours out of the bathroom, we can call the fire department. They—he, she—will not go *in* the bathroom unless there is an emergency. I am being clear about this, I hope? We don't want to start fires, that's all we don't want to do."

Pipes in a KMET disc jockey who's playing a disc jockey named Paraquat in the movie, "You should know that there are real police here. So you should be cool." A scattering of boos at this advice. Paraquat, defensively: "Hey, it's the Hollywood Palladium, the Hollywood Chamber of Commerce. So give me a break!"

*** *** ***

They are at last ready to shoot, and Landis explains again to the crowd what they're doing here: "This is *not* a rock & roll concert. I have to stress that again. This is the Palace Hotel in Lake Wazzapamanie, Illinois, and you've come to see a rhythm & blues revue. They get pretty rowdy once they start, but this is not a rock concert, it's a very different thing. If you have a bag or a book or a newspaper, put it under your seat, okay? If you have a knife or a gun, you're under arrest. If you have drugs, I'd like to buy them…"

He's trying to get the crowd to *not* react to the vamping band and the entrance of the Blues Brothers. The joke is that the audience sits on its hands and couldn't care less.

"You're not impressed at all," Landis tells them. "Who are these guys? From the CIA?"

Adds Aykroyd, after all have crossed their arms and sit rigid, "Everybody should look like Secret Service men—a little menace, kinda hostile. Very, very still. Like death. This will be a major laugh to audiences around the world, and this is your laugh."

*** *** ***

Yet another delay. I'm beginning seriously to wonder how people in the glamorous movie business put up with the boredom.

Landis starts rapping to the audience, like they're all *one* friend of his and they're hanging out getting high and trading stories. He tells them about shooting in Chicago and at any given moment having sixty cop cars at your disposal.

"Can you imagine the power? I could say, 'All right, you guys, get in your cars and go do this—'" He adds as an afterthought, "It was one of the high points of my life."

I can dig it. Like other dread unwitting longhairs during the famous '68 Chicago Democratic Convention, I've never forgotten or forgiven being teargassed and chased through alleys by Chicago's Finest. We Serve And Protect. Right…each other. I *never* particularly liked cops, but in '68 I discovered I had reason.

Landis tells me later: "I don't trust police. Except when I'm suing people. Then I go, hey, if you can't trust the police, who can you trust? But in Chicago, the police were told to cooperate with us one hundred percent."

I think but do not say that this just *might* be because Murphy Dunne, who plays one of the band members, just happens to be the son of George Dunne, who, as Chairman of the Cook County Board, pretty much ran the city for Mayor Daley and who is still probably the most powerful person in the city government after Mayor Jane. Murphy is talented and a nice guy and all of that, but, still, in Chicago these things don't hurt. I flash on this as Landis continues:

"So I found myself in the position of saying, 'Say, can I have that sidewalk cleared?' And they were going, 'All right, move your fucking asses off the fucking sidewalk!'

"There was an officer, and I won't say his name, but I had him on the Maxwell Street scene. We got into a fight on the set. It was real interesting. I arrive on Maxwell Street, and there are like 600 extras. They're almost all black. And the guy's got a loudspeaker. This is how he starts the morning: 'All right, if anyone fucks up, I'm gonna put them in jail! Do you understand me? You're going to jail!'

"And I'm going, 'Wait! What are you talking about? They're going to work for us!'

"And he turns to me and says through the loudspeaker, 'You don't understand these people. We're not dealing with normal people.' And I shouted, 'What are we dealing with? Negroes?' And we had this huge screaming match. It was incredible."

*** *** ***

Anticlimactically, after all this waiting and preparation, the crowd does its take in two quick tries. Landis tells them, "Boy, are you good. Thank you."

Aykroyd says, "I'm gonna go give Belushi a massage now, and then we'll be back and do a few songs for ya."

Cheers as they split to their star Winnebagoes parked on the street.

And I decide to quit for the day. The endless hanging out is driving me crazy.

On the way out, one of the surfer extras is telling a bored girl, "You just gotta resign yourself to the whole thing, that's what I did." He adds as an afterthought, "I woulda stayed home and got high all day anyway."

*** *** ***

The next morning when I show up there's a fat long line of extras curling out of the Palladium and around onto Sunset, since the first shot of the day will be of the crowd filing into the hall. I go inside, past a crew member in an army jacket and beard, who's wearing a tee-shirt that says in loud caps: I SURVIVED CHICAGO.

Written on a box of accessories on a camera mount, in large black pentel, DISCO SUCKS! And I notice another bearded crewman's tee-shirt, really showing the right attitude: KILL THE BEE GEES—DISCO SUCKS!

Much of the morning is spent shooting the crowd filing in, and then reacting with increasing frenzy to the theoretical Blues Brothers, who are presently here in spirit only on playback. Landis, trying to get scattered catcalls out of the audience, tells them, "I have to shoot you escalating. Pretend it's Southeast Asia."

But they overdo it. Quickly, *everyone* is hooting & whistling. Landis, trying for a lower reaction from them, says, "If you made noise last time and you're...*Chinese* don't make noise this time."

Word comes in that someone out on Sunset has fainted, and that a nurse is needed.

David the A.D., to the crowd, explaining: "Nothing to worry about. Somebody fainted—it happens all the time. We're ready now. Movie magic! Here we go!"

After the shot, Landis deadpans to the crowd: "We've just received word. There's been a terrible earthquake, and San Francisco has been destroyed." This provokes both cheers and boos. "Thousands are dead...so if you have any loved ones—no, I was lying."

*** *** ***

When a break comes for a camera change, I head with much of the crowd for the sunshine outside—and the roach in the ashtray of my Rent-A-Toyota. On the way back in from my toke break, I spot a kid who'd walked out the same time I did. Fatigue jacket and stringy long hair. His face, formerly pale and pasty, now glows a rosy pink, and he's staring up in awed, amazed wonder at a tree growing in a patch of lawn between the sidewalk and the street.

I agree.

*** *** ***

I catch Landis for a few minutes during the lunch break. We talk a little about *Animal House*, since I was one of two writers who made the trek to Eugene to watch them shoot it. Landis tells me that working with Belushi is different now that he's a superstar, but doesn't elaborate. We talk about the *Animal House* script, and he relates how he had the writers tear it up after he first saw it. "You couldn't tell the difference between the Deltas and the Omegas—they were both disgusting." Which leads me to ask about his version of the current project.

"What happened was, I was going to produce the movie. You know, before the concert that created the album, they were going to make a movie about these guys. But the album was this phenomenal success—it was like double platinum. So there was this acceleration.

"Were you here when they performed *Soul Man*? Mediocre performance of *Soul Man*. They were tired, or something like that. But the place goes *berserk*. Belushi and Aykroyd are so well loved. And also these people have been applauding and cheering and working for 12 hours.

"Anyway, the process was…John and Danny were making up the legend of Jake & Elwood on their own. And I took elements of that and made up a real simple plot, and gave it to Danny and then walked away. This is when I was producing it. A long time later, Danny turned in this enormous manuscript. It was like 300 pages. Unbelievable. It was truly an awesome work, and it had amazing things in it, but it just wasn't a movie.

"So now I'm the director, and I did what I always do, which is make changes. So I ended up rewriting it. By rewriting I don't mean…it doesn't mean that everything in the movie is mine. Because it's not. I literally rewrote it and I put a lot of things in it, different things…"

"What sort of things?"

"I put in more movie. I made the characters more defined. I also shortened it considerably. The movie is designed to be an epic, and when you see it, it is. In terms of definition, it's epic and the size is epic. The characters I believe to be epic characters—you'll have to see the movie for that to make sense. Also the look at the United States…the scope is enormous. You go from the wealthiest, wealthiest white, white, white, to the poor black, and everything in between. Everything from Howard Johnson's to fancy French. It's a movie about Americans. It takes place in America, it's about American music."

While we're talking, Steve Cropper ambles up with a very attractive woman on his arm. To rock & roll junkies such as myself, Cropper is something of a walking legend, and of all the greats and near-greats running around here, he's the only one I get a little rush from meeting. I first saw him perform in a fraternity basement in '64, doing the now-classic *Green Onions* with Booker T & The MG's.

"One reason there's been no publicity is that it's a secret that these cameos"—Landis pokes Cropper in the brown western-shirted belly—"actually *act.* I guarantee the critics will say Aretha Franklin's *acting* is one of the surprises of the film."

Landis begins jumping up and down happily.

"That's what I love about making the movie. People will walk down the street, point, and say, 'You're Steve Cropper!'"

Which, in fact, *is* nice.

Landis then launches into a story about how he was called to Martha's Vineyard to perhaps help fix a then-soggy *Jaws.* How it was raining, nothing happening, and Spielberg relates saying to Richard Dreyfuss: "I don't get it. You've been laid dozens of times since we've been here, and I haven't gotten laid once—and I'm the *director!*" Sez Dreyfuss: "Well, I have a head *fourteen feet tall!*"

*** *** ***

Seems to be my day for stray showbiz gossip.

Backstage a little later I overhear one crewman telling another, "So Kristofferson says to Jon Peters while they're shooting the Streisand thing, *A Star Is Born*, Kristofferson says to Peters, the *producer* of the fucking movie, and it goes out over the mike, 'If I want any shit from you, I'll squeeze your head!'"

*** *** ***

Not far away Belushi sits on a trunk, next to a delicious sweet peach in gauzy white sultan slacks, lean athletic thighs through a poof! of fabric, and a GUEST patch on her gauzy black blouse. He's waggling his famous eyebrows appreciatively at her while discussing samurai movies with some guy in the crew.

A good ole actor who plays one of the Good Ole Boys—a country & western group the Blues Brothers have on their tail along with all the cops in the world—comes up to Belushi and insists that Belushi say howdy to his ole buddy, Alex Burger, who's out in the audience, come all the way from Texas.

Belushi assures him that he will, and goes back to talking samurai movies & checking out the peach next to him.

When he's on stage next, instead of forgetting all about it, he actually calls out and finds ole Alex Burger, up in the balcony, who happily stands and salutes the crowd. Belushi has an apparently deserved reputation among his friends as something of a colorful beast. Not for nothing, I hear, did he star in a *SatNiteLive* skit called "The Thing That Wouldn't Leave," and his lapses from the usual social contracts are legendary. Belushi himself told me at one point during this, re former friends and working acquaintances who in his judgment have turned into turkeys, "You gotta have talent to be an asshole. I'm a big asshole, but I'm a big talent, too." He may in fact be an asshole—I don't know him well enough to say—but there is a piece of him that seems genuinely to be a Very Nice Guy, and his saying howdy to ole Alex seems as good an emblem of it as any.

*** *** ***

Finally on Friday I get to see the Blues Brothers perform.

I walk in on Belushi standing onstage next to a stunt man double. He's the guy who's been wandering around for two days with his hair up in curlers, the better to approximate Belushi's devil-may-care locks, and what appears to be a life preserver belt under his shirt to reproduce the actual Belushi gut over his flat acrobat's stomach.

The effect of the two of them standing together is a little startling.

Belushi is again talking samurai movies, this time with his stunt double and Landis's assistant. He's saying that the first samurai bit they did on *SatNite-Live*, rebroadcast two days earlier on *The Best of*, was the best he ever did.

The stunt they're trying to do is a running front-flip-hand-slap move that will be Belushi's concert entrance in the movie.

Mumbles Belushi, "I don't think it's gonna work."

Belushi seems to be right. The flip repeatedly is a bit...troublesome. Stunt Belushi either lands all right but forgets the slap, doesn't land right at all, or, in one heartbreaker, makes the flip & accomplishes the hand slap, barely, only to suffer time-lag balance loss and fall on his ass a full second after the slap.

Actual Belushi sits on the apron to the stage, signing autographs and schmoozing with Landis's assistant.

Stunt Belushi tries again and again.

*** *** ***

A crewmember's random take: "Jewish guy? Looks Mexican?"

*** *** ***

It went on like this, but you don't want to hear about it.

Making movies is duller than laying cement.

I finally got to see the Blues Brothers perform, sorta live, since the band were all there, and they were actually singing & dancing about to *Sweet Home*

Chicago, but the music had all been recorded back in Chicago in July, so all concerned were doing a Dick Clark *Bandstand* lip-synch on the grand scale.

So I gave up again.

From good canned *Sweet Home Chicago* I get on the radio of my Rent-A-Toyota some girl who's singing sounds like whipped cream substitute, toodling in this sappy Elevator Welk style...*I'm only 4 feet 11, but I'm goin' to Heaven, and it makes me feel 10 feet tall...* LA radio!

*** *** ***

That night writing out my notes in the West Hollywood apartment of a friend, around midnight, the doorbell rings. It's some lean guy carrying a guitar case, wearing a black leather jacket and hair...hair that looks to me like it's somewhere between shocking pink and danger-ahead fuchsia. Like Jack Paar, I kid you not. It looks like electric Pepto-Bismol. Definitely no color any human has every grown.

I'm cool, he's cool, so we don't mention the hair. He's looking for some guy who wants to buy his motorcycle. We talk for a couple of minutes. Finally I can't take it. The hick in me comes out. I ask about the hair.

"Oh," he says, nonchalantly, like it's so natural he forgot about it, "I'm in a movie."

Sweet Home Chicago, here I come...and not a minute too soon.

- 1980

Six thousand miles is a long way to travel for a bummer. At first blush it seemed like a gift: A free trip to Buenos Aires for a week, and then another week in Rio de Janeiro—and during Carnival, no less. Where do I sign up? But nothing is ever free. What would I be paying for this free trip? Well, it came with a big kicker. That would be Freddie Mercury and his bandmates in Queen.

It was the same old story I'd already been through with Kiss and Led Zeppelin. Queen has sold more records and filled more stadiums worldwide than anybody but crooked accountants could calculate, but the rock press remained unimpressed. Why Queen—or their record company either—gave a shit was beyond me. But apparently fountains of money and teen adulation forever pouring down upon them simply weren't enough. As I said in the lead to the piece here, the failure of the press to admire them sufficiently evidently remained the pea in the mattress of their well-being. Nobody ever said this outright, of course, but what other possible motive could there be to dropping thousands of dollars to lure a dozen or more scuzzy rock journalists like me from both the U.S. and Europe to fly to Buenos Aires to see them do two stadium shows there, and then throw in a week in Rio during Carnival to make sure the bait seemed sufficiently succulent and juicy for us to take the hook?

I for one have always done my best to have no morals, so I bit right away. And remain enough of a deviant that I'm glad I did, even though by almost every measure it was an awful experience—or at least the part in Argentina was.

I've been back a couple of times since the trip described here, and have come to love the place. But back in 1981 life in Argentina consisted of hard cheese. The so-called "Dirty War" being conducted by a junta led by Roberto Viola was waging state terrorism against political dissidents—chiefly by making them 'disappear'—an estimated 30,000 or more before it was over. Mass assassinations, victims pitched from airplanes into the ocean, tortures, prisoners stashed in over 300 concentration camps across the country. Many of these 'disappeared' were trade-unionists, students, left-wing radicals, journalists, leading intellectuals—and their families.

A pall of fear and suspicion lay over the country. So thick you could cut it, and obvious even to a clueless largely apolitical junketeer like yours truly. I could feel the bad vibe the moment I stepped off the plane. And the next morning one of the braver newspapers led with frontpage headlines about a middle-of-the night sweep in which two dozen of Argentina's most prominent intellectuals had been spirited away by government goons.

I know rock groups are seldom politically astute—or even aware of non-rock-life things like politics, or crazy stuff like right and wrong—but I soon found myself wondering: Why the fuck would Queen want to bring its brand of glam stadium rock to such a creepy police state? Why give Viola and his thugs their tacit endorsement by showing up to play two concerts here?

But they did. And you'll see the outcome of such decision-making in the piece. To complete the slightly sour note, I would have to add that sitting through both concerts—maybe living through them is a better way to say it—did not change my feeling about Queen's music. The world would be a far, far better place without We will, we will, rock you!

QUEEN IN ARGENTINA
ROCKING OUT DURING
THE DIRTY WAR

For reasons having more to do with hubris than anything, and not my own for a change, I'm winging my way to Argentina to watch the rock group Queen play two stadium shows in Buenos Aires, as part of what is being billed as the first major rock tour of South America.

Queen, after ten years together and as many albums, with such a worldwide following that their *Another One Bites The Dust* was the #1 single on Earth last year, after becoming as rich and famous as anyone could possibly need, were now trying to gain the approval of the press as well, its absence apparently being the one remaining pea in the mattress of their well-being.

Like Styx and REO Speedwagon and a few others, Queen is enormously popular with real people, but the critics tend to dump on them often as not, writers for *Rolling Stone* being especial repeat offenders.

So at their own expense (except for incidentals, which prove not to be so incidental) they're bringing in writers from the United States, England, Spain, Chile, and Scandinavia, among others, to witness this historic event, and presumably, to write glowing accounts of it when they get home.

My flight from Kennedy to Miami is empty & nice as such things get, but from Miami to Buenos Aires it's absolutely jammed. Many families with many kids. More children, in fact, than I've ever seen on a flight. They're all returning from long summer vacations in Florida, parents bringing the kids home to start the fall school term, which begins on March 2nd.

Argentines with means apparently escape the summer heat and the up, up, and away inflation at home by fleeing to Florida, where the weather's more pleasant and goodies like Betamaxes & Sony TVs & such are much cheaper than they are back in Argentina. One woman who spoke English said she & her family travel to Florida every third year, where she buys all her family's clothes for the next three years, since even including the air fare & hotel bills it's still cheaper than buying them at home.

So as we pour ourselves off the plane in Buenos Aries after a long hot squashed flight we are met and semi-whisked through customs by a smiling silver-haired gent representing the government. They seem to be taking this visit by Queen and the foreign press seriously.

We are, among others, Fred Schreurs (*Penthouse*), Jim Henke (*Rolling Stone*), Ray Coleman (Editor-in-Chief of *Melody Maker*), Deane Zimmerman (*New York Times* syndicate), Mike Reynolds (Robt. W. Morgan radio show), Lars Stahre (Swedish magazine syndicate), and me, unattached.

We wait around for our luggage, watching people everywhere pushing airport carts loaded with snazzy electric gear in THIS SIDE UP cardboard boxes, like this is a Pacific Stereo warehouse instead of a baggage claim area.

After much waiting around for our passports to be processed, during which time our man from the government repeatedly uses his favorite two English words, if not the only ones he knows, smiling broadly and saying, "No problem…no problem," he aims us upstairs to a restaurant/bar area & shells out for beers and sandwiches for all, and has enough clout to have them open a closed section especially for us. While we sit there some guys rightly figure the section's been opened for everyone and make to sit down at one of the tables. But they're stopped cold by a staff member who shooes them quickly out of there. They leave obediently, offering no argument. My first glimpse at how things are done in Argentina.

We pile at last onto an air-conditioned bus and head for town, to the Sheraton—what else?—a new highrise near the waterfront that faces a little park dominated by a Georgian brick clock tower commemorating Anglo-Argentine solidarity or somesuch.

*** *** ***

Buenos Aires looks like a hasty sketch of Paris drawn by someone who's never been there. Like it's trying desperately to look like a major European capital but just not making it. One main drag called Avenida del Constitucion, for instance, was clearly designed with the Champs Elysees in mind; but instead of climaxing in a great arch or grand park, Constitucion peters out into half-torn-down half-built-buildings, grassy empty lots and finally a gray corrugated metal fence, beyond which are the railroad yards.

The architecture is a mix of European-style neoclassic stone buildings, some of which are quite beautiful, blended uncomfortably with uninspired modern gray concrete highrises, which, generally speaking, are not so beautiful. And instead of being strung out along some nice shiny blue ocean, as Rio de Janeiro is, say, or even the Seine, as in Paris, Buenos Aires extends along the wide yawning mouth of the Rio de la Plata, hopefully if dead-wrongfully named, the water stretching nearly far as the eye not even close to silvery, but rather a yurky yellowbrown shade of mud, and the low ridge of land nearly on the horizon is the coast of Uruguay. It made me nostalgic for Lakewood and Lake Erie; but if you're not from around Cleveland I'm afraid it's not what you'd exactly call heartwarming.

*** *** ***

We find ourselves mostly marveling at the prices. London and Paris are cheap by comparison, thanks to a galloping inflation rate running right around 100% a year. The contracts of factory workers in Argentina have a clause written into them guaranteeing cost-of-living increases *every three months*. At the moment one hundred wobbly U.S. dollars will buy you approximately 230,000 Argentine pesos. That might sound pretty good until you find out that a single local *cerveza* will cost you in the neighborhood of 17,000 of those pesos. Right around seven dollars. I sat at a regular everyday sidewalk café, had a plain cheese sandwich and a beer, and it cost me just over fifteen bucks. Somebody who'd forgotten to bring his bathing suit went looking for one in the hotel shops. The cheapest he could find was $73.00[2].

*** *** ***

So in lieu of being able to buy anything with our colorful Argentine money, we went window-shopping instead along Avenida Florida—an ironic name, given Argentine shopping habits—a street nearly two miles long that's been sidewalked over and turned into an open-air shopping mall.

*** *** ***

On Friday night we're to get our first look at the band. They're having a press conference out at the stadium where they'll be playing on the two nights

---

[2] This was in 1980. In 2017 dollars, this means the beer and cheese sandwich cost $21.31, and the bathing suit cost $222.19.

following. We'd been told repeatedly before the trip to bring along decent grownup dressy clothes, that not only are things more formal here, we will be brushing shoulders with many high-level Argentine dignitaries as well. So we all dutifully put on our best duds and pile once more into what we quickly come to think of as the press bus. We thank the Lord for air conditioning on the bus, since we're having the privilege of experiencing the hottest night of the summer, humidity thick as bacon grease, doomy stormclouds stacking up in the sky. It's about 8 o'clock at night, and we're heading through the center of town, close to the famous Pink House. This is the presidential building, Argentina's answer to the White House.

*** *** ***

Soon we are stuck in the most godawful traffic jam since Goddard's *Weekend*. Old-fashioned buses in many colors, most boasting extravagant chrome hubcaps, each seeming to represent a different line, point at each other like pickup sticks on the wide tree-lined thoroughfare, every which way. Our bus noses against the midriff of one, while inches away next to us bored passengers in another hang out windows for air and try not to stare at the peculiar people all dressed up in the fancy bus.

I take it as nothing more than weekend rush hour, Latin style. But through José, a journalist from Spain who's also along for the ride, our driver tells us it's this bad because the government has closed all the streets within four blocks of the Pink House. This is something they do down here periodically, without warning or noticeable reason, except perhaps for the fun of it, or simply to create grand, epic traffic jams as some new avant-garde art form.

The likelihood tonight, actually, is that it's practice. A new old retired General has been named el Presidente, and since overthrowing the government is a favored form of political protest in South America, things for the moment are in the sensitive condition of changing over.

General Viola is reported to be even more liberal than his predecessor. In support of this, people point to the fact that he gave the final nod to letting Queen in to do two huge stadium shows for the young people in the country, who are fond enough of Queen to have made a couple of their albums double platinum in Argentina. As Fred Schruers will point out later perceptively and with good cause, however, Marcuse among others was onto such scams as, what the Roman satirist Juvenal wrote around AD100, giving the people "bread and circuses" instead of fundamental freedoms and economic well-being—but that comes a little later.

At last we inch through the last of the traffic jam and are moving again.

We enter the concrete trough of a feeder to Autopista #1—Argentina's first, and as far as I know only, expressway. It is a model of modern planning. After finally deciding to go ahead and build it, the government gave the people living in the right-of-way exactly two weeks to get out. At least that's what we were told. And the view along the Autopista tends to confirm it: many buildings not even entirely torn down, just sheared off, as far as was needed to build it, leaving ghosts of former cozy apartments in patchwork aqua, pink & green on the remaining walls. Then we're passing block after block of low two-story stucco apartments, many with rooftop garden patios, many in use by people trying to beat the heat. And then we're on an exit ramp that coils around the stadium itself. We turn a corner featuring dueling sidewalk café pizzerias (pizza being very popular here, if somewhat evolved away from the platonic ideal) and pull up in front of the stadium, built in 1978 for the World Cup Soccer Championships and looking pretty much like any new stadium anywhere, except perhaps for the *moat* separating the visiting team stands from the playing field, a wide 20-foot drop to scummy green water below.

Just as we come to a stop, the heavy black sky explodes rain in torrents. Howard Bloom, the publicist who'd assembled the American contingent of writers, advises that since we're late and missing it, we really ought to brave the downpour. Deane Zimmerman, who's barely five feet tall and on the light side of 85 pounds, leads the howl of protest inside the bus.

"Are you crazy?" she asks. "This is *silk*! I'm not going out there!"

A couple of enthusiasts make the dash, but most of us, despite Howard's gentle urging, stay put until the rain lets up enough to get in without getting soaked.

Like I said, we'd been told that this was going to be our close encounter with the Argentine bigwigs, that we in a way would be representing our country, the implicit suggestion being to clean up our acts, not look & act like slovenly wiseasses like rock writers usually do.

I mean, they were so forceful and convincing that I even went to Mister Hair and had my pony tail cut off. I also bought over a hundred dollars' worth of clothes, an event for someone like me who lives habitually in jeans and old promotional t-shirts celebrating defunct rock groups.

I had had visions of attending a toney cocktail party at the consulate, in some ornate salon with chandeliers hanging from fancy ceilings covered with friezes, thirty feet overhead; candlelight gleaming from the polished wood of elegant Victorian couches and settees; ancient butlers in penguin suits, creaking about offering champagne and caviar; a few retired Generals in flashy uniforms, bent by the weight of the medals on their chests, carrying about them somehow an aura of Germany, reminiscing about the good old days of the Third Reich.

This was the scene I conjured from our admonishments, anyway. I knew it wouldn't be that way when I heard the press conference had been moved—unaccountably, at the last minute, no noticeable reason—to the stadium. But I wasn't prepared for it to be in a brown cinderblock combination VIP parking area/volleyball court inside the stadium.

Or for the scene inside, which is your basic madhouse.

The press conference is for the local press, not us, and they're eating Queen alive, the group members arrayed in chairs along a brown wall, sweating under hot glaring television lights while answering TV journalists who squat before them asking questions and poking microphones into their faces as they respond. The TV technical assistants are twitching and jumping like tree shrews as they move the equipment around for new shots fast as they can.

Several uniformed policemen work at keeping the TV crew and the band separate from the crush of fans, most of whom are the children of various muckety-mucks, and most of whom, like the Keyport Cheerleaders—a platoon of them, hired to be definitely living advertisements for the local beer, scattered in the crowd, wearing white shorts and white t-shirts saying KEYPORT in red letters undulating over their breasts—are extremely cute girls, teenagers or barely beyond.

Whatever else you might say about Argentina, the women are among the most beautiful in the world. And they dress to let you know about it, many of them here at the press conference in dazzling slinky summer designer originals from Paris, although another popular look seems to be circa '69 cosmic cowgal, featuring bona fide Dale Evans leather fringe & cowboy boots, and I saw one or two wild, leopard-spotted Sheenas in the crowd, one of them having her ranch and jungle too by wearing a scanty Me-Jane outfit with gold cowboy boots.

They're generally lighter than their Brazilian neighbors, hair and complexion tending toward reddish and blondish, possibly yet another suggestion of Deutchland as diluted in the local gene pool? This may just be fanciful racism on my part, brought on by Mel Brooks' old routine about the Oberst in the Peruvian Indians, but if a *soupçon* of good solid Aryan stock is responsible for the full, wonderful bottoms of Argentine women, then we should give credit where credit is due, don't you think?

So the girlwatching is terrific, but we're fairly thin on dignitaries.

Atavistically, we distinguished members of the foreign press, prevented by poverty and inflation from indulging in such incidentals as eating or drinking much of anything so far today, aim straight for the two long tables laid out with *hors d'oeuvres* and cold green bottles of local white wine; those, or one of the two refrigerator carts dispensing Keyport on foaming draft. We're concerned with more basic issues than how Queen likes being in Argentina or what their metaphysical goals in life are.

Somewhere in Argentina, there must be a Bread Crust Burial Ground, a place where all the crusts cut off all the sandwiches served in Argentina go to die. Not even little old ladies in England are resolute as Argentine cooks about chopping off crusts to attain a dainty aesthetic effect, no matter that most of the vitamins and minerals are lost in the process.

But free empty calories are better than no calories at all, I figure, so I grab and devour two or three, washing them down with plastic tumblers of white wine, something they are much better at making here than sandwiches. I pour myself another and stroll over to where the group is being grilled.

I've never seen any of them up close before, so I wander around the edge of the media frenzy trying to get a look. Aha! There's Freddie Mercury, the lead singer and chief sex object in the group. He reminds me a little of Rudolph Valentino, although the overbite suggests just a dash of Bugs Bunny as well. He looks like he's very tired of doing this, and exchanges a weary glance with Brian May, lead guitarist and Queen's resident brain, the press releases never failing to remind us that before all this he was a Ph.d. candidate in Astro-Physics. He's the one I'm most interested in talking to, in fact, since I'm hoping he'll be able to show me where to find the Southern Cross in the night sky.

But not tonight.

Abruptly, the press conference is over and the band & bodyguards are zipping away to dinner in plain unmarked sedans. We are to follow in the bus and join them for dinner, but this is Argentina. When we head outside for our bus, we find that it's no longer there. Nobody knows where it's gone, or why. Much confusion and milling around. How to get all these writers to the restaurant? More confusion. After half an hour some cars are turned up, if not really enough of them, so many of us jam into one small compact and we are off, chauffeured by an affable maniac who, like most Argentine drivers, makes even the most gung-ho New York cab drivers look like old folks on a Sunday drive in the country.

This is true psychotic mania I'm talking about, not merely near-fatal reckless driving. He tears toward a bunch of cars stopped ahead for a red light, showing absolutely no intention of slowing down, and in fact not doing so, just sailing into this cloud of cars on the faith that something good will develop. And it does, daylight opening just enough to keep flying right on through, without waiting for the light to turn green or anything mundane like that. His grin widens as he pulls it off, and he offers everyone cigarettes while accelerating even faster.

When Deane observes that a lot of people seem to smoke here, he nods in agreement like it's natural law. "Sure," he says. "Everybody smoke in Argentina."

He doesn't speak much English, but his buddy, crammed into the open area behind the back seat, does. So our driver talks to us in time-lag through his pal. He tells us, when we ask him to drive less *rapido* and maybe not flash his lights so much at offending slower vehicles ahead of us, that he's doing it all for us, that the flashing lights inform the other drivers that he's carrying very important visitors from North America, saying this and other such charming lies while tearing breakneck through traffic, executing hair-raising maneuvers like some flawless death-defying *matador*, blowing through red light after red light with total aplomb.

I'm in the back seat with Lars and Deane and a couple of other people. Like me, Lars has been hitting the *vino blanco*, having had the good sense to cop a bottle for the road before we left. He's a good-looking Scandinavian in his late twenties, and he's just a little smashed. There's a mischievous sparkle in his eyes and voice as he leans forward toward the driver. "You taking us on a tour?" inquires Lars cheerfully. "To all the political prisons, maybe?" Then he turns to the buddy in back. "How about you? Are you a spy? Taking notes? Huh?" Lars has the charm to pull this off, and everybody laughs. But Lars turns to me in all seriousness and says quietly, "People disappear here, you know. They just grab you and—" He makes the motion of turning a final key and tossing it out the window.

As you might imagine, we're at the restaurant in no time.

It's a loud bright steak joint in a restaurant row right on the water, close by the airport. Nice enough, except maybe for the planes taking off every few minutes about eight feet overhead, rattling the windows and drowning out conversations in the roar of exhaust. Truly a *tres chic* setting.

As we walk in, we see Queen and their party at a long table against one wall. By their glazed looks and ravaged plates it's clear they're practically finished eating. And there's nowhere to sit near them anyway; it's moving up on midnight, but the place is packed.

Well, we've only come 6000 miles or so for the story; why should we actually spend any time with them? We stand around in the aisles watching other people eat while they get a table in another room ready for us. Finally we sit down and everyone orders steak, which as you probably know is the national dish.

When our entrees arrive I begin wishing I'd had a couple fewer sandwiches back at the stadium. The chunk of steak before me is the size of a football. It's delicious, which I guess it ought to be for $75 or so, but I barely make a dent in it. Not only the brutal heat and the bad sandwiches and too much *vino blanco*, but ol' jet lag's got me too.

I stare at this huge prodigy of a steak and sort of space out into a strange meat meditation, involuntarily hearing snatches of Kerouac reading his *Wheel of the Quivering Meat Conception*, punctuated by the occasional screaming roar of a jet taking off or landing or crashing just nearby. Serious jet-lag brainfry. Luckily, my new-found friends in the press get me out of there and back to the hotel before I begin launching into philosophic dialog with my dinner.

*** *** ***

On Saturday morning the hot spell has gone elsewhere and it's a cool, breezy, thoroughly pleasant day. We're to receive some sort of briefing about what's happening in the next two days from one Jim Beach, the British chap who actually hacked his way through the bureaucracy and red tape to make these concerts come off. But that's not until early afternoon, so a bunch of us jump into two taxis to go cruise the zoo and the adjoining botanical gardens.

The zoo grounds are reminiscent of sections of Central Park, sycamore-lined walks curving around ponds and the various exhibits. But the net effect is sort of depressing. This is partly because the enclosures for the various animals look like a whacko Depression-era theme park. Somebody obviously had the bright idea to dramatize the worldwideness of the collection by housing the animals in buildings of characteristic regional designs. So the bears are in a sort of Parthenon, antelopes scuffle in the dust before a scaled-down Taj Mahal, and two llamas lazily mate in the shade of a primitive jungle hut, rendered, sticks and all, entirely in concrete.

And most of the animals look a little beat. Most are stuck in cramped enclosures more like jails than not, and the whole thing is pretty dreary and dismal.

Happiest are the ones running loose everywhere in the zoo grounds, light brown little suckers that look like the result of a ménage among a white-tailed deer, a prairie dog and a miniature kangaroo—wheat-colored rodents the size of a small spaniel, hopping around all over the place. They're Patagonian maras, endemic in the Argentine grasslands extending more than a thousand miles. Their ubiquitous presence leads Fred Schreuers to speculate on where last night's restaurant gets its meat. Also present in noticeable numbers—and not counting all the weightwatcher pigeons, a more svelte variety than we have back home—are various specimens of *el gato domestico*.

We see even more of them at the botanical gardens across the street. Not all that much in the way of dazzling exotic plants to thrill and delight you, but tranquil gravel walks through little parklets and groves of this or that quiet greenery—and cats practically everywhere you look, like the plants are there so the cats will have a nice place to hang out. T.S. Eliot would have liked it.

[3] Or $30.44 in 2017 dollars for those keeping track.

*** *** ***

Our briefing takes place in the lounge bar area of the hotel lobby, where a gin & tonic costs a measley 23,000 pesos[3] —exactly ten dollars. Luckily, we are being briefed by Jim Beach, Queen's Business Manager, and he's British gentleman enough to buy a round for all while filling us in on what he takes to be salient details and answering whatever questions we have.

Mr. Beach concentrates on firsts.

After everything really important in rock & roll has been done already, about two hundred times, what else is left but to list aftershock conquests?

This is the first major tour of South America, Mr. Beach tells us, and is the first ever rock tour to play huge outdoor soccer stadiums. "The tour arose because Queen wanted to come to South America," he says. "They've taken a big gamble to come here." He adds that until now, with the exception of a recent Earth, Wind & Fire tour—which, he hastens to point out, was merely *indoors* and played to a third fewer people than the 300,000 this one will attract—only rock groups on their way *down* have played South America.

It's true. In the past, groups have usually come here riding some final worn out wave of culture lag. Most rock music is created and first consumed in the United States and Europe, of course; and then, often more slowly than you'd think, the music and the groups making it drift along a sort of Entropy Trail, gradually penetrating increasingly obscure parts of the Earth, until even burned-out Joseph Conrad types gone native in cannibal Papua New Guinea backwaters have heard of you.

At least if the initial surge was great enough. If it wasn't, after you've exhausted your audience in the primary markets—which is to say, when nobody in the real world will pay money to see you anymore—that's when you hit the Entropy Trail, the first stop usually being Japan. People like Suzi Quatro and Gregg Allman were boffo in Japan when they couldn't get arrested back home, and Kiss is still a new idea there. But it's mainly downhill after Japan, until finally you peter out somewhere in New Zealand, or can't fill a high school auditorium in the Philippines.

That's usually when you think of Argentina.

But this is definitely not the case with Queen—at least not in terms of popularity and revenue. They're still peaking, as Mr. Beach carefully points out, marshalling statistics as proof: After being together nearly a decade, Queen presently has 10 albums in active catalog; and yet after all this time, over 60% of all their record sales have taken place in the last ten months.

Another One Bites the Dust is the #1 single here as elsewhere, and has been for the last six weeks. *The Game* has gone double platinum, which in Argentina means sales of 120,000 units, as they so vividly put it in the record biz.

Mr. Beach moves on to details of tonight's concert.

To properly mount the show, they've flown in 75 *tons* of equipment from various parts of the world, at least 20 tons of which came in on its own 747 directly from Japan—sort of like a group pleasure excursion for robots.

This, as you might imagine, is another first.

Wisely trusting nothing to Argentine construction skills, they've had the stage scaffolding built in Florida and shipped in from there. And from California, where, naturally, it's made, three tons of artificial grass have been trucked to Miami and flown in from there. This is not polyethylene Sonoma sinsamillea we're talking about, but real artificial turf to protect the actual grass on the field during the concerts. Three tons of it.

This is definitely a first.

The stadium is sold out: 16,000 in the stands, 15,000 "populares" in a standing general admission area at the far end of the field behind a fence, and about 3,500 of the wealthy and/or privileged—tickets costing about $45—on the grass directly in front of the stage. Altogether, about 35,000 people.

Another first.

According to Mr. Beach, no one in Argentina has ever seen a concert of this magnitude; never before have the authorities permitted stadium-sized rock shows. The only two acts who have ever played stadiums here in the past are Frank Sinatra and The Pope.

"We're involved in a cultural revolution here," says Mr. Beach. "Thirty-five thousand people have no idea what's going to happen to them. Nobody here has really come across this kind of show.

"The pure volume may confuse them, may excite them," he says, adding, "The volume of Queen shows reaches the pain threshold, and it's absolutely calculated and deliberate."

Queen is due to go on at ten p.m. They had trouble finding a local Argentine group to open for them—easy to understand why—but finally came up with some brave sacrificial goats called Zas. They will be preceded by the simultaneous raising of the Argentine flag and the Union Jack, as yet another symbol of Anglo-Argentine solidarity, and this will be accompanied by the music that was played in celebration when Argentina won the World Cup Soccer Championships in 1978.

This part of the world, after all, is one major center of soccer madness.

Witness the *moat* as a functional part of the stadium's design—they tend to rampage and kill each other over big games in these parts.

So the question is, how will these people, totally unused to such goings on, react to the flags and the emotional nationalistic soccer anthem, followed by

Queen's fairly flamboyant two hours onstage?

During our briefing, Mr. Beach hints darkly, with an unerring instinct for PR, that they really don't know *what* is going to happen tonight, implying that everyone just might go berserk and create another first—Argentina's first rock & roll riot—that things just might turn wild and out of hand, the further implication being, of course, that Queen's show is so powerful and magnificent as to stir such strong responses.

*** *** ***

Our bus, returned today as mysteriously as it disappeared yesterday, pulls up at the stadium a little before 9 p.m. There are kids swarming around everywhere outside. Some of them have been here all day, lining up for the "populares" standing area starting early this morning, and exhibiting while they wait more patience and cooperation than crowds at home—making the waiting more comfortable by sitting cooperatively in line with their knees up, leaning against the knees behind them, lines of them extending like long human zippers from the entrance gate.

A phalanx of cops stretches across the press and VIP entrance. Several of them scrupulously inspect our backstage passes, which feature a sexy cartoon of two nude women, one South American and one Japanese, embracing. The South American *Chiquita* holds a half-peeled banana against the bare hip of her Oriental girlfriend, the design symbolic of the fact that Queen has come here directly from a tour of Japan.

The backstage passes have gone through their own little Argentine saga. On seeing them, the customs inspector at the airport decided they were obscene and temporarily confiscated them, along with a copy of the current issue of *Playboy*.

*** *** ***

Past the first phalanx of cops and through the doors, we're confronted by yet another batch of cops and official types who also want to inspect our backstage passes.

There are cops everywhere.

They wear an assortment of blue uniforms, in old-fashioned designs left over from the Thirties, quaint in a sinister sort of way. Some wear high black boots with the trouser legs tucked in. All carry guns, some serious enough as to require two hands to handle. They seem to be a mixture of the local police and the Army, plus a scattering of private security hired by the promoter and Queen.

Here just inside the doors, anyway, it looks more like a Nuremberg Rally than a rock concert.

We walk out on the field—or "the pitch" as the British members of our group say. Covering the half closest to the stage is the well-travelled three tons of artificial grass, many long wide ribbons of it. Well, it's almost covering the real grass, except in all those places where people keep tripping over the edges and kicking it up into useless snarls.

The stage they've constructed is heavy with outer-space equipment. The standard tall piles of black killer amps and speakers on either side, piano and drums and all that between, with three very large high-tech banks of mobile pod lights hovering in an arc high overhead under the rainguard roof that covers the whole thing.

The "populares" area, corresponding to the bleachers in a baseball stadium, is jammed; but so far, anyway, the stands themselves aren't yet full, even though Zas is already dutifully plugging its way through a mercifully brief opening set.

Several hawkers cruise the field, giving away posters of Queen made from an ancient picture of them when they all still had long leftover Sixties hair; and, more inexplicably, a white plastic strip that says only *fiorucci copyright 1981* and has absolutely no observable function. You got me.

The Keyport Cheerleaders are back in their cute white summer camp outfits, tonight carrying large KEYPORT banners, which, as Zas leaves the stage to listless applause, they unfurl, and, two to a banner, commence running around the perimeter of the field with enthusiastic cheers from the crowd following them in waves.

So little experience with mega-rock concerts do these people have, they've reverted to earlier models, specifically soccer matches, where partisan banners are trotted around the field before games. It's a sign of a certain innocence about exactly what goes on at such giant concerts, and it continues in different forms all night.

As for instance in a few minutes, when the stadium goes black in portentious prelude to the raising of the flags and the playing of the soccer anthem. The crowd begins lighting matches, either not knowing or caring that this is something that's done at the end, to lure the precious superstars back for another encore, not before they've even hit the stage.

And if they're supposed to go berserk when a single spotlight traces the raising of the blue-and-white Argentine flag, accompanied by the song that's supposed to be a symbol of Argentine victory in the international soccer wars, well, apparently nobody told them about it. They cheer and whistle, but it seems more in anticipation of Queen finally coming on than true gung-ho patriotism or incipient displaced soccer frenzy.

*** *** ***

And then blam! blam! blam!

Cannisters explode smoking into the air from the stage as the speakers fill with thunder and the close-encounter light banks pulse blindingly again and again through stark rainbows of color that carve changing beams in the smoke, while hard distant spotlights slice through it all to reveal…Queen!

We will, we will…rock you!
We will, we will…rock you!

*** *** ***

Well, maybe and maybe not.

While the kids in the crowd are all standing and screaming in electric joy at Queen's pyrotechnic opening, this is probably the place to admit I'm not exactly Queen's biggest fan. How to say this politely? I mean, they *are* our hosts and all. But I'm afraid they seem a little like dinosaurs to me. Jim Henke, I think, said it most accurately and least judgmentally, calling them the epitome of a Seventies group—or something very close to that. And it's true. Queen was/ is one of the great Seventies groups, if "great Seventies group" isn't an oxymoron. They came from the same historical context and sensibility that also gave us Kiss and Elton John during his most feathery period, an overblown chapter in rock history, and precisely what all the Punks and the New Wave rockers have been reacting against.

They're not *bad*, mind you, and in fact the choral/theatric/operatic overlay Queen put on good old heavy metal *was* a brand new twist, one resulting in a number of singles—among them, *Keep Yourself Alive*, *Killer Queen*, *Bohemian Rhapsody*, *Crazy Little Thing Called Love*, and, most recently, *Flash's Theme* from their Flash Gordon movie soundtrack—which even nonbelievers like me can get off on. In general, though, they stray too far from the blues/rockabilly roots of rock & roll for my taste, and I am among the sad pitiful minority who are certain our lives would have been far better if we had never heard *Another One Bites The Dust*.

*** *** ***

But hey, who am I to carp?

The kids love it. Not only do they love it, they *know* it.

The crowd is really *sweet*. As a group, these Argentine kids are warm and responsive and open to a degree you just don't see much anymore in Chicago. They cheer familiar opening notes, and sing along with Freddie Mercury as he struts and frets in skintight red plastic pants. On one new song they know all the lyrics, and at Mercury's direction and encouragement they sing most of it without him, virtually everyone in the now-brimming stands and "populares" joining in spontaneously and happily—and singing together more melodically than any crowd I've ever heard in 25 years of going to concerts. It's like a great children's choir, thousands of young voices raised and echoing among the stands.

Some one or two of us in the foreign press mention Woodstock, but it's purer than that, more pristine—nobody lying in the mud paralyzed on bad acid, for one thing. The kids' singing together is my favorite music of the night.

*** *** ***

Freddie Mercury has changed for the encore, returning shirtless in short tight cutoffs, what used to be called "walking shorts" years ago in the Village and may still be. In fact, with the short-billed yachting/motorcycle cap he looks like a lost member of the Village People, or a regular at The Anvil.

But he's less interesting than the crowd.

Remember the part of tripping when the walls and furniture start *melting* a little? Just before the part where the whole room starts breathing with you? Well, from where I stand on the field, that's what the crowd in the far stands appears to be doing, as they sway *en masse*, if out of synch, to the music, like water rippling over shallows.

*** *** ***

But like Fred said, bread and circuses.

As far as I could figure later, it was precisely at this beautiful communal moment—almost exactly at midnight—that elsewhere in town, General Viola's secret police were breaking into separate residences and offices and hauling away the first of nine leading human rights activists in Argentina, among them physicist Jose Federico Westerkamp, one of Argentina's top scientists. They are people who in recent years have been grabbed and locked up in political prisons after being duly tried by a compliant judiciary.

On Sunday morning the headlines in the English-language *Buenos Aires Herald* are: RIGHTS WORKERS ARRESTED IN BA. On Monday: LOCAL RIGHTS ACTIVISTS HELD INCOMMUNICADO. That story began, "Six of the nine human-rights activists arrested over the last 48 hours in Buenos Aires are still being held incommunicado by the federal police, while several political and legal groups have demanded their immediate release, their relatives said yesterday."

I'm no political reporter, but a constant refrain in conversations during the next couple of days was Ronald Reagan. That General Viola & Co. perceived a climate under Reagan where such behavior would bring no moral outrage from the United States, or, worse, any economic sanctions against Argentina.

They figured they could get away with it, so why not?

And as I write this in mid-March, there's a story on the front page of *The New York Times* saying that the Reagan administration is thinking seriously about giving greatly increased aid to General Viola, a good chunk of it in guns & ammo & other basic necessities.

*** *** ***

Meanwhile, back at the circus, the show is over and we're all hanging out in the same volleyball area inside the stadium building where the press conference took place yesterday, being pacified by more cold wine and Keyport, nibbling on strange things on crackers while someone takes the collective emotional temperature of the band.

If they're happy about tonight, on balance, then they'll be sure to talk to us press; but if they feel bad, if some ominous omen beclouds them, then no. Until the soothsayer divines their regal mood, we mere visitors to the Court will have to wait.

Queen is not alone in this basically medieval/feudal structure/atmosphere. Almost all superstar retinues are this way, with a King or Queen at the top, and a closed, extremely structured society that depends entirely on them for its well-being, with all the familiar roles represented, right down to the Jesters (often the Road Manager, Photographer or Visiting Writers) and the hard-working Serfs who schlep the equipment, otherwise known as Roadies. There are also the Ladies in Waiting and far-travelled Merchants with rare herbs and spices for sale.

The main trouble with it, if you are not yourself the King or Queen, is that it means an endless amount of waiting around and hanging out. And that for my money is the single worst thing about the rock & roll life. Accounting offers more thrills 'n chills than most of the time spent on the road.

But luckily for us, the hare had a heart and no owls died.

The band admit us to their dressing room, where it's the usual scene— air thick with cigarette smoke, a table of assorted liquor, a tubful of beers on ice, everybody drinking & smoking & talking like mad among the benches & gym lockers, like it's halftime in the locker room for some new sports team franchise, the LA Degenerates, maybe.

*** *** ***

We didn't know it, but some of General Viola's karma was drifting our way.

By now it's two a.m., and the concert has been over nearly two hours.

While we've been hanging out inside, at least a fourth of the crowd, several thousand of them anyway, have been waiting outside the stadium for a glimpse of Queen when they're whisked away. Most of them line the driveway leading from the VIP parking area inside out to the street; two lines of various cops stretched out along both curbs hold them back. The kids stand on tiptoe and peer around the police, their eyes all focused on the garage-sized doorway, and the cars and people inside.

Now, Fred Schreuers, who grew up in Jersey, can be fairly...*exuberant*, not to say downright bold. And for the last two days he's been taking pictures right and left with his Insta-Flash, capturing Henke with a zebra, little kids at play, whatever strikes his fancy—at least until he learns the price of film here, which is around $16 for 20 exposures.

So the band makes to leave. They're being piled into this boxy squarish tanklike gun-metal-colored armored car you could have seen rolling through the streets of Paris in 1942—I mean the *exact one*—all it lacks is the right insignia.

While they're climbing into this anachronism, Fred spots the crowd and the line of cops outside and decides to bop over that way for a few pictures.

This is the last we will see of him for quite a while.

After the band is spirited inviolably away in the glyptodont truck, those of us in the press begin drifting outside and across the street to our bus, which, remarkably, is still there. More remarkably, it seems already to be full.

As we climb on, quickly filling the remaining seats and accumulating standing room only in the aisles, there's a palpable bad vibe in the air, as the Beach Boys used to say. As it happens, most of these people are from California—they're a good proportion of the roadies and crew.

I'm standing about halfway back, and don't really see the first of it develop. The crew as we continue to get in begins grumbling audibly, and then led by one or two active malcontents, they begin to leave the bus, most of them pausing as they pass the driver to leave him with some parting thoughts of the you-stupid-Argentine-fuckhead persuasion.

Then there's an explosion of glass shattering and falling to the street. A sudden turmoil of movement up by the front door. It's a fight. The driver has gone after whoever took a wine bottle to his headlight.

"He's got a hammer!"

"You motherfucker!"

And one pleased cowboy, "Oh boy, havin' some fun now!" as he dives into the thick of it.

Lightning bolts of adrenaline zapping everywhere.

And then it's over suddenly as it began.

True to their school, all the crew people leave the bus together, saying so long to us with a wide variety of sneers and hateful looks.

This isn't really their fault. It has, once again, to do with the feudal structure of such little self-contained superstar societies. At only one or two removes, the crew lead the lives of superstars—*sort of.* They travel as much and get as many girls and all that, but they don't get the mass love and attention, and in fact a lot of what they do is pretty much shit work. And they often—as these are—stay in a different and slightly inferior hotel than the band (and in this case the press). So it's not unusual for a crew to develop a certain inferiority complex, which can show itself in such little boogies as just went down.

The band had an Army escort out of here, but the crew, apparently, were left to shift for themselves—and upon spotting the nice fancy bus, decided to appropriate it. But our driver, tonight a little more steadfast than last, refused to leave without his designated charges—us writers. And then when all of us piled on, he said he couldn't leave because standing in the aisles wasn't permitted, and since most of the standees were the people he'd been waiting for—well, you get the picture.

All this comes through Josè our driver, understandably boggled by the experience, who can't find the *entrada* to the Autopista, and so José instead takes us on a brief tour of narrow residential streets before locating it.

Sadly, all this is nothing in comparison to Fred's recent adventure.

The short violent freakout still hovers in the air when we see that Fred is red-faced mad and terribly shaken up about something.

His story comes out in pieces, laced with a succession of short inventive scenarios of revenge. We learn that he did indeed go over to take his pictures of the crowd waiting outside. But he apparently caught two undercover cops on film in the process. They jumped on him, spread him, they want the film. As Fred begins to refuse, flashing his press pass, etc., one of them bends back Fred's middle finger like unto breaking, and whips out a cigar-tip cutter, which the undercover cop deftly slides over it, indicating with a smile that he will slice the tendon if Fred doesn't cough up the camera. Fred, shaking, gives. They empty the camera, ripping out the film, and turn him loose.

Nice friendly place.

Back at the hotel, we help Fred calm down by taking over the hotel coffee shop and drinking there until nearly dawn, $7 beer after $10 rum punch, plus *hamburguesas* etc., toasting each new image of revenge, and finally charging it all to Howard Bloom or Freddie Mercury's room, I forget which.

*** *** ***

I drag myself out of bed at noon on Sunday and find the headlines about the arrests of the human rights activists awaiting me. Then we are all invited to an awards luncheon up in the penthouse suite of the hotel, a little bash being thrown by Argentine EMI, Queen's label here.

The room has a spectacular view of the city in three directions, and an open-air vertigo-inducing rooftop patio. In the center is a table arranged with delicacies, dominated by a huge dadaist food sculpture of a giant parrot done in shingles of glazed ham & sliced cheeses & various cold cuts & sliced hard-boiled eggs laid out in patterns of feathers, like an edible entry in *Peterson's Field Guide*—the rarely sighted Amazonian Lunchmeat Macaw.

After luring us all down here Argentine way, thousands of miles from home, the band members haven't felt like being interviewed by any of us, putting us off to the extent it's become a standing joke. Mike Reynolds wants to make up t-shirts: *The interview is tomorrow—Howard Bloom*. That on the back, and ARGENTINA '81 on the front.

So after many postponements, this luncheon is to be our big chance to exchange more than 15 words with the band.

But I can't get into it.

Three of us arrange ourselves around a card table and Queen's drummer, Roger Taylor. Our cassette recorders sit in front of him like curious black geometric tropical bugs. I ask as politely as possible what he thinks of New Wave. With an appearance of disinterested analysis, he is intelligently defensive about the stuff, but I do not care. I realize as he talks that this is it. I've had it. This is the last junket. I can no longer stand to spend my time recording the halfbaked opinions of inarticulate musicians. I can't take it anymore.

Then four of us are similarly gathered around Brian May. I figure maybe I'll start some conversation. I'll spare us from the usual boring record chitchat by talking about science. "Say," I say, "particle physics is pretty exciting these days, isn't it? All those charmed quarks and all?" He does a sort of gliding understated doubletake and resumes talking about the *Flash Gordon* soundtrack with someone else. But at the right moment, I strike again. "Can you show me how to find the Southern Cross?"

Bonkers, flash his eyes, totally bonkers, this one.

But he's British and a gentleman, and Deane Zimmerman is now wondering along with me, so he takes a cocktail napkin and draws the configuration, identifying the brightest stars in the group, and trying to explain where we ought to look for it in the sky. He lifts his eyes as if to see through the ceiling and show us the precise spot. Tilted that way his face seems to rest like a large pointed egg in the brown nest of his long hair.

*** *** ***

By the middle of the concert Sunday night, I am ready as I've ever been to be on my way back home. I'm lying on my back on the field, far as I can get from the *Sturm und Drang* onstage, staring up at broken clouds sailing along under a fat waxing moon, searching in vain for the Southern Cross.

What better place for a mid-life crisis?

I find myself wondering obsessively, over and over again, just what I am doing here, in this faraway uptight place, following a rock & roll band. Worse, a rock & roll band whose music makes me want to weep and run far far away. And then coming home and spending more time writing about it. Is this the behavior of a sane person? I mean, at my age, and after all that education, and all that support from Mom? Is wasting my life like this any way to repay her?

Maybe a teaching gig—I'm still in touch with a few of my former professors. No, it's definitely time to write The Novel. But who cares any more, really? I'll just finally learn Spanish and move to Mexico and disappear, like Ambrose Bierce and B. Traven. No, maybe a screenplay exposing how dull & boring the rock & roll life really is. *Life In The Fast Lane*; or, *Asleep At The Wheel*. And this spring I'll finally start the wildflower garden, it's absolutely time to do that…

- 1980

Failure can have surprising rewards. This profile of Willie Nelson is a good example. The assignment was to do the Playboy Interview *with him. The magazine at the time required a minimum of ten hours on tape with the subject—ten interesting hours, it should be added—which is a really long time for anyone to take with an interviewer. Especially somebody like Willie. He had been interviewed about a million times, and was sick of telling the same old stories. Also he hates being pinned down for very long for anything, other than occupying a stage making music. Of course I didn't know any of this when I got the assignment.*

Willie had me fly to Reno, where the band was playing, for an audition. Naturally he wanted to know what this stranger he was supposed to spend so much time with was like. I was seated next to him at a big dinner, and I guess we hit it off. I think I sealed the deal when I answered with a big smile when he asked if I'd like to retire to his suite with him for a smoke. A really superior smoke, since Willie smokes only the most potent weed on God's green earth, this night gorgeous aromatic Hawaiian buds worthy of a High Times *centerfold.*

So I got the okay, but this didn't mean he wouldn't find all kinds of reasons to avoid sitting down for interview sessions with me, and after he couldn't avoid it any longer, ranging from reluctant to nonverbal when I tried to get him to tell me the good old stories. Over several months I would fly in to where he was playing a gig, nab him for another half hour or so on tape, and then fly back to Chicago with little or nothing usable. My editor was getting antsy, as was the PR person at Willie's end, so there came a plan: I would ride with him and the guys in the band on the band bus for a week or so during a springtime tour of the southeast, from Louisiana to Georgia. How could he possibly avoid being interviewed if I was underfoot 24 hours a day?

Well, Willie is many things, and one of them is crafty. One little thing after another came up. I had the time of my life, but never did manage to do a decent job of interviewing him. I failed miserably. And the Playboy Interview *never happened. But all this prolonged failure meant I got to go back and try again and again, and over that time I got a better sense of who he is than any interview could provide. I got to see him living his life, not just talking about it.*

I came to know this as well: I have been a journalist nearly all my life, have met and interviewed and hung out with every sort of person under the sun, and Willie is the only one I have ever encountered about whom I would use the word charismatic. Again and again in my time chasing him around, I saw it happen: He wouldn't have to say a single word, but when people got within about a 20-foot distance or less from him, you could practically see them undergoing a sort of beatific meltdown. You could see them tangibly change, feel better, look more peaceful, have some sort of lowlevel spiritual experience. As a journalist I try to be as cynical as possible, but it even happened to me. What can I say? Not long after this I named my son Willie. And titled this profile "Saint Willie." I was not quite even half kidding...

SAINT WILLIE

IN EVERY AUDIENCE, THERE ARE
THOSE WHO COME NOT JUST TO HEAR
WILLIE NELSON, BUT TO BE HEALED

It's two hours into the show, and I'm sitting behind and below the one-night-only stage, blissed out like a Moonie on the music. Outside, the Lord appears to be having a go at recreating The Flood for the good folks of Louisiana. It's been the wettest spring in memory, and, if you listen for it through the music, you can hear the dull ceaseless thud of rain pounding the roof of this drab all-purpose sports dome somewhere inside of Baton Rouge.

I feel a hand soft and warm upon my knee, and look to see that it belongs to a pretty girl in her late 20s. She has long sandy hair and wears a thin green blouse whose neckline plunges down between firm centerfold breasts.

She's sitting in a wheelchair. And she's a little drunk. She smiles, grasping her legs and rearranging them a little. They move stiffly, like pieces of cordwood. "Hi," she says brightly. "How about a drink?"

Why not? I shrug, smiling back.

She reaches behind her, into the backpack strapped to her chair. She pulls out a quart of bloody marys, already sipped on some, and a quart of screwdrivers, pristine.

"I used to tend bar in Boca Raton. Used to get backstage with all the groups, Deep Purple, the Allman Brothers. That was before"—she makes a pistol of thumb and forefinger, turning it against her solar plexus—"pow!" Lightly, she cups a breast in each hand. "He missed these, though. Lotta good it does me. Can you fix it so I can say hi to Willie?"

I should have known. Girls this cute never just spontaneously fall for me. She's attracted to my full-access backstage pass. And Willie.

Now she's, well, she's caressing my thigh.

"You're nice," she tells me, vamping hard as she can. "Please? I have to say hi to Willie."

I try to explain there's no way she'll meet Willie back here tonight, that the moment the show's over, he's whisked offstage and into the bus, flanked by Snake and Poodie and Poodie's security guys. That she just might have a chance out by the bus, but it's practically Hurricane Hilda out there. I add philosophically that it's the music that counts, anyway, that meeting him isn't what really matters.

That is apparently *too* philosophical for her. She leaves in search of greener avenues to Willie.

Then, much later, as the band swings into its signature *Whiskey River,* a reprise of the opener and closing parenthesis to the show, I see her stationed at the base of the stage stairway down which Willie will have to pass on his way to the bus. She's steadfastly refusing to hear a security cop who's explaining that she can't be there, that the area has to be cleared for Willie's getaway. She's not budging. Her hands clamp down like emergency brakes on the chair's wheels. She's beginning to look a little wild-eyed and hysterical.

The guard takes her chair by its handles and begins gently but forcibly to move her away from the stairway. There's a sudden confused flurry of motion and, unheard among the swells of *Whiskey River,* she lurches screaming from her wheelchair onto the electrical cables covering the floor like a convention of blacksnakes.

Two strong security guards put her back into the wheelchair, which they lift and start carrying away.

"You fucks! Assholes! I have to say hi to Willie! *I have to!*"

She wails this through brokenhearted sobs deeper and sadder than mere hysterical fandom. She's carried off anyway.

She'll never know how close she got. Seconds after she's carried off, the show's over and Willie and the band are hurrying down the stairs and up through a long ascending exit ramp. Since temporarily at least, in the Pranksters' telling phrase, I am on the bus, I follow along closely after.

We near the end of the concrete corridor and someone throws open the metal fire doors. Standing there in the continuing downpour, drenched to the skin, is another young woman. Backlit almost blindingly by cars leaving the parking lot behind her, hair clinging like a sodden old mop, she supports her twisted body on aluminum arm-brace crutches.

When she sees Willie, her eyes widen and melt. She looks up searchingly at him, beyond words.

And here, I think, is an important piece of why Willie is Willie these days.

It doesn't even occur to him to ignore her and make a dash through the deluge for the bus. Instead, he steps out into the rain and walks slowly up to her, taking the hand she has raised. Astonished happy tears well in her eyes and are lost among the raindrops splattering her cheeks. He's rapidly getting soaked too, but stands there talking to her in tones only she can hear. As he does this, the look on his face—one I will see often over the next months—is positively beatific. Like he's clicked into a state of grace the rest of us are missing most of the time. The sort of face they give Saint Francis holding a handful of happy chipmunks.

Saint Willie.

I ask him later if he thinks his concerts might replace church for some people.

"Yeah," he says. "I like that part of it. I really do. There's a lot of people who I'm sure experience religious experiences during *Amazing Grace* and *Uncloudy Day*. They receive religious experiences without knowing it. Without knowing they're receiving one. But they're certainly acting like people we've seen receiving them before."

As the bus pulls out, I wave goodbye to my bloated red rent-a-car parked there in the lot under the TOW-AWAY ZONE sign. So I can get some time with Willie on the bus, and so they can hang out here a little longer with friends, Jody Payne and Mickey Raphael of the band have offered to follow us in it later. This is very kind of them, but, somehow, I have a sinking feeling I'll never see it again. Actually, it's sort of *thrilling* simply to abandon it like that—a dash of Hunter Thompson in my usual Dagwood life. I mean, it's not in flaming ruins with the radio blaring at the airport, but it's something—and the TOW-AWAY ZONE sign definitely helps.

No matter anyway—I am on the bus.

It's a standard Greyhound customized to the teeth. It's been divided into thirds. The first part is a sort of lounge area, with a Beta-Max connected to not one but two color TVs, and a stereo tuner/cassette sound system that won't quit, all this built-in directly above and behind the driver's seat and stairs. There are three swivel easy chairs, a diner-style booth with low-backed bench seats, a small couch facing it across the aisle, and a tiny galley kitchen featuring a two-case ice chest filled with cold Budweiser. Across from the galley is a john the size of an airplane john, and beyond them toward the back, the Pullman section—two tight stacks of four sleeping berths each, separated by the aisle. The final third, reached through a door denoting rank as much as for privacy, is Willie's bedroom, with a double bed, a couch, and its own ice chest abrim with cold Bud.

It's a little like *essence du frat house*, as if the basics had been distilled down to bus size and wheels added. Altogether not exactly a horrible way to travel.

Or an uneventful one, I quickly find.

We're barely beyond the city limits when Bee Spears is suddenly seized by inspiration: I must be introduced to the pillowcase bong.

Bee is one of two bass players in the band, and has Willie's personal endorsement as the craziest person he knows—this choice from a group that includes Waylon Jennings, Johnny Paycheck and Kris Kristofferson among other heavyweight contenders. Bee started playing for Willie when he was 17, and has with one hiatus been with him ever since, having snagged the job on someone's recommendation to Willie saying that, "He don't play very good, but he smokes a lot of dope." These days he does play very good, and still smokes a lot of dope.

His pillowcase bong is a recent discovery in a lifetime of research.

It consists of a pillowcase with a small hole cut in the closed end. A long cardboard tube is inserted partway into the hole. Near the end of the part sticking out, a smaller hole has been poked. Sticking out of that is a fat joint of Hawaiian buds retailing at $3750 the pound. This all develops back in Willie's room. He watches smiling as Bee produces his invention, and, with the help of Billy Cooper, an amiable assistant road manager known by all as B.C., proceeds to demonstrate.

Bee slips the pillowcase over his own head and signals to B.C. to fire up the joint. It glows cherry red and a quarter-inch of it disappears. Explosive coughing inside. "Damn!" More coughing. "That's the stuff, all right!"

The test, I am told, is to survive an entire joint in there.

I find out later there's something of a tradition among the band of "burning 'em down," as they so colorfully put it. Regularly smoking the most potent grass known to mankind, they find it great fun to oversmoke visiting writers and photographers and the like until they can't remember their own names, much less ask dumb questions or take pictures or whatever. Willie, I am to learn, uses it as a way of ending interviews which in his estimation have gone overly long.

Bee knocks off the joint in nothing flat and emerges from the pillowcase red-eyed and grinning.

Now it's my turn.

The pillowcase goes over my head.

"Don't open your eyes is all," advises Bee regarding technique. "And just breathe like normal."

The smoke comes rolling in. Soon there's nothing to breathe but smoke. Hmm. I'm beginning to feel like Fat Freddie trying out for the fire department. I can't resist opening my eyes. It's like a climactic closeup from *The Towering Inferno*. Vague light, diffused through smoke. Then my eyes close sympathetically as I'm racked by coughing. I flash first on Doc Holliday, followed by Hans Castorp and Wile E. Coyote.

"Hang in, you're almost there."

No, I'm already there. I'm just not finished yet.

It's a little later, and I am marshalling my remaining wits to interview Willie. He's graciously responding to whatever I manage to ask.

"*Night Life*…let's see…I was driving from my house in Pasadena, Texas, over to Houston, to a club called The Esquire Club. On the way over, I started the song. The idea that the night life ain't a good life but it's my life came to me. I wrote half of it going over, and I finished it after I played the job and was driving back. The easiest place for me to write is in a car, moving."

Why ain't the night life a good life?

"Well, back then it wasn't. And from a religious standpoint, it's not the good life. The night life is beer joints and the women of the evening and the honest man blowing his hard earned money in some beer joint on some dance-hall floozy. That's what the night life is thought of by a lot of people. Plus the fact that it *is* a hard life for a musician who works six nights a week, four hours a night, for just a little money. At the time I think I was getting ten dollars a night, six nights a week. And I was trying to raise a family and pay rent, buy groceries and pay electric bills and buy clothes and send the kids to school on that kind of money. So the night life wasn't the good life in that respect even. But now, the night life is a great life."

Big grin.

What do you like best about it?

"The fact that we're moving. And we get to play to a new audience every night. We get to see new places. We get to ride up and down the highways in a nice bus. And there are no phones. It's very private out here, like being on a ship or a sailboat. And you have to get your bus legs out here, just like you have to get your sea legs on a ship. Once you get them, you can dance up and down the aisles like everybody else."

It's somewhere after one a.m., and there's a card game in progress at the diner-booth table up front. Grady Martin and Willie sit across from Bee and Chris Etheridge. B.C. and Johnny Gimble are kibitzing from the couch.

Everybody's still coming down from the concert buzz, an understandable high brought on by prolonged mass love and attention—a 2 ½ hour dose.

Grady leans against a window and rests his cards on his Buddha belly, frowning down at them through his salt-and-pepper beard. Like Willie, he's been around for what you would call forever. He played on Elvis sessions in the 50s, and is responsible for those hot licks on Brenda Lee's early hits. After years as a top Nashville session man, he decided about a year ago to hit the road again with Willie. In Willie's estimation, he's the greatest guitar player going. Nightly, when it's Grady's turn for a long lead, Willie will stop in his tracks and simply watch, his face suffused with a rapt look of pleasure tinged with awe. It's not misplaced. Grady may look like a crusty, slightly grumpy good ole boy, but there's lyrical liquid mercury in his fingers, a fast fluid style that loses no punch by being melodic.

Studying his own cards directly across from Grady is Chris Etheridge, the other bass player. A native of this Gulf Coast we're going along through outside the bus, he combines longish hippie-style locks with the penetrating eyes and habitually sober face of a country preacher. It's a face with echoes of Faulkner about it, the eyes especially, which seem sometimes to burn darkly in search of something serious that hasn't shown up yet.

To people like me, he too is something of a legend.

At a little over 30, he's been on the road over half his life. He was for a long time one of the genuine Byrds, and then along with Gram Parsons as an important part of The Flying Burrito Brothers. He joined Willie a few years ago when Bee decided for a time to call it quits. And then when Bee undecided, Willie found himself with two bass players and wisely chose to keep both, giving the band a complex bottom unrivalled in country or rock.

Presently sitting right next to Chris, Bee also examines his cards intently—so intently, in fact, that he fails to notice that the eyes of the other players repeatedly flash above and behind his head. Snake, the road manager, has angled a rearview bus mirror so all can see what Bee holds. Too bad for Bee, he's bluffing. The others struggle to avoid cracking up as he makes raise after confident raise. Snake's grin gets wider with each one.

Snake is a lank six-footer with a little beer paunch and straight brown hair dropping longish from a crown starting toward bald. His background includes time in the Marines, a few days of which he spent as part of the Bay of Pigs invasion. As you might imagine, Snake wasn't always his name. At birth in Baltimore in the early 40s, he was named something he thought drab and ordinary. So he became Mr. T. Snake—just plain Snake to his friends—some years ago in Nashville, when a fellow promotion guy suggested he move on up from the ho-hum everyday to something memorable. And it is that, as countless stupefied hotel operators who've been asked for him can testify.

"Mr. T. Snake, please."

"Who?"

"Mr. Snake. S-N-A-K-E."

Bee finally realizes he's being had and launches into vivid protest, cut short by Johnny Gimble, who'd disappeared in back some minutes before and is now making a dramatic re-entrance wearing crispy-clean blue flannel pajamas. Look on the back of practically any Nashville album you own, and you'll find Johnny Gimble listed as one of the fiddle players. Like Grady Martin, he's seen 50 come and go. With his silvery hair and carriage on the portly side, he reminds you of a decent W.C. Fields, one who's never had a mean thought nor taken a drink. He's here in his clean blue jammies to wish us all a good night before he retires to one of the berths.

Now it's somewhere after four in the morning. Practically everybody has crashed by now, Grady right in the spot where he was playing cards. Only Snake is still awake, sitting up front with Allen the driver, shooting the shit about this and that. I'm just behind them, settled to the point of growing roots in one of the easy chairs. Technically speaking I guess I am also awake, albeit too far swacked on dread killer weed to move or speak technically.

Finally even Snake peels off and heads for a berth, pausing to slip the Bud from Grady's sleeping grasp and drop it in the trash can already overflowing with crumpled Bar-B-Que Chips bags, shredded Chips Ahoy sacks, and squashed Marlboro boxes among the beer cans.

I may be turning into silly putty, but I can't pass up a little time in Snake's vacated shotgun seat. On atavistic will alone I manage to launch myself forward and flop down beside Allen the driver. Allen is very cordial, telling me how much more he likes driving for Willie than for other bands he's hauled around—especially some extremely famous and disagreeable British art-rock faggots who shall remain nameless. It's great gossip from a unique point of view, but I'm too road-zonked to pay proper attention. The passing scenery has me hooked.

The rain has stopped, but the bus still sizzles over wet pavement, its headlights tunneling into the mountain of darkness outside. We're on an empty two lane blacktop. Kudzu covers the road cuts on both sides, devouring all it touches—fences, bushes, trees, even telephone poles—in bites slow and green. The blip blip blip of the white line is a sad plaintive appeal in some unknown language.

Okay, I admit it. I'm practically in heaven. Whatever the road disease is, I've got it too.

I awoke to shouts.

"Where is it? Where's the damn golf course?"

Golf course?

I slide out of my berth to find most of the band glued to various windows, searching the visible countryside for, yes, a golf course. It's early morning and we're in the cowpasture outskirts of Hattiesburg, Mississippi.

"There's gotta be a country club! You comin' out with us, Grady?"

Bee more or less hollers this out of pure enthusiasm.

It seems one of the band's current passions is golf. Most carry their own private set of clubs down among the baggage in the guts of the bus. Willie says none of them is any good, himself included.

"We average about seven strokes a hole. That's a normal hole. That could be a par three, or a par five. It doesn't matter. We have as much trouble with one as we do the other. I get real pissed off when I miss a shot. But whenever I hit one, I feel better—I guess. It's a frustrating game. You can go out one day and play like a pro, and then you go out the next and you can't hit the ball. I think golf is good for that reason. Because it's hard and frustrating and you've got to concentrate on that, and you can't think about anything else."

Allen wheels the bus into the parking lot of today's Holiday Inn. At the hiss of the brakes Bee is out the door heading for the front desk to ask the whereabouts of the nearest course.

Willie and the boys claim their rooms—all in a row on the first floor facing the pool except for Willie's, which is somewhere Top Secret, its location to be learned only through Snake, or so they hope at least.

And then led by Willie and Bee, both of whom look fresh and rested and ready to go, those presently consumed by golf fever are off to the country club, which should be an experience for the sedate local gentry puttering around on the golf course, these longhaired crazies whooping and hollering and waving their mashies at each other. Definitely something to see if I weren't feeling like last night's ashtray. But I'm not up to all that sunshine and good cheer, so I salute their long-ball hitting and opt instead for some room service breakfast with *Rocky & Bullwinkle* before a long morning nap.

This time I awake to the sound of—can it be? Yes, by god, it's a live marching band murdering *Whiskey River* at extremely close range. I pull back the orange Naugahyde drapes and there they are in the parking lot, formed up regimentally in full dress uniform and playing this impromptu tribute to Willie without mercy.

The whole place is crawling with teenagers in a variety of high school band uniforms—from the traditional fat kids in thick hornrims lugging tubas to cute tutued majorettes flashing silken thighs while sending their batons aloft like so many spinning silver stars. It's the Mississippi state finals or something, and several of the bands are staying here—every single member of which has discovered that *the* Willie Nelson is also staying at this very same nowhere motel.

By mid-afternoon, Willie has already changed rooms twice to no avail.

Persistent little bastards that they are, the kids keep finding him and lining up for autographs—which he is unusually generous about, given how many he's signed by now, but enough is enough.

He now appears on the second-floor walkway wearing his running gear, waving howdy and thanks to the marching band in the parking lot just as *Whiskey River* is reaching its sour conclusion.

And then he's off on his afternoon run.

I think Willie's much-publicized fondness for running is connected to his fondness for buses. During most of his waking hours, somebody or other wants a piece of him—an autograph, an interview, just one more song. The bus is one refuge from phones and loving fans, and running is another, a socially acceptable way to steal a little time alone in the hallowed name of health. He averages between five and ten miles a day, and while his legs might belong to a college halfback, it's a credit to the night life, the munchies in particular, that he still manages to maintain a slight roll around his waist in spite of the distance.

When we talk next I ask what made him start running three years ago.

"I was getting too fat."

But why running as opposed to the other sports you might try?

"Just the fact that I was running, out there making some effort to take care of myself made me feel better. Because I was destroying myself every night, so I was having to do something the next day to counteract it, or else. Back then I was abusing myself terribly, drinking and smoking. Running and smoking was agonizing, so eventually I knew I was gonna have to quit one of the two. I just feel better doing it. I think it's natural that it should make you feel good. Back when we were kids, we ran all the time. And then we got out of the habit of doing it. We thought we were too grown up to go out and run around. But we weren't, really."

A month later, in mid-June, over a thousand of us test this philosophy about 40 miles outside of Austin, as participants in the First Willie Nelson Distance Classic—a 10K race over hill and dale in the general vicinity of the Perdenales Country Club—which, among much else in Austin & environs, Willie owns.

The race begins on Sunday morning at some gruesome early hour.

So I am riding with Mark Rothbaum and Paula Batson over empty freeways through gray false dawn. We are to pick up Willie at his ranch and then all go to the race from there. Paula, a friend and publicist for CBS Records, has wisely decided to stay on the sidelines and watch. But I am a sucker and something of a junk runner myself. I seldom manage half of today's distance, but I figure I can only die trying.

Mark, on the other hand, is the true runner in Willie's crowd. Like a deer during hunting season, he lopes ten or fifteen miles a day over the Connecticut hills surrounding his house. Mark is what you would call personable, a fast and funny New Yorker who at 31 has to be the youngest manager of someone in Willie's league that you can find. His sole other client is Miles Davis, whom he's known most of his life, having grown up haunting New York recording studios because his parents were in the business.

He got his job managing Willie by going to jail. At least indirectly so. Remember the famed Waylon Jennings coke bust of a few years ago? Well, when the dust settled, Mark ended up doing the time for that one. He'd been working as an assistant in the management company which then handled both Waylon and Willie, and they nailed him on the technicality that his name was on the return address of the package the Feds intercepted in Nashville. A law school graduate, he found himself doing six months in a Connecticut prison. He told Paula and me all this at dinner the night before, and said that at the time, of everyone he knew, that Willie, and especially Willie's wife Connie, gave him the most ongoing support—to the extent that Willie hired him as his new personal manager when Mark got out.

We turn onto the side road leading to Willie's ranch. The fields and trees somehow look more Midwestern than Texas ought to, like parts of southern Indiana—except for the scattered jackrabbits sitting at attention near the road, twitching their ridiculous cartoon ears.

The road swerves down into a wash on a curve, and is quickly nothing but a narrow concrete slab hanging over the streambed, without guardrails or room for mistakes, the drop being only a couple of feet into a shallow muddy pool, but enough to make you notice.

Mark roars over it with easy, hair-raising familiarity, noting that on occasion in former more rip-roaring times Willie himself has landed in the drink here.

From the outside, approaching along the road, Willie's ranch looks like a minimum-security work farm. The property line starts where a high stone fence with barbed-wire strung along the top. You follow it a while before turning in and stopping before a serious gate across the long driveway. Then you announce yourself to a stone pillar with an all-weather mike built into it, while a closed circuit TV camera checks you out and relays what it sees to a monitor in the house a quarter-mile away. If you pass inspection, the gate seems to open of its own accord, and you are driving toward the inner sanctum.

The house is sprawling Texas modern. It's back on a rise above a little stream dammed to form a pond fringed by willows, a swing rope hanging from a tall branch of one, pure idyllic Huck Finn.

Parked in the open garage is a sleek gray Mercedes.

Willie comes out to say hi wearing his running gear. His hair this morning is in a single plaited braid, curling around his neck onto his chest like a friendly pet copperhead.

He directs us through a door leading into an enclosed porch dominated by a pool table. It more or less melds into the kitchen, which is on a level one step up. The surface of the pool table is a tranquil green sea beneath a full Lone Star sign moon. The kitchen is clutter and disarray, the kitchen of busy people more interested in other things and no servants. On an oblong oak table a couple of shoebox tops contain miniature haymounds of marijuana and packs of E-Z WIDERS.

Willie is cordial and soft-spoken, offering coffee and a pre-race joint and maybe a quick game of pool if anybody's interested. It's barely 7 a.m., but in this world there is apparently no time too early or too late for a joint, even if we are about to run over six miles. Well, why not? If he can take it, so can I.

We share a joint while Willie and I split two quick inept games of 8-ball. A lifetime each of bar pool hasn't improved either of us. He takes the tie-breaker when I plop the eight in the corner on the break.

Then we all pile into his Mercedes to go to the race. Willie drives. He heads up the long driveway and stops at a stone pillar on this side of the gate. This one wants the right key stuck in it before it will let us out. Unfortunately, after much searching of pockets & visors & seat cracks, Willie doesn't have it with him, so we have to go back to the house. But instead of turning the Mercedes around on the hard dry lawn, or backing up at a slow decent pace, a little gleam appears in Willie's eyes and he floors it, tearing expertly backward at 40 miles an hour and loving every second of it.

As we get close to Willie's country club, we see the main drive is clogged by a slowly crawling line of cars, vans, and pickups full of people on their way to the race.

Willie has a flash. We turn around and head off over a road roughly paralleling the club grounds, in search of a semi-hidden shortcut. But it's too well hidden, Willie can't find it. We drive back to the clogged main entrance-way and Willie has another flash. This is after all his country club. He executes a flanking maneuver and we're suddenly tearing along the grassy margin next to the drive. People's faces instantly transform from outrage to radiant recognition as they see that this gray outlaw Mercedes speeding by is being piloted by Willie himself.

Then we're off overland. Drive em, cowboy! The Mercedes bucks down a hill and then up a long bumpy fairway, flying between sandtraps and flat manicured greens.

We come to rest next to a cyclone fence enclosing another in Willie's collection of houses, this one modest by Texas standards, but nice enough to relax in after 18 holes and a swim in the near-Olympic-size pool shimmering in the sun below the clubhouse nearby.

The race is scheduled to start in a few minutes, from a spot about 50 yards away. Most of the thousand-plus entrants are already here. Everywhere you look people dance obscure private ballets of stretching exercises to stay loose in the cool air. But as word of Willie's arrival spreads, increasing numbers abandon their warm-ups in favor of fandom, and Willie is gently mobbed by admirers. I go over to pay my five dollars at the signup table, and am awarded #692, a number which proves to be prophetic.

The race begins, and the first couple of miles are cake. I feel great. This is because I don't know yet that some cardiac arrest sadist has designed the course, and that the final two miles are virtually all uphill.

Into the third mile, I catch up to Willie and hold a few yards behind him for a while. He's going along at a pace so slow and easy that nearly everyone is inexorably passing him—which is to say, slow and easy enough that anybody who feels like it can say hi or fall into stride with him for a while—to which Willie again and again graciously responds, that beatific look clicking in again as his smoky eyes lock for an instant onto those he's just encountered. Most just want to be, however briefly, in the presence, so they can tell their grandchildren how they once went running with Willie Nelson one fine morning in Texas.

I pick up my pace and pass him. But a mile later my heart is quaking like a palsied dog. My breath comes in short pants and an occasional pair of trousers. If my forehead weren't exploding, I'd probably be enjoying the scenery, pretty rolling hills and a lake at the bottom of rocky bluffs in the distance. But it is now all uphill, and my legs have turned to jelly. I'm wheezing, gulping air, constellations of blood-red stars pinwheeling before me. I love running.

Mark and Paula are together just beyond the finish line as I come collapsing across in 1:04 or so. Mark, whose time was a little over half of mine, looks like he's done nothing more strenuous than watch the Sunday Morning Movie. Paula hands me the most welcome cold beer of my life, and we stand there waiting for Willie to finish.

Seconds later there he is topping the last hill, chugging along at the same pace he was doing when I last saw him three miles or so earlier. A lesson there, certainly. He hits the finish line behind a TV news team jogging backwards before him to record the event on videotape.

He stops off to one side, sweating like crazy, red bandanna soaked black, chest heaving deeply, trying to catch his breath. The TV sportscaster asks how he feels right now.

"Fine," answers Willie, breathing heavily but recovering quickly. "I ran the whole way, anyhow."

Mark hands him a fresh open Lone Star. He accepts and salutes the camera's eye with it before tilting the can and drinking half of it down in two gulps.

Now the sportscaster wants to know what he thinks of his time—1:14:27.

"It's okay. I wasn't racin' against anybody—except Father Time, maybe."

The TV sportscaster asks him another.

Willie has tremendous patience for this sort of shit. Or, more precisely, does when he's finally trapped and caught. As my many days of hanging out in motel rooms waiting for an interview session attest, he can be extremely elusive and unpredictable. A constant refrain among the people around him is "Where's Willie? Anybody seen Will?"

For the rest of today, he's due to officiate at the awards ceremony immediately after the race, and then he's scheduled for a news conference to be followed by several individual interviews, these to be followed by yet another with me out at his ranch, and then a show tonight at the Austin Opry House—which, incidentally, he also owns.

But the moment the TV sportscaster's done with him, Willie disappears through the off-limits clubhouse for a recuperative dip in the pool. And then also disappears from there, entirely forgetting, it appears, about the awards.

A crowd gathers and gets fidgety around a flatbed truck parked outside the clubhouse for use as a makeshift stage. "Where's Willie?" those on duty ask each other. "You seen ol' Will?"

Finally he is captured and produced.

He climbs up on the flatbed to give away the prizes looking like there's nothing else he'd rather be doing at the moment. And in fact when it's over, he actually lingers by the front of the truck, leaning against the fender signing autographs, on tee-shirt or back or running shoe or breast, depending on the desires of the autographee, until everyone who might have wanted one has had his chance.

After nearly three hours of fans and interviews, we drive back to the ranch, where I am to steal yet another hour of his life with questions. When we get there, he again disappears as if by magic—re-appearing half an hour later ready to go.

He sits at the oak table rolling a joint while I fire away.

I figure after all this interviewing, I can at least ask about something interesting. So I ask about sex. Have there been periods when he was freely sampling the offerings when he was on the road?

"Yes, this is a problem. It's been a problem all my life. Whenever I was looking for companionship, it usually was there. I didn't have to go looking for it."

So on the road it can be a daily crash course in getting to know someone very intimately…

"And then they're gone. Of course, there's a lot of people that like it that way. Just one-night stands is all they're looking for. Most musicians who travel around from town to town and country to country will do that. They enjoy that type of relationship as opposed to any long-term relationships, which they've always had bad experiences with. So what happens is, a guy turns 60 and he's had a wild, hot life. But all of a sudden there's nobody around anymore. That's one of the big problems."

Do you think of yourself as a romantic?

"Probably so."

Is that a word that means something to you?

"I take it to be associated with the word love. And I seem always to be involved with love in one way or another."

It seems like your songs, more than any other male's in country music, grasp the woman's point of view in various situations. Do you have any idea why?

"I've had the woman's point of view pointed out to me several times."

Do you find sex as important now as when you were 20? Has its meaning changed for you at all?

"I may be more appreciative these days than maybe when I was younger. I think a good woman, from whatever way you consider her—mental, spiritual, sexual, whatever—is always more appreciated the older you get. I think the same thing applies to women. They appreciate a good man the older they get."

Houston. Every few hundred yards along the freeway, triangular signs advise me to DRIVE FRIENDLY. One on a long pole beyond the road says only INTERIORS in blue neon against a moons-of-Jupiter-peach evening sky. TOTALLY NUDE GIRLS!! This in a trumpeting sideshow typeface, like they're some newly-discovered freak species on display at a carnival, a dog-faced boy or the world's smallest horse. Another simply asks, FAT?

Three times on the elevated expressway on my way from the airport to where I'm staying with a friend on the far west side, tall goofy TOYS 'R' US giraffes loom up out of nowhere and seem to hang their inquisitive cartoon heads over the guardrail.

My friend Scott lives in a development that was desolate fields hardly months ago, but where the building of ersatz British country manors and zip-pop! traditional colonial houses is presently so frenzied that even on Sunday, at first light, I was jolted awake by some eager beaver with a chainsaw, cutting and framing as fast as he can.

It's September, and I'm here because Willie & Family are performing a benefit for Jimmy Carter on Saturday night.

I drive to their downtown hotel about three or so in the afternoon, and am just walking toward the entrance when who comes driving up in a weathered old sedan, waving as he turns in to the hotel, but Chris Etheridge. Bee, Snake, and Grady Martin are in the car with him.

They've all driven here together from Dallas, five hours away, all jammed into one cheapo rental car when all of them could afford to charter separate Lear jets if they felt like it. There's no getting around it. They really do like hanging out together.

They look a little glazed as they get out and stretch and look around. And there's a problem: they've lost the trunk key. They're in the lobby checking in and discussing the situation, when out front a sleek black limo glides to a stop.

From it steps drummer Paul English, a friend of Willie's now for 25 years, wearing his regular gear—black shirt, spear-pointed red cowboy boots with shiny pointed cleats over the toes, and a black cowboy hat alive with medallions. All this and his black salt-and-pepper Mephistopheles beard and mustache make him look generally like what you'd suspect people around Nashville would think of as The Devil.

He comes in clutching a small bulging black leather kit bag, and embraces the guys in turn, California touchie-feelie having arrived even this far, and, anyway, they're glad to see each other again.

"You got a knife?" Snake asks him, getting back to the trunk problem. English shakes his head no. "Anybody got a knife?" Snake inquires generally. Nobody does. But moments later, Chris has somehow come up with a big long-handled screwdriver. We go outside and gather around the trunk to watch him go at it. He digs at the lock cylinder and quickly pops it like a champagne cork. A little more digging around in the resulting hole pops the trunk lid, too. It's a good thing these guys are gainfully employed. They grab their luggage and head for their rooms, leaving the traumatized Rent-a-Chevy to the doorman.

"So what *did* finally happen to it?"

It's 20 minutes later, and I'm sitting with a few others in someone's room, talking desultorily with Mickey Raphael while everybody half-watches a somnolent Yul Brynner western on TV. I can't resist asking the fate of my own abandoned rent-a-car of a few months back. I'd finally gotten the bill, and all I could tell from it was that it was turned in a week after I last saw it in the Baton Rouge parking lot.

"Oh, we just left it there. We couldn't find it when we wanted to leave, and then we didn't need it. But I called in the morning and said you couldn't get it started because of the rain, and that you had to leave, and I told them where it was."

I thank him for this, since at the time I was having visions of the thing just sitting there collecting tickets and accumulating rental time until it was finally stolen and totaled by MDA-crazed teenagers.

Around 5 p.m. I'm standing with Snake and Jody Payne outside the lobby waiting for a limo to take us to the sound check. It's Snake's job to see that everything's going smoothly, and Jody and I are coming along for the ride.

He is yet another guitarist in the band (which, counting Willie, makes three). He handles most of the backup vocals and sings lead on *The Working Man's Blues* in every show, in a whiskey-and-cigarettes voice you can tell has really been there. He's currently at work on a solo album on which most of the guys in the band will be playing.

He is also newly married and working on a house outside Mobile.

While we wait for the limo, we mutually rhapsodize about south Alabama for a while, a beautiful and undiscovered piece of America. Jody says that in what little spare time he's got he's been doing some fishing too back home in Austin, so then we trade fishing stories until the limo glides up.

The gig tonight is in yet another sports dome, this one holding about 20,000 people. One end is sliced off by the stage, which is alive with roadies as we walk in. Snake and Jody encounter and embrace several roadies by way of saying hi.

"How ya doin', Jody?"

"Oh, keepin' between the ditches."

We head for the press lounge, where The Beast is about ready to serve dinner, and where the Houston Oilers—Kansas City Chiefs game is on TV. We sit and have a beer and watch the game, which is being played here in town.

There's been much general lamenting all day about the competition for crowds tonight in Houston. The best guess is that they won't fill the place, a circumstance rare as hen's teeth for Willie Nelson concerts. Not only is there the Oilers-Chiefs game to contend with, worse, they're also up against the final climactic game in the Astros-Phillies playoff series, which everyone in Houston will be watching on TV exactly when they're onstage. And worst of all, Carter is about as popular as food poisoning in these parts, so they'd be in trouble even without the competing football and baseball.

It turns out they were right. The place is half empty, but nobody seems to mind. They're all out of their seats screaming at the sound of the first notes. It's Willie's usual crowd, which is to say every manner and age of person you can imagine.

In watching a dozen concerts over a 6-month period, I've been continually amazed at the range of Willie's followers, from blue-haired little old ladies to kids under ten goofing in the aisles, and everything in between. He simply appeals to everybody who can stand anything remotely like country music— although among the 40 or more songs he sings bits and snatches of every night, you will hear blues and jazz and western swing influences as well.

The favorite bands of Willie & Family are The Band and Duke Ellington. And like both, Willie's magic is never better than when live. Not one of his many records, not even *Willie & Family Live*, one I've played daily for over eight months now and not tired of yet, quite captures the sound and the spirit. His group can all play their asses off—this very much including Willie himself, whose guitar playing goes generally unmentioned but which is bluesy and muscular and fast when need be, so good that Grady Martin told me in all seriousness he thinks Willie is one of the best there is—and they do it differently every night, improvising, throwing in this and that. It's as close to being a jazz band as a so-called country group can be. There's nothing else like it.

So it is a little like going to church. To experience it, you have to be a follower, you have to go to it for whatever spiritual rewards might ensue.

In all my months with Willie, one scene sticks out. It was after the show that night in Austin, the concert Willie and the guys put on following the 10K race at Willie's country club.

The Austin Opry House is low cinderblock in the popular bowling alley school of architecture. Inside it's a Rorschach-test show bar, two separate not-quite equal rooms back to back under one roof, with a humongous kitchen off one of them that can handle dinner for 400. As you come through the front doors, the larger room on the right is a vast empty dancehall decorated like someone's vaguely remembered dream of frontier Victorian splendor. The show that night was in the smaller room on the left, with a bigger stage and rising arc of theater-style seats.

It was a packed hometown crowd, chiefly cowboys and cowgals. On this hot, muggy night their collective body heat was too much for the air conditioning, even though it was cranked up to Ice Age. The stripped-down, utilitarian bar near the stage did land office business in draft beer and surprisingly good margaritas.

I dropped into a seat margarita in hand and was quickly lost in the music, closing my eyes and drifting away, just like you're supposed to on the good stuff. Then suddenly it was two hours later and everybody was filing out.

I went prowling through the backstage area to see what, if anything, was happening. Everybody had gone. I wandered through the backstage rooms into a long unpainted cinderblock hallway, lit by a succession of harsh unshaded bulbs on the ceiling. And every few feet on the concrete floor there were crimson smears. Not a lot of it, but definitely blood. Probably a cut bare foot hobbling toward the parking lot. My eyes followed this bright trail forward, and there at the end of it, by complete coincidence, was Willie. He was bending over a bit, the better to chat with a midget couple standing there beaming and holding hands and craning their necks to get a good look at that beatific face, clearly so overjoyed they could burst.

Good ol' Saint Willie.

- 1981

You never outgrow your need for comic books. At least I never have.
My love for them started before I could even read. But it began with a
movie.

When I was four, my mother took me to see Walt Disney's Bambi [4]. *It is*
almost impossible to convey how utterly earthshaking and lifechanging and little-
young-mind-blowing was sitting in a theater watching those giant cartoon creatures.
I had never been to a movie before, period, and to be dropped into this colorful
dream world where fawns and rabbits and skunks and owls can talk and have
adventures was, well, so thrilling and wonderful I found it almost unbearable.

But as any kid who first saw Bambi *that young can tell you, the movie not*
only enchanted and delighted me, it also scared the living shit out of me. The scene
of the fire gave me nightmares long afterward, and what four-year-old wants to

---

[4] If you will pardon a small David Foster Wallace moment here, it is maybe worth noting
that walking into a theater and seeing an animated movie in color on such a huge screen was
something rare and extraordinary back then—this would have been about 1945—in a way
that generations who have grown up with color cartoons endlessly pouring from TV sets
probably can't really understand or appreciate. The only time you could see cartoons was to
go to the Saturday matinee (25¢—a dime for a ticket, a dime for popcorn, 5¢ for a candy
bar), where, if you were very lucky, you might see two short color cartoons that clocked in at
slightly under 8 minutes each. And that was the only cartoon fix you got for the entire week.
Fifteen minutes' worth. Disney had only pioneered full-length color animated features a few
years earlier, and in 1945 you could pretty much count the total number of such movies in
existence on one hand. It's really too bad that Disney turned into the Evil Empire, because
at first in these movies—*Fantasia, Sleeping Beauty, Dumbo, Pinnochio, Bambi*—were letting
little kids like me enter what truly seemed like a Magic Kingdom.

encounter the idea that mothers can die? And those big bruiser stags with their lethal racks of antlers, crashing against each other—this was love?? No thanks.

Quickly the awe won out, and I couldn't stop thinking about the movie. Or talking about it. So either to gratify this obsession, or simply to get me to shut up, my mom bought me my first comic book—a telling of Bambi in comic book form. I couldn't read it, of course, but my mother's aunt, Maude, was a sucker for kids, and with buddhalike patience I certainly didn't appreciate at the time, would read it to me again and again, until I had memorized every single word and would on occasion, being a little snot, correct her when she varied from the True Text. But she didn't mind, thought it was funny, in fact.

From this first Bambi, my comic book collection grew and grew. At first I remained partial to the Disneys, particularly Uncle Scrooge, and other "comic" comics—Archie, Little Lulu, etc. But as I got a little older—eight or nine—I began shifting over to Superman and Batman, plus Wonder Woman, Blackhawk, Captain Midnight, Aquaman, and Captain Marvel (dorky though he was, I loved the Shazam! transformation from Billy Batson boy radio reporter into big over-muscled red-suited Captain Marvel, and his nemesis, evil weaselly bald little Dr. Sivana). By the time I was a sophisticated 6th grader, I had discovered Pogo, a passion considered in the article here—I still very much go Pogo.

I was like Uncle Scrooge with my comics, fussy, fastidious with them. My mother donated the bottom section of a big linen closet upstairs for me to keep them in, my precious vault, and I would sit there on the floor with them for hours, pull them out, visually caress the covers, make stacks, practically swim around in them the way Scrooge did with his money.

Then in the early 50s the comic book world changed and I was right there with it. Who needs Batman or Archie and Veronica when you can have…The Vault of Horror, Tales From The Crypt, Weird Science…Comics had reached a creepy adolescence, and so did I. EC Comics were delightfully lurid and gruesome, just what a 13-year-old boy needs!

In October 1952 EC dropped a considerably bigger H-bomb on the world of comics: the first issue of Mad. It was a comic book for the first 24 issues, and it changed the world—mine, anyway, and everyone else's of the right age and sensibility. It made fun of everything,without apology. Superman? No, cloddy Superduperman. Tarzan? No, Melvin of the Apes….

What, me worry? Mad was the antidote for the tedium and conformity of the early Fifties, with Ike genially mangling the English language in the White House (when he wasn't out on the links, waving his wedgie) and How Much Is That Doggie In The Window? rode the top of the music charts for weeks on end. It was also a time when Joeseph McCarthy, the honorable mad Senator from Wisconsin, began hallucinating Commies wherever he looked, and gradeshool kids like me were taken out of class twice a week down to basement hallways where we practised crouching and kissing our little asses goodbye in preparation for the bright day when The Bomb dropped and its mushroom cloud melted downtown. Many of us were issued dogtags, so our charbroiled young remains could be identified by any survivors.

But Mad was a sharp stick in the eye to all that blandness and paranoia. The genius behind it was Harvey Kurtzman, who wrote and drew most of the first issues, aided by "the usual gang of idiots," which included Wally Wood, Will Elder and Jack Davis. But Kurtzman was the guiding spirit, and I had a new hero.

And here's where it got weird and wonderful for me. Flash forward to the early 1970s, and I am a junior editor at Playboy magazine. Years earlier, starting in 1962, Hefner—also a lifelong comics fan, one of his most admirable traits—had hired Kurtzman to write and draw a recurring comic strip for the magazine, a very sexy parody of Little Orphan Annie called Little Annie Fannie. Cartoon Editor Michelle Urry was then overseeing it, and she and I had become friends, first from running into each other on the 151 bus many mornings, and then because when I felt like fucking off and not working, I would drop by her large 9th floor office to hang out and poke through the batches of original submissions by famous cartoonists she always had around. One day I started telling her about my boyhood hero worship of Harvey Kurtzman, and she laughed, and said, well, you can work with him if you want. Hunh???? I responded, taken aback. "Sure," she said, "he's always looking for good ideas for Little Annie Fannie stories, he's been doing it forever now, and you're the funny guy who started the college humor magazine, aren't you? I can put you two together if you like." If I liked??? So by what seemed a miracle, twenty years after seeing that first issue of Mad, I actually began working with Harvey Kurtzman, sending him ideas, him sending notes and encouragement back, talking on the phone occasionally. I don't know that a single idea I had ever made its way into the actual strip, I'm pretty sure none did, but still…how often do you get to know and work with a childhood hero? Then and now, I felt very lucky indeed.

And it happened again while I was at Playboy, just a few years later.

Another new wrinkle in comics that had come along in the late Sixties and continued to flourish into the Seventies were socalled "underground comics." Or comix, as some spelled it to distinguish them from the cornball mainstream titles. These were bent on breaking every single existing rule of comicdom that they could think of, and succeeding with heartwarming regularity. They made stars of individual artists. R. Crumb became and remains the most famous, but there were also gory S. Clay Wilson, Skip Williamson (whose main character, Snappy Sammy Smoot always advised "Don't forget to smash the state, kids!" and who for a time was an Art Director at Playboy and a friend—whenever some project calling for weird came up, they would pair Skip and me), plus Vaughn Bodé, Jay Lynch, and last, but one of the best, Gilbert Shelton.

Shelton had been an early comix pioneer, starting with his character Wonder Wart Hog, a Superman parody that made Mad's seem genteel and restrained, who made some of his first appearances in 1962 in the Texas Ranger, the campus humor magazine in Austin which Shelton edited while he was in grad school there—and whose cartoons I cheerfully "borrowed" for Plague, the off-campus humor magazine I co-founded and edited during those same years at Miami U. in Ohio. But of all his characters—including Fat Freddy's Cat—the ones I loved most were The Fabulous Furry Freak Brothers. How could you not admire the wisdom of their motto: "Dope will get you through times of no money better than money will get you through times of no dope"? Anybody else remember the awful long dry pot drought in the summer of '69?

So I had been a fan of Shelton's since back when we were both avoiding the Army in the name of pretending to be graduate scholars. And at Playboy articles meetings I began bringing him and the Freak Brothers up, suggesting that we try to get him to do an original Freak Brothers story for the magazine. The other young editors liked the idea too, and we won over doubting older editors fearful of seeming unhip. I contacted Shelton—he was then living in Venice, California— and he agreed to meet with me, if I would come to him. A couple of weeks later I was at his door, the house a funky little bungalow facing one of Venice's funky little canals. Shelton came to the door looking a little tentative—was I a narc?—but then relaxed when I told him who I was, his face opening into a warm smile beneath wavy touseled hair complemented by an old west mustache. I don't exactly remember our conversation—a good host, he had produced a wowie-zowie joint for us to share—but he did agree to do the strip for us, and didn't quite hate the idea I had suggested for it: that somehow the Freak Brothers find themselves transported back to the boring repressive 1950s, and have to deal with the cultural jolts of the timewarp. I went back to Chicago and began working on a storyboard. We traded ideas back and forth, and he actually ended up liking and using many of mine. It ran at six color pages in the magazine, and I had gotten to collaborate on a Freak Brothers story with Gilbert Shelton. My name didn't appear anywhere on it, of course, but I didn't really care. Getting to do it with him was what counted.

Then in the mid-70s, I talked the editor in charge of the Books section to let me do a longish essay/appreciation of Marvel Comics, on how they had during the last 10 years or so reinvented the comic superhero, giving them all sorts of neuroses and doubts and everyday regular problems. This is old news now, of course, but back then the mainstream media had barely begun to notice the Marvel Universe, so the piece was maybe an inch or two forward-thinking. To research it—well, in the name of research, I contacted Marvel, and was put right through to Stan Lee himself. The comic book dweeb in me was thrilled, though the would-be journalist did his best not to show it. We had a 45 minute phone conversation, which I taped, about the ideas behind Marvel and its growth since 1962 when Peter Parker got bitten by that radioactive spider. Lee was friendly and generous with his time, and at the end of the call said he would send me "a few" samples of recent issues and titles. Well, a week later, a rather large box arrived at the Playboy offices with my name on it— crammed full of Marvel comics, a year's run of every title they were publishing at the time. I had died and gone to heaven.

Jeff Norman, a buddy from Miami U., or so I thought at the time, was also an editor at the magazine, thanks to a little finagling on my part, but that's another story. Jeff was originally from south Alabama, and loved fishing. At the time he was learning his way around the intricate arcana of fly fishing, climbing the angler social ladder from his humble spinning-rod bass fishing roots up to the trouty elegance of tied flies and hatches and single malt scotch at the country club. He suggested we take a long weekend, for a roadtrip up to the fabled Pere Marquette River in northern Michigan for a little fly fishing. Margaret, my wife at the time, was more than game for any excuse to get out in the country, so she cheerfully agreed to go along. She found us a sweet rustic rental cabin with an expansive screened porch and a view of the river, and she and Jeff fished their brains out for three solid days.

Me?

Well, I had brought along that fabulous box I mentioned earlier, and my long weekend consisted mostly of sitting on that cool shady porch with a frosty Heineken or three, and an occasional toke, doing vital research—happily swimming in those Marvel comics, just like when I was eight or nine, playing Uncle Scrooge with my comic collection. True to my school, I didn't set foot on the river once the whole time we were there. And truth be told, during the six hour drive back to Chicago, I have to confess that I sat in back with my nose in Fantastic Four, The Hulk, Iron Man, Amazing Spider-Man, and the rest, while Jeff and Margaret sat up front pleasantly passing the time together like regular civilized human beings. My behavior during this trip, while only a small drop in the large bucket of my deficiencies, was a telling one, and emblematic of why Margaret was wise to ask for a divorce a couple years later. I am pretty useless when it comes to most things.

By the mid-90s I had been married and divorced for a third time—I really was lousy at marriage, though I clearly liked the idea—but that union had produced two children, Maude and Willie, who are by far the brightest shining lights in my life. They are the best kids who ever breathed air, and ever since they were little, I have felt lucky to be around them.

But in 1997, following a truly melodramatic years-long alcoholic swan dive on my part, a bottom that is the ugly equal of any other I have heard in 20 years of AA meetings, I was newly sober, and newly divorced, and Willie was 11 years old. In the divorce settlement my ex-wife Carol had understandably given me only limited time with the kids, pending proof of mending my amber ways, but Willie and I got most Saturday mornings together—and we filled many of them in the next year or so by, yes, driving to every comic book store within 50 miles, and beginning Willie's comic book collection. Showing innate good taste, he was only interested in Amazing Spider-Man—well, mainly at least—so we prowled comic shop after comic shop, with a list of the issues we needed, looking for bargains and only drooling over those precious expensive issues with numbers under 100—since I was far from back on my feet, and the money I got from what freelance writing I was able to sell mostly melted away far too quickly. But I always managed to find a few bucks for at least a few Spider-Mans every week, and, anyway, the hunt, the chase, was the most fun for both of us on those Saturday mornings. Willie is now in his late 20s, and unlike me, never let a fit of romance or, god forbid, attempted maturity, destroy his collection—a painful tale recounted in the article here, and one that still hurts me—although one young criminal friend of his did put a sad serious dent in it when he was in junior high school, the young thug while visiting Willie at home, when no one was looking, rifled the collection and stole many of the true gems, a betrayal that so disheartened Willie that his mother and I never managed to get him to let us pursue it and bring in the cops. The truth is that for Willie and me it broke our hearts, since those lost comics represented all those Saturday mornings together. Uncharitable, I guess, but I am happy to say that the creep thief not long after that ended up doing several years in Joliet for some other thuggish enterprise. But to Willie's credit, this didn't put him off comics or collecting, and slowly if intermittently he has been rebuilding his collection, with occasional help from dear old Dad at Christmas or birthdays. Maybe it's genetic.

And one final scene to complete my life in comic books:

In the 1980s my longtime lawyer friend, Ken Levin, became a co-founder of First Comics, headquartered in Evanston, and part of yet another new wave in comics, with titles that included Grimjack, American Flagg and Jon Sable—though my own favorite was their English translation of the Japanese manga series, Lone Wolf and Cub, *the story of a disgraced former executioner for the Shogun and his very young son, who wander the countryside as ronin, assassins-for-hire bent on revenge on those who murdered—well, it's way too tangled to explain here.*

Naturally I quickly became a fan, and wrote a short piece about First for Chicago *magazine in 1985. First had a pretty good run, but due to a complicated host of problems, they had to cease publication in 1991—though they proved to be down, but not out.*

Ken revived First in 2011, partnering with Devil's Due *publishing in June 2015, with a new main focus, though not exclusively, on graphic novels. (They're also reprinting* Lone Wolf and Cub, *along with other original First titles from the eighties.) The company is now called Devil's Due/1First Comics—and they are the publishers of the book you're holding. Ken has always had a faith in me that I never really felt I deserved but have greatly appreciated. Back in the mid-70s he talked several dentists into putting up money for me to produce and direct* Secret Saga, *a radio soap opera parody I had written with my pal Jerry Bovim back at Miami, and now Ken has done it again. Can't thank him enough.*

But the final scene…

A couple of weeks ago, while I was working on these introductions, another big box arrived at my apartment—this one full of an assortment of new graphic novels First had published in the last year or so. Thank you, Ken. It was great to get them—but I still really haven't had a chance to read them. The day after they arrived, Willie came over for a visit, and his eyes lit up when he saw them. Willie is now 31, and right after he graduated from the University of Denver with a journalism degree in 2008, he and a buddy took off on an enviable six month backpacking trip though southeast Asia—the Philippines, Maylasia, Singapore, Laos, Cambodia, Vietnam, Thailand, Bali, Papua New Guinea, East Timor… I was of course deeply jealous. He took batches of notes during the trip, filling four journals, and lots of pictures, and has been planning to write a nonfiction book about it.

But when he saw these graphic novels, he remembered a conversation he'd had with Ken a few years ago, in which Ken had urged him to do it not as plain prose, but as a graphic novel. Willie had adventures that gave me pause as his father to hear about, if great material for a book. Life intruded, as it will, and the Asia book receded to a far back burner—until, that is, Willie started looking through these graphic novels, which he found impressive and cool. I could tell from his eyes that he was all excited. "I gotta do it," he said as he flipped through them, shaking his head, gaining determination, "I gotta do it…"

And what he did was nab my box of new graphic novels and head for home with them, there to dig out all the journal entries (which he's transcribed) and begin working on a storyboard. Ken said that he could put him together with an illustrator, and said he'd be happy to help them along and would like to publish it if they actually do it.

I think my work here is done.

ANYBODY HERE SEEN GRUNDOON?

BEWITCHED, BEBOTHERED AND BEMILDRED
AT THE CHICAGO COMICON

In a lifetime of error and folly that includes two ruined marriages and the decision to become a freelance writer, the dumbest thing I ever did happened when I was a senior in high school. I was in love for the first time, but that wasn't the dumb part. Her name was Charlene, and she was wonderful. Sometimes I miss her still. It was spring and we were going steady and I'd never been so happy before. And so as a grand gesture of my love, and to show her how grownup I was, I gave her little brother my whole comic book collection. Well over a thousand of them, all in spiffy shape, some dating back to 1945 when I was four years old and started talking grownups into buying them for me. It pains me still to think about it. And it didn't do a bit of good. She dumped me for a returning college guy in May anyway; and her stupid little brother shredded and ruined these comics I had kept so carefully for so long. But I'd do it all over again if it had postponed her getting rid of me by even a little. She died a few years later when she was just 22, and like I say sometimes I miss her still—and can't help thinking about her whenever I see old comic books.

So walking into the 10th Annual Comicon at the Ramada O'Hare over Fourth of July weekend yanked me right back to that green April with her so long ago. God knows how many other such internal detonations were going on around me, since these two rooms of comics and allied low rent forms on display represented untold megatons of nostalgia gathered under one roof. The place was dangerous.

It's become the biggest comics convention in the country. Space at 178 tables was sold to more than 100 different dealers and vendors from all over. There were also discussion panels featuring comic artists and writers from such powers as Marvel and DC—as well as newcomers like Kitchen Sink, which largely devotes itself to Will Eisner, reprinting old Spirit Comics from the 40s and publishing his new stuff too; and Evanston's First Comics, whose titles *Grimjack, John Sable Freelance, Nexus, Badger* and *American Flagg* among others represent the new leading edge in comics, a generational shift, trying to steal Marvel's thunder just as Marvel did to DC in the early sixties.

Off in another sector of the Ramada, which was being torn up for remodeling during the three days of the Comicon, there were a couple of "artists' rooms," where various celeb artists sat selling sketches and signing autographs and for a small fee showing young aspiring artists how to improve their sketches. And on Sunday there was an original art auction of donated material whose proceeds went to some charitable cause or other. For comic books, altogether a fairly big deal.

Gary Columbuono, a participating dealer with three comics shops in the north suburbs, said there had never been more golden age comics—from the 1930s to the early 1950s—for sale in one place before. There were even three *Action* #1s from June 1938—the most prized comic in comicdom, since it marks Superman's debut and tells the story of his origins for the first time. (This incidentally was before he could fly; he got around making giant frog leaps; the flying came later.)

Certainly it was a visual treat—even if also a minefield of blasts from the past.

The main room had three wide aisles lined with tables mainly bearing box after box of comics stored upright in Mylar bags; and then on backdrop panels reaching nearly to the ceiling, the prizes and treasures were arranged on individual display—*hundreds* of them forming inviting seductive colorful gantlets, sweet bits and shreds of your past and mine everywhere I looked.

A *Whiz* comic I used to have, with dopey old Captain Marvel looking mighty and dopey on the cover, wearing his red longjohns and golden cape, throwing a car through a brick wall, Li'l Abner turned superhero. But I always liked him myself—and his nemesis Doctor Sivana, bald old scheming weasel that he was.

Stuff upon stuff. A Mickey Mouse mystery featuring inky creatures called The Blots, one I'd also owned way back when. Sets of bubblegum cards in a glass case, *Leave It To Beaver* cards and two sets of J.F.K. cards, the top one a family portrait on the White House lawn, Jackie in a pillbox hat and the kids so young. An enclave of movie posters, *The New Mutants* and *The Mummy*. A tableful of Japanese robot toys. One vendor with an incredible stash of fat squat Better Little Books—*Ken Maynard & The Gun Wolves of the Gila, Flash Gordon & The Witch Queen of Mongo, Jungle Jim & The Vampire Woman, Tail-*

spin Tommy & The Famous Payroll Mystery... Another table loaded with ancient newspaper comic strips gathered in globs, *Buck Rogers* from the 1930s, and even some *Little Nemos*, an opium dream of a strip from before the first World War. Original art panels from all periods, among them a dandy color Sunday *Pogo* strip going for $1500. *Godzilla* monster toys. A copy of *Sex Kitten* magazine proclaiming an all-Brigitte Bardot issue, a smiling BB in a very '58 party dress on the cover. Dr. Who books and paraphernalia. A Ricky Nelson comic, *The Hong Kong Adventure.* A *Joan of Arc Starring Ingrid Bergman* comic. An old Howdy Doody puppet lying crumpled but ever agrin. Some sheet music. Barbershop pinup calendars from the 40s, just like my grandfather used to have up in his basement workshop. A book dealer specializing in science fiction. Mint condition *TV Guides* from the 50s. But mostly comics, a sea of comics.

And some of them pretty expensive.

As part of the art market, which I guess they are, comics are fairly low rent—not that you can't drop a bundle on them if you keep at it. But the Rembrandts and Van Goghs here, all sell for less than $25,000—and these are only a handful. That *Action* #1 introducing Superman lists in the current *Comic Book Price Guide 1985* at $17,000 for a mint copy. But few golden age comics are mint, and the three for sale at the Comicon were going for around $2500. Another big one is *Detective* #27, where Batman made his first appearance in June 1939. A mint copy lists at $10,000. Yes, an appreciation of 170,000% and 100,000% respectively, since they both cost a dime when they came out, isn't too shabby. But the dollar figures are peanuts compared to other art markets.

Still, there are thousands on sale at the Comicon for around $20 apiece, which can add up real quick, and hundreds and hundreds more up around the $200+ range—some of them relatively new, such as Marvels from the early sixties, the first numbers of *Spiderman* and *Fantastic Four*, etc. *Fantastic Four* #1 from November 1961 lists mint at $1100. The second issue drops to $440 mint, down to $350 for #3 and $260 for #4—with issues down to 16 through 20 still fetching $44 each. While this isn't big bux, it still adds up if you go for a complete run.

Luckily, I'm a reformed collector myself.

I began collecting things as soon as I was old enough to have things, starting with comic books when I was four. Over the years I collected cigar bands, baseball cards, beetles, Tom Corbett Space Cadet cards, coins, stamps, *Galaxy* magazines (I still have those) and science fiction paperbacks, rocks, 45 records, and, starting in high school, old books I liked. Then came several years of ascetic poverty otherwise known as college, in which every spare cent went to draft beer and chasing girls. Vietnam improved my education by several years, and so from 1959 to 1967 while in school my collecting habit went on hold, except for cheap used books, which I told myself was not collecting but building resources, whatever that meant.

Then in 1967 I left school for a job on Michigan Avenue, and suddenly I had the impossible—extra money! My collecting habit kicked right back in. Remember those antique Wells Fargo belt buckles that suddenly appeared in the late sixties? Well, I collected them, even after they all proved to be fakes newly cast from old dies. Also I got into records in a big way, mostly rock & roll, which my sometime job as a record reviewer fueled quite nicely. And first editions. Piddley little stuff among serious book collectors, but first editions of books I loved: A few Mark Twains I could afford, including a beatup but genuine 1st of *Huckleberry Finn*; firsts with dustjackets of *On the Road* and *Dharma Bums*; an extravagant—for me—first of Melville's *Pierre*, my favorite Melville novel; and a few Faulkners, among them a beauty of *Light in August*. Also a signed *Other Voices, Other Rooms* and a *Young Manhood of Studs Lonigan*. Along with firsts of all of Pynchon's novels, and my *Galaxys*, plus a short run of early bound *Rolling Stone*s, these comprise my meager treasure trove.

So I used to be a collector, in a modest way, even as a grownup, but then I started freelancing. And bought an old house wracked with rot and neglect. And got married for a third and final time and last year had a new daughter, Maude. Now we're trying for a boy, whose name at the moment is Elvis. I figure my collecting days are pretty well over.

Also the gleam went out of it for me somewhere along the line. I think I maybe took enough acid back when we were doing that, that I kind of stopped believing in collecting, for myself anyway. I knew firsthand the pleasure of assaulting the chaos and meaninglessness all around by carving out a little corner of order within it by collecting something, anything, selecting from the absurd rushing mess a bit of order, meaning—and doing it yourself, just like Camus said you should. He was talking about moral social commitment more than accumulating souvenir tea spoons or *X-Men* comics, but you do what you can. So I understood the pleasures of collecting, had often bathed in them myself. Collecting anything. I know of a Federal Judge in Washington, D.C., who had the most complete collection of coprolites—yes, that's fossil doo-doo—outside the Smithsonian and the American Museum in New York. Each coprolite was kept under its own bell jar on varnished wooden shelves in his study. People will collect any goddamned thing. It gives us the impression we're contributing to the greater order of the universe, diminishing chaos by a notch. Also it's nice to have pleasing stuff around. But the acid or something reminded me of entropy, and I kept seeing or so I thought the sadness and futility of it—since it's all flux and flow, you know? Collecting seemed like trying to pin down the river, drive nails in water.

At least that's what I thought I thought before walking into the barrage of the Comicon. But once inside I wasn't so sure. I found myself wanting all of them, yearning for them, wanting to swim around in them the way Uncle Scrooge did with his money. So much for learning spiritual lessons and growing up. I missed my comic books! *Waaaaaaa…*

Summoning a measure of control, I decided to look for an old *Pogo*. It would give me an excuse to look through everything else, and with luck I would find one featuring Grundoon. As the old man of the sea in the crowd I now find myself in, only one other coot and myself remember the glory that was Pogo. Because no one can stop me, it's a Christmas tradition in our house to sing *Deck Us All With Boston Charlie, Walla Walla Wash, and Kalamazoo* at least three or four times over the holiday season. I still go Pogo. And I particularly wanted to find one with Grundoon in it, Miz Groundhog's chile, who would stand at the edge of the swamp and in musical gibberish sing the fishes onto land—because my 15-month-old daughter Maude constantly reminds me of him, being in what I think of as "Grundoon state." But only the other coot and I get the reference, so I wanted one with Grundoon to show my wife, Carol, what I was talking about.

I quickly found I wasn't the only one who still goes Pogo. In all these thousands of comics there were only a few—which means people who own them are hanging onto them. And none of them for sale at the Comicon had Grundoon in it—not that I could really afford them anyway. There weren't that many comic book appearances of Pogo in the first place. A December 1941 debut in *Animal Comics* which lists mint at $580. Another 25 or so appearances there; a stray *Albert the Alligator and Pogo Possum* from 1946 that's $325 in perfect shape; a one-time annual *Pogo Parade* from 1953 ($110 mint); and a run of 16 *Pogo Possums* from 1946-1954 that range from $45 to $325 apiece, mint. Too rich for my blood, and academic anyway since there were only a few well-read *Pogo Possums* on sale here. But some of them were chipped and spine-broke enough to be going for as little as $12. Hmmm, I began thinking, Grundoon or no Grundoon, it's still Pogo…

So now I am the proud owner of *Pogo Possum* #4, Feb-April 1951. On the cover Pogo is jumping through ringmaster Albert's hoop on a pogo stick and landing on poor Albert's tail, while a sleepy bored bluebird looks on. It's real nice—and not the beginning, I dearly hope, of a new comics collection.

The dealer I bought it from said Pogo is way up now—especially the Pogo paperback books from the mid-50s on. He had *The Pogo Puce Catalog*, yet another I used to own, shrinkwrapped and priced at $95. He said they go for so much because most of them haven't been reprinted in years, and people like me still want to read them—not just own them, he said. Pogo freaks usually

213

want them to read over and over—and the only way to do so is pay $100 a pop for these books that were $1.25 not thirty years ago.

While we were talking Pogo, the dealer next to us was talking Beatles to a couple of guys in their early twenties. They're all inspecting a group of four small Beatles movie posters, the kind that go in the small windows beneath the main poster. They're bargaining over price on what the dealer tells them baldly are Canadian piracies—known fakes, counterfeits, mind you—and are hundreds of dollars cheaper than the real thing, but which still are fetching $400. The dealer saying they're good to put up on your walls, you don't have to worry about destroying something valuable—something you'd never do with the real thing, of course. "This is even cheap for the piracies," he tells them. Another guy comes up and asks, "Can I see the #100 of *The Avengers?*" He's handed one. "Pristine mint copies," intones the dealer, "$20 apiece, guide. That's last year's guide, actually. Everybody who was an Avenger up to that time is in it. This is a classy cover..."

*** *** ***

In three days of wandering around, I noticed a couple of things.

First, that this is an almost exclusively male preoccupation. This didn't surprise me; it was more like proof that things hadn't changed in all those years since I'd been into it in a serious way, before love blinded me for the first of many times. It was guys then, and it's guys now. I hasten to add that I think it's because women have better sense. With few exceptions those I saw present at the Comicon were there as a kindness to some guy they were somehow connect-ed to—in a crowded hot room packed with all this old stuff, instead of at Fullerton Beach or picnicking in the back yard or anything else sane people did over the Fourth of July. It was overwhelmingly men pawing through the boxes of comics and asking dealers if they had this issue or that.

The demographics were what I think they call a bimodal curve. One large glob clustered in the 12-14 range when comics passion usually burns brightest, along with those other grotty male teen preoccupations—like science fiction and record collecting, not to mention heavy metal. I've heard Def Leppard concert crowds referred to as "Men Without Dates." And I once went to an early Sunday morning rock & roll swap meet in the parking lot of Capitol Records in Los Angeles, and not only was it all male, most of them had the complexions of cave fish, looked like they'd crawled out from under rocks—and this in sunny LA. The crowd at the Comicon looked generally healthier than that, but it did seem like there were maybe more people per square foot than in the general population who were overweight in really unusual ways.

But then there was also more long hair too, which is refreshing these days.

And then demographically there was a smaller glob, whose wallets only were fat, in the 35-45 range, lawyers and admen and brain surgeons who never got it out of their system and now had the money to buy on, to paraphrase Daredevil. Though not necessarily the taste. I saw one 3-piece sort drop seven or eight hundred dollars for a stack of *Classics Comics*. Ugh! Yuk! They were to both comics and the books they were based on the comic book equivalent of Muzak. Fek!

The other thing I noticed, after pawing through these bins for three days myself, was how this Comicon was a treasurechest of comics it hurt me to not own, the mere sight of them churning up emotion and memory like some Mixmaster whirring inside, stirring ambiguous strangely deep feelings more than a little sad in their reminder of sunny green days, bringing on true nostalgia, which the dictionaries say is a longing for home, homesickness—not the warm fuzzy remembrance of things past it's usually taken to mean, but hunger to go home, which seems to be located in the past. The trouble is you have to be Dr. Who to get there, since it's a dimensional not geographical yearning.

But looking through them I also noticed the exact opposite, that many of the comics gathered here were also a repository of the utterly forgotten, the never loved, the unimportant, of poignant Freudian significance to no one. Comics that never made it into our national mythology, barely even pop culture. They were published and they're still around, that's all; and now for sale here. It was a reminder that the comic book business is a business, no matter what dreamy types it attracts as customers; and that it too acted on those two time-honored principles, namely, throw it against the wall and see what sticks, and, when in doubt imitate success.

Have you ever heard, for instance, of *Buster Bunny*? *Vic Verity*? *Supermouse*? *Dopey Duck*? *Dizzy Duck, Dippy Duck or Dinky Duck*? Well, they all had their own comics. Remember *The Arizona Kid*? Me either. He lasted 6 issues in 1951. How about *Little Aspirin*, who lasted three issues in 1949? The mint #1 of it goes for $24—because Harvey Kurtzman, who went on to *Mad* and *Little Annie Fannie*, was the artist. Or these other *Littles: Little Ambrose, Little Audrey, Little Beaver, Little Dot, Little Groucho, Little Ike, Little Joe, Little Klinker, Little Lana, Little Lenny, Little Lizzy, Little Lotta, Little Max, Little Roquefort, Little Spunky...* How about *Fantoman* from 1940? His mint #1 lists at $245. *Moon Girl* from 1947? Her #1 is $315. *Wambi, The Jungle Boy*? He's mint #1 at $110. Or how about *War Against Crime* #11, the cover featuring an Indiana Jones type studying a manuscript in an Egyptian tomb, with a mummy leaning on a shovel in the background? The sell says "Another tale from The Vault of Horror." The asking price on this obscurity from February

1950 is \$145—but there's some slim excuse on this one. It was the precursor of *Vault of Horror* comics, one of the classic creepy E.C.s from the early fifties. But I mean the comic of the movie *Rhythm of the River* starring Bing Crosby, Mary Martin and Basil Rathbone? *Wacky Duck, Wacky Witch, Wacky Woodpecker* or *Wacky Quacky? Jim Solar Space Sheriff? Naza, Stone Age Warrior?*

*** *** ***

By Sunday afternoon I was ODing on comic books and so was practically everyone else. A few of the dealers had already packed up and split, so as to at least enjoy a bit of the long summer weekend outdoors. Even Wonder Woman was getting tired. She was a sweet Linda Carter semi-lookalike in authentic WW costume who was part of the DC booth and promotional display. Patiently all weekend she'd had her picture taken with kids and families, gracefully dodging an onslaught of bad jokes from would-be admirers. But by Sunday afternoon she was admitting to one young fan that her feet hurt, that the boots were custom made size 9 while her feet were a 10, and she couldn't wait to get them off. I knew exactly what she meant.

So I cut out early to catch a little of the Cubs game and forget about comic books for a while. Besides, there was another smaller Comicon coming up in October anyway; plenty of time to study the Price Guide and get the juices flowing again.

- 1985

I guess the article here might suggest that my notions of good parenting were slightly deranged, but you do the best you can. I just wanted my daughter Maude's musical education to begin as early as possible, that's all. So why wait until she was born?

The essay pretty much speaks for itself. I wrote it for Chicago *magazine in 1985. What strikes me about it all these years later—Maude turned 33 in April 2017—is that* Chicago *magazine would never publish an odd little article like this today. Which is less a diss on them than an emblem of how the world, and magazines along with it, has changed in that time.*

We didn't really think of ourselves as living in a more innocent era back then—doesn't every generation think it's the coolest, and that life is as fast and complicated and difficult as it has ever been in history?—but compared to today, and especially today's post-nuke media landscape in the wake of the I-Bomb, those were simpler, more easy-going times.

Magazines had plenty of ads then, so there were pages and pages of space to fill—since editorial material exists in magazines largely to keep the ads apart, of course—so why not devote a page or two to something as inconsequential as this piece? It contained no breaking news, no vital new information, nothing of any particular import…and, for Chicago *magazine in particular today, nothing about real estate, a trendy new restaurant, political scandal, top doctors, or money in its many enviable manifestations. Useless, you know?*

But that wasn't always the case. Over the years Chicago *magazine let me, again and again, write pieces for them that had little redeeming value beyond, I hoped, being good reads. My first article for them, in 1980, was called* Search for the Sagawau, *a mock-heroic account of an "expedition" down to a Forest Preserve on* the Southwest Side, where we explored "the only true Canyon in Cook County"—a dinky little affair, with a stream easily as wide as a double bed, and walls that had to tower, unquestionably, ten or fifteen feet above it. I wrote it in a portentious tone, as if we were Powell and company bravely risking our lives shooting the Colorado River through the Grand Canyon—and Chicago magazine didn't have anything better to do at the time than run it as a feature, with several pictures to boot. Knowing I could never get an actual assignment for something so loopy, I simply wrote it on speculation, without knowing a soul at the magazine, and sent it in cold.

Well, not quite cold. I am mainly writing this introduction as a big tip-of-the-hat to my longtime editor at Chicago magazine, Christine Newman. She and I had known each other slightly when we were both at Playboy magazine. It was she in whose lap the Sagawau piece landed, and she who championed publishing it to the other editors. And Maude Learns All About Music wouldn't have existed without her encouragment and shepherding through the wolf pack gantlet otherwise known as the editorial process. She was the most understanding and careful of editors, writing long handwritten edit notes to me using an actual fountain pen, and with flawless cursive penmanship, gently suggesting areas of improvement and pointing out deficiencies in a clear but friendly way, and then going over every single comma in the final edit. She was one of those rare editors—and I have suffered under dozens and dozens—whose editing actually improved my pieces, instead of steamrollering the voice or inserting discordant baloney into them, like so many who will go nameless here.

So, after Maude, this one's for Chris.

MAUDE LEARNS ALL ABOUT MUSIC

BEGINNING WITH A LITTLE
PRE-NATAL MOZART

It began I guess last February, a couple of months before my daughter Maude was born, with a Prenatal Mozart Concert. My wife, Carol, was lying in bed wearing a white flannel nightgown, the soft fabric clinging to the top of her epic belly's swell and falling softly from it in ski-slope miniatures. *The New Yorker* was resting on the apex, open to the latest Ann Beattie short story.

One reason Carol and I get along is that generally we find each other's peculiarities amusing, not insufferable material for divorce court. So when Carol saw me stalking toward her, Sony Walkman and headphones in hand, a strange grin on my face as I placed the headphones astride her belly and pressed the green button to start the tape, instead of calling the cops she said with a smile, "Doctor Benway, I presume?"

This was Maude's first exposure to music, although at the time she was named Willie or Emily or Ethan or K.E.—short for Kennedy Expressway.

I had never actually read, you understand, any of the mounds and pounds of baby books that Carol's fellow mom friends had lent her by the bagful. But I knew that babies were squirming little sponges who soaked up whatever was aimed their way, for better and worse. And that what went into you the first three years pretty much determined the way you dealt with the rest of the whole three-score-and-ten boogie, from your happy passions to your weird unspeakable neuroses, your values for life already setting the cement before you even hit play school.

So I figured we couldn't begin too early with one of the biggest passions:

Music.

I grew up in a household where music didn't exist—unless you count Julius LaRosa, the McGuire Sisters, Haleloke, and the rest of the gang who sang on my mother's beloved Arthur Godfrey radio show. We had no phonograph records to speak of. I remember only one fat 78 album of the *Nutcracker Suite* that got trotted out for the holidays. And my father, a paint company sales manager with a travelin' man's tastes, had a short stack of "party" records by a guy named Larry Vincent (and the Lookout Boys) that he'd play for the boys. One of my favorites—*I Used to Work in Chicago (In a Department Store)*—went in part: *Lady came in for a lamp, / I said, 'What kind did you come for?' / 'Floor,' she said, and floor 'er I did, / and they threw me out the door.* The only other titles by him I remember were *Wong Had the Longest Tong in China* and *She Has Freckles On Her But She Is Nice.*

Such was the rich musical environment of my early childhood.

So I was determined when Maude came along last April that she would do better than I had. Actually, she had little choice. One result of my early deprivation was that I became a music junkie.

For me, all music began in July 1955 with Chuck Berry's *Maybellene*. I'd just turned 14, and when I heard the first ringing guitar chords of *Maybellene* I knew that something new and wonderful was going on besides my hormones exploding.

Now I listen to music almost all the time, and will listen to almost anything except disco and grand opera—although I'm weakening on the latter. In a given week I'll play Cream, Howlin' Wolf, Brahms, Bob Marley, Peruvian flute music, apocalyptic gospel bluegrass by the Marshall Family or fine plain bluegrass by the Stanley Brothers, Elvis Costello, the Ink Spots, Miles Davis, the Dead Kennedys, Duke Ellington, the Budapest String Quartet, Marvin Gaye, the Doors, the Grateful Dead, Django Reinhart, Waylon Jennings, Willie, Little Feat, Kiss, Led Zeppelin, the Heptones, Buddy Holly, Wayne Fontana and the Mindbenders—plus the obvious Beatles and Rolling Stones and so on. The rest of the time I listen to whatever turns up on WFMT (an unsolicited testimonial).

Because I work at home and watch Maude for at least a couple of hours every day, she gets her daily dose like it or not, along with impromptu, lengthy, and untrained music lectures from me about what she's hearing.

For the first six weeks, she was still in a wide-eyed space-visitor E.T. state, when the look in her gray bright eyes said, Well, this is all great, but I don't get any of it, not one single thing. And she couldn't do anything yet like laugh or smile or happily pound the floor and coo or otherwise go, Swell, Pop, I dig this one. So I can't say for sure what kind of music Maude liked most at first.

Early on she was like Lefty, our cat who was displaced by Maude's arrival. (Lefty is now leading the gay bachelor life in a San Francisco condo.) I was always impressed with the way Lefty could totally ignore my sound system. Even with *Live at Leeds* or *Live Cream* or *Get Your Ya Ya's Out*—contrary to the usual production-brained studiophile thinking, live albums, as I've told Maude, are always the best, since they bring out the humanity, not the machinery—one or the other cranked up so far that the speakers were shredding and books were vibrating off the shelves, the way God intended. As I've explained to Maude, as a general principle, loud is good and louder is better. But for Lefty, the music, no matter how loud, was a new version of Zen silence. The sound simply didn't exist. Lefty used to like sleeping on my speakers with Led Zeppelin crashing below or Jimi Hendrix launching himself like Explorer 4 out toward Saturn.

And Maude, at first, was like the cat, at least with all recorded music. True, to save her ears for later, I mainly kept the volume down, her lessons about loud still chiefly theory unless I got excited. But in the beginning the music seemed to pass through her unnoticed, like gamma rays or made-for-TV movies.

Then one night last June, when Maude was pushing two months, we all went to dinner at our friends the Sullivans' apartment. After New Orleans-style meat loaf and a few beers, Jerry dragged out his old acoustic guitar and accompanied himself while singing us some nice old populist Woodie Guthrie song.

Maude went bananas. She was down on the floor as usual, baby surfing on her belly, going nowhere, with all four arms and legs waving in the breeze, like Mighty Mouse up in the cartoon clouds. But when Jerry started playing, she did her very first baby pushup and, arching her back, raised her head and grinned in wonder. Then she started laughing, a succession of happy goat sounds. This wasn't her first recorded laugh—that came about while she was taking a close look at her dear old dad's face—but it was among the first. Maude was delighted.

Which is how we eventually arrived at Baby Mozart Hour.

She had seemed to like the simple clarity and presence of Jerry's guitar, so the next morning, instead of continuing our history of doo-wop, I began to think, simple, clear, less is more; nursery minimalism.

I thought I'd start with an album of Baroque lute music, try her out on a little Johann Pachelbel and Dietrich Buxtehude, with J.S. Bach's Suite in G Minor on the flip side. As the record began to play, I told Maude that lutes were a distant old relative of that quintessential instrument, the electric guitar; that in Shakespeare's time lutes were extremely popular but that by the mid-1700s their vogue was gone, partly because of changing fashion brought on by new technology (the piano, for instance, was invented in Florence in 1709). And this was not so different from the eclipse suffered by the saxophone and the trumpet, which had been the instruments of the 1940s, until the electric guitar started taking over in the 1950s. In both cases the inheriting instrument could be played louder than what went before, further proof of the natural superiority of loud.

Maude found the Baroque lutes and my erudite commentary so fascinating that she fell asleep on the rug. This was the auspicious beginning of Baby Mozart Hour. Thereafter I played Maude a daily sampling of things I thought she might like. At first I struck out.

I tried John Fahey, and she did look toward the speaker once during a waterfall cascade of notes, but even on solo guitar Fahey was a little too busy and advanced. During a clean, clocklike Bach quartet, she preferred staring at lint on the rug. Reggae was OK as long as I sang along, but I knew that my goofiness was what she really liked—and it seemed a little early to be singing *Get up, stand up, stand up for your rights* to her, since she couldn't even crawl yet. An accidental brush with Barry Manilow on the radio made her cry, so I knew that she took after me, was my girl.

But O, O, O, that Amadeus rag! It's so elegant, so intelligent…

It was Mozart's Piano Sonata No. 1 in C Major, K. 279, played by Lili Kraus, that did it—the very same one I'd played for her before she was born. The sweet, simple trills and rills of the first movement, like green blooming spring itself, had Maude beaming and searching the room for the source. I had a flash that the sonata was a happy correlative, that it sounded like the inside of Maude's brain—bright, sunny, uncorrupted morning in there.

So then every day for a month I played this same Mozart sonata for Maude, and expressed my feeling to her that Mozart is the golden mean between mathematical Bach and *Stürm und Dräng* Beethoven, geniuses both but often out of touch with the pleasing cosmic harmony that came to Mozart as unconsciously as breathing. Who cares if he was into toilet jokes? Personally he might have been Buddy Hackett—which isn't so bad—but until Duke Ellington, I told Maude, Mozart's music comes closest to being the music of the spheres.

I came to look forward to Baby Mozart Hour as my morning music—a drastic change for someone who for years, just to get my mean, scarred old heart going, had started most days with the *Crossroads* side of *Wheels of Fire* turned up to state-of-the-art loud. Maude at three months had already taught me about lightening up with Mozart in the morning.

And then came Mojo Motion!

Gradually, Maude was learning to work those appendages branching out of her. From tranquil, immobile space creature she was soon goating around the floor looking for the next thing to stuff into her mouth, her grandest baby dream being, I am certain, to stuff the entire world at once into her mouth. That would be heaven itself.

As soon as she could move in even the shakiest, least certain fashion, slipping and sliding on the carpet, taking a header every so often, she went straight for my record boxes.

True, she was more intrigued by the cellophane still on some of the albums than anything else. She loved to take a tiny pinch and hear it crinkle before jamming it into her mouth. So I got rid of all the cellophane and plastic wrap on the albums she could reach. But she still went for them.

Maude's first personal album selection was *Deguello*, a 1979 album by ZZ Top. She pulled it out while I wasn't looking and was chewing contentedly on it when I finally noticed.

So I played it for her, not telling her that *deguello* is Spanish for a slaughtering, or butchery. No point in encouraging any nascent New Wave tendencies yet. I did tell her that she could have done worse, that ZZ Top is a group of three white Texas guys who play black urban blues with a Texas rocker kick; that while it wasn't the real thing like Howlin' Wolf or Muddy Waters or John Lee Hooker or Little Walter, they were at least stealing water from the right well.

And there was a semi-inspired version of Elmore James's *Dust My Broom* on the album, which led me to tell her all about how lucky she was to be born in Chicago, where the electric urban blues that led to rock and roll were born and where you could still hear the real thing. And that these were the guys the Rolling Stones were stealing from when they came along, and how they got rich while the bluesmen at best got by.

But this was all too heavy for Maude at five months.

The next album she picked was one I didn't know I owned, one James Boyk in concert at Cal Tech playing Robert Schumann's *Scenes from Childhood*, Opus 15, on solo piano. I swear, I'd never listened to it (I used to review records, and albums have slipped unplayed into my collection over the years), so we did. It proved sweeter than the Mozart, and less inspired for it, but definitely in the same ballpark. I guess Maude told me.

I have to admit that I'm a little disturbed by the latest phase in Maude's musical development. It started a week or so ago. She's seven months old now and still loves to pull out my albums. I figure it's as good as the *I Ching*, so I usually play them for her. She's also working on entering the third dimension—big stuff like sitting up on her own and, miracle of miracles, pulling herself up into a standing position.

When Maude pulled out the Rolling Stones' *It's Only Rock 'n' Roll (But I Like It)*, I simply took it as another instance of her innate good taste and put it on for her. As usual I was futzing around at my desk, and sat back down and began typing. But the title cut always gets me going, and when I looked up to point out Keith Richard's tasty rhythm guitar to Maude, I found her standing up, holding on to her red playpen with one hand and shaking a red rattle with the other. When she started sort of goat-shouting along, I really got worried. I had an awful premonition.

"Please be careful, Maude," I told her. "*Please.* I want you to love this stuff, but you stay away from that Mick Jagger. Keith Richard, too. He has his blood changed to cross international borders. I know they'll be nearly 60 when you're 15, but I don't trust either one of them. Please, Maude—don't ever take food or rides from strangers, or ever be a backup singer for the Rolling Stones!"

It was my first parental epigraph for her.

Maude just grinned and shook the rattle harder, goat-shouting away.

- 1984

I grew up geographically deprived. It's probably why I've been driven all my life to travel as much as I could possibly manage—including a 20-year stint as a freelance writer, during which I wrote as many travel pieces as I could, no matter how badly paying, just so I could get to someplace new. The reason for this was simple: Cleveland, Ohio. Tom Passavant, a friend from earlier days at Playboy *magazine, and the longtime editor of* Diversion *magazine, for whom I wrote nearly 50 articles between 1984 and 2000, used to say he enjoyed my pieces because I liked everywhere he sent me. Again, Cleveland: Anywhere seemed better and more interesting. That's not entirely fair to Cleveland, of course, but the moment I first went elsewhere—by train on the Empire Builder, from Cleveland all the way to Portland, Oregon, with my Aunt Maude, when I was 11—the cruel secret was revealed. I had been born in the wrong place. I remember the exact moment: We were having lunch in the dining car, at a table set with a white linen tablecloth and shining heavy silverware. A white-jacketed black waiter put my lunch plate before me—the very first trout I had ever eaten—while he pointed out the window to make sure I didn't miss the herd of elk gathered there on a dry meadow, with mountains as backdrop. Mountains!*

We were going through Glacier National Park, and my life was forever changed. This fabulous assault of the new—the dining car, the trout, the elk out the window, the mountains, all as we sped along to the rolling clickclack sound of the moving train—was almost too much for me. And it hit me in a flash: What else lay beyond flat drab rusting Cleveland, asleep on the frothy brown polluted south rim of America's first official Dead Lake? I had to find out.

I didn't realize at the time that Aunt Maude had offered to take me to visit my mother's sister in Salem, Oregon, largely because she loved opening up the world to kids, me especially, but also as a way of shielding me from some of the uglier realities my mother was going through in getting a divorce, finally unable to put up with my colorful but useless alcoholic father, whose drinking had by then moved beyond colorful into dangerous and abusive, so extreme that my mother, despite the conservative tsk tsk tsk values of the time that considered divorce a desperate unthinkable act, was forced to do it, for her own safety and mine.

I mention all this because it meant we went from being sorta semi upper middle class—Pop the showboat bought a new car almost every year, and we had the very first TV on our block, in 1948, when TV barely existed, and was such a modern wonder that I remember neighbor kids sometimes peeking in our front window to see this marvel firsthand. But my mother hadn't had a job in nearly 10 years, and before that was a secretary at the American Can Company—so right after the divorce we moved in with my grandparents, and when she finally got a job, as a clerk in the repairs department of a Ford agency, we were closer to being poor than I ever quite realized at the time. And of course my father seldom came up with alimony or child support.

So any dreams of further travel I entertained remained just that, dreams. About then I began collecting postage stamps, starting with those bags of mixed stamps from countries all over the world, sorting them, looking up the countries in the World Book Encyclopedia *my old man had bought us before his downward spiral, dreaming as I read of what these places might be like to see, dreaming, dreaming...*

And even though I guess they were pretty lame as music, songs on the radio fed these dreams too. I'd like to get you on a slow boat to China....Far away places with strange sounding names...

One in particular caught my imagination. Probably due to my age—I was a high school sophomore in 1957 when it came out—and not only did it evoke an enchanting place, it was also about sadly leaving a girl behind. In my experience so far the girls had pretty much left me *behind, but still it spoke to the dreaming traveler in me...*

Down the way where the nights are gay
And the sun shines daily on the mountain top
I took a trip on a sailing ship
And when I reached Jamaica I made a stop

Down at the market you can hear
Ladies cry out while on their heads they bear
'Akey' rice, salt fish are nice
And the rum is fine any time of year

Sounds of laughter everywhere
And the dancing girls swing to and fro
I must declare my heart is there
Though I've been from Maine to Mexico

Something about the song made me yearn to see this exotic place—a place so exotic to me that it became the talisman of all those places I had never seen, and probably would never see. Jamaica became my own personal Shangri La.

But sometimes miracles do happen. And sometimes more than once.

By the time I went to Jamaica to watch them make Club Paradise *in 1985, I had been lucky enough to get there three times before—and unlike so much of life, Jamaica hadn't disappointed me. The more often I went, the more seductive it became.*

I didn't get there until 1980, when I was almost 40—but it did happen at last.

The first time was a socalled "press trip"—which is travel industry code for "junket." It was me and a handful of other lowrent freeloading travel writers, on a freebie sponsored by the Jamaican government, with a focus on…are you ready?… birdwatching opportunities around the island. I confess. It's another of my character defects. And one thing among many that I like about it is the fact that it takes you to places you wouldn't go otherwise. So we spent zero time at the north shore resorts or Negril—but we did go to a spot up in the hills above Montego Bay, near the village of Anchovy, to visit Lisa Salmon, a locally famous birdwoman, at home, the back patio of her modest little country house festooned with feeders of all kinds, including sugar-water-drip tubes for hummingbirds. A substantial heavyset woman of indeterminate late middle age, she was a sort of "bird whisperer," so familiar and friendly to the birds that came there that these wild lovely creatures would land on her extended finger and perch on her ample shoulders, feeling completely safe and at home with her. For a small fee to pay for the feeders and the privilege of being there with her, you could sit for an hour or two on that patio drinking tea while being close to a shifting crowd of colorful birds most people only saw distantly through binoculars if at all. This included a number of "doctor birds," or streamertail hummingbirds, with shimmering tails twice as long as their bodies, that are Jamaica's spectacular national bird, and represented on its $2 bill.

On that trip too we ventured into the "cockpit country," a part of the island few tourists see, which begins about ten miles south of the north coast not quite halfway between the resort enclaves of Montego Bay and Ocho Rios, and extends from there another ten miles or so into the interior. It is a wild rugged up-and-down landscape that provided a hideout for the Maroons in their rebellion against Spanish and British rule, a place still lightly populated, and home to a traditonal way of life—lots of donkeys instead of cars—far from the zip and pop around the resorts or in Kingston. Here too remains the largest contiguous rainforest on the island. We spent a day exploring this little visited part of Jamaica, truly out in the country, and even saw a Jamaican Lizard Cuckoo. I know that cuckoos are nest parasites—the Mayzie the Lazy Bird of real birds—depositing their eggs in nests made by other species, for more responsible mothers to raise while they head for the beach or a bar, but despite their disreputable habits, they sure are great-looking.

The next trip, a couple of years later, was something else entirely, and far less memorable for it. This was another junket, and even more of a freeloader's dream I guess, but not for this freeloader: A tour to sample a number of the island's most high end rental villas, a different $500 a night joint for seven days. I still pretty cheerfully live like a graduate student—one bedroom apartment, junker '89 Buick my son is embarrased to be in—so this one didn't hit any of my own fantasies.

But the one after that, in January 1985, just a few months before the Club Paradise *trip covered in the article here, was memorable in quite another way. Kim and Mary Angelo, friends of Carol's—wife #3 for those keeping score—had rented a modest villa on the north shore a few miles east of Ocho Rios, right on the ocean, and it had a couple of extra bedrooms, so they invited us, and Maude, our new 9-month-old daughter, to join them for a week or so. Get out of Chicago in January? Where do I sign up? Beachy peace and quiet, with, they told us, its own lime tree in the yard for absolutely perfect gin & tonics. We were there.*

Except it wasn't quite the tranquil tropical experience we had anticipated. We'd been there all of one day when the whole island went up for grabs. The government had announced a noticeable hike in the gasoline tax, and people were pissed—pissed enough to stage protests all over the island. I hadn't known before this that one common accepted form protest takes in Jamaica is creating roadblocks by piling old tires, preferably fat truck tires, in the middle of the highway circling the island, and setting fire to them. Big stinky smoky traffic-stopping fires. Despite the way it was reported back home, the situation wasn't particularly scary, and the people shot in Kingston were members of rival parties, out being rivals—but it did mean we couldn't go sightseeing round the island for recreation.

But hey, no problem, mon. We didn't want to go anywhere anyway. We had that glorious white sand beach right out the front door, Kim and Mary had hired a terrific cook who dazzled us with local dishes, we had a boombox that played great reggae when it wasn't giving updates on the "disturbances"—and we had that lime tree, plus an ample supply of Beefeater's.

But don't misunderstand. We didn't stay bombed all the time—there was sweet new Maude to care for. In fact my favorite memory of the time there was getting up with, well, the birds, and taking Maude out to look at them with me. Exploring the enclave of villas, I had found a forlorn unused busted-blacktop road cut along a hillside through thick scrub and trees, relic of some developer's failed dreams. Its only present use was as a freelance garbage dump, and at intervals along it trash heaps accumulating on the downhill side of the road. In most respects a blemish on the paradisical face of Jamaica—except for the birds.

So early every morning during the few days of the roadblocks, I would lash Maude to my chest in her blue snuggly, and we would take a slow peaceful walk along this decaying overgrown road—which provided an "edge" through the greenery, useful both to my purposes and those of the birds, providing a small open convergence of habitats where there is more action, foodwise, than deep in the thickets.

Maude cooing & kicking & grabbing at my binoculars also made it more of a challenge than it might have been otherwise. Even so we saw some amazing birds—probably the best were the Doctor Birds, hovering at a flower like some bright dream. But we also saw a clangorous flock of Smooth-Billed Anis complaining for space in the same palm tree, and they look like great fat crows with Jimmy Durante beaks. Also Jamaican Orioles, snazzier even than the Baltimore, plus Zenaida Doves, Stripe-Headed Tanagers, Jamaican Euphonias—and a small flock of Guiana Parrotlets, limegreen birds feeding high in a tree, the first parrotish birds I'd ever seen that weren't behind bars. And all this on a road that would seem ugly and useless to most people.

Then early one evening as the falling sun slowly set fire to the sea, I headed for the beach by myself for a final dip, and ran into a couple of local kids sporting serious dreadlocks, 500-watt smiles, and one looked around before reaching into a cloth shoulder bag in bright rasta colors, red, gold, and green, pulling out a truly impressive spliff and offering it to me. Well, why not? We split the joint while admiring the flaming sea, and they said they had more if I was interested. So we talked price a bit, settled that, but there was one kicker—the ganja was back at their village a couple of miles up in the hills. Could I drive them up there to get it? Now, I figured this was maybe not the most sensible thing I had ever contemplated doing—heading into the hills as darkness fell with two guys whose reliability credentials consisted of sharing a a joint with me—but it was a really topnotch joint, you know? So I said wait a minute, and went back up to the villa to see if Kim might be talked into lending me his rental car. When I explained the errand I saw smiling disbelief on Kim's face, but he just asked, "Are you really sure you want to do this?" while handing me the keys. The car was an ultra-basic little stick shift model, it should be added. So soon we were off into the darkling hills on a narrow bumpy dirt road with not a streetlight in sight, and me, the stoned driver, trying to keep track of fleeting landmarks briefly illuminated by the headlights. "Right here, turn you right." I hooked the right onto a narrower dirt track that was even steeper, and in moments we were in a gathering of plain small unpainted concrete buildings more suggestive of bunkers than not. They told me to stop here. "Soon come, mon." It's hard to describe this next. While they went into one of these little concrete buildings, I realized that my car was on this impossibly narrow street pointing more straight up than not, or so it seemed, but I noticed a turnout and so decided while they were gone I would see if I could turn the car around using it. Baaaad idea. As I turned onto the pulloff I realized, rather too late, that it only extended not very many feet at all before doing an undrivably steep plunge into darkness. Hit those brakes, Dave! I tried putting it in reverse, but as I said, it was stick shift, and before I could get the gears engaged, the car slipped forward another couple of feet toward a slope steeper than any car would handle without careening down out of control. I was fucked for sure. By then my "friends" had reappeared, and, seeing the predicament I'd gotten myself into, naturally burst into truly joyful laughter—they hadn't expected anything this funny. Myself, I was picturing rolling down the declivity, crashing the car, seeing many $$$$$$ for car repairs, more for the towtruck if one could even be found, and the deep profound embarassment, the folly of heading into the pitch black hills with a couple of teenagers I'd never seen before an hour earlier, the expense, stupidity and shame of it all—how right they were to be laughing, they and the crowd of their neighbors that had spontaneously materialized in the couple of minutes all this had taken.

But here is one of the many reasons I love Jamaica. Without even discussing it as far as I could tell, about ten or so of the biggest strongest guys in the gathered crowd just got their hands on the car, most in front but others grabbing handholds through the windows, and, still grinning and laughing, told me to put it in neutral, and then as if the car were weightless, easily pushing it back toward the little track and turning it so it was aiming back the way we came. The two teenagers and I did our little deal—it did prove to be primo buds—and I was heading back down the hill, which proved easier than I had thought it might be because, doh! all I had to do *was follow the track downhill until I hit the main road. Soon I had a gin and tonic in hand, with pungent smoke rising in silver swirls above my head.*

Which leads to the article here, the last and most memorable of my Jamaica adventures.

Please read on…

COOL RUNNINS

IT'S A LONG WAY FROM CLUB SANDWICH
TO CLUB PARADISE

Sweet early morning along a country road outside Port Antonio, Jamaica. It's almost heaven. Green, exotic, serene, gorgeous in an aggressive tropical way, the seductive beautiful threat of jungle everywhere, even in the cleared fields and yellowgreen banana orchards and tiny pastel houses set like painted saltboxes on scraped-out lots along a road rising dipping and curving through hills which if left to their own devices would really rather be rainforest. The only sound in the cool early air is a musical contention of rival mockingbirds, chasing and scolding each other over love and real estate.

But then turning a corner onto a yet smaller gravel lane, heading north toward the sea, which should be even quieter, it is instead total mayhem. Cars and vans everywhere, parked or snarled in a traffic jam at this nowhere intersection on this nowhere little country byway. Guys shouting into two-way radios spitting static at them. A roadblock marked NO PRIVATE VEHICLES BEYOND THIS POINT. Noise and confusion. Locals lounging at the corner watching it all.

It may look like an outing of the Jamaica Traffic Jam Fanciers Society, but this is really the fringes of Hollywood. Down below on the beach, they're making a movie called *Club Paradise*.

Hired drivers in vans shuttle visitors down and up the narrow twisty gravel road to the beach, which is an adventure every time since it's a brushy one-way track supporting heavy two-way traffic, with bailout widespot turnouts every so often, rearview mirrors rubbing ears as they pass.

There's a line of trucks parked a quarter mile up the hill from the beach, blocking the road, so we get out and walk, me and Don Levy, the movie's publicist, whose job I am this week as the Announced Journalist.

At the bottom is the entrance to Club Paradise, the funky-but-nice beach resort. And which they will tear down when they're done shooting, since it's all just fake façades, otherwise known as movie magic.

Standing around the entranceway are a mixed covey of Jamaican police and private security guards, the police with their sporty distinctive red stripe down the seam of their black trousers, the security guards in army brown shirts and black trousers. I don't know who's responsible for security, but Mayor Daley would have approved.

The level of chaos on the beach is even higher, human Brownian movement.

On the beach over in a far corner of the cove, a wind machine is filling a silky red-and-yellow parasail. The stunt crew is working on Andrea Martin's broken-rope parasailing scene, where she lands, an exhilarated new woman, in the palm trees.

In that scene, Steve McClosky *is* Andrea Martin. He's a sandy-mustached stuntman from Orlando, who as Andrea will wear a dark wig and be seen from a distance only.

They're having a problem with the prevailing wind.

The wind machine and powerboat combo are getting Steve up from the beach, but above the rocky bluff the wind he hits wants to blow him down against the rocks. I watch one try where he seems barely to miss scraping his ass or worse as he soars low over the point before heading out to sea. He told me he preferred jumping out of airplanes to this.

Not far down the beach another cell of crew spends the morning swarming over a large long black steel thing getting longer, building it like the neck of a life-sized erector set brontosaurus, something for use in a long tracking shot along the beach. In their obscure busy purpose they remind me of ants, but then aren't we all?

Skinny shirtless British assistant directors running all over the place, two-way radios always in hand, riding herd like sheepdogs, getting things and people to where they belong under ever-shifting conditions.

This includes keeping track of all the extras, many of them dreamy and unprofessional, since they were recruiting for background tourists here in May, on a part of the island where there basically aren't any tourists this time of year.

No wonder all the A.D.s look like marathoners and frown a lot while on duty.

The whole crew is British, somehow cheaper than an American crew because they're shooting in Jamaica, but also by general consent better than any other location crews.

Lee Brothers Electric, the sparks, out of London, are legendary. They'll go anywhere without blinking an eye. The matto grosso of Bolivia, the Green Hell from which no one has ever emerged alive? You got it, guv.

They're shooting in May, hotter and rainier than the winter months, because Warner Brothers was so desirous of having Bill Murray play Island Jack. And Warner's was so betting that since Murray and director Harold Ramis were old pals, and since Ramis had cowritten the final script with Murray's very own brother Brian Doyle, well, they were so sure he'd go for it they booked a million dollars' worth of hotel rooms here in January.

But then Murray didn't want to do it anyway, telling Ramis he felt like he'd done the character before, that it reminded him of *Meatballs* with grownups.

And so the studio *ate* the million dollars worth of high season resort hotel bookings, and now they're shooting in May with Robin Williams playing Island Jack.

It's ultimately a much better choice, actually, judging from the bits and shreds I saw them shoot over a week's time, Williams bringing an *edge* to the character it's hard to imagine pussycat Murray bringing to the part. Williams may not be as bankable as Murray right now—but then who is these days?—but he seems better for this one.

This morning they're shooting an establishing shot of Club Paradise.

The planeload of guests has survived its arrival on Joe's Airlines ("The Charter They Come"), piloted by a fearful drunken and nearsighted Joe Flaherty, in a performance that brought cheers during the dailies.

The lucky-to-be alive guests are now being driven to Club Paradise by co-owners Island Jack and Curtis Reed, the latter played by Jimmy Cliff, in his first movie since *The Harder They Come.*

So the scene is all of them rattling down the hill in Cool Runnins, the *Club Paradise* Bus, onto the grounds for the first time.

They've mounted a camera behind the driver's seat of Cool Runnins, for a new-guest's-eye view of coming onto the club grounds. Jimmy Cliff in a sunny yellow shirt is driving, and Robin Williams in his bogey straw hat and red print shirt is riding shotgun, turned back toward the camera, reassuring the new arrivals imagined there.

Behind the camera sits director Harold Ramis in a pink LaCoste shirt, smoking an unfiltered cigarette, leaning his head out a window for a breath of air. By now it's mid-day, and the breeze has disappeared. It's murderously hot, humidity weighing like layers of lead plate. Fit only for comic mad dogs and Englishmen making movies. And so there goes Harold in his pink shirt, placidly smoking, riding down and up the hill again and again, take after take, with that same semi-smile on his face, in this killer heat.

The background choreography of happy vacationing extras is repeated and repeated with slight variation, like *Last Year at Marienbad Meets Where The Boys Are.*

Thank god moviemaking is so slow and boring and repetitious. Otherwise it would be a *totally* enviable way to make a living. Hanging out in the best places in the world, the love and adulation of total strangers, plus more zeroes at the end of paychecks than most of us manage even to dream about. But thank the good lord it is dull tedious work. There is at least that. As Peter O'Toole, who's also in this, playing the dotty island governor, put it to me: "I get paid the fabulous sums for the bloody waiting. The acting I do for the fun of it."

The amount of detail, the convergence of energy, thousands of man-hours worth, that goes into getting 90 minutes of comedy out the other end is absolutely mindboggling.

They've taken over an entire resort for office space, for instance. The draftsmen, art department, transportation people, assistants to the assistants, all have as offices duplex resort suites, with little kitchens and green views of the landscaped grounds.

They so dried up the local vehicle pool they had to convince the local LAAT dealer—this is an eastern bloc vehicle that makes old Russian jokes live again—to turn out all the new cars in his showroom on lease to the movie company.

On the far side of Port Antonio, they've turned a big warehouse into the carpentry shop, from which the fake Club Paradise set was built.

They're even rebuilding and spiffing up the downtown square a bit, to make it look, I guess, more authentically Caribbean, repairing reality one more time.

All this $19 million activity is all the stranger to me because none of it would be happening if Chris Miller and I hadn't had a terrible time at a Club Med in March 1979.

He was recovering from oral surgery. I was suffering from the aftershocks of a divorce, entirely my doing, which made it hurt even more. So Chris suggested that we go to a Club Med, the swinging one on Guadelupe. I knew it was a bad idea but had nothing better to do.

We were wildly out of place, at least 10 years older than everyone else, a group tending toward young nurses and boy execs on their first tropical vacations.

It was awful, like being trapped in a singles bar for a week.

I did have one romantic interlude. She was a nurse from the Mayo

Clinic, radiant in her trade, and we strolled one night along the beach holding hands beneath the Milky Way's creamy smear across a velvet sky, while she told me with great love and affection about the magical sound of open heart surgery, the deep moving crunch like timber cracking when they broke open the chestbone, what a thrill it was, sighing and looking up at the sky at the wonder of it all.

When we got back, Chris and I decided to write a humor piece about it for *Playboy* or *Oui*, one of those—at the very least to vent our spleen, and more importantly, to write off the trip for the IRS. We sat in my living room tossing around ideas for a couple of hours, getting deeper and deeper into libel and slander. Then we both sort of simultaneously had the same flash: this would make a great movie. And so was born *Club Sandwich*. Carol, my then-new girl-friend and final wife-to-be, thought of the title.

Chris, along with Doug Kenney and Harold Ramis, had been one of the writers of *Animal House*. Doug had since formed a production company with Michael Shamberg, now producer of *Club Paradise*, and Allen Greisman, who's executive producer. They had an arrangement with 20th Century Fox and were looking for properties.

So Chris went out to Hollywood to pitch *Club Sandwich*. And then wonder of wonders, they said yes. We had a deal.

Chris now refers to this project as his Vietnam. It was mine too.

Neither of us, it turned out, really knew how to write a screenplay. I had never written one before, and Chris had co-written only one, huge success though it was.

And while all three of them had contributed to the actual writing of *Animal House*, Chris's chief contribution had been his *life*. It was his real-life experiences at Dartmouth in the early '60s that the whole thing started from. But it had been Harold who supplied most of the structure, with Doug providing inspired loony thoughts along the way.

We worked on our script for more than a year, daily sinking deeper and deeper into the quagmire, the Lyndon & Nixon of screen comedy. Don't misunderstand. We wrote some very funny stuff. But none of it ever hung together. We had lots of nice shiny ornaments but no Christmas tree.

Among our main characters in the first draft of this beach comedy was a creature from outer space, taking a vacation tour of this part of the universe. Like a giant friendly mop, the Alien had many tentacles and six eyes on long stalks, and had learned English by listening to Henry Kissinger voice tapes. "Vell? Volleybowl anyvon?" He was sweet—or rather *it* was. Another character in that one was Sol the Shark, the actual shark from *Jaws*, now wearing gold chains and visiting Club Sandwich to get away from the phonies in Hollywood.

There was a time warp in that one, too, with a samurai warrior suddenly appearing on the nude beach. And the head nurse seems at first to be a Nazi-built android, but proved to be another alien from outer space, an evil one which like Proteus can change its shape, which it turns out our friendly alien can do too, and the end was a battle of giant aliens on the nude beach.

Our main characters were a hapless pair of 60s-vintage dope dealers named Woodstock Nathan and Fillmore West, who are trying to hide out from the law in this square, awful resort. We were hoping for Tim Matheson for Fillmore and John Belushi for Woodstock, that's how long ago this was.

Our producers, including Doug, weren't exactly thrilled by this draft, and in retrospect it's hard to blame them.

They brought us out to Hollywood and put us up in suites at the Chateau Marmont for a month of meetings and rewrites. They explained that the only people interested in old hippies are other old hippies.

This was the summer of 1980, and would be Doug Kenney's last, though no one knew that in June.

For me it was heady stuff.

Getting our daily visitors' pass to the 20th Century Fox lot, past the two blocks or so of city streets circa 1900, a bit of London among the palm trees. A $170K Lamborghini in the parking lot with the vanity plate RERITE. Stars everywhere. I even got to meet Mel Brooks' desk. Mel was out at the time. Glamorous foxy Fox president Sherry Lansing sitting two tables away at lunch, other tables variously filled with firemen or eskimos depending on what they're shooting that day. Sitting next to Starsky himself at the Imperial Gardens sushi bar on Sunset, getting advice from him regarding California roll and other west coast sushi creations I'd never heard of. Drinks at the Whiskey with Doug and Brian Doyle Murray and the real Johnny LaRue, John Candy. Being passed a joint by Father Guido Sarducci at an early roughcut screening of *Caddy Shack*, which Harold and Doug were just finishing that summer, a pre-cleaned-up Chevy Chase puffy and sitting there looking zoned. On and on. One afternoon in Beverly Hills I saw the back of what looked like a dry cleaner's van open, and out stepped Burt Lancaster in a suit. I swear. This was all a long way from my usual haunts and pursuits.

Poor Doug was falling apart. His attention span was getting shorter and shorter. Weird-looking characters in restaurants would hand him vials of coke under tables. The only objects in the living room of his new Laurel Canyon house were a couch and a big green Hefty bag full of topnotch Hawaiian dope. One morning at a 9 o'clock meeting at Fox, we all watched amazed as Doug paced like a cat trapped until his coke connection arrived, laying a ridge of it from elbow to wrist along his arm and snorting it all up, smiling for the first time that day. And this was our producer. In fact, he wanted to direct *Club Sandwich*.

Even in this condition Doug was usually smarter about things than the rest of us put together. That's what did him in, I think. As P.J. O'Rourke wrote in a recent *National Lampoon* memorial issue to Doug, he was just too smart for his own good. I could tell that in June. Doug couldn't help seeing the void lurking everywhere around the edges of things, couldn't' shove it aside with the mundane pleasures and distractions like the rest of us. As O'Rourke says, you got the feeling he saw all the implications of everything, all the time, and couldn't shut it off, or could do so only through the most extreme derangement of the senses.

Here's one about Doug: He and Henry Beard were still co-editing the *Lampoon* in New York. Doug showed up at his usual after-work cocktails joint one afternoon already a little greased, continuing through happy hour with a certain dedication. There was probably some artificial energy in there too, because as I was told this, Doug didn't sleep all night, but found himself at his own apartment around the time regular people go to work. And Doug was a moral creature, something else that probably did him in. All-night fucked-up on this particular morning, but a moral thoughtful man. So he dug out a handgun he'd gotten somewhere, went downstairs and hailed a cab for the *Lampoon* offices. He went straight to Matty Simmons' office—he the originator of the Diner's Club Card in the 50s and the publisher/major investor of the *Lampoon*. Maybe you have to have heard Matty Simmons stories to appreciate this. But Doug went straight to his office, the big boss's office, and pulled a gun on him. Then Doug reached for the phone and dialed 911. When the police answered, he gave the address and said: "Get over here fast as you can. I've cornered a dangerous criminal!"

Doug's advice to us on our rewrite of *Club Sandwich*, repeated often enough we came to believe him, was: "Follow your own worst instincts."

This we interpreted to mean do whatever pleased us most, despite Shamberg & Greisman's repeated pleas that we bring it back to Earth and make it less surreal.

Doug agreed that the Alien had to go, though mainly because it would be too expensive to build and manipulate. He suggested we replace it with the Creature from the Black Lagoon, the rights to whose much simpler suit the studio already owned. It sounded good to us.

So in the new improved saner toned-down version, the Creature from the Black Lagoon was now one of the main love interests. We came up with an evil dictator named Moussakka, so tough when he accidentally sticks his hard-on in a fan, the fan breaks. And a group of fake Rastafarians we called

Palookas, who worshipped Joe. They were all named after cigarettes—Winston, Marlboro Lights, like that. And an island restaurant called The Mangled Parrot, specializing in the local *cuisine vivant*—in one scene, a loving couple are holding hands and dreaming over dinner, only to find that certain parts of it, covered with sauce, begin to hop off their plates and across the restaurant floor. There was a handsome goofy Frenchman named Marcel who did ventriloquism with his dick to impress girls ("Sokay?" "Sallright."), and, in a true Chris Miller touch, one scene ending as a projectile gob of cum hits a light bulb and blows it out.

It would have been a classic.

Robin Williams, who's read all 6 versions of the script, characterized Chris's and my initial two drafts to me as "Buñuel Meets the Marx Brothers." He didn't mean this as a compliment. But he hit it right on the head—at least what in our mistaken ambition we were trying for. A double feature we had screened early on for inspiration was *The Discreet Charm of the Bourgeoisie* and *Duck Soup.*

Hey, call us irresponsible.

Then late in August Doug fell or jumped off that cliff in Hawaii.

The joke went around that he accidentally fell while looking for a good place to jump. Harold Ramis told me he visited the spot afterward, and that it's not a likely candidate for a place to jump, more a crumbly steep hill than a nice dramatic cliff—though I heard too that Doug had written I Love You in lipstick on the bathroom mirror of his hotel suite, and that his moccasins had been found left neatly at the cliff's edge, which doesn't necessarily mean anything either I guess. Harold said that Doug was uncomfortable with all the money he'd made, would sometimes go around randomly telling strangers he was rich, tipping car schleppers $100 a pop, like that. Harold also said that particular Hawaiian island is one where tourists flashing rolls are sometimes not seen alive again. And a rumor that made the rounds was that he'd stumbled on some secret dope fields, and was killed by the growers, so it could have been something out of *Magnum, P.I.* like that.

Doug's death like his life seemed ambiguous, complex.

Chris and I were hard at work on the second draft in a country house near Woodstock, New York, when we got the news. Chris was devastated. Doug, though younger than Chris, had been a sort of fatherly guiding light to him, I think. I hadn't known Doug very well, but I felt gut-punched too. He really had been the best and the brightest. He was to be buried somewhere in Connecticut. Because Chris simply didn't seem up to it, I drove him to the funeral, one of the saddest and strangest days of my life—many of the funniest people in the country gathered red-eyed and tearful and choking back sobs on a sunny hillside as they planted what was left of Doug.

It seemed an incidental loss that *Club Sandwich* was now a goner too.

That autumn Chris and I finished our second draft, but our hearts weren't in it. All along Shamberg & Greisman had been begging for realism, characters the audience could cuddle up to, a host of things we had either been unable or unwilling to provide.

So after a decent interval, they said thanks guys and handed it over to two other writers, and the project became *Club Paradise*, the title shift alone a fairly reliable indicator of the attitudinal shift of gears that was going on generally in regard to the piece.

These two other guys, whose names I have resolutely refused to remember, wrote it twice more.

Then last March, Harold sent Chris and me copies of the final version of the script, which he'd written with Brian Doyle Murray. The note attached to mine read: "David—This is *Island Jack*, six years from *Club Sandwich*. I hope you will like it and that you'll consider visiting us in Jamaica while we're shooting. There's even some extra work in it for you if you're up to it. Hope you like it. All the best, Harold."

This is maybe the place to mention—and is further proof of my theory that there are only 43 people in the world—that Harold and I used to work together on *Playboy* magazine. I was the first full-time Party Jokes Editor, and when I began getting batty and asked that I either be given something else to do or be fired, they hired Harold as the second full-time Party Jokes Editor. We were never buddies, but we worked in the same small office for a couple of years as junior editors terrorized by the same senior editors, and got along all right.

Reading Harold and Brian's script—their second version, bringing the number of writers and drafts to 6 each in 6 years—reminded me again why I'd fled back to regular writing with its many fewer zeroes at the end of checks.

Theirs was so much sleeker than ours. It had formal elegance, was seamless, economical, graceful, smooth. Its humming structure made our earlier attempts seem like a friendly Frankenstein monster lurching along with bolts in its neck. Reading it made me think Chris's & my credit should read "Evolved and Domesticated From a Pair of Wild Primitive Scripts by Chris Miller & David Standish."

While Chris and I had sat around writing down dreams, they did research.

Associate producer Trevor Albert is an easy-going native Californian who got into the movie business, as Harold put it, "by going to UCLA film school and then walking Jon Peters' dog." He and Harold have been working together since *Caddy Shack*, and for this one he scouted locations on 18 islands, starting on Trinidad and working his way north. Tough job, eh?

He and Harold and Michael Shamberg went back to three or four of them several times before landing on this section of Jamaica outside snoozing little Port Antonio, largely because it offered the most varied paradisiacal settings closest together.

They were drawn to St. Kitts and Nevis, Harold told me, but the logistics proved too tough—although it was from these islands, he said, that they took their main inspiration for their island of St. Nicholas, and for the political subplot, in which a fabulously wealthy sheikh is negotiating with the prime minister basically to buy the entire government, legal system and all. "We'll never be able to go back there again," said Harold with his usual small smile.

It is, in Michael Shamberg's phrase, "the comedy of realism."

It is also comedy made by grownups.

Most of the cast and crew were staying at the Marbella Club on Dragon Bay, six miles outside Port Antonio. The setting is ridiculously beautiful, a pale yellow and white stucco Spanish Riviera style resort of villas and courtyards arranged in a pleasing jumble on a hillside overlooking a perfect little lagoon, whose clear extraordinary water is seventeen shades of blue and green all at once. There's a freshwater pool on a wide lawn facing the sea, and a private beach protected by a reef. Simply hard to beat.

The Sunday night I arrived, tables and white linen tablecloths, set for dinner, were arranged in an outdoor courtyard around a fountain centerpiece. It was that time of evening gloaming, a sprinkle of early stars in a violet sky, candles lit inside curving clear hurricane lamps on all the tables, just swell.

I'm sitting happy to be there after a long day's journey from Chicago, much of it on relatives of Joe's Airlines. But the last part from Kingston was a 3-hour drive through rainforest mountains, partly along a picturesque boulder-strewn stream called in one section the Ugly River, though not so to me. I found it seriously exotic and gorgeous, and well worth our many barely-averted head-on collisions on the narrow twisty hairpin roads.

The cold bottle of Red Stripe beer I was working on didn't hurt a bit. I was feeling better and better. I mean, Jesus, there standing against a white stucco wall I recognized Jimmy Cliff, *the* Jimmy Cliff standing right there, wearing a classy red leather jockey's cap, leaning and checking it out, smiling just in general like a friendly imp from Shakespeare. Cool Runnins if ever it did exist. This is a big one for me. I mean, you know, movie stars are okay, but that was *Many Rivers to Cross* himself over there not thirty feet away.

I took another sip of Red Stripe. Dis already be all right, mon.

Then wobbly running and squealing with delight, scooting among the tables, is this little kid, who's being pursued by none other than Robin Williams, with a happy grin on his own face, playing good old I'm-gonna-get-you with his

2-year-old son through the maze of the candlelit tables. They roughly described a simple polygon around the tables and then were gone. It just added to the sweet placid feeling of the evening.

And then a few minutes later, as they came into the courtyard, I saw Harold Ramis and Michael Shamberg for the first time. Both had their tired over-sunned daughters in tow, both Dads taking them home to get ready for bed. I had a flash that Cecil B. and Jack Warner probably never done it this'a way, that here were the director and the producer of this thing, sans moms and nannies too, marching off into the sunset with their tired crabby kids, putting in a little quality Dagwood time with them.

Thus do creatures of the 60s move into power in Hollywood, it struck me, with an egalitarian leftover-hippie edge, even as they become the new comedy moguls and hang out in places like this and drink Montrechet with their langouste and talk about real estate.

It strikes me that it's the new Hollywood establishment, comedy division, congealing before my very eyes. And sliding smoothly into grownupdom. And this is how they live—camping for months at one of the most pleasant beach resorts in the Caribbean, with their wives and husbands and kids and friends along too, and they call it work.

I felt like Robin-Leach-for-a-Week.

But I had no inkling of the *extent* of this G-ratedness until the next morning, on my way to breakfast in the colonial-greathouse-style dining room facing the lagoon. Everywhere you looked, there were kids and moms and nannies. It was like the world's fanciest daycare center, new baby boom central.

I especially liked one morning in mid-week, a rainy day at Movie Camp.

Walking into the dining room for breakfast, I discovered that the covered porch had been converted into the rainy-day games center for the tots and their various caretakers, while up in the dining room most of the cast were sitting around drinking coffee, also waiting for the sun to come out, and playing their own rainy day games.

Robin Williams' large bearded assistant was calling out questions from a Genius version of Trivial Pursuit, and people were just yelling out guesses and answers instead of keeping score.

It's Joe Flaherty, Mary Gross, Robin Duke, Rick Moranis, Twiggy, Eugene Levy, Robin Williams and a few others shouting out answers and cracking wise over the questions.

If it weren't for all the household faces, it could be a summer house rainy day on Cape Cod or East Hampton or somewhere along the Lake Michigan shore.

A card comes up: Which of the Mackenzie Brothers wore earmuffs?

Well, one of the Mackenzie Brothers is sitting right there.

A little later: Who played an axe murderess on *Mork & Mindy*? And of course Mork's right there too.

As Joe Flaherty's Count Floyd would say, pretty scary, eh, keeds?

Then twitchy with nervous energy Williams pops up from his seat and looks out on the lawn, commencing, in an ironworker's voice, a harangue at one of the peacocks strutting there: "C'mon, be a man! Get out of that drag and make something of yourself, like your mother and I have prayed you would! Eddie, come to your senses, boy!"

This was about as wild and crazy as it got. There will be no stories of bizarre ganja parties among the stars reported here. I know there had to be some around, but I didn't smell a whiff of the stuff all week, and not one single person offered to sell me any. What's this country coming to, anyway?

And everyone's working these long days in the heat—7:30 a.m. calls, wrapping for the day around 6, then dailies from 6:30 to 7 or so, then a quick cleanup and dinner—so by 10 o'clock, everybody's worn out, yr. faithful parasite among them.

This is the 80s. We're not partying, we're all working our asses off, making it—though of course some of us are just working our asses off.

It sure was different from the shooting of *Animal House* in Eugene, Oregon, back in the autumn of 1977, under gloomy doomy skies the few days I was there. Chris Miller had invited me out to watch, and it was hard to tell where the movie left off in the afternoon and real life set in at night, except the drugs were better at night.

I vaguely remember one night, a bunch of the cast and crew crammed into one little Rodeway Inn room watching some big fight on TV. Even John Vernon, dread Dean Wormer, was there hanging out. It's vague because of the fat joints that kept circulating and circulating. And the night after that, Chris and Doug Kenney and Bruce "D-Day" McGill and Karen Allen and I and maybe a couple of others, spent much of the evening in Doug's room, listening to tapes of greasy R & B, some of us passing a joint now and then, drinking beer and shooting the shit and hanging out, like decent people should. There was a large cardboard box in one corner that Doug spent a certain portion of the evening in, doing strange puppeteer riffs from it every so often.

But in Jamaica there were at least a few night owls who sometimes closed the bar at one a.m. or so, among them Verna Hampton, a wonderful woman from Boston who plays a native woman named Pansy, the perpetual bringer of bad news to poor Jack. A scene they were shooting while I was there involved Jack arriving with all the new guests, and Pansy behind the desk exclaiming loudly: "Cook she vex' 'cause the generator go bust and melt up the freezer. And I try to call Mr. Skeet the plumber 'cause the sewer line back up, and we got poo-poo in all the rooms on this side!"

Her reading of "poo-poo" is birdlike, lyrical, a delight.

In her mid-30s, deliberately 10 or 15 pounds overweight to play plump Pansy, she is still seriously cute, and a serious, interesting woman. She's a single parent, with a 12-year-old son named Gregory who, yes, was on his way down to Jamaica after school was out next week. Until he got there, her sister Elaine was keeping her company and giving moral support. Mainly Hampton is a teacher, and has taught in such outposts as the New York prison system as a volunteer, but at the age of 30 she just decided to go be an actress. And from what I saw, she'll be the surprise hit of the movie.

Since she and a few others helped close the bar a couple of nights I was there, it wasn't a total loss hanging out-wise.

And there were some good moments hanging around the set for the better part of a week. True, it all moves along at the pace of primordial ooze, but amazingly it does make headway.

And one thing I noticed was that contrary to the prevailing flat lean hard-work 80s style here, practically everybody smokes, Harold leading the pack as it were with no-fooling-around Galoises. I took it up again for the duration myself. It is after all something to do amidst the endless waiting.

One morning gathered in the shade of one of the magnificent old trees right on the beach, the assembled extras were being given a sunburn seminar by a woman from makeup. Twenty or so of them gathered in an arc around her. She's insisting like a drill sergeant that they stay out of the sun whenever they can, because they had to tan on the movie's schedule, not their own. And not, horror of horrors, get too sunburned to work. She then demonstrates Too Much Sun by pressing a thumb on a handy sunburned fellow nearby. Her finger leaves a whitish afterimage on his red skin. "That's trouble, that's too much sun." Pipes some local dreadlocked black guy, one of several gathered for the sunburn seminar: "Does that mean me, too?" This brings smiles for his boldness from other of the local black extras, laughs from everyone else.

Standing there watching I strike up a conversation with a thin bearded fellow named Fisher, who tells me he was from Boston before he took off for the islands to work on his windsurfing. He's presently working on it as an extra in the movie, at $30 U.S. per day, and is one of the guys tooling around the lagoon on a windsurfer in the establishing shot.

At first blush he seemed like the real Island Jack, since the Robin Williams character has chucked a job as a Chicago fireman to bail out to the islands, and Fisher here had chucked 15 years of rehabbing and real estate in Boston to come hang out in the islands and just think about it for five years.

But the thing is, it turns out what he's thinking about is still real estate. Like associate producer Trevor Albert, he too has been scouting locations—but for a place to build his own beach resort. And he likes this beach a *lot*, he told me. Another yuppie in beachcomber's clothing.

Also standing around watching is a young local guy who goes by the name of Tiger. He's around 20, slight, and not very tall, his dreadlocks up under a round knitted hat, his sparse beard also diverging into dreadlocks.

Tiger is a go-getter. He's working on the movie as a mechanic's assistant; later in the day I saw him tearing apart the hindquarters of a broken truck. But he's also a dub dj in Port Antonio, he tells us, sometimes at The Roof, the loud racy disco in town where they are reputedly advanced enough to have bar girls hustling for drinks—there and at a couple of other spots around town, one of them a vacant lot near his house, where they're playing Saturday night. They set up an open-air bandstand, somebody brings cold drinks for sale, and they boogie—or rather reggae—late into the night.

Tiger also has a *song*, just like Jimmy Cliff's character did in *Harder They Come*, the song he believed would change his life and make him rich and famous if someone didn't steal it from him or worse.

And since Tiger is an outgoing sort, and we're all just standing around in the heat anyway, we convince him to sing a little of it for us. Before beginning he dedicates the song to the five or so of us listening. Providing his own occasional rhythm and bass highlights, he begins. And it's pretty good, he has a nice voice, and the message of his song is love. Some of the folks also hanging out in the shade, local people tending impromptu stands selling cold beer and cigarettes and such, they clap and begin to boogie—I mean reggae—a little as Tiger performs his song, a free spontaneous concert among the tedium on the beach. It was a treat.

And made all the nicer because not far from us, Jimmy Cliff himself was sitting on the porch of his fake movie beach bungalow, smiling at the sea. The living dream and its model not 50 feet from each other.

One afternoon I managed to overhear some killing-time improv between Robin Williams and Eugene Levy. Mary Gross and Robin Duke, who seem to be real-life buddies, just as their characters are in the movie, and Rick Moranis were also nearby.

For no noticeable reason, Williams breaks into a blue magic act.

"See these little ropes?" he says to Levy. "Now they're gone. And if you'll look in your pants, you'll find them tied around your penis. Isn't that amazing? And I believe you had a watch? You'll find that up your ass!"

Levy mimes removing it and holding it up gingerly.

"Yes," he says, going into John Cameron Swayze, "it takes a licking and goes on ticking."

"Oh, no," groans Mary Gross.

Then Williams doing his John Cameron Swayze, conjuring a tub of water and the growl of an Evinrude as he tosses in the watch and cranks the outboard. He relates how on live TV he saw this and the watch disintegrated or something, they couldn't find it. Then: "Yes, we took our Timex to a leather bar on the lower west side. And after 15 guys..."

Mary Gross groaning again.

Toward the end of the week Don the publicist's charter excursion to Montego Bay on Sunday for an afternoon of golf began falling apart. One of the tragic deficiencies of the Port Antonio area, to all these Californians, is the absence of golf courses—so Don had set up an air charter for 8 or 9 of them, mostly the sparks. Yes, $150 each plus greens fees for an afternoon of golf is a little steep, but if ya gotta have it...

Then on Thursday or so he got word from somebody that the sparks were bailing out, largely because they'd gotten into the black market in a heavy way, and didn't want to part with the chips.

This is the result of Jamaica's new stiff monetary laws. Only Jamaican money may be used on the island—dread U.S. dollars are forbidden, in hopes of propping up the local currency. So everybody's getting paid his per diem money in Jamaican. But you can't change Jamaican money back to dollars or pounds in any amount over what you have receipts for changing at a bank or hotel. So they either have to spend all this Jamaican money while they're here on location, or play the black market. The official exchange rate hovers around 5 Jamaican dollars to 1 dollar U.S. So on the black market they're paying 6 or more per U.S. dollar, and stockpiling the dollars to take home.

Which means it's goodbye, golf game, and hello money market.

During lunch break one day I had a good long talk with Harold, sitting at one of the tables in the semi-open-air Club Paradise lounge over frosty Red Stripes. I hadn't seen him for years, but far as I could tell he hadn't changed very much, with that same easy relaxed manner.

Over and over the week I was there people of all sorts—from Peter O'Toole and Robin Williams and the rest of the stars, to the grizzled experienced crew and new first-time assistants recruited from Port Antonio—they all kept variously volunteering to me for various reasons how good he was to work for, many of the old hands saying this one had the best vibes of any location they'd ever been on.

Being in Jamaica, the prettiest part of Jamaica, doesn't hurt, certainly. But it's also Harold, and a little of that leftover hippie thing again, I think. Harold and his wife Anne in Chicago lived in a pad that was *seriously* Sixties, and I think he still carries around the best of those attitudes with him, rich and famous though he is these days.

Harold has his own style of cool runnins.

Certainly he doesn't take himself too seriously. He said that he'd had no real directing experience before *Caddy Shack*, that the studio basically handed him and Doug $10 million and said, go, guys. Starting out on that one, he told me, that constant semi-smile on his face, he didn't even know what the assistant directors *did*. When I asked why he thought *Ghostbusters* had succeeded so hugely, he said after thinking a moment that it was because it wasn't dirty. How parents would come up to him, thanking him for making a movie their kids liked that was neither pornographic nor incited them to revolution. And his capsule comment on *Club Paradise* was that it had long been his dream to make a movie where nothing blew up in the end.

But the one with the coolest runnins by far is Peter O'Toole.

He wasn't working the week I was there, and had his own villa by the sea in toward Port Antonio, so had been nowhere in evidence. I tried to convince Don the publicist that I absolutely had to talk to Peter O'Toole or the story would fail utterly. It wasn't exactly true, and we all knew it, but O'Toole graciously agreed to come down to the set one afternoon and talk with me.

Kids again.

I get my first live glimpse of Peter O'Toole as he's sitting in the shade of the lunch tent laughing with a young local woman and her cute roly-poly little baby. In fact he is leaning toward the tot and comically growling at him like some fierce beast, O'Toole's elegantly wasted face lighting up yet more when the baby squeals with delight each time.

When Don introduces me, he says, "Let's piss off to my beach shack and talk." We take this to mean his fake beach bungalow on the set. He says just a second, and heads off at a good clip down the beach to say something to Harold, hanging out down the beach with him and Joe Flaherty (who told me quite seriously that it was seeing *Lawrence of Arabia* that made him want to become an actor) and Steve Kampmann and some others.

Just as everyone likes Harold, they are openly in awe of O'Toole—Harold, Robin Williams, the lot. And well they should be. Marching there down the beach is Lawrence and Becket and Lord Jim and all the rest of them.

So no problem, mon. I sit beneath the big tree by the Club Paradise beach bar and read some more of *Nostromo*, Conrad's Caribbean novel. Soon come, you know? And then he's marching across the sand back toward us.

It turns out the beach shack he meant is his villa. We'll go there and have tea. I'm to go with him and Don will follow in the Latka. I've been chasing around the great and near-great for 15 years as a journalist, but I still feel nervous and a little giddy.

I needn't have. He's been around so much—he characterized himself as "The Old Man of Locations" to me—that he has seen everything and everyone before, including me. And he still finds the vanity fair tremendously amusing.

Of all the people imported here to make this movie, O'Toole seemed most comfortable, naturally friendly, easily at home with the local black Jamaicans. To the ulcer-inducing horror of the head of Warner Brothers, since he might get hurt and god forbid screw up the shooting schedule, O'Toole has tried out for and made a serious local cricket team, making him both the only white person on it and the oldest by a good ten years—and of course the only international star.

As we walk toward his car on the set, he stops for some cricket chitchat with a few of the red-striped Jamaican police.

On the way up the hill the cricket continues. He says he first heard of the West Indies and Jamaica in 1948, in a calypso song about cricket that was popular in England, and proceeds to sing me a bit of it as we rattle up the road. At the top he stops for some more cricket chitchat, and then we're off on the main road to his place.

He's been horseback riding a lot, he says, both in a young cocopalm plantation by the sea that's exquisite, and on trails up in the hills—where he's been visiting the Maroons who live up there, a semi-mysterious separatist group descended from runaway slaves, who claim the island is theirs and want it back.

His villa is spectacular, right on the water, with its own little crescent of private beach. Soon we are served tea by the housekeeper, and O'Toole, with little prodding, is telling one good story after another.

Like when they were shooting *Lord Jim* on the Mekong Delta, and the Vietnam war started up right around them. He said they woke up one morning and there were four dead Americans outside the compound, and they got out of there as fast as they could—ruining the picture as well, he felt.

And saying when pressed that of all of them, *Lawrence* was the one that mattered most to him—saying out loud for the first time, he told me, that to him it was the masterpiece, was the one. And incidentally that *Lawrence* was also the worst location he'd ever been on, two years of heat and sand.

But my favorites were two stories about the shooting of *What's New, Pussycat?* with Peter Sellers. They were all living in the hotel that the last part of the movie takes place in. When I suggested that must have been a zoo, he agreed. And naming no names, but indicating that the other person in the story was one of the several beautiful female stars of the movie, he began thusly:

"Well, I was climbing out of a window. I couldn't go up, so I went down—and found myself in the bedroom of this woman, who was lying there nude in bed. I began to make my apologies, but she said no, don't go, and hurried into the bathroom. I thought she was after a robe or something. But in a minute she came back, still quite naked, but wearing her false eyelashes!"

The thought of it still makes him laugh to this day. And he never did explain why he was climbing out of a window in the first place—a master storyteller's touch, I thought.

The other story involves the invention of Inspector Clouseau as O'Toole recalls it. There was actually working at the hotel as the desk clerk, a young Spanish guy whose English wasn't as good as he thought it was. Also small misfortunes kept befalling him. He'd pick up a telephone, and the bottom would fall out. And then he'd try to look cool, like nothing had happened. O'Toole said that Sellers picked up on this, and used him as the model for the Clouseau character. He was also playing the desk clerk in the movie, and in one scene was required to give an inventory of who was doing what to whom in which suites. O'Toole does the voices:

Desk Clerk: "There are two Boy Scouts and their scoutmaster in the Marie Antoinette suite, and in the Napoleon suite, there is a man *sheeting* on his wife—"

Director: "Cut, hold it. That's cheating! Ch!...ch!"

Desk Clerk:"Yes, there is a man *sheeting* on his wife..."

The last night I was there, spinning with it all, I found myself, after dinner, stretched out in the dark on one of the beach chairs, staring up into the sky, wondering what I thought of it all.

The complacent moon one day past full was rising through the trees, coming up over the blueblack presence of the mountains behind an inky fat cloud, so searchlight strong it lit the cloud's ragged edge like neon sculpture of the chiaroscuro school.

So I stretched out to watch moonrise—the only sensible time to be on the beach. I've always thought man evolved from the sea for a reason, and sunshine is extremely overrated in my opinion. Also I've never properly appreciated sand. But at night it was all right.

So I sat there staring up at the real stars with my last Red Stripe, wondering what to make of it. To get even a token writing credit and a few of those zeroes would send the hound, who's been gaining on us lately, howling in painful retreat. And naturally that would be a relief. But it didn't seem likely. And then too, we've sort of gotten used to having him yapping there on our heels—and, you know, I've read *Bleak House*. The ever elusive possible payoff seems like Jarndyce & Jarndyce revisited, even though Chris's and my Club Med stumblings were what set this whole big wheel turning.

Was it possible that I didn't care? Or rather that a few of me did—my Dagwood family man and my Sammy Glick among them—but that the other 12 or so of us just didn't give much of a shit? Apparently so.

Even though I wished them well, I felt fairly remote from the movie they were making here. It is sensible grownup comedy, and there is no friendly tentacled alien or Creature From the Black Lagoon in it. Not one single major character of another species or from another part of the universe, you know?

It was all a large reminder that Doug was dead and the world had changed. Although I did like the warm family G-ratedness of this new grownup-dom all around—the joys of kids finally being discovered by a generation that had tried almost everything else first as a substitute for such cornball pleasures. And that those of us who are left seem to be gaining our balance at last, all of us slightly safer and duller survivors who flirted with the edge but seem to have mainly made it safely back to center.

I sat there watching the rising moon electrocute a fat dark cloud, missing old friends, and knew it was time to get back home.

- 1985

This was a happy accident. So many articles happen that way. You start trying to do one thing, and then something happens that you never expected. This article was to be a group profile about the three Holsteins brothers, who were co-owners of a folk music club and bar on the Chicago Lincoln Avenue saloon strip, a block or two north of the Biograph Theater, infamously known for the 1934 shooting of bank robber John Dillinger by FBI agent Melvin Purvis. The bar, of course, was called Holsteins. I had fun reporting it, but the moment—the accident—was when I went in on a Friday during a howling rainstorm that had driven most of the customers back home. The place was almost empty. And who, I discovered, was headlining, for this sparse scattered soggy twenty or so devoted, was Dave Van Ronk. And even luckier, between sets, I spotted him sitting at the bar by himself. He sported a railroad cap, perched above chipmunk cheeks and a rubicund complexion gained by lifelong application. I sat down on the stool next to him and asked him if I might buy him a beer. He said sure, why not. So there I was, as the man said, sitting right there shooting the shit with Dave Van Ronk! I was delighted.

Many of you might ask—who?

I can say two words: Bob Dylan.

Critic Robert Shelton—whose New York Times *1961 review of Bob Dylan's performance at Gerde's Folk City in the west Village launched his career—wrote this about Van Ronk:*

"A tall, garrulous hairy man of three quarters, or, more accurately, three fifths Irish descent. Topped by light brownish hair and a leonine beard, which he smoothed down several times a minute, he resembled an unmade bed strewn with books, record jackets, pipes, empty whiskey bottles, lines from obscure poets, finger picks, and broken guitar strings. He was Bob Dylan's first New York guru. Van

Ronk was a walking museum of the blues. Through an early interest in jazz, he had gravitated toward black music—its jazz pole, its jug-band and ragtime center, its blues bedrock... his manner was rough and testy, disguising a warm, sensitive core. Van Ronk retold the blues intimately... for a time, his most dedicated follower was Bob Dylan."

Shelton also called Van Ronk "the musical mayor of McDougal Street."

So I felt fortunate to spend some time with him in such casual circumstances. With a little prodding, I steered our talk to the summer of 1962 in the West Village. I did so because it brought me back to my green youth, realizing years later that 1962 proved to be my Favorite Year.

I had been in my junior year at wholesome pastoral dull Miami University in Oxford, Ohio, surrounded on all sides by cornfields and cows. I had grown up in Cleveland, so you would have to say that up until then, I had never been anywhere. But that spring my girlfriend Beth and I had managed to get jobs together as counselors at a summer camp in upstate New York, within the vast rugged Adirondack Park, nearly ten thousand square miles in extent. The camp sat on Lake Placid's northern edge, beneath the brooding fastness of Whiteface Mountain, fifth highest peak in New York State. The forest surrounding the camp was primeval, uncorrupted, autochthonous, where you might encounter Natty Bumpo, Chicgachgook, and Uncas, tramping through trackless wilderness. Now more than fifty years later, I can still taste the crisp fresh invigorating mountain air, so sweet you could bite it like an apple.

On rainy days, I loved retreating to my bunk, raindrops on the screens a whisper, open to the vast sea of Of Time and the River, Thomas Wolfe's boundless novel about becoming a writer, its words pouring from the pages like the rainfall itself. It was a fat brown brick of a book, a library copy, and I never did get around to returning it. It sits in my bookshelf today, its March 10 1962 late notice yet another stain on my permanent record. Some nights Beth and I would grab a blanket and go out to the end of the pier, the lake a black shiny sable presence, beneath the greater blackness of the night sky, smeared white with stars, painting the Milky Way with infinity's brush. One of my campers would let us borrow his transistor radio, and we would lie down on the blanket, listening to distant signals from Boston's WBZ or New York's WABC...Summertime, Summertime...Count Every Star...Moon River...Please Mr. Postman...Born To Lose...Love Letters (Straight From Your Heart)...I Can't Stop Loving You...The Way You Look Tonight... This last, by The Lettermen, was "our song," and I remember hearing it on that dark pier there with Beth, cuddled together listening, in love with each other, the night, the lake, the stars.

But in very few weeks it all ended abruptly for Beth and me and Camp Birchwood. The camp owner, a Long Island gym teacher named Irv Platnik, fired both of us, on the most specious reasons, and told us to get out the next day. We realized afterward that the camp was failing, and Irv couldn't afford to pay us, so he cooked up a bunch of bullshit reasons and booted us out. The next day we were on a bus to New York City. Beth went home to her parents in Long Island, and soon got a waitressing job at the Garden City Hotel—while I scored, thanks to a friend from Miami University, Carole Smith, who was sharing a room in a cramped apartment on Sheridan Square, while at summer school in Columbia, studying James Joyce with

William York Tindall himself—sort of like studying God with Jesus Christ himself. But Carole was like that, fearsomely brilliant, if often too finely tuned. By the time I visited her, Carole, as was her wont, had the Village wired. And when I told her I was broke and jobless and looking at a long dreary summer with my mother at home in Cleveland—well, Carole took me right over to the Bleecker Street Tavern, between Sullivan and Thompson, and introduced to me Mama, the owner, and insisted that she give me a job waiting tables. I was living in the Village! As we used to say back then, it was a gas!

I sat at the bar at Holsteins next to Van Ronk, reminiscing of sweet hip times with him. And remembering the same old joints. Just around McDougal and Bleecker alone, circa 1962: Gerde's Folk City, the Night Owl, the Café Wha, the Gaslight, the Café Bizarre, the Kettle of Fish, the Minetta Tavern, the Fat Black Pussycat, the Caffe Reggio, the Café Rienzo, the San Remo, Le Figaro Café, the Village Gate, the Mills Tavern, Googies, the Bitter End, the Dugout, and my own joint, briefly anyway, the Bleecker Street Tavern.

To be honest, I lived there that summer not even two whole months, but it was enough.

Only later did I quite realize how revolutionary the time there was—and for me. At first I felt I was too late, that I had missed it: All the true beats, Kerouac and Ginsberg and Burroughs and Corso and the rest, had split, had hit the road for other scenes by the time I got there. So it seemed we could only see their ghosts, too late. But something is happening here, but you don't know what it is, do you Mister Jones? Or rather, Mister Dylan. He first landed in the Village in January 1961, on a 7th Avenue subway stop at Sheridan Square, and went straight to the Café Wha on Mcdougal Street, and asked if he could play a set. Like many of these "baskethouses," the performers passed a basket after a set, and the change was how much you made. Over the next two years, Dylan played there a lot—as well as the Gaslight, a basement joint next door—and I used to hang out at both places, so I am certain I saw him there. But I have to be honest here: I was no fan of folksingers back then. I was a resolute rock & roller, with Chuck Berry in my blood, and in truth, I never really got Dylan until he went electric at the Newport Folk Festival on July 25, 1965. But I was fortuitous enough to see him at the fount—even if I hadn't exactly appreciated it. Dylan in the Village was a sign: the old hip 50s guard of beatniks and poetry was giving way to a new generation of musicians. Not only was Dylan playing at the Café Wha, but in very few years, by the mid-60s, so were Jimi Hendrix, the Fugs, and the Mothers of Invention headlining there. The Night Owl, on W. 3rd St. and Macdougal, was an all-night restaurant/café the summer of 1962 when I was there, where we would have breakfast after working until 4am, before heading off to some loft in the East Village to party until noon or so, and then catching a few hours of sleep in the afternoon before going to work at 6pm. The good life! Not long after that, the Night Owl soon began jamming a tiny stage in there, where John Sebastian and The Lovin' Spoonful were regulars, along with The Blues Magoos (forgotten, but early psychedelia), James Taylor, The Blues Project, Fred Neil, Tim Buckley, Stephen Stills, the Mamas & The Papas.

So Van Ronk and I talked about the Night Owl, and then I asked if he remembered a character named Von, who owned the Café Raffio on Bleecker, another *basket house. My friend Carole had a big crush on him then— her and just about every other would-be cute beatnik chick nearby. Von was about 30, and had seriously long hair, back when absolutely no one had that yet, was thin, handsome, and cultivated a look like he could have modeled for Sunday-school prints of The Lord Almighty himself, right down to his riveting blue eyes and perfect cheekbones. The girls simply had to stand in line. He had started Café Raffio in the late 50s, and cleaned up: those baskets full of quarters amounted to a cool pad he owned in St. Marks Place, and various expensive toys, including several classic cars, and a snazzy yellow Vespa you would see him tooling around the Village, usually with some new young honey riding behind him. A lot of people, including me, thought he was a poseur, a jive artist. I didn't like him, no doubt because he was always hitting on Carole when we were in there, but I had remembered him, and asked Van Ronk about him. "You never heard?" he said. "Murdered. Must have been March 1963. Pop pop pop, three shots, right in front of the Raffio. He was expanding the Raffio, and was evicting an old Italian guy who had been living in an apartment behind the café. He confronted Von in front on Bleecker, and when Von told him to fuck himself, the old guy pulled out an old revolver and shot him three times. Von stumbled down the street, and died in front of a liquor store. You could see the blood for days. Von was a dork, but still…just another New York story, and over what? Real estate. The apartment was the old guy's home, you dig, and Von didn't give a shit—he was seeing more profit, more dollar signs in his eye, and fuck the old guy."*

Van Ronk also remembered The Bleecker Street Tavern, a couple blocks east of the Raffio, where I used to work. My few weeks there were great. The characters. Jimmy the bartender, black Irish, maybe 40 years old. He was finishing his fourth novel, though none had been published, but he knew this one would be the one. When the place closed at 4am, Jimmy would give me my daily bartending lesson, teaching me how to make classic drinks, along with their histories—including the Bellini (puréed white peaches and Prosecco, an Italian sparkling wine, created around 1940 in Harry's Bar in Venice, its unique pink color reminded him of the toga of a saint in a painting by 15th-century Venetian artist Giovanni Bellini), the Sazerac (first concocted in 1838 in New Orleans, Sazerac French brandy and Peychaud's Bitters, plus originally a dash of absinthe), and one I got fond of, the Sidecar (named for the dashing motorcycle accessory, created in the Ritz of Paris during World I, equal parts cognac, Cointreau, and lemon juice, the bee's knees during the Twenties). Another guy I knew there, Ragnar Svarstad, always sat at the same burstool by the front window. He was a young lank Norwegian sailor on a freighter yoyoing between Oslo and New York. He seemed isolated and lonely, staring at his beer night after night. We started talking one night when it wasn't busy, and said he wanted to practice his English, he would give me $20 for a few minutes when I had time. So I asked him about Norway, and it was great. He told me his grandfather, Anders Svarstad, had been a noted avant-garde Norwegian painter who married Sigrid Undset in 1912 in Rome, she to be the author of Kristin Lavransdatter *and winner of the Nobel Prize in 1928—and, Ragnar said, quite a beauty when she was young. Strictly, Ragnar wasn't related to her—his grandfather had had three sons by an earlier family before marrying her, and Ragnar was the father of one those sons—but Undset raised Svarstad's sons as if they were her own, so Ragnar told me he thought of her as his* grandmother. Ragnar kept an old worn picture of her in his wallet. She's currently on the Norwegian 500 kroner bill, looking fetching.

Ragnar loved Norway. His halting English nevertheless shone with poetry about its incomparable landscape, and I could be right there with him strolling through an alpine meadow quilted by wildflowers, or canoeing, sliding silently through a peaceful fjord, between massive cliffs laced by ribbons of delicate waterfalls spilling from high above. Norway seemed clean, pristine, innocent. I liked talking with him. And I liked the bar too. Van Ronk asked me if the big murals were still there when I was there. I said I didn't remember them. "Too bad," he said. "Franz Kline did 10 of them in 1940, supposedly paid five buck per canvas, and they were still there when I used to go there in the 50s. They weren't like the black abstract smears like he later did—these were burlesque images, strippers, dancers, jazz bands. One mural was a couple dancing in the bar, and he looked at her with all the love in the world. Entranced." Through the miracle of Google, I recently researched the murals, and found that of the original ten, eight were sold in 1960, and two were either lost or stolen. So like so much in my life, I just missed it. But I did find the couple, and discovered that the couple was Kline and his wife, and the back room shown in the painting is exactly as it looked like when I worked there, including the ersatz-New Orleans staircase and balcony that always seemed to be a stage dressing.

Quickly my summer in the Village ended, too soon. Mama said I could work there as long as I wanted, but my real mother, in Cleveland, began insisting that I had to come home and earn some college money before September. She was right. But there was one more adventure before heading for forlorn Ohio. Carole came into The Bleecker and said, "David, we gotta split to P-Town, it's a scene." Carole was always ahead of me, and I had no clue what she meant, but I tried a stab at it. "Why should we go to Pittsburgh?" I asked. "You poor thing," she said. "I mean Provincetown. On Cape Cod. This wiggy artist I know is putting up a huge tent on the beach and every-body's invited. Should be a blast. And Joe Denmark has wheels. We're gonna split after he works. Outta sight!" Well, it was one way to get to Cleveland, I guess, so why not? I was planning to quit the bar anyway. So it was off to Cape Cod in the middle of the night. Naturally, not much happened the way it was supposed to. When we got there the next afternoon, of course, no huge tent. And nowhere to sleep for the night— no room at any inns—except on the beach itself. As the sun dropped and twilight dwindled, a breeze stiffened from offshore, and the temperature fell. "This way," Carole said, heading toward the dunes beyond the shingle, climbing upward into the dune grass, me following dutifully along behind. She found a pocket among the dunes, protected from the chilly wind. We sat close to each other. "Spoons," she said, backing herself against me, drawing my arms around her, cupping my hands nicely against her breasts, our zipper bags as makeshift pillows. Soon the only sound was respiration, the serene sighing of the ocean's rhythmic breathing, and our own breath as counterpoint, as if the two were one. We slept like this for several hours, hardly moving, quiet, peace-ful. Once in the middle of the night I looked up into the night sky, a smear of stars and distant galaxies, the full moon flooded with some color between silver and bleached bones. But even though we snuggled together in our natural foxhole, by long before dawn we were both chilled throughout—and decided by first light that hitching back to the Village seemed the smartest thought, since Joe Denmark had disappeared after the tent didn't materialize and we had no other ride. But it seemed too that no one was driving back from Provincetown that early. So we stood on the side of the road not getting a thumb for a very long time. By noon we had only made it to New Bedford, a hundred miles, where our ride dropped us over the bridge at the Achusnet River. Seeing the sign across the river gave me a little zolt! Even then I was hooked on Melville, and the Achusnet of course was the name of the whaling ship Melville signed up for in 1841, sailing out right here in New Bedford. And I somehow found it a nice omen that Melville was 21 when he first climbed aboard the Achusnet, and I had turned 21 just three months earlier myself, and I dearly prayed that like him I too would have adventures and far-flung travels ahead, dreaming too that some Moby Dick may lay in my own future. Not far from the riverbank we saw oversized striped tents with dramatic pennants waving above them saying New Bedford Scallop Festival. "Lunch!" said Carole, "and maybe more." Smelled good to me. We paid, and were treated to all we could eat. And while we were eating, Carole chatted up various people nearby us, and, after not long, she found us someone heading right to New York City, and we had one long ride all the way back. It was getting toward midnight when we got back to the city, and discovered that Carole's roommate was there, and she was too uptight to allow me to crash there. So I told Carole I finally had to head for Cleveland anyway, saying goodbye, regretfully, and went to the 7th Avenue subway up to Penn Station, where I discovered that the bus to Cleveland wouldn't leave until 10 in morning the next day. Rather than sit in the station for all that time, I went back to the subway to Grand Central, looked at the map, took the longest route I could find, and then yo-yo'd out to Jamaica station and back, back and forth, until it was time for the bus. At least I could feel the city throbbing around me for a few more hours, and, too, a current Broadway hit at the time was Subways Are For Sleeping.

All of this flashed through me as I sat there next to the bar with Van Ronk, and I realized, again, that it was my favorite year. It was a gas!

A RAINY NIGHT WITH DAVE VAN RONK

AT HOLSTEIN'S, A CHICAGO FOLK CLUB
OWNED BY BROTHERS THREE

It's a fine Saturday night in late October, moon crumbling just past full—just too nice out to stay home and miss this last warm gasp of summer—and everybody's out, including me. Next week it might be the new Ice Age. So the streets are alive and lively, bars and restaurants doing land-office business on this fool-about-my-money-don't-try-to-save night kind of week. I'm on my way to see Dave van Ronk at Holsteins, myself.

Holsteins is a block north of the Biograph Theater on the west side of Lincoln Avenue. Saloon historians remember that it was once Rasto's—my wife, Carol, waited tables there when she first came to Chicago after college—and it was a vegetarian restaurant before that, but March 1986 marks the three Holstein brothers' fifth anniversary as proprietors here of a folk-music club—and one of the pleasantest live-music joints in town.

This is due in part to the space itself, which is actually two separate storefronts with doors in between. The first one you come into is the bar, which when empty or close to it may seem a little sparse—a fancy old wooden bar and back bar with just a few plain utilitarian tables scattered around, a color TV built into the back wall on high—and in the adjoining music room, three tiers of tables facing a black storefront stage, with brick walls painted a deep red: altogether considerably nicer than when it was Ratso's, if nothing to write home about. It's the separation that counts. In most music clubs it's impossible to sort out the chatters and laughers from those there to listen, but at Holsteins they can be separated like oil and water—you have your loud, friendly bar and your sensitive singer-songwriter room, and you can go from one to the other easily.

The second thing I like about Holsteins is that the owners define folk music about as broadly as you can, and they bring in anything but an unceasing stream of guys and girls with guitars singing the latest newly discovered Woody Guthrie song. Over the past year, for instance, they've booked a Swedish folk-singing group, bluegrass bands, traditional Irish, Yiddish, Peruvian, you-name-it—plus a constant succession of name performers such as John Hartford and Melanie and the like. Middle brother Ed handles all the bookings, and he really mixes it up. It's not quite an open-stage policy, but he says if he gets a call from a group that sounds promising, and they'll guarantee bringing along 20 or 30 friends to drink and pay the cover charge, he'll book them for a night. So there's no telling what sort of music will turn up next at Holsteins; and of course each different kind of performer draws a slightly different kind of audience.

It's not the easiest or most profitable business. But the Holsteins seem to love it, and survive in part because of their brotherly divide-and-conquer strategy. Ed credits WFMT's Ray Nordstrand with the idea. Both Ed and Fred had worked as performers on the folk circuit here, but while Fred continued, Ed gradually shifted over to the business side of things, working at the Earl of Old Town, the Somebody Else's Troubles, then booking folk acts into Stages up on Clark near Wrigley Field. As Stages began going more New Wave, Ed began looking around for something else to do. "And Nordstrand said, 'You guys should really look for a place; you have three noncompetitive abilities,'" Ed told me. "And then John Davis, who's a mutual friend of Ray's and ours—he owns Geja's, and we've known John for a long time—he got interested. And this place became available, and we started talking to John, and we tied it up real fast."

Fred Holstein, in his early 40's, is the oldest. A fixture on the local folk circuit for many years now, Fred is Holsteins' musician-in-residence, working as an opening act some nights, headlining when nobody else is booked—so they can always fill the stage. And the graffiti in the women's room, my wife, Carol, tells me, attests to his continuing sex appeal and popularity, and would account for a scrawl in the men's room that reads BETTER FRED THAN DEAD. Ed in the middle is four years younger, and he's the front man/booking agency/public-relations firm/man on the door/emcee. Youngest brother Allen, 32 and recently married, handles the bar, from ordering supplies to bartending—which he'd been doing next door at Orphan's before they started Holsteins. The brothers even do porter duties themselves, and clean the johns, so all they need in the way of employees are a couple of waitresses. The brothers split all the other chores of running the place. This familial low overhead has allowed them to survive when a more conventionally run business might have gone under, because no matter how much you love it, or how you cut it, folk music just doesn't mean big bucks. Just ask Dave van Ronk, which I did.

Saturday was his second night there, and I'd liked it so much on Friday that I'd come back for more. For one thing, if you ever wonder what happened to the early sixties, the van Ronk crowd at Holsteins provides some answer: Graying and a little plump maybe, but here they are in beards and even a few hipster railroad caps—van Ronk himself sporting a modified version he found in Europe. And some of the women, praise the Lord, with their hair hanging long. Contrary to the usual party lines these days, the feelings and lessons of the sixties didn't conveniently disappear in a puff of smoke, and not all sixties types have gone over to Lean Cuisine and BMWs and the cosmic rewards of shopping.

As I come in, I spot van Ronk at the bar, talking with some guy wearing a brown corduroy hipster cap and full beard. He's asking van Ronk what ever happened to his favorite folk singer, Patrick Sky, and van Ronk is filling him in. Van Ronk is a big man, with large, crooked shoulders and friendly chipmunk cheeks above a trimmed little graying beard, railroad cap, and dark, nondescript wool sports coat. You can tell he's been dressing the same way since 1957. He's sipping a glass of red wine and happily chatting away. Now, I covered rock and roll for *Playboy* for more than ten years; and much as I love it, this is just something that doesn't happen in rock and roll. You just don't get to sit down and casually talk it over with Mick or Bruce or Prince before a gig; but in folk music, the scale is still human, and you can. I'd had my chance to talk to him between sets the night before.

The Friday-night weather was out of a club owner's nightmare—steady sheets of heavy rain blowing white across Lincoln as they struck the street, a miserable night. The music room holds 150 people comfortably, but there were 30 people tops at the first set and half that at the second. Still, van Ronk put on an enthusiastic, professional show. His repertoire and styles are eclectic to say the least, from light, gentle kids' songs to real growlers—the last a little too much for a few of the patrons, who exchanged dumbfounded glances and then discreetly split early on. The rest of us had a very good time.

Finding myself at the bar next to him after the first set, I couldn't help asking if he was fond of Howlin' Wolf. He laughed and understood and launched into a wonderful story about his first visit to Chicago in 1956, when he was 20, here to cover an anarchists' conference in Hyde Park for an anarchist publication he wrote for back in New York—chiefly remembering, he said, running out at night to the blues clubs and discovering Howlin' Wolf, then and now his favorite blues singer. I couldn't resist asking a few groupie questions—since van Ronk has lived in Greenwich Village as part of the folk scene since the mid-fifties, and has seen such lights as Bob Dylan, a good friend of his, and the Kerouac-Ginsberg Beat crowd, not such good friends, come and go. Of Dylan he said he was always twitchy, a little distracted and withdrawn, terrible company even among close old friends; and of the famous beatniks I asked about he said they were the other crowd, that at the time he thought they were all poseurs who couldn't write, saying he'd reviewed *Howl* as bad as Whitman in his anarchist magazine; but the old critique was leavened by a smile and the view from nearly 30 years farther downstream.

Was he going back to New York on Sunday, I asked. And he said no, he couldn't get a cheap enough flight until Monday. So he was going to hang out at Ed's place—he was staying there—and spend the afternoon reading the Dizzy Gillespie biography he was working on, hastening to add that it was like every other musician's life there ever was: Gillespie started blowin', quit Cab Calloway because he wouldn't pay, got high, got some chicks, went to Paris…he laughs… all the same. Van Ronk would like to get home to his wife, but all the cheapo flights are booked; it was left unsaid that the difference in flights of maybe $100 would noticeably affect his profit margin on this little trip. He smilingly attributes it to genetics—the absence of the profit gene, a major deficiency in these capitalist United States. So for another few minutes we laughed and wondered over working hard and remaining broke, and then he went in and played an exuberant second set to 14 wet people.

On Saturday night the room was nearly full for both sets. Before the first I ran into Fred Holstein wearing a black wool turtleneck and carrying a small sack full of cassette tapes. He was again opening for van Ronk, but said he planned to tape both of van Ronk's sets through the house sound system— something he does regularly with the performers who come through, he said— excusing it to me as a lazy man's way to learn new songs (guessing when I asked that he probably knew about 2,000 now), but I could see the unreconstructed fan in his eyes. That's another nice thing about the Holsteins; like Br'er Rabbit, they have been thrown into the briar patch and seem very happy about having landed there. Filial camaraderie and musicians you love coming through the door to play night after night aren't bad at all. And the Holsteins have loved this stuff for a long time, both Fred and Ed being walking histories of the Chicago folk scene in the late fifties.

They grew up on the South Side, where their father was a pharmacist. Ed, though younger than Fred—and Allen hardly a toddler—was apparently the true music junkie early on. When he was eight at any rate, in 1955, he was already going to George's House of Music at 79th and Halsted and buying either 78s or 45s. He remembers his first purchase being *Rags to Riches* by Tony Bennett. Fred says his was *Chick-a-Boom* by Guy Mitchell, about the same time.

They quickly discovered rock and roll, but disagreed as to their main men: Fred favored Elvis, while Ed went for Fats Domino. But George the record-store man, whom Ed credits as his first musical mentor, played Ed a Bob Gibson album, and he was hooked. For Fred it was the discovery of Pete Seeger, his earliest folk hero and inspiration. And they were off and folking. The next stop was the Fret Shop on Stony Island, where you could "try out" the various fine guitars and banjos on sale for hours on end with no one hassling you, sit there and learn to play while saving up to buy one. And both have fond memories of the Point during this time, with sometimes nearly a thousand people out there at night at the lake east of 55th Street, pickers and singers and watchers of all persuasions, all getting along and unfearful of being there at night. How times change. By the mid-sixties both Fred and Ed were performing, in joints now gone over to saloon history: the Yellow Unicorn, Mother Blues, the Fickle Pickle, Rising Moon, and all the others.

Allen, 11 years younger than Fred, says that back then, when he was in grade school, he didn't have the slightest idea what they were doing, only that somehow Fred magically got to sleep late every morning, when he had to go off to school. Allen, too, tried to follow in the brotherly tradition, and one day asked Fred to teach him guitar. So Fred handed him an old 12-string and suggested that Allen buy a book, as he had. When Allen protested that 12-strings were too hard, Fred told him to just take six of them off. Allen says he never did really learn—and, on hearing a tape of his voice, decided that going to hear his brothers at the Earl of Old Town with a girlfriend was good enough for him, since Earl would let him in even though he was underage (as long as he drank Cokes) and sometimes Earl would come up with a hamburger on the house.

Talking with them about these old days leaves me with a sort of warm glow, for a couple of reasons. Before working on this piece, I'd been in the club but didn't really know the Holsteins. We found out quickly that we had a few dozen mutual friends, which I took as proof of my theory that there are only 43 people in the world. But it was also proof of another of my feelings, namely that Chicago is the biggest small town in the country—and I say that with a positive, not a negative, spin.

Along the way Ed had worked for Earl Pionke, who put the "Earl" in The Earl of Old Town, his longtime folk saloon on Wells Street—who now drinks recreationally at Doninger's, my friendly corner tavern, so Earl and I hang out once in a while. Working at the Earl, Ed knew lots of people from Second City, right across the street. We talked about John Belushi, whom I knew slightly through my friend Eugenie Ross-Leming, who was in the same Second City company with him. Ed said Belushi used to come into the Earl between sets and was mainly quite regular and reserved, more the shy nice guy from Wheaton eager to please than any drugged-out maniac (my own impression then, too). And Fred knows Eugenie's former husband, Warren Leming—my oldest friend in Chicago—and remembers him as one of the first and best banjo frailers in town, before Warren went over to rock and roll and Wilderness Road with Nate Herman, another mutual friend. Back in 1967 when I met Warren, he and a bunch of other guys were sharing a town house on Orchard by the John Barleycorn which they called Fat Chance House. One of them was math whiz and boy-wonder novelist Paul Tyner; and Fred and Ed knew him, too; and we talked about Paul's sad, long goodbye and remembered him together for a time. Belushi told me that it was at a Hyde Park party—the Holsteins were probably there, too—that sitting in some little room away from the main noise with Paul and Warren, listening to them riff and rap, do their shining improv chitchat, the bebop of fast, funny talk; listening to them was what blew the lid off his straight Wheaton head, and that they had talked him into moving to Chicago and trying out for Second City. So in a small way, Paul and Warren invented Belushi at that party, according to his own testimony. And in this small town, we all sort of knew one another. Circles and circles, round and round.

I don't mean to wax nostalgic here, or be unduly sentimental. But hanging around at Holsteins and talking to the brothers remind me that the city isn't just the awful random blood-spattered horrors of the daily news; that there is friendly community and continuity here, too; that life in the big city isn't all strangers and scary disruption, by any means. It's our home, no matter how many of us there are—and eventually we get to know one another. So there's something reassuring about Holsteins. Merely a music bar, it is true, but emblem and metaphor nonetheless. Allen behind the bar, Fred on stage, and Ed in a snazzy wool hipster hat greeting and shmoozing and showing people to their tables. And God is in His folk heaven, and all is right with the world.

- 1986

Magazines are always in a rush. Rush to come up with the newest idea. Rush to get the article written. Rush to have it edited. Rush to put it into the first possible issue. Rush rush rush…

So here's what happened to this profile of Jimmy Buffett, which I wrote for Playboy.

As I explain in the article, I moved to Key West for a few months early spring 1972, pretty much fleeing from a bunch of bad judgments on my part, and one of first people I got to know there was Buffett, and we got to be friends, well before he was famous. Which continued after I moved back to Chicago and returned to working at Playboy *as an editor and staff writer. When at first he would come to Chicago to play gigs at The Quiet Knight or The Earl of Old Town or some other dinky folk club, he would often crash on my couch, and I'd drive him to the gig in my old Mustang, his whole band consisting of his guitar case. I even dragged all my friends at* Playboy *to have him play for them in my living room, and convinced them to let me write a short On the Scene piece on him in the magazine—the first piece about him, I am pretty sure, ever published in a national magazine. I was quickly a fan, and we were pals, too. He had studied journalism at Tennessee before launching his music career, so at night after his gigs, we'd go back to my place and sit up into the wee hours shooting the shit about writers we liked and music we thought was cool.*

By 1991, of course, Jimmy had an empire, and Margaritaville was its name. By then, too, there had many profiles written about him. I thought it would be fun to write one anyway, but magazines, like hit singles, always need a hook. But what? Then I thought of it—to do a profile of him focusing mainly on him as a businessman. So I thought I could pitch it to Playboy.

Something I learned after years of pitching story ideas to magazine editors is that a good catchy title can sell the idea all by itself. And I had an idea for one: The CEO of Margaritaville. *The hook worked—I had an assignment. I called Jimmy to tell him about it, and asked if we could get together somewhere for us to talk and catch up with what he'd been doing. Always generous, Jimmy said sure, why don't we meet at a place he'd recently bought in southern Georgia, a handsome 600-hundred acre bird hunting plantation formerly owned by the Orvis folks from Maine. So I went there for the better part of a week, and then I came home to Chicago to write the piece.*

Of course, Playboy *was in a rush. I had gone to Georgia in March 1991, and* Playboy *wanted to put it in the August issue. That meant I had to finish by late April, since big monthly magazines like* Playboy *needed a three-month lapse from editing and actual printing. I am not the fastest writer, but I managed to hit the deadline. It was going to be published.*

Tick tick tick…

Since writers are babies, always in need of whatever shreds of encouragement and solace we can grasp, I was eager to see the piece in the August issue. An article with your byline in a magazine always seems like some slim proof that you actually exist, that your name on a byline somehow shows that you might not, after all, be the worthless piece of shit you really know you are down deep. So as always I was excited to see my piece about Buffett in the August issue.

But guess what? Not long before it was due to be on the stands, I got a phone call from Jonathan Black, Playboy's *Managing Editor and a good friend, telling me that the piece had to be pulled out of August, that they had to cut pages because ad pages were short, and the piece about Buffett would have to be 86'd, really sorry. Well, I had been working for* Playboy *for 25 years by this time, so I knew that this happened with a certain frequency. And Jonathan assured me that they would get the piece into another issue soon. But I was concerned on another front—namely, how I was going to tell Jimmy about it? He had spent a lot of time letting me interview him in Georgia, and he was happy that* Playboy *was doing a major profile on him. But I bit the bullet and called him, giving the news. Jimmy wasn't exactly thrilled, but he too had been in these wars long enough to understand. And I promised him that it would be published soon, as Jonathan guaranteed. So we were cool.*

Tick tick tick…

After a few months, I checked in with Jonathan to see when it would be scheduled. Jonathan was apologetic, genuinely so, but told me they were still planning to publish it. I called him again after a few more months, with the same apologetic result. Jimmy, thank god, hadn't called me to push about it, and I maintained radio silence to him about it. I was scrambling to make a life as a freelancer at that time, so I was chasing after new assignments and writing new pieces all the time and pretty much forgot about the Buffett profile.

Then two years later, in 1993, Jonathan called. The magazine wanted to publish the profile, finally. One problem—could you get in touch with Jimmy and do a little updating of what he had been up to since we had talked. I checked his concert schedule, and saw that he would be playing in Milwaukee two weeks. So I called Jimmy's longtime assistant, Sunshine, and explained that Playboy *wanted to publish the profile at last. I also apologized profusely about the long wait, and Sunshine said that Jimmy was a little peeved that it hadn't run in 1991, that he'd told a bunch of*

*people that I was coming out, so he was embarrassed when it didn't appear. I apolo-
gized again, more profusely, and said that* Playboy *promised that this time it would
run—all I needed was half an hour or so to update my questions. Please? Sunshine
checked with Jimmy, and, again generously, he agreed to meet me in Milwaukee. I
went there, and loved the concert—his concerts are always good fun—and we talked
for a while after the show. The piece didn't need too much work, so I sent the revision
into Jonathan Black, he liked it, and it was on.*

Tick tick tick…

*You guessed it. The issue came and went. No profile. This time Jimmy called
me after it didn't appear, and he was pissed. I told him that I was pissed at* Playboy
*myself, that it sucked for what passed for my professional reputation—that I was
embarrassed and sorry about it. Jimmy said a few curt words and hung up. And I
didn't blame him.*

*So I had pretty much written that one off. I should add that Jonathan Black
was unhappy about this outcome, but he couldn't do anything about it—his boss,
Arthur Kretchmer, had kept it in inventory, but never put it in another issue. So as I
say, I decided it was a casualty of war. Best to forget it and keep moving.*

Tick tick tick…

*Then in October 1997—yes, six years after I turned in the original version
of the piece—I got a call from Jonathan Black. "Good news," he said, "we're going
to publish the Jimmy Buffett." "Really?" I said. "Really?" He could hear the irony
dripping in my voice. "I swear," Jonathan said. "We want it for the February 1998
issue." "Great," I said, though I wasn't so sure it was. "But there's one problem," he
said. "What's that?" I asked. And he said, "It's late!"*

*That's right—after six years, it was late. Jonathan explained that they had
decided to cram the piece into that issue at the last minute. "But it needs to be
updated," Jonathan said, "and the deadline is two weeks away. Can you get in touch
with Buffett in the phone and update it? We can pay you two thousand dollars if
you can." That seemed like good incentive, so I said I'd see what it could do. I called
Sunshine, and tried to explain. "You're kidding, right?" was her answer. I begged,
wheedled, begged some more, and she finally said she would pass it to Jimmy. She
called back in about ten minutes. "Not a chance," she said. "He doesn't want to talk
you again. Ever." Click. I should say that I thought he was right. The whole thing had
turned into a soup sandwich—I was as pissed and embarrassed as he was, no, more.
I had fucked myself with an old pal. Didn't blame him a bit. So I called Jonathan
and told him that Jimmy wouldn't talk—not a chance, sorry. But Jonathan took
Sunshine's phone number from me, and said he'd see what he could do. Good luck,
was my thought, thinking it was over.*

*I don't know what magical powers of persuasions Jonathan worked, but
somehow he convinced Sunshine to convince Jimmy to talk with me by phone. I
started by telling him how truly deeply sorry about all these years-long fuck ups.
Jimmy chewed me out for a while, but his old generousness showed itself, and after a
few minutes' rough patch, we had a good talk.*

And, miracle of miracles, the piece actually ran in the February 1998 issue.

*I would have to say, though, that the version that ran in that issue was itself
a fuck up. It was cut, chopped, and covered with scar tissue from the many revisions*

and edits. A botch.

So for the version of the article here, I've gone back to the very first draft. And again, truly sorry, Jimmy.

THE CEO OF MARGARITAVILLE

JIMMY BUFFETT MEANS BUSINESS

I had moved for a while to Key West, bailing out from a marriage gone sour and an affair gone sad. You don't want to hear about it. I rented half of a little white frame conch house, borrowed a bike, bought myself some flipflops and a cheap used blender, and worked on feeling sorry for myself—wasting away in Margaritaville, even before it was incorporated.

This was spring 1972.

My friend Tom Corcoran had landed in Key West after a tour of duty in the Navy, and told me it was a scene. Everyone went out and applauded sunset every night. Bales of marijuana washing up on shore. Great cheap Cuban restaurants. I had nowhere better to go. Key West seemed like The End, East Coast Division—a common reason people wind up there, especially writers, artists, musicians, other interesting derelicts, drawn by the idea that Key West is the final stroke, a last comma in the map of the United States, suggesting more to come but maybe not.

I met Buffett my first night there. Corcoran said there was a good party we had to go to, at Tom McGuane's house. McGuane's close friend and former college roommate Jim Harrison was there, and so was Jerry Jeff Walker, along with a few other members of Club Mandible, a social club McGuane had created whose only act so far had been the making of Club Mandible tee-shirts.

Buffett was sitting outside on the porch when we walked up, but I didn't know who he was at the time. Nor did anyone else in particular. What I saw was a longhaired hippie sitting crosslegged practically in the dark on the wooden porch floor with a honeycolored Martin cradled in his lap, singing an old Coasters hit…

> *I been searchin'…*
> *Oh Lord, I been searchin'…*
> *Searchin' every whi-i-i-i-chee way yay yay…*

…more for his own enjoyment than anything, though a few people were enjoying it along with him, while the main part of the party went on inside.

Buffett was then living in spare cheeseburger rooms like mine. To make a living he was playing for beer and tips at a bar on Duval Street. He was 25, and had landed in Key West a few months earlier, bailing out from a few things himself, including a busted early marriage to his high school sweetheart, and a semi-unsuccessful assault on Nashville that had led to a couple of obscure albums that had sold about nine copies each.

In Nashville he'd met Jerry Jeff Walker, who said he should come on down to Coconut Grove, where Walker was hanging out for a while. And one day they decided to take a spin in a vintage 40s Packard that Walker had just gotten; and the next thing they knew, they were driving to Key West—and Buffett decided to stay. My pal Corcoran, tending bar at the Pier House at the time, served Buffett his very first beer in Key West, an act that began a longtime close friendship.

"He became sort of an instant mini-celebrity," Corcoran told me, "because he was fun to be around. Jerry Jeff could get mean when he was drunk, but Jimmy would just have more and more fun until he passed out. Plus the girls thought he was cute, and he sang some funny songs. He was sort of magnetic that way. And shortly after he arrived, he was writing songs about Key West, and everybody got a big charge out of that."

The first place Buffett worked was a club called Crazy Ophelia's, often sharing the stage with a washboard player doing accompaniment and three six-foot ladies—Tall Donna, Sonia, and Cydall—who stood behind (and over) him doing fake backup singing and Hawaiian moves, unconcerned that they didn't know the words.

A couple of days after the party at McGuane's, I went to see Buffett play at Howie's Lounge. Normally I wasn't crazy about guys sitting on stools strumming acoustic guitars and telling you endlessly their life stories, otherwise known as folk music, but Buffett had major league charm. And his songs were, well, *smarter* than most, not about the usual stuff.

Though he didn't quite know it himself at the time, Buffett was in the process of inventing his own unique amalgam, Gulf & Western music—a little folk , a little country, some rock, and calypso too, and lyrics most often on happy-go-lucky beachbum Caribbean themes, plus some such as *He Went To Paris* and *A Pirate Looks At Forty* that showed a deeper, poetic side.

It was music about to become essential listening on yachts around the world—and for everyone dreaming of being on one instead of where they were. In the years since, Buffett's many albums have created their own legendary geography, that elusive mythical place whose capital is Margaritaville.

It is a measure of his faithful following that he fills 20,000-size venues night after night, without having had a hit single in a long time now. He's really only had two, *Come Monday* and *Margaritaville*. Despite not being played much at all on the radio—a peeve of his we'll come back to—he has annual record sales (or rather cassette and CD sales these days) of around a million "units". A new album can be counted on to sell 400,000 or so, minimum. And catalog sales, thanks in part to the arrival of the CD, account for another half million or so. These sales, plus the paycheck from the big summer concerts—sometimes as much as $80,000 a night for him after expenses—add up to what a mere regular person might consider noticeable cash.

Today, along with his current sailboat, the Savannah Jane, and his Lake seaplane—his flying boat is his latest passion—Buffett owns a bar right on Duval Street, next door to one of the joints where he used to play for beers nearly twenty years ago, proving not only that what goes around comes around, but that sometimes you're able to buy it. The Margaritaville Store adjoins the Margaritaville bar. He also owns a piece of a Class A minor league baseball team in Miami (fellow Cubs fan Bill Murray is a co-owner); a small hotel on St. Barth's, probably the most chi-chi frenchy island in the Caribbean; rents a house in Malibu, where his ex-wife Jane lives much of the time with their 10-year-old daughter Savannah Jane; owns another house in Key West, though it is his old waterfront apartment that is accorded the same tour-bus status as those of Ernest Hemingway and Tennessee Williams; keeps a small *pied a terre* in Paris; and two years ago bought a splendid 600-acre wooded birdhunting plantation in the wilds of southern Georgia.

All of this comes from the fact that this wan't just music, it was, to use the dread word, a lifestyle. Pop music has always been about style, of course. But Buffett's touched our beachy pirate dreams and has found a following whose loyalty may only be beaten by the sweetly fanatic Deadheads—except their scruffy tiedyed legions don't buy as many clothes and accessories as Buffett's fans do.

He calls them Parrotheads.

For these devoted there is *The Coconut Telegraph*, a free occasion-al Buffett newsletter and catalog of Buffett stuff—would you call it Parrotalia?—available for sale. Margaritaville margarita glasses, naturally. Your very own Lost Shaker of Salt. Hats, tee-shirts, beer steins, Margaritaville University sweatshirts—Banana Republic for Buffettheads. For them too there is 1-800-COCOTEL, which accepts credit card orders, answers Buffett trivia questions and provides information on his upcoming performance whereabouts.

There's a downhome grassroots quality to it all, right along with the capitalism in action.

"We got a letter to *The Coconut Telegraph* from some bankers in Cleveland I think it was," Buffett told me. "They were complaining that they were Parrotheads but had to wear suits and ties to work, and everything we sold was too casual for them to make a Parrothead statement at the office. So they sent in a design for a Parrothead *tie*, which we went ahead and made. We gave them a percentage for thinking of it, and it's selling real well."

Buffett's recent book of short stories, *Tales From Margaritaville*, stayed on *The New York Times* hardback bestseller list for 27 weeks. This says a couple of things. You might expect his hardcore fanatic fans to buy enough copies to put the book on the bestseller list for a few weeks—but not for six months at $17 a pop. So people had to be liking it well enough to recommend it to others—quite a few others.

That it's good—far from being just another celebrity ego trip—isn't that surprising. One of Buffett's strengths as a songwriter is his natural storytelling ability. Before his career as a performer, he was a history major at the University of Tennessee. "I was sort of a history buff as a kid," he told me. "Particularly as it pertained to the Antilles, the Greater and Lesser Antilles. I think *Treasure Island* was the thing that got me going. I was fascinated by it, young Jim Hawkins was my favorite character." During his short stay at UT, he also took some journalism courses, and worked briefly as a stringer for *Billboard* in Nashville. Most of his closest old friends are writers. He told me recently that his book of Margaritaville stories represents what he originally wanted to do, that his music career could be considered a 20-year detour. He said that from now on, he would rather be known as a writer than as a performer.

The best and longest of the stories is about a Montana cowboy who leaves the snowy mountains, and takes his horse, Mr. Twain, south to the warm sunshine. At the end he sends a postcard back to a girl he's met, asking her to leave the cold and the diner where she works to join him in this funky Caribbean paradise, and it's postmarked Margaritaville—the essence of the myth so many people are drawn to.

Ecologists call this finding a niche.

Buffett realized that he had one, one rotten winter day in Pittsburgh.

He had already made several well-received albums—including *A White*

Sport Coat and a Pink Crustacian, *Living and Dying in ¾ Time* and *A1A*—which pretty much defined the borders of Margaritaville.

He was on tour, a southern boy in cold northern cities.

"It was February, freezing ass. You know what Pittsburgh is like in the wintertime. We had sold out some big auditorium. Snow and ice outside. And they all showed up wearing Hawaiian shirts.

"That afternoon I'd been walking around killing time. For lack of anything else to do on the road, I'd always go find a good hardware store, Army-Navy store, or a book store to browse in. So I was on this boring browsing run and went into this Army-Navy store, and the guy recognized me. He said, 'Man, I love it when you come to town. I sell every goddamn tacky tropical shirt I can get my hands on for people to go to your shows.'

"When I saw all those Hawaiian shirts out there that night I started thinking, well, why don't I do that? Why should somebody else make these shirts for me? Why don't I own and control this? And I guess I was one of the first artists to own his own tee-shirt concession, which are now multimillion dollar corporations."

So began the diversification of Margaritaville Incorporated.

Buffett now owns his own tee-shirt company, based not in Taiwan or Korea or Indonesia, but in Kentucky. At those 20,000-size venues he packs around the country night after night in the summertime, nearly everyone in the audience is wearing—or buying at the concessions—those tacky tropical shirts. Which now come with a Jimmy Buffett label, and bring in an income that rivals what he gets from albums and concerts.

While these days he has a fleet of lawyers and accountants and such, he's always stayed on top of the business stuff himself, and directed what he calls "the tentacles" he's put out into various enterprises. And he's made tough decisions when they seemed necessary.

He remembers the first such as leaving Don Light—who'd been his manager and supporter and friend in Nashville—for Irving Azoff, then a new powerhouse manager in LA. This was after the success of Buffett's first few ABC albums, in the mid-seventies.

"It was hard, because I'm pretty loyal. And Don Light was probably the most honest guy in a business full of thieves and sharks. But I knew that he could only take me so far. He was in Nashville. There was a good ole boy kind of mentality there, which was great, but up against the realities of Los Angeles and New York, they'd eat him alive in a contract negotiation. And I realized that if I wanted to go on, I needed somebody with more powerful connections who could get me the jobs I wanted."

Enter Glenn Frey and Don Henley of The Eagles, and their chew-em-up manager, Irving Azoff—who had a reputation as a portly shark himself. He had made his start in Champaign, Illinois, managing Dan Fogelberg and REO Speedwagon. By then, Azoff had The Eagles, whose summer tour was the big concert news of the year.

The Eagles were the hot new band, but they were also Buffett fans.

"We opened one show for them in the South somewhere. Henley and Frey and I became very good friends right off the bat. And they were at the top of the heap at that time. I met Irving through them. There was some chemistry that happened, and I saw that as the opportunity.

"Not too long after that I was working a club in San Diego, and The Eagles were doing a big anti-nuke benefit up in Sacramento. It was going to be The Eagles, Jackson Browne, Linda Ronstadt and a couple other people. But Jackson Browne's first wife committed suicide, and he had to be off the show and they had to fill the bill.

"So I got the call from Irving, and he said, I really need some help here. And I realized if I help him out, the way business is done here, he's going to remember that. We did our own show Friday night. I got on a plane at 5:30 Saturday morning and flew to Sacramento. Did an afternoon show for him. Got on a plane and flew back to San Diego and did our two-show set that night. I mean it was a run.

"But it really helped him out, and then a couple of months later The Eagles' *Hotel California* album came out, and the tour was going to be the hottest rock & roll tour of the summer. And I got a call one morning from Irving. He said, I'd like you to open for The Eagles, and you've got the whole tour if you want it for the summer. I realized that the whole transaction happened without Don Light having a thing to do with it. And I realized too that Irving and I were now in this relationship. I said, this is the guy who can take me to the top, and he knew that, too."

Buffett and Light worked out a fairly friendly parting which Buffett describes as being like a divorce, with Light continuing to participate in certain royalties. "I'm still good friends with Don Light," Buffett said. "And Irving and I are still together. We've never had a written contract. With his help, my career took off."

It wasn't tossed in Buffett's lap. He has worked hard for it—but then he likes work. Even back in high school in Mobile, though his family was comfortably middle class, he always worked part-time jobs, "so I could have my own money, and some old car to go to the beach in."

He describes himself in high school as being an "altar boy," under the intellectual spell of the Jesuits. His epiphany came one night at a folk club in Biloxi, Mississippi, when he was 18. He saw these guys sitting up there playing guitars and singing these songs with stories to them—and all these cute girls in the audience just oohing and aahhing. He thought is was really cool, especially, being no fool, the part about the girls.

"It was probably girls more than money or fame or anything in the beginning," he told me. "I had a friend show me how to play guitar so I could meet girls."

So he began learning to play guitar and writing his own songs—just like 12 million other guys then and now. The difference was his songs were good—and that instead of sitting around dreaming about fame and fortune, Buffett did something. He went about selling himself, at first as a songwriter, not a performer.

"My first break came from a guy named Milton Brown, who had a little studio in Mobile. A guy who had worked for him had just gone to work in a studio in Nashville. They liked the songs and were interested. It all started with people being interested in my song writing from a publishing situation. There wasn't any interest in me as a performer. But I was interested in being a performer. So I'd do gigs wherever I could, mostly doing cover songs in places like the lounge of the Admiral Semmes Hotel in Mobile. Which wasn't bad. It was better than working at the Mini-Mart. I was making 700 bucks a week, that wasn't bad money back then.

"But I was writing my own songs, and so during the third set, at 3:30 in the morning, I'd get my courage up and do one or two of my own for the drunks that were still there. I figured they wouldn't mind—or notice much. And if they liked it, they might come in early the next night and say, hey, play that song that you wrote. And that started happening. So gradually I got up the nerve to do more and more of my own songs."

He also pounded the pavement. Driving hundreds of miles to perform semi-unwanted at college booking conferences, get-togethers where schools decided on their entertainment schedules for the year. He stayed on the case in Nashville, and had his own album released when he was 21—something else the rest of us guitar-playing songwriters were just dreaming about. It didn't sell very well, but nobody's perfect.

He's worked hard. Part of the reason he has such a loyal, extensive following is that he's toured his brains out, in the early days hitting every dinky club that would have him. When he first began playing Chicago, where I was again living, he used to crash on my couch, both to save a little money and to see a friendly face, and we would head in my old Mustang for some little club, The Earl of Old Town or The Quiet Knight, or some other 100-seat joint, back when the entire Coral Reefer Band consisted of his guitar in its case. He has earned the big toys he has today.

But all work and no play wouldn't be Jimmy Buffett.

I should maybe say here that having known him slightly for all this time, I don't think he was ever mainly in it for the money, though he didn't mind its arrival either—he wasn't crazy. And there is an on-the-case business man lurking beneath that Hawaiian shirt. But primarily it was the action, the fun, the life. "It was never the money," he said, "never was. They had to tell me when I was rich."

In a gesture you just gotta love, after four albums and a hard contract renegotiation with ABC Dunhill, Buffett had gotten a $30,000 signing bonus, which back then was pretty good money in the record business. He went straight out and bought himself a sailboat. A 33-foot Cheoy Lee ketch he named Euphoria. Tom Corcoran was along for the maiden voyage. According to him, Buffett said, "I may never see this chunk of change again, and I've always dreamed of having my own boat—and I don't have one. So if my career goes down the tubes, I can sail off into the sunset and not regret a minute of it."

They were taking the Euphoria from West Palm Beach to Miami, where Buffett had to be at Criteria Studios to cut a new album. Corcoran came along as crew and semi-navigator. "But it turned out the weather was too rough on the ocean," Corcoran said, "so we brought it down the Intercoastal Waterway, in what turned out to be a crazy all-night bender—having to wake up bridge tenders, throw things at their windows to wake them up, drinking a few beers and staying up all night shouting ourselves hoarse. After which Jimmy walked into the studio, having yelled all night long, and recorded *Margaritaville*."

Corcoran recalls a few more times sailing with Buffett and Groovy Gray, today the permanent captain of the Euphoria II, Buffett's 50-foot upgrade from his first sailboat.

"Once we were a thousand miles out in the Atlantic, and the steering blew. The cable snapped in the steering, and a storm was coming in. The sky was yellow, the waves were starting to build, and we had to go to work, just get the tools out and do the best we could to reconstruct the steering before the storm hit. At one point Groovy was down underneath in the bilge, Jimmy was up top, everybody was greasy from head to foot with grease from the cable—and we fixed it. There were things where each of us had to do his part, or it wouldn't have gotten done. So now we could look at each other and know that now we can get things done together. It was neat, sort of a bonding thing. I don't know where he got it, but Jimmy has a real respect for the ocean. He knows when it's time to party, and when it's time to get to work."

Onshore for a while there it was pedal-to-the-metal party time.

I remember one at some bar up in New York's trendy East Side. It was called J.P.'s or P.J.'s or J.J.'s or one of those. They had closed the place down for a private party celebrating Buffett's first gold record. It was August, boiling outside, but the factory air was icing down the bar, and when I got there around 10 at night things were almost hopping, breaking loose from the manic business schmoozing that usually begins such get-togethers. I hadn't been there long when Jimmy said hey, come on downstairs and meet my lawyer. What? We went down steps into a definitely *not* air conditioned basement, and I was directed toward what my grandmother would have called a "fruit cellar"—a basement compartment with a plank door on it. Four people were already crammed inside, one of them sitting on a folding chair cutting up cocaine on a fat phone book. Jimmy and I crammed in and shut the door, all of us sweating like pigs. I was introduced to the guy lining out the coke as being Jimmy's lawyer. But as we shook hands I realized this was no lawyer, this was a face I was used to seeing on national news programs on television, mainly *Sixty Minutes*— none other than Ed Bradley himself chopping up that coke for all of us. Bradley and Buffett had been good friends for a considerable time.

Then it was later that same night, in a penthouse suite at the Sherry-Netherland. It must have been four in the morning by then. And poor Buffett was exhausted, gone, slunched down in a big comfortable easy chair, a hand shading eyes that were closed, a big hospitable smile still on his face, sound asleep, zonked, while around him the party continued.

There are lots of party-down stories about Buffett from what he now calls "our crazy period." Like the night he met Hunter Thompson. I wasn't there. From what I heard, someone had half an ounce of bolivian marching powder. A big framed poster was taken down from the wall, and someone else created an elaborate labyrinth for those who chose to sniff away the maze, like the bird in *Alice in Wonderland* with a wiskbroom for a beak, that sweeps away the trail Alice is trying to follow. Hunter reportedly was cheerfully waving guns and otherwise doing his usual best to be the gentle host.

Another sailor friend of Buffett's remembers trying to take the Euphoria up the Atlantic coast with Buffett, the goal being Martha's Vineyard. Again they ran into rotten weather—which seems always the case in these sailing stories—up around Palm Beach. As the weather got worse, according to this sailing friend, Buffett increasingly began suggesting they anchor somewhere and boogie out the storm, send the boat up on a flatcar if need be, but have some fun in the meantime. Which they did, anchoring the boat and cranking without sleep for nearly three days. "In 43 years," Buffett told me, "I have been *up* longer than most people have been alive."

During this party period of Buffett's, I was once backstage doing a story at a Delbert McClinton concert in my sweet home Chicago. The backstage area was the usual feudal chaos. I found myself talking to the road manager—one of the world's hardest jobs—who told me he'd recently quit being Buffett's road manager. I asked him why. He looked at me and said: "I got tired of picking him up out of the bushes."

But that was the wild old days.

And even during this boogie period, which ended five or six years ago, Buffett was still taking care of business. He never missed a show, and always did his best to put on a good one. One member of a tour during this time remembers knocking on his hotel room door in mid-afternoon. Buffett came to the door, saw who it was, and said come on in, but don't tell anybody. Inside, instead of naked groupies sprawled about, there were stacks of paper everywhere—receipts and chits and accountants' reports. He was doing his homework, checking up on how things were going—and didn't want anyone to know about it.

We talked about business recently when I visited him at his south Georgia plantation, his current favorite hideout. I sure didn't blame him. It is off some side road in the middle of nowhere, a genteel old birdhunting planta-tion, his 600 acres adjoining another 6000 acres of manicured woods with an occasional token cornfield and pond to lure the birds in, and a few sandy jeep tracks winding unobtrusively through it all. A quiet place whose main house is reached on a curving quarter-mile gravel lane shaded by twin rows of patrician live oaks dripping Spanish moss. This long driveway is flanked by wood-fenced horse pastures and stands of old pine beyond. The house, built in 1928 by the Orvis sporting goods family, has the look of a big elegant log cabin, built in an H shape, more like a 19th century Adirondack great lodge than the southern gothic country houses that are more common around here.

It was early March, gray late winter back home, but spring here, the bushes already heavy with white and purple flowers, mockingbirds calling, the air soft and gently warm.

I knocked on the front door, and Sunshine answered.

"I thought it was Savannah Jane," she said by way of greeting. "Nobody else ever uses this door."

Sunshine Smith is an old friend of Buffett's from Key West. She might have been a hippie once; there is a sunny organic look to her now. She manages and owns a share of Buffett's tee-shirt store in Key West. Laughing she told me he gets it both ways: profit from making the tee-shirts, and then profit again for selling them to his own store. She also serves sometimes as his administrative assistant, fielding whatever comes along, from journalists to lunch. They decided years ago that this would be a hands-off friendship, and it's lasted. Buffett is currently among the formerly married, and is lucky to have her around—Sunshine enviably combines the qualities of business partner, execu-tive secretary, nanny, cook, and understanding pal.

The house inside is natural wood, like some unpainted rustic cabin raised to a state of simple elegance. A small fleet of maids in green uniforms were bustling around cleaning—an enviable perk in itself.

Sunshine led me through a study with a nice big fireplace, passing a 'family room' dominated by a Mitsubishi television set with a screen the size of a garage door. Buffett was in a small room whose window overlooked a tree and bushes hung with bird feeders, and lots of birds digging in, including at the moment a Carolina chickadee, a boffo rose-breasted grosbeak, and the scarlet splashes of several cardinals. Who would have thought! Mr. Margaritaville a birdwatcher!

He was fussing with some new equipment, setting up a little home studio in this room. Wearing a shortsleeved yellow shirt and khaki pants, no mustache, light golden toast tan, he looked alarmingly healthy and fit.

After turning, as he put it, "from a Catholic altar boy to a roaring party animal," five years or so ago he decided to clean up the act. He said a series of brutal anxiety attacks onstage—in front of thousands of people—did the trick, along with feelings of responsibility to his daughter and the other people who depended on him. Once in a while Catholic guilt works for you. That and going to the funerals of too many friends who had boogied too close to the edge. He entered no rehab clinics, just did it. Today there is Corona in the refrigerator and a rack of prime-vintage wine nearby in the kitchen, but he said said goodbye to the substances that provided that illegal gleam for so long.

On this morning he'd just gotten back from Tallahassee, where mostly for the television stations, on the statehouse steps, the Governor had presented him and a few others with one of the first Florida license plates with a manatee and your vanity word of choice on them. The extra money people will pay for them goes toward the protection of manatees. Buffett put a song about them on an album a while back; they are one among a number of environmental causes he gives time and money to. His manatee license plate read BUFFET. Apparently the state needs to hire a proofreader or two. Later on the five o'clock news I saw him hold it up to the camera, grinning, saying "I just wish they could get my name right."

He showed Sunshine and me the license plate. He said he was invited that night to a celebrity dinner for these license plates, where he would have a chance to meet Michelle Pfeiffer. (Still meeting girls!) But his parents were driving up for a visit, so he'd be staying home with them.

We moved into the sunny kitchen, where Sunshine made shrimp salad sandwiches while Buffett looked for a particular cassette and put it in the kitchen boom box. Out came Stevie Winwood doing *Green Onions*. Outstanding.

While we listened, Buffett told me that this was his latest business interest—a small new record company being put together in Memphis by long-time Nashville record producer Norbert Putnam. The idea is to make records having that great sixties Memphis/Motown/New Orleans sound, but which are mostly new songs written in the same jukebox beach party vein. And using some of the original performers: The Neville Brothers, parts of Booker T. and the MGs, Stevie Winwood—who in a bow to the actual old has cut this radiant version of *Green Onions* we were listening to, one that rivals Winwood's classic *Gimme Some Lovin'*, which is going some. Buffett is writing a few songs for the Neville Brothers. It could be interesting.

"Shit," Buffett said, "when Norbert told me about it, I said I'd invest $50,000 in something like that *any* time. So now I figure I'm an accountant's nightmare. I own a boat, an airplane, a bar and a record company. Everything a wise accountant advises you not to be in.

"Oh, I have good conservative lawyers and accountants and such advising me on investments, but I do what I want. I bought this farm sight unseen. I was in England on tour, and my friend Guy called and told me about it. The guy who was training my bird dogs was also a caretaker here, and told Guy it was going up for sale.

"I think I've got a pretty good business sense. It goes back to my old days, it was a necessity when I was a one-man show traveling around in a station wagon. I booked myself around, ran my own sound, paid my taxes. I was 21, self-contained. The guys who become leaders of bands are the ones who take care of business—hassle club owners over the gate, get bookings—they are the ones who are still around. And I've always liked working. Because it gave me an independence. I was strongly independent as a kid and I still am now. I turned down The Mouse!" he said grinning.

He'd been approached by Disney to put a Margaritaville in Disneyworld. Proof that there are still bizarre ideas out there in the business community. The Margarativille crowd in there with the Frontierland crowd? Just hard to imagine. But the potential numbers were such that he considered it, finally turning to his Dad for advice—something he does fairly regularly, Buffett told me. "He said, well, you've got enough money to do whatever you want to do, right? And I said, yeah. He said, then you decide what you want out of it. Don't commit to anything you feel uncomfortable doing." And so Buffett came up with a counter-offer, reverting to old musician's instincts. "I asked for a percentage of the gate on the nights that I played. I told them, I work on 80-20 splits most of the tme doing concerts, so I want 20% of the whole gate on the nights I work. Twenty percent of everything you take in that night. Their mouths dropped open. And that was that. No deal. Also Disney was too clean and pristine. In Margaritaville you expect to see dope dealers, rifraff, Captain Tony—and

Disneyworld is too clean. I could have made a jillion dollars doing it, but I would get the feeling I'd sold out, and I think the people who look to me would feel that way too. So I turned down The Mouse."

While we ate Sunshine's excellent shrimp sandwiches, I asked if there had been any time when he thought his career might be going belly up, and he said yes, in the early eighties, when his record sales dropped like a rock. "The music changed. And our time was supposedly over."

It was the coming of videos, rap music, synthesizers, the re-ascendancy of Pop, the Brill Building triumphant over good old blues-and-country-based rock & roll. Suddenly the kind of music Buffett made was old-fashioned—or so thought the record companies anyway. Warner Brothers unceremoniously axed several major names—including Van Morrison and Bonnie Raitt—whose music no longer seemed profitably hip to them. Buffett figured he might be next, 86'd from the label he was on.

"I felt lucky. I'd had a run. Most people hadn't gotten that far. But all of a sudden, I saw things going down, and it's something you have to think of. It's a reality. This ain't going to go on forever. I thought, if it was really over, I'd retire. Because I will not be working a Holiday Inn as a has-been. I will never do that. And that was my greatest fear that kept me moving."

But then all that touring paid off. While his record sales in the early eighties dropped noticeably, his concert attendance didn't. People knew they were going to have a good time at a Jimmy Buffett concert. Unlike other 70s artists who'd been able to fill football stadiums and were now playing the casino lounge in Tunica, Mississippi, Buffett's hardcore crowd of Parrotheads hung in there with him, and kept growing. "Before that," he said, "I was selling more records and playing to less people than I do now, and now I play to more people and sell less records."

"But," he said, "I've had a 20-year battle with my record company. I've never felt they've adequately done what they can to promote me. When I see Bonnie Raitt with four Grammies this year, I get pissed off." He quickly adds that this is nothing against Bonnie Raitt, of whom he is a great admirer. "But I think I do as good work as she does. It's my record company. They don't understand how to promote what I'm doing."

This may have something to do with his newfound career as a writer.

"I always have a Plan B," he told me. "And I want to work regular shows maybe five more years, and then only occasionally. I want to be working on books instead."

This is the current buzz among his friends: he wants to be thought of as a writer now, has gone into competition with his pals Jim Harrison and Tom McGuane, by my lights two of the very best writers going. (McGuane is also his brother-in-law, having married Buffett's sister twelve years ago.) Both Harrison and McGuane have recent novels that barely scratched the bestseller lists, while *Margarativille* keeps sailing along. Word is that this has caused some strife in this tangled famous extended family, but Buffett says no, not true, that brother-in-law McGuane called right away with congratulations as soon as it started happening.

It's a savvy career move, and one not available to most fortyish musicians getting a bit weary of the road. The sales of *Tales from Margaritaville* have been such that he's gotten a hefty advance on a novel—enough money to induce him to spend most of his time writing it for a fall deadline, which has to be a lot. I didn't ask how much.

The novel is about Frank Bama, seaplane pilot. Buffett was inspired by flying in a Grumman Goose on Chalk's Airlines from Miami to Bimini. Flying on these old seaplanes is like getting into the belly of an aluminum duck, takeoff is a wet desperate affair seen through windshield wipers and spray—and plopping down at the other end, the plane waddling out of the water onto a patch of black-top on Bimini, is also a splashy experience.

There are only a few of these Grumman Gooses left, and their former pilots are getting old. Buffett has sought out several of the pilots and talked to them for their stories; he's also done research on the planes in several libraries—the star as journalist and historian. And, since he also has a star's money, he's found a Grumman Goose in pieces in Miami that he's this close to buying and having restored, at a cost of about $300,000.

"I can sell my other airplane and be in it. And it makes no sense at all—a radial engine, an airplane built in 1947. But there are only about 30 left in the world."

His accountants should love that one.

Another of about 16 new enterprises is a Broadway show that's in the works. He and Glenn Frey are writing the songs, and Larry L. King (who wrote *The Best Little Whorehouse in Texas*) is doing the book. Frey plans to be in it—trying to make a "career move"—but Buffett seems to be doing it more for the fun of it than anything, a fairly basic motive for him it seems. After talking about how Broadway music has longevity, isn't quickly perishable if it becomes a hit, and the appeals of that, his shorthand take was: "Another one to cross off life's list."

It struck me as we talked that far more than most of us, Buffett has lived out his fantasies. Existentialsim in action: you are what you do, not what you talk about. And what you do depends on what you let yourself think of. Buffett has let his imagination roam freely, and done just about everything he could think of. Sailing off Bora-Bora. Singing the *Star Spangled Banner* at Wrigley Field. Having a star-spangled circle of friends in which "Jack said at dinner" means Jack

Nicholson. On and on.

I asked him, out of all these adventures and experiences, what's been the top kick of all? He beamed. "Easy. Taking off and landing on an aircraft carrier in an F-14 Navy jet fighter—top of the list. I rode in the navigator's seat. Unbelievable. There's nothing else like it. It's beyond anything you can describe. I fly, but this takes flying to another level.

"I always wanted to do it," he said. "I used to drive over to Pensacola from Mobile, and see all the Navy officers in flight training. I'd see these guys tearing up the sky, then driving sports cars, and they'd have their uniforms on, and it looked pretty snappy. If I had not become a musician, I probably would have become a pilot. Something had to get me out of my dull existence in Mobile. I wanted to see the world, and these guys moved, traveled, and I wanted to go. That was just in my blood. I always was a Road Dog."

- 1991

For a number of reasons, this article is one of my favorites. First and foremost, because it features my daughter, Maude, as the main character. I had convinced my editor at Universal Press Syndicate, Harriet Choice, to let me do a piece about the stretch of Highway 61 between Memphis and Vicksburg, often called "Blues Alley"— since this section of Highway 61 cuts through the Mississippi Delta, the home of the blues. As it happened, I was about to leave for the trip when Maude said she had spring vacation that week, hint hint hint. Of course I said sure, and we jumped on a plane to Memphis. Maude was fourteen at the time. Beyond this excuse to hang out with Maude for a week, and loving the blues from the first time I heard it, I had another secret agenda for going, for which I blame Bob Dylan. I've always had a special oddball connection with Dylan—we are almost exactly the same age, barely a month apart. Somehow that accident of shared time has resonated for me in his music—kinda nuts, I guess, but true. And one of my all-time Dylan songs has been Highway 61 Revisited. *Listen again if you haven't recently. Hilarious, brilliant, shining with speed and riffing on Kierkegaard. I am only one of millions who were inspired by the song to attempt to see every foot of Highway 61. And doing this section of it, added a major, and important, section of that main vein, which runs from Duluth all the way to New Orleans. So this trip also represented another of my pointless quests.*

There's a footnote about the editing history of this article. As I said, I wrote it for Harriet Choice at UPS. It should be noted that UPS is a newspaper syndicate. I've spent most of my life writing for magazines, and they are a different animal. And it should be said that I have never been much good at following rules of any kind. I sort of fake it, however that leads me. I should add too that Harriet is a terrific editor, and we have worked a lot together over the years, but we've had a few dustups from time to time as well. In fact, full disclosure, I have at times been a pain in the ass to editors over the years. Harriet, in fact, used to call me "Tootsie"—from the Dustin Hoffman movie, where he was a terrific actor but such a prick to work with that he had to start dressing as a woman in order to get any work. So that's the context. I sent the first draft piece to Harriet, and, well, let's just say that she was so pissed that I could have heard her screaming at me without needing the phone—I could have heard her without it. My offense? I had put Maude in the piece as a character. And it was all in first person! This was not how UPS operated! As she cited my myriad deep fuckups on the phone, I could practically see her percolating differing shades of red while we talked, or rather blistered. Take out all mention of Maude! No one cares about your children! Put it in decent sensible third person! Don't you know anything? And do it by next week! So I revised it completely, no Maude, no first person. Harriet liked the revision, and it ran. Shortly after this, I was on the phone with my friend Tom Passavant, the EIC of Diversion magazine and a long time friend, and, as writers will, I started tell him about my screwup with UPS. Tom was curious, and asked if I would send him the first version, just out of curiosity, he had an idea. So I sent it to him. He read it and called me back. He'd like to publish the earlier version, with Maude and first person, but he did want me to do some revisions on it. What was that, I asked. "Just one thing," said Tom. "I want you to put in more Maude!" So goes editors. The version here is the one Tom published in Diversion. I know why Harriet insisted on my changes, but, like Tom, and as always, I wanted more Maude!

DELTA
DREAMIN'
ON THE ROAD WITH MAUDE &
KODIAK MAN OF CHIPPICHAK

It was just a big plain handpainted sign on the side of a ramshackle old barn on a country road a few miles east of Highway 61, outside Cleveland, Mississippi:

DOCKERY FARMS
ESTAB. 1895

So why was the hair on the back of my neck standing on end?

Because this was the *source*, the cotton plantation where in the early years of this century Charlie Patton, the first great delta bluesman, worked and lived—and influenced generations of blues musicians leading right down to the present. Robert Johnson, a key figure in early delta blues, learned from him. His music also inspired Howlin' Wolf, Muddy Waters and others who moved to Chicago in the 1940s, where their music became the "electric urban blues" that were the headwaters of rock & roll. Without them, Elvis would never have become The King, and Mick and Keith wouldn't be counting their money in villas on Mallorca today.

A gravel road not far from the Dockery barn cuts straight across empty fields for nearly two miles before ending at a treeline. The dark ground was newly plowed in this spring season. Until the machinery that displaced them started coming along after World War II, this road had been lined with the wooden shacks of more than 2500 black farm laborers and their families. Ghosts now.

They had lived here and worked some of the richest earth on Earth, left by eons of Aprils when the Mississippi River overflowed its banks and its water spread shining for miles over the flat land, leaving behind more topsoil each time it withdrew again.

That's what the Mississippi Delta is. Not the fan of land that accumulates at the mouth of a river when it reaches the sea, but rather a vast floodplain that stretches nearly two hundred miles from Memphis to Vicksburg and extends as much as 30 miles on either side of the river's current course. Until the Civil War it had been soggy ground covered with hardwoods, but in the years that followed, the trees were nearly all cut and levees built to control the river.

By the time Charlie Patton came to work at Dockery's, it was becoming as it is now, farmland as far as the eye can see. There is a stark beauty to the unrelentingly flat landscape, which has nurtured the blues as lovingly as it has cotton and other crops.

We began our roadtrip pilgrimage along Highway 61—this stretch of it known as 'Blues Alley'—in Memphis.

I'd brought along my 14-year-old daughter Maude. She'd been hoping for Jamaica or Hawaii, but life isn't perfect, and she ended up having a lot more fun than she'd expected to on this excursion through the origins of her Dad's record collection.

Our first stop, since it's ten minutes from the Memphis airport right on the way to Highway 61 south, and somehow as inevitable as death and Disney World, was Graceland. Poor Elvis. The mansion, which seemed unexpectedly dinky as mansions go, faces what is now called Elvis Presley Boulevard, in the middle of one of the ugliest strips of commercial gabonga I've ever seen. Graceland Dodge. Elvis Presley Storage. Elvis Presley Motors. Egad. But we took the tour and were glad we did. I was just the right age when Elvis came along. The increasingly garish—and increasingly large—jumpsuits on display in the memorabilia room adjoining the mansion attest to his long sad fall, but for a while there he was as cool as it got. Looking at the early pictures of him performing when he was first starting out, like some handsome untamed panther, powerful and wild, even thoroughly modern Maude agreed. We skipped the sweet potato pie at the Heartbreak Hotel Restaurant, and also passed up the Elvis Presley Early Days Screen Saver in the gift shop, but did buy a few souvenir postcards and were on our way.

Soon we were on Highway 61. As we were to discover again and again on the trip, driving through this part of the South is often like time travel. On our right on the outskirts of Memphis, Maude pointed and said, "What's that?" It was a true anachronism, a drive-in movie theater, still a going concern—the first she'd ever seen.

Then we were out in the country, many of the fields a bright sea of yellow wildflowers, glowing in the soft afternoon light. The telephone poles were the skinny, slightly crooked, old-fashioned kind, the power lines drooping and drooping to the horizon.

Yet another form of time travel was evident on the billboards lining the road at regular intervals. There are riverboat gambling casinos now in Mississippi, and the entertainment mainstays in their showrooms seem also to be blasts from the past. In the 20 mile stretch to Tunica, we saw signs trumpeting upcoming performances by Johnny Rivers, Frankie Valli, Eric Burden, Tony Bennett, and, believe it or not, Grand Funk Railroad—which I'd thought had been off rusting on a siding somewhere since the 70s.

But the real time travel comes when you leave the main highway to check out the small towns lurking just a few miles away. We were hungry, so we turned off toward Tunica, three miles distant, which looked at first to be fast asleep, its main square practically empty and most of the storefronts—relics of an earlier and more prosperous time—closed.

We parked and began walking around anyway, and on a sidestreet just off the square seriously lucked out. Café Marie, in an old hotel, seemed an anomaly with its CAPPUCCINO sign in the window and its spiffy modern interior; and, our stomachs were delighted to find, it was delicious. We were the only customers, and the cook himself brought out my broiled catfish filet with cajun spice the moment it was ready. Maude was most impressed with their "Chocolate Chip Cookie Blast" dessert, which begins on a base of a huge homemade cookie and adds three scoops of ice cream, fudge sauce and bits of Heath Bars—an invention, our waitress told us, of her mother's one slow afternoon when she began having chocolate daydreams.

Afterward we drove to the river a few miles west. The sun was setting, the county road paralleling a remnant of cypress swamp, its still water the pinky color of the sky, dark gnarled stumps rising from it. Beyond the levee, along the riverbank, resided a fishing camp, of the truly downhome variety. More than a few of the riverside 'cabins' were actually old aluminum mobile homes up on stilts—to protect them from flooding. We got out to stretch our legs and admire the sun going down over the river, both of us feeling happily far from home.

We spent the next morning exploring Clarksdale, 40 miles south on 61. With 15,000 people, Clarksdale is one of the bigger cities in the delta. And it's ground zero when it comes to delta blues. Even former Led Zeps Jimmy Page and Robert Plant know it—their most recent semi-reunion album is titled *Walkin' To Clarksdale*. The roster of important blues artists that came from around here is simply amazing—including Muddy Waters, Howlin' Wolf, John Lee Hooker, Son House, Ike Turner, and many others.

The sharecropper's cabin on the outskirts of town, where Muddy lived for many years, is, after a fashion, still standing—or will be again soon. While we were there, it was on tour (which seemed sort of perfect), being taken around to various House of Blues clubs for display. It's scheduled to be put back up where it belongs, but right now the site is a grassy lot. The little brick train depot where Muddy got on the Illinois Central for Chicago in 1943—taken as the beginning of the electric blues he created after he got there—is long shut down, but you can stand on the platform just like he did. She wasn't from Clarksdale, but Bessie Smith, one of the first ladies of the blues, died after a car accident on 61 at the now-decrepit Riverside Hotel on Sunflower Street (rooms still for rent, but only the brave need apply), where countless classic blues performers stayed while playing local juke joints—a few of which are still very much in business.

But *the* legendary spot is the intersection of old highway 61 and 49 under two miles southeast of the Delta Blues Museum, on Clarksdale's outskirts. Others in the delta make the claim, but this seems to be the favorite choice as the crossroads where Robert Johnson supposedly sold his soul to the Devil one dark midnight in exchange for playing guitar and singing the blues like a tormented angel. It's the one in his *Crossroads*, arguably the quintessential delta blues of the 30s, electrified with a vengeance by Cream in 1968 into one of the most kickass rock songs of all time. Today the intersection, for a non-blues fan, is unremarkable or worse. It's not the spooky rural meeting place of gravel tracks in the legend—rather a faceoff of a Fuel Mart, a Church's Chicken, and The Delta Donut Shop right next to Abe's Barbecue. Changed just a *bit* since Johnson's time, true, but for me at least, still kind of a thrill to see after all these years of listening to the song.

As was the green rusty metal THREE FORKS STORE sign hanging on a wall of the Delta Blues Museum, housed in part of the Carnegie Public Library downtown. This is the actual sign from the juke joint not too many miles away where Johnson died in 1938 at the age of 27, poisoned—according to most accounts—by drinking from an open bottle of whiskey laced with strychnine, generously offered him by the owner as a reward for Johnson's having been flagrantly fooling around with his woman, the final payoff of Johnson's deal with the Devil.

We checked out the rest of the small musuem—the 'Muddywood' guitar, made of wood from his cabin, was especially cool—and then drove over to the St. George Episcopal Church on Sharkey Street to see the rectory where Tennessee Williams spent the first years of his life, living with his grandfather Dakin, who was pastor of the church (this after Williams' father proved too footloose and flaky to take care of the family).

Dakin also tended a church in Tunica, making the 40-mile trip by mule-drawn wagon. He would often overnight about halfway at the Moon Lake Club, a small unassuming resort on a fishing lake, then owned by a relative, and Williams sometimes went along. It was pretty wild—with a dancehall, a little casino upstairs, and private rooms where things went on that decent folks didn't talk about. Great material for little Tom—years later in fictional form it became the setting for his heavy-breathing play *Summer and Smoke*.

It's still in business, though now as a genteel and charming country b & b and restaurant called Uncle Henry's, so we drove out to take a look. Which proved to be a little more than that. As Sarah Wright, the pleasant silver-haired owner, graciously gave us the tour, Maude fell in love.

"Oh, daddy, can we stay here?"

Sure can. The building, dating from 1926, is a rambling old frame affair. Mrs. Wright has planted lovely flower gardens all around, and decorated the inside in period stuff from the 30s and earlier, including a lot of family memorabilia. Her mother's dresses and hats on mannequins were Maude's favorites, but the canopied four-poster bed in what would be 'her' room is what did the trick, I think.

As Mrs. Wright showed us around, she told us nice stories about growing up here. And about Elvis. As a girl she'd sometimes go to Memphis to the movies, at the Loew's State Theater, where Elvis was working as an usher. "He was so thoughtful," she said. "He always remembered just where I liked to sit. He was such a nice boy, so polite and handsome—except for all that grease he wore in his hair!"

The restaurant features splendid southern-style seafood cooked by her son, who's an accomplished chef. Uncle Henry's is a terrific rural retreat, only about 5 miles off Highway 61, and at $65 a night, including a lavish breakfast, it's a far, far better thing than some dismal bland motel at the same price on the main highway.

Maude wanted simply to move in. But the next morning we headed down the road to Cleveland, about 50 miles south. It rained pitchforks all day, but Maude and I didn't mind. It was Saturday, and there was an all-day-and-into-the-night blues festival going on at the Airport Grocery at the edge of town on the road to Rosedale.

Formerly a grocery store near the airport—cleverly enough—it's now a funky bar/restaurant with a stage at one end. The decor is *roadside chic*, with old metal Texaco Skychief, Drink Barque's, and Dr. Pepper signs on the walls, dangling lights with rusty gray buckets as shades, tables covered with green oilcloths.

We spent most of the afternoon there. The Grocery has a good-time family atmosphere, and the food is as authentic as the music.

To her great credit—she is a northern city girl, after all—Maude didn't even hesitate when the heaping platter of boiled crawfish, heads and crawly appendages still attached, was set in front of us. Her instructions to other first-timers: "All you have to do is twist off their tails, rip off the shell, and eat the meat. A lot of people like to suck the juice from their heads. They call them 'mudbugs'. They're really good."

Truly my girl—she'd brought along *On The Road* as recreational reading for the trip—she even dug the bands and was happy to linger. For a music so much about bad times and sorrow, listening to live blues sure is a lot of *fun*. Maude got into a long gin rummy game with several other kids, and when I wasn't just sitting back soaking up the music, I struck up easy conversations with other blues fans and performers too.

It was a great rainy day.

But Sunday proved bright and sunny with soft poofy clouds in crystal blue sky, and a mild gentle breeze—perfect spring. Our goal that morning was Robert Johnson's gravesite in Morgan City. Probably the single thing Maude and I enjoyed most about the whole trip was taking these semilost, exploratory excursions off Highway 61 into the country. On back roads so back some have no number, it's peaceful and redolent of more tranquil times in ways you just don't get in Chicago, much as we both love it.

We were on some empty highway heading in the general direction of Morgan City, not really concerned about getting a little lost, when Maude pointed out a definite home-fashion statement: A house trailer come to rest in the middle of a big lawn, painted the most electrically exuberent purple I'd ever seen in my life.

"We need a picture," Maude said as we whizzed by. I agreed, though it seemed unlikely that film could do it justice. So we stopped and turned around. As we got out with the camera, so did the trailer's owner, and the two rotweilers in a pen behind the trailer set up a ferocious din. But all was cool. The owner, an older man, gave us a smile and waved hello. He shushed the dogs, and said by way of greeting, "Don't mine them, they's jus' happy t' see ya."

Riiiight, was my thought, but they were fenced in and would probably take at least a few minutes to gnaw their way through the chainlink to get to us. We all said hello, and he told Maude to go right ahead with the picture, he liked the color too. We asked what he called it. "Beats the hell out of me," he said. "Just a color." He tried shushing the dogs again, but no luck. "They're just like my chirrens," he said. Maude asked their names. "Theobaldus is the baby, and the big one, he's Kodiak Man of Chippichak." Along with color choice, he got an A in my book for dog-naming too. We talked some more—he warned us about snakes in this wet spring weather—and then were off again.

Morgan City must have been named in a fit of someone's optimism. It's just a blip on a blue highway, little more than a cotton gin, a grocery store, and a small clump of houses. We had to ask directions at the grocery for the Mt. Zion churchyard, on a side lane a mile past town. It seemed nearly forgotten, the little white-siding church, hardly bigger than a double garage, closed tight on this Sunday morning, nothing but farm fields in every direction. But the gray granite grave marker was there, and we stood looking at it for a while, the quote on it from one of his songs come true: "You may bury my body down by the highway side, so my evil old spirit can get a Greyhound bus and ride."

It seemed somehow fitting that Johnson, so elusive and mysterious during his brief lifetime, had finally come to rest in this out of the way place.

Heading back toward Highway 61, we crossed a bridge over a small placid green river, and stopped to get out and envy the turtles peacefully sunning themselves on a big log sticking out into the water. Another to add to my reincarnation wishlist.

But Maude had spotted a limegreen flash zipping around and was off in pursuit. She's never had this *eeeuuuuw!* thing about various creatures that girls are supposed to have. Soon she was hurrying back wearing a big grin and holding up one softly closed fist. "Look, daddy! I caught a lizard! Can we keep him? We can call him Kodiak Man of Chippichak!"

We found a box to put him in temporarily, and discussed it in the car on the way to the Memphis airport.

I pointed out that the airlines probably frowned on bringing live lizards onboard. But then I've never been exactly perfect at following rules, and Kodiak Man of Chippichak was both cute and fairly small, and seemed unlikely to cause any major disruptions, or to set off the metal detectors, so I said why not?

Maude tucked him in the front pocket of her thriftshop Boy Scouts shirt, buttoned the flap, gave him a gentle friendly pat, and aboard we went with our contraband. Maude must have peeked at him about 36 times during the short flight to Chicago, but no one noticed, and our cold-blooded smuggling run was a success.

Kodiak Man of Chippichak, formerly of the Mississippi delta, has a new home.

- 1998

I didn't know it at the time, but this proved to be a milestone—after forty years, I was hanging up my rock and roll shoes. Don't get me wrong. I still crank up my sound system until the speakers are shredding on occasion. And I'm one of those who blasts Led Zep or Cream or Hendrix in the car while I'm tooling along waving my AARP card out the window. I am with Dylan Thomas: Do not go gentle to that good night, old age should burn and rage at the close of day, rage, rage (loudly!) against the dying of the life. *So I haven't wimped out entirely. But the article here—about the opening of Cleveland's Rock & Roll Museum and killer six-hour concert in mouldering Cleveland Stadium on the lakeshore next door—did prove to be the last piece I ever wrote about rock. And it couldn't have been a better farewell. Turn it up!*

THEY'RE ROCKIN'
IN CLEVELAND!
OPENING WEEKEND AT THE ROCK AND
ROLL HALL OF FAME AND MUSEUM

I grew up there, so I'm prejudiced, but you have to admire a city that throws a huge civically-sponsored downtown parade to honor the history of rock & roll. This is sort of like honoring The History of Teenage Sin and Delinquency, and it was great. Especially the huge 20-foot Elvis puppet shaking his hips down East 9th Street, and the similarly enormous Madonna with more than proportionate breasts.

Cleveland did this to celebrate the opening of the lakefront's Rock and Roll Hall of Fame and Museum last Labor Day weekend.

I went to my first rock concert ever in Cleveland in 1955. I was fourteen. It was at one of the ornate old three-balcony movie theaters downtown near Terminal Tower, then Cleveland's only highrise and a very funny name for a building, I have always thought. The headliners were Bill Haley & The Comets, but a far, far better thing was the opening act—none other than Chuck Berry. Chuck was wearing an electric-green iridescent suit and when he duck-walked across the stage, his red Gibson slung gunslinger low, chug chug chugging out *Maybelline*—well, the hair on the back of my neck went tingling, and my life was changed.

The Labor Day weekend Saturday night concert to celebrate the opening of the museum was at mouldering old brown concrete Cleveland Stadium, hovering like some glacial boulder over the post-postmodernist I.M. Pei building built for the rock museum close by—which looks, as one of my Cleveland cousins put it, like an abstract white RCA 45rpm record changer from the 50s, with a triangular greenhouse falling crashing against it.

As a 7-year-old with my Dad I had seen a couple of games at the Stadium in 1948 when the Indians won the Series and creamed everybody—even the Yankees! And as a first-generation TV-child a year or so later had pleaded and begged to be taken there to see a personal appearance by Hopalong Cassidy and his faithful horse (anybody remember?) Topper. Gray-haired and grinning, he was perhaps the first and last geriatric cowboy hero. I never had any taste. Seeing Hoppy there in 1950 was the last time I'd been to the Stadium.

It hadn't changed much, nicely grubby then and now.

The concert opened with Chuck himself doing *Johnny B. Goode*, with Bruce Springsteen and the E. Street Band as his backup group. Heaven. All these years later, Chuck was still at it, and so was I.

And so were my wife, Carol, and the kids, Willie 9 and Maude 11.

We had turned this into a family road trip, a generational rock & roll initiation for the kids, and even rented a fancy all-frills new black Lincoln Continental for the drive from Chicago. If you've lived in the Midwest long enough, the farms of northern Indiana and Ohio along the old turnpikes seem beautiful in late-summer sunlight, and then when we got there we were in a Radisson suite-hotel right downtown. It wasn't the Four Seasons, but Willie and Maude were thrilled to find that our suite had not one but two TVs with cable.

Naturally they had to cruise the hotel.

And in their wanderings—Willie, I'll never forgive you!—in the 5th-floor lobby sitting room, Willie ran into Little Richard, who was staying there too. Willie knew who he was (what a kid!), said hello and shook hands with him and they talked for a while. I'll be forever envious.

The Saturday night concert was great foreplay for going to the museum the next day. At seven-plus hours it was a marathon even for us veterans. But Carol and the kids hung in there. Walking across the parking lot back toward our hotel at 3 in the morning, poor Willie was dragging a little but still determined and game, and as we walked holding hands some guy in his twenties noticed us, and said, nodding a look at Willie, "How old is he?" I said nine and the guy grinned. "Cool!" was all he said. When we got back to the hotel, despite how late it was, we were all so buzzed we had to sit up and talk about it for another hour. Rock and roll will do that to you.

Right there on that stage had been Chuck, Bruce, Aretha, Little Richard, Dr. John, Jackson Browne, Al Greene, James Brown, The Pretenders, Booker T. & the MGS, 'Soul Man' Dave Robinson, Robbie Robertson, The Kinks, The Allman Brothers, spaceman George Clinton, and for me, the best, surprise guest Bob Dylan, with yet another new hot young band doing *Highway 61*, one of my own personal top five rock songs.

We were definitely primed to see the museum on Sunday. Tired, but primed.

The Rock & Roll Museum is in Cleveland because rock & roll was invented there. In 1951 Alan Freed went on the air on Cleveland's WJW with his nighttime "Moondog House," often opening the show with one called *Sixty Minute Man* by The Dominoes. Sixty minutes of what? Things beyond what was going on with little fifth-grade me, that was for sure. I was 10 at the time, and it seemed proof, both wonderful and scary, that there truly was another world out there after all, far beyond *Shrimp Boats Are A'Comin'* and *How Much Is That Doggie in the Window?* Freed was picking up on the fact that white teenagers had started buying and loving black rhythm and blues records, epitomized by the urban Chicago blues, which is the true wellspring of rock—and on the radio in Cleveland he had named this black music that white kids were starting to like "Rock and Roll," longtime black slang for just what you might imagine. Hard to believe, but for a while there, Cleveland was the hippest location in the nation. We invented it, folks. Well, okay—at least we named it.

Still, I confess that I have become cynical enough that I was ready for the Rock & Roll Museum to be nothing more than a Hard Rock Café on the grand scale. But I am lococentrically proud to say that it's far better than that, a qualitative leap.

It is something done well.

You could spend two whole days there, easy. Okay, I could. For anyone with a rock & roll heart, the collections, are, well, thrilling. There's all this actual stuff from everyone you ever listened to when you were growing up and in love with that teen angel or hurting from teen heartbreak, the artifacts of all our emotional histories there to see.

Where to start?

Inside, the building is sort of a five-floor pyramid of diminishing size as you go up, with the most displays in the basement, in the Ahmet Ertegun Exhibition Hall, where the history (and pre-history) of rock is there in chronological order through an amazing array of objects and interactive computers and TV loops of various decent people from the 50s denouncing rock & roll as a pernicious influence on innocent teens. Which it was. That's what we liked about it. When it first came along, rock & roll was like *Mad* magazine with a good beat. Only better. Far more subversive, *and* you could dance to it.

I guess my favorite single thing in the Ertegun Hall—he and his brother started Atlantic Records in the early 50s, which became one of the main purveyors of this pernicious influence—is John Lennon's report card from 11th grade or whatever its British equivalent is. Among many disparaging comments, was this from his religion teacher: "Lazy, seldom shows interest, and when he does, it's usually misplaced." But even better, the simple handwritten comment of his Latin teacher. You can almost see him sighing and shaking his head as he wrote the single word: "Hopeless." Lennon was already cool.

On a yellow legal pad page they have Jimi Hendrix' original pencil-scribbled lyrics for *Purple Haze*—and many other original handwritten lyrics similarly displayed. All these songwriters seem to have shared two things—cheap office supplies and questionable handwriting. Except for Paul Simon, whose handwritten lyrics for *Graceland*, while also on a big yellow legal pad page, get an A for neatness.

A lot of costumes/stars' outfits have been donated, and placed on mannequins, so there's a certain weird clothing store aspect to this part of the museum too—except this is the true collarless natty black suit Ringo wore in 1966; John Lennon's greaser black leather jacket from Hamburg days; also his psychedelic-military outfit from the cover of *Sergeant Pepper*; extravagant original gowns worn by The Supremes; an Elvis Presley jumpsuit from 1970, which is fairly scary; a 1977 Jimmy Page white silk suit with embroidered snakes and orentelia on the back; a Gene Simmons Kiss bat outfit; and Michael Jackson's original glittery sequined glove, twirling slowly on a glass pedestal.

They also have Janis Joplin's hippie Porsche convertible, cartoon painted all over with scenes of mountain and sunny skies like some automotive 60s Peter Max poster. Guess she never got that Mercedes Benz, but Porsches are cooler anyway. Another don't miss are the industrial-strength all-metal ZZ Top guitar and bass that look like they were made out of old truck parts, instruments from a band in a *Mad Max* movie. Also Jim Morrison's birth certificate and adorable little baby footprints. And his blue 1950 Cub Scout shirt with merit badges sewn on it. Not quite The Lizard King yet.

Altogether the museum is a fairly wild assault on the senses. And while it's a word not generally associated with rock & roll, it's, yes, educational. This is not simply a stray assemblage of rock junk. It's carefully thought out and arranged, and for those with the time and inclination, it's possible to learn the whole history of rock here.

This is largely thanks to head curator Jim Henke, who was managing editor at *Rolling Stone* for many years, and grew up about five blocks from where I did on the west side of Cleveland, although in a different time zone.

The other five floors of the museum, while each is smaller as you go up, as I can't help repeating, if you have a rock & roll heart, are mind-blowing. Sam Phillips donated the original equipment and furniture from his Sun Records studio, so the place where Elvis and Jerry Lee Lewis first recorded is replicated here. The 12-string Richenbacher that began The Byrds' *Turn, Turn, Turn*. Sad moving photographs of Jerry Garcia looking happy and Buddha-like. The first issue of *Rolling Stone* and other rockzines. There's an arc-shaped radio room with portable radios from the 40s through the 60s on display and interactive computer terminals and headphones where you can find the city and date of your precious youth and hear the disc jockey who was on when you were parked in the dark watching the submarine races with someone somewhere.

Before heading back to Chicago, in fact, I dragged the family around to some of the stations of the cross of my own precious youth on Cleveland's west side. They got to see what used to be Prange's Diner, where we hung out in junior high, listening to *Speedo* by The Cadillacs on the jukebox and checking out our arm muscles. And a spot or two in the still-beautiful Valley (our name for the woodsy metropolitan park that winds along Rocky River for miles) where a few years later I used to park in the dark with Charlene Jirsa, my first true love, with Mad Daddy on the radio as our background make out music. You can hear Mad Daddy at the Rock Museum, and I did, longing more than a little for lost Charlene. The house I lived in during high school is now airspace over the I-71 expressway that's been dug through the old neighborhood, but we found its coordinates and visited its ghost anyway. Carol and Maude and Willie were sweetly tolerant of Dave's Not-So-Magical History Tour.

All the way back to Chicago we listened to the tapes I'd made of the whole Saturday night concert—which was just about the same length as the drive.

And I kept thinking about all that wonderful *stuff* at the Rock & Roll Museum. The roughhewn wooden squared-off guitar that Bo Diddley made for himself in a Chicago vocational high school. Elvis's draft card. Stop me before I list more.

But Maude who's 11 said I had to put in her favorite: John Lennon's small round 60s eyeglasses, her feeling being that they were still cool after all these years. Carol's pick hit was Janis Joplin's crepe Hawaiian-style flowered necklace. And Willie wants me to mention his own favorite, the wig made from Green Day's lead guitarist Billy Joe's hair that's all the colors of the rainbow, which Willie says are all the colors BJ has dyed his hair at various times. Sounds like Dennis Rodman with a guitar to me, but apparently major league if you're 9 and into alternate rock like Willie is. And Green Day is from Cleveland. I was more moved by those scratched-up lyrics to *Purple Haze*, but hey, pass it on to the kids. Isn't that the idea?

- 1995

If only I were a poet, not the lowrent nonfiction writer I am, instead of the article here I would create a poignant elegy, worthy of Keats or Shelley, to say a farewell to my lifelong devoted friend since my youth, now cast aside on the junkyard of history, its lights now dark, its cheerful music forever silent. I am talking of course about pinball machines.

We are about the same age. Pinball machines truly came into their own a year or so after World War II, with the invention of flippers in 1947, on a game called Humpty-Dumpty, *when I was six years old. I may have played it back then, since part of my cultural background among the men in our family, chiefly my father and grandfather, was frequently to bring me along with them "up to the corner"—our local family saloon—where I would be given a kiddie cocktail, usually a Coke loaded with maraschino cherries, and was handed a few nickels to play the shiny new pinball game. Just as I did years later with my kids, Maude and Willie, when our "corner" was Doninger's, where Floyd served up kiddie cocktails for them, where a pinball machine still had an honored place.*

But no more. Pinball has gone the way of rotary telephones, typewriters, cassette tapes, Polaroid cameras, and free air. Dead, extinct. By 2000 no new pinball machines were being manufactured—though in the years since there have been a few sporadic attempts to revive them. Our local Cineplex has a spiffy Rolling Stones *pinball machine in its little game room, for instance, built in 2011 by Stern. But these are rarities, anomalies, sports, the last few remaining specimens of a bird that once darkened the sky with its numbers.*

So I lament their passing. I have measured out my life with pinball machines. They are perfect—there is no better, or more pleasing, complete utter waste of time. And each game is its own little microcosmic lesson, you're caught for a few moments in a fleeting present beyond future and past where nothing has meaning except trying to keep the silver shining balls in play, though, no matter how hard you try, at the end, one by one, they drop into the out hole and you're done. The only winner is gravity. Every time. Truly existential. Pinball might have been designed by Camus and Sartre, with inspiration by Kierkegaard. And unlike dumb video games, which aren't capable of such subtlety, pinball can exert a measure of human free will, and can influence the outcome. By strategic body english, light deft wrist action, you can imperceptibly alter the playboard by microns and change your fate, send the ball to live again, for a brief time anyway. No video game, trapped by its rigid humorless algorithm, can say that. Freedom! And there is hubris lurking as well. One reckless pushy move, and it's TILT!—the pinball gods' saying you have committed overweening pride. So not only are pinball machines great fun, they're packed with metaphysics!

I walked into the pinball convention described in this article, and found dozens of pinball machines in one expansive room, all of them lit up and ready to go, all set on free play—three days of a pinball binge, just costing the price of admission. I was in heaven, of course. My son Willie, then twelve, was eager to join me, since he was even then a smart kid with a good sense of values. As you'll see in the article, we both had a ball.

But all these years laters—Willie turns 29 next week as I write this, and now prefers to be called Wil—and looking back, I find myself feeling a certain wave of sadness about it. Not about the experience, but... All those old pinball games, all in one place like that, seem now to me like phantasms, shades of the passing of pinball. I see that convention room full of pinball machines like a gathering of bright ghosts, each one an individual, each one standing for a single time and place. A noisy chorus of garrulous old geezers, bent on telling their stories at top volume, and no one listening. You can see why I'm empathizing here. But I could do worse than being reincarnated as a pinball machine. You can read the piece to see which one I'd be.

PINBALL LIZARD
SPARE FIREBALL? SPARE FIREBALL?

Here's true addiction:

A buddy and I were on our way home from college for Christmas vacation, somewhere in cold empty northern Ohio, on a Greyhound bus. This was fancy travel for me in those days, when hitchhiking was my usual way of getting around. It was snowing hard when the bus pulled into the parking lot of a diner for a rest stop. Its name was Coffee Pete's. I remember because I ended up spending most of the afternoon there, long after the bus left, hooked.

I had no choice. The inescapable siren song of cheery blings and dings had me the moment I walked in. It was *4 Roses*, a brand-new machine I'd never played. The backglass was a sexy pinup parade of blonde bathing beauties, with more smiling up from the playing field. I had to try it.

I got my turn right away, and it was great. I didn't even bother to order a burger. And I had the knack. It was mine. I hit a big bonus and heard the sweetest sound in the world, that deep satisfying KA-THUNK! signaling that I'd won a free game. I'd racked up six more by the time the bus driver started honking to get everyone moving. My buddy and I looked at each other. We didn't even have to speak. Get back on the bus? You're kidding, right? He ran out to the bus for our luggage while I kept playing. The diner emptied out, and we just kept racking up free games. We must have played for two hours on the same dime. Heaven. True, later, standing in the dark on the side of Route 42 with our thumbs out, wind howling and the blizzard getting worse, it did seem like it might not have been the smartest thing we ever did, but I'd probably do it again.

And over the years, I've found that once addicted, you never outgrow your need for pinball. So when I saw a piece in the paper last October announcing the 14th annual Pinball Expo at the Ramada Inn near O'Hare, I heard that siren song calling yet again. The article said that the 4-day extravaganza was the only one of its kind in the world, and would include over 200 machines, of all vintages, which, for the $10 per day admission, *could all be played for free*. For as long as you liked—it was going to be open all night on Friday and Saturday. I managed not to start drooling on the newspaper.

Since I have raised him properly, inculcating sound values, my 12-year-old son, Willie, also loves pinball and was eager to go. He invited his friend Eric, and we all headed out there Friday afternoon right after they got out of school. Once inside the Ramada, the Expo rooms weren't hard to find. All we had to do was head toward the wonderful din of pinball noise.

We paid our admission and signed up for the tournament—a semi-outrageous $5 for two plays on a new *Godzilla*. You could enter as often as you liked, naturally, since all the money went into the promoter's pocket. But then the winner did get to take home one of the *Godzillas*. Along with the main competition, there were a juniors, a women's, and a seniors division on a vintage 1973 *Spanish Eyes* for golden oldies like me.

We walked into two large convention rooms full of pinball machines going, I guess you could say, full tilt. Immediately in front of us were a dozen *Godzillas* in two rows back to back, every one of them being played by a wannabe tournament winner, with a long line of competitors waiting their turn. The place was packed, and the crowd nearly all male, which was no surprise since pinball falls into a zone also occupied by comic books, science fiction, heavy metal and other such forever-teen testosterone-based cultural pursuits. The range of actual ages was a bell curve probably centering around 35 or thereabouts, but if I'm at all typical, I'd say the average developmental age hovered somewhere around 14 or so. We don't *want* to grow up!

It wasn't exactly an elegant scene. More like a post-nuke Mad Max arcade from *Road Warrior*. The Expo is mainly aimed at hardcore pinball fanatics, and they literally come from all over the world. Many are there for supplies to fix up and refurbish the machines they have at home. Or to buy one or two more, however wounded. (I saw one guy walking around with a big kick-me style handlettered sign pasted to his back that said WANTED: GOTTLIEB GOLD STRIKE.) So among the working games, there were booths with bins full of arcane pinball parts, leaning stacks of backglasses, nonworking games in all imagineable states for sale (as were almost all of those being played), tables loaded with pinball t-shirts & keychains & decals and other paraphernalia—a pleasant chaotic messiness to it all, like some bright electronic junkyard.

Okay, I admit it. I went nuts. Over the next three days I tried to play every game there.

On Friday afternoon, so many people were wanting to play the newer games, cued up in front of them, and patience not being one of my long suits, that I started out on the older machines that weren't as sought-after. Which was okay with me, being an older machine myself.

Also, on these, true greed hadn't kicked in yet, so you get *five* balls per play instead of the current three—a qualitative change for the worse that to me spoils the cosmic harmony of pinball. Five balls permit a bit of dreaming and spacing out—if one goes straight down the tubes there's still time for redemption. But three balls per play are unforgiving, emblematic of what passes for reality these days. Life is harder and faster—just one screwup, and it's so long, sucker.

So I began by pooting around on a few neglected classics: Gottleib's 1960 four-player *Texan*, whose backglass featured a handsome Roy Rogers-oid cowboy wearing two ornate sixguns and with a manly cigarette dangling from his lips—how times have changed. Then *Hot Shot*, a 1973 game with a maniacal-looking character shooting pool on its backglass.

And *Lady Luck*, from 1968, a pinball version of blackjack where a dealer's number comes up and the player tries to beat the machine's hand by hitting various targets while racking up points. The art on this one features several raggedy beatniks a la Maynard G. Krebs—since pinball machine themes often try to cash in on current fads, but also are often a little behind the times. A better one for 1968 would be one called *Acid Test*, with longhaired hippies, where a "high score" could take on new meaning.

Willie and Eric had been in line for the tournament all this time. I wandered over there just as Willie was about to get his turn on one of the *Godzillas*. And saw a quintessential pinball obsessive-compulsive in action. This guy walked up to the machine like a wary gunfighter heading for the O.K. Corral. He pulled several Handiwipes out of his pocket, carefully cleaning all possible smears off the glass, and getting the grease and taint of previous players off the flipper buttons. He got his feet in precise playing position, scruffing his right pressed-forward foot on the carpeting several times to be sure of a solid non-slip grip, outstretched his arms and gave his hands and wrists a good warmup shake, just like swimmers do on the block right before a race. Placing his fingers just so, he gave the flipper buttons a few test pushes. With incredible focus and concentration, taking and holding a deep breath, he pressed the start button. Samurai pinball!

I didn't get to see the result—Willie was up. I thought he did pretty well—28 million on the first try, and 83 million on the second. But then the eventual tournament winner scored 3 billion and change—these numbers representing the latest in the inflationary spiral regarding possible high scores that's been going on for some time now. Some of the earliest machines I played, from the 50s and early 60s, had a top possible score of 999 before they turned over, something they no longer do since electronic readouts replaced the old numbered cylinders in the late 70s.

But more is always better these days. And these scores in realms up there with denominations on South American currencies are also signs of a certain desperation among pinball manufacturers today to make the games more exciting—or at least seem so. It's led, unfortunately, to a sort of rococo overabundance and overcomplication.

The playing fields on new machines like *Godzilla* are sometimes so gunked up with multilevel ramps and hideyholes and gadgetry that you can't even see where the ball is half the time. And thanks to the miracle of microchips, the sound effects have gotten so sophisticated and omnipresent that they can be positively annoying. On some it's fun—*Star Trek: The Next Generation*, for instance, has Picard, Data and Worf offering encouragement and advice, plus the show's themesong. But *Godzilla* sounds like rush hour moments before an atomic attack—screams, horns honking, tires screeching, some manic dork shouting "Gun it, gun it, go go go, gun it!" every fourteen seconds. Where are the simple soothing blings and dings of yesteryear? I play pinball to *relax*, you know?

For me, pinball hit its apotheosis in 1972 with *Fireball*. I was an editor at *Playboy* magazine at the time. One of Hugh Hefner's most admirable qualities is his lifelong love of pinball, and he had a brand-new *Fireball*, set on free play, put in the editorial conference room. It sure was an effective way to build staff comaraderie, and rivalry. I hate to admit how many hours the other editors and I put in on it after work (never during office hours, of course!). And I am proud to say that I had the highest score. *Fireball* was the first game with multiball— three of them zapping around at once when you managed to "Release Fire Gods"—and there was a big berzerker spinner just above the flippers that sent them unpredictable whichways. Even better, it was truly a game of skill. If you got good at it, you could control what happened. Well, occasionally, anyway. When I win the lottery next week, the first thing I'm going to buy is a *Fireball* in perfect condition.

And they're not *that* expensive. I searched in vain for a *Fireball* at the Expo, but I was too late. Somebody had brought one in primo shape there for play and for sale, but it was snapped up about an hour after the Expo opened by a Japanese guy who'd come all the way from Tokyo looking for one. I'm not alone in my love for it. The cost? Just $1500. And *Fireball* is one of the most sought-after, collectible vintage machines. Even older, rarer ones don't go for that much. *Triple Action*, for instance, from 1948. Another game called *Humpty-Dumpty* had been the first to introduce flippers in 1947, revolutionizing pinball, but *Triple Action* was the first to put them where God intended, at the bottom on either side of the "out hole," as it's known in the trade. There are only a handful of them still around in working condition, and it's sort of the first-Superman appearance *Action Comics #1* of pinball. But while *Action #1* goes for nearly $100,000 in near-mint condition these days, you can pick up a *Triple Action* for a measly $15,000 or so.

Pinball always has been sort of low-rent—one of its many appeals.

There was a big TV monitor near the Expo entrance where the tournament scores were being posted. Willie and Eric and I were standing around it with a bunch of other people, waiting to see where they were in the kids' standings, and struck up a conversation with an exuberant woman who was checking out how she'd fared in the Ladies Division.

"Oh, look!" she said when the scores came up. "I'm in 6th place! I'll have to try again!" She was a full-bore pinball enthusiast. "I came all the way here from Tucson just for this—just for the tournament," she told us. "I love to play, and I want to add a *Godzilla* to my collection."

"Your collection?"

"I have *Circus Voltaire, Scared Stiff, Party Monsters, Trail Drive, Fin Car, Dry Hole, Orbiter…*and a few others."

"Where do you keep them all?"

"I have a game room, I've got some in the bedroom, I've got *Judge Dredd* in the living room…" The last especially is a statement few can make. I resisted asking how he liked it.

We were both impressed and envious. I asked which was her favorite.

"Probably *Creature From the Black Lagoon*. It's a John Troudeau game, Kevin O'Connor art, can't beat it."

It was great being around so much pinball mania, but there was a certain sadness to the Expo, too. It's the only one in the world of its kind for a reason. Pinball as a pastime—for me, the most pleasing utter waste of time there is—is going down the tubes. Video games are the chief and most obvious villain. Why anyone would prefer to play a cold, impersonal *Tekken 3* or *Time Crisis 2* over almost any warm, cuddly pinball game is beyond me. But they do. And the Pinball Expo is a sort of Elephant's Graveyard. I'm very sorry to say, but pinball is going the way of spats and running boards and girdles. Pinball accounts for less than 5% of coin-operated game revenue these days. Because of the ever-shrinking market, companies such as Bally and Williams, which used to produce 10 or 15 new games a year, are now down to one or two.

John Mohr, who fixes slot machines by day at a Native American casino near Minneapolis, and repairs old pinball machines as a hobby by night, is a pinball diehard. This was his 7th trip to the Expo. "I bought my first pinball machine when I was in second grade," he told me. "I had a paper route, saved up, and bought a *Midway Raceway* for $50. I still have it."

He had some thoughts on the current sad state of pinball.

"Pinball has been in the dumps before," he said, "and it's my hope that it will come back again. But it's as bad now as it was in the early 80s when video games first came along. It's hard to say what *the* reason is today. I don't know if it's the Internet, or Nintendo and Playstation, those type of things. And while it's gotten more complicated, it hasn't really changed since 1948 when flippers came along. It's like cars—cars have gotten more complex, but they're still cars. It's a bleak outlook. There are lots of collectors, but collectors can't keep a factory in business. Collectors like me, we're the ones that keep the old stuff going. And if you keep the old stuff going, you don't need new."

Somebody else I talked to, who works in Chicago at the Williams factory, which made the still hugely popular *Addams Family*, had the same complaint.

"I think our biggest problem is that we've been making the machines too well over the last few years. They last too long. We sold 25,000 *Addams Familys*, and they're still on location, earning as much money as new games do. It's very difficult to compete with yourself, when you've got 6-year-old games that are still on location, and with half an hour of scrubbing they still look and work like new. We need to figure out some way to make pinball new and exciting, so nobody wants to play those games any more."

But he sounded more wistful than genuinely hopeful.

I didn't have a chance to try many of the newer games until late Saturday night—or rather very early Sunday morning. My advice to other true pinball lizards is to take a good long nap and show up at the Expo around midnight on Friday or Saturday night, when the weenie day-trippers and faint-hearted have gone home to bed, and you practically have the place to yourself. All those untenanted recent games set on free play, just waiting, are like dying and going to Pinball Heaven.

In the name of dedicated research I played until about 3 a.m. Among the newer games, I agreed with the lady from Tucson about *Creature From The Black Lagoon* being the most fun. Others in my Top Five were *Tales From The Crypt* (which commences a deep earthquakelike shaking when things get exciting), *Star Trek: The Next Generation* (the one I played was for sale at just $1250), *Terminator 2* (really advanced when it came out in 1991, but which now seems sweetly quaint), and *Twilight Zone* (the most internally complex game ever made).

Being a right-wing conservative when it comes to pinball, I was put off at first by the gunked-up playing field on *Creature*. But like *Fireball*, it's one that you play; it doesn't play you. Once you get a few games under your belt, there's a learning curve, a sense of strategy emerges, and you gain a degree of control over what's going on. My scores went up pretty steadily, from a mere 12 million on the first try to 110,464,000 on the last—which, when I passed the 96 million mark, awarded me with that magic KA-THUNK! signalling a free game.

But instead of playing on, I walked away. It seemed a perfect time to call it a night. Maybe I've at least learned *something* since that snowy winter afternoon in Coffee Pete's. But then again, they were all free anyway, so probably not.

- 1998

I OWE IT ALL TO

Allegra Reniff, J.P. Standish, Herb Reniff, Florence Reniff, Maude Reynolds, Bob Reniff, Rollin Reniff, Jane Reniff, Rennie Ricker, Kay Henderson, Peter Goudinoff, Stanley Yeager, Jim Mitchell, Linda Armstrong, Lynn Bobula, Cathy Fredericks, Pam Alexander, Tim McDevitt, David Seilstad, Sharleen Morris, Dorothy Bleish, Mrs. Robinson, Mrs. Main, Doug Cooper, Donna DeWitt, Joan Ainsworth, Joe Nafsinger, Cynthia Yuhas, Judy Dean, David Dreshar, Phil Rouse, Bruce Henrikson, Tom Swartwood, Ma Bates, Ann Wells, Sharie McCue, Art Dodge, Don Baltes, Susie Ricker, Robbie Ricker, Nancy Grapentine, Lois Swinson, Kay Kujala, Scott Guthery, Barbara Hartford, Charlene Jirsa, John Chamberlin, Kathe Merta, Mary Pat Smagola, Phyllis Smagola, J.C. West, Alison Kyle, Anika Dogger, Bob Babiak, Bonnie Hamilton, Carolyn Graham, Judy Mead, John Weigel, Milton White, Edgar Branch, Kathy Allmon, Ellen Holland, Carol Smith, Walter Havighurst, Jerry Bovim, Joe Zucker, Beth Lee, Dee Dee Martin, Bill Bartlett, Tom Corcoran, Lyle Johnston, Karla Moore, David Altman, Karl von Ausdal, Janice Legow, David Humphries, Jack Warshaw, Cathy Davis, Rick Shaw, Paul Somers, Dick Fisher, Bob Scheute, Joy Krausser, Neva Ferguson, Marv Friedenn, Lou Borok, Ken Haker, Bob and Peggy Harris, Kay Peterka, Frank Lalli, Dick Close, Joel Baron, Ruth Ann Schroeder, Penny Chaloupka, Paul Tyner, Howard Dixon, Larry Woiwode, David Moritz, Carole Peterson, Stan Wallace, Ira Berkow, Mike Erhardt, CyAnn McNary, Barbara Popp, Jim Vykopal, Barbara Buehner, Dick Dunbar, Margaret Globig, Ann Kindberg, Dottie Wilder, Judy Feazell, Dick Mallot, Ron & Myrna Beach, Leslie Morgan, Lisa Standish, Geoffrey Stuart, Michael Nushawg, Bill Foster, P.J. O'Rourke, Louie Penner, Margaret Wolf, Henry Collins, Mrs. Benje, Tony Brazis, Robert Dudak, Jeff Norman, Peter Montague, Walter Nugent, David Smith, George Meredith, Michael Laurence, Jim Goode, Warren Leming, Nate Herman, Jerry Sullivan, Dan Zapp, Abe Peck, Glenda Daniel, Eugenie Ross-Leming, Alan & Maria Ravage, Carol Wrubel, Chick Richards, David Butler, Harold Ramis, Barbara Nellis, Jean Butler, Nancy Siegel, Susie Weiss, Carl Snyder, Craig Vetter, Barbara Biederman, Laurence Gonzales, Arthur Kretchmer, Maria Nekam, Larry Linderman, Reg Potterton, Bob Post, Nat Lehrman, Bob Shea, Tim Johnson, Ingrid Miller, Ken Levin, Carol Hissong, Barry Golson, Jim Petersen, Skip Williamson, Nate Herman, Andy Haban, Kurt Vonnegut, Chris Miller, Nora Ephron, Hunter Thompson, Tom Passavant, Robert Easter, Jimmy Buffett, Jane Butler, Lee & Len Herzenberg, Janet Herzenberg, Judd Klinger, Cameron Crowe, Neal Preston, Janet Lever, Eleanor Sullivan, Jim Mayhercy, Stanley Meises, Carl Arrington, Mark Gilbertson, Dana Planck, Al Jaramillo, Floyd Saunders, John Doninger, Dr. Briskus, Jeff Smith, Jonathan Black, Chris Newman, Carol Ehlers, Nancy Melvin, Tom Melvin, Gretchen Brown, Louise Schnorr, Patty Carroll, Jake Ehlers, Pete Ehlers, Glen & Helen William, Kim & Mary Angelo, Margaret Deacey, Gail Greiner, Shashi Caudill, Claudia Olney, Tony Armour, Mike Dillon, Peter Kuttner, Tim & Max Pollack, Beverly Logan, Alex Paull, Carl Arrington, Stan Meises, Harriet Choice, Patricia Smith, Bob Higgins, Willie Nelson, Paula Batson, Lisa Lawley, Joan Yee, Maude Standish, Wilson Standish, Bill Roth, Lanet Jarret, Lori Rotenberk, Eric Schwartz, Terry Moore, John Chandler, Anita David, Edie Jarolim, Rich Stewart, Molly Stewart, Bailey Stewart, May Melvin, Laura Villanueva, Amanda Rivkin, Meredith Pillon, Margaret & Brooks Darrah, Susie & Marshall Philipson, John Starrs, Dr. Ann DeClue, Lucie Singh, Jerry Detra, Elaine Steinbeck, Randi Schreiber, Patricia Arrigoni, Susan Katzman, David Abrahamson, Patti Wolter, Charles Whitaker, Doug Foster, Bob McClory, Roger Boye, Rich Gordon, Mango Curtis, Laurie Kutche, Queenie Burns, Pierce Hollingsworth, Janice Castro, Jack Doppelt, Michelle Bitoun, Abigail Forestner, Loren Ghilione, Jon Marshall, Bill Handy, Joshua Dunn, Kathleen Burke, Josh Karp, Maggie Sullivan, David Wasserman, Mike Benoist, Mike Haney, Kate Ashford, Brooke Barrier, Robin Terry, Emily Howald, Dorothea Hunter, Rachel Davis, Ericka Mellon, Alana Price, Jeff Fleischer, Sarah Schaale, Aranya Tomseth, Anat Rubin, Karen Hawkins, Fawn Ring, Melissa Bell, Jim Distasio, Laura Schocker, Willow Duttge, Evan Smith, Leslie Breed, Patricia Kroll, Roy Carlson, Dr. Jayshree Dhali, Kenn Kaufman, David Bernstein, Lanny Jones, Karen Springen, Janet Fitch, Julianne Hill, Chris Sweeney, Christa Hilstrom, Ariel Ramchandani, Elisa Coakley-Koch, Todd Koch, Gary Shlifka, Sandra Song, Catie L'Heureux, Sunny Kang, Jennie Ross, Emilie Syberg, Nick Accardi, Rory Forrest and Mingo Dabney.